TRANSFORMING PHILOSOPHY AND RELIGION

Indiana Series in the Philosophy of Religion
Merold Westphal, editor

Transforming Philosophy and Religion

Love's Wisdom

Edited by Norman Wirzba & Bruce Ellis Benson

INDIANA UNIVERSITY PRESS
Bloomington & Indianapolis

This book is a publication of

Indiana University Press
601 North Morton Street
Bloomington, IN 47404-3797 USA

http://iupress.indiana.edu

Telephone orders   800-842-6796
Fax orders   812-855-7931
Orders by e-mail   iuporder@indiana.edu

The paper used in this publication meets the minimum
requirements of American National Standard for Information
Sciences—Permanence of Paper for Printed Library Materials,
ANSI Z39.48-1984.

Manufactured in the United States of America

Library of Congress Cataloging-in-Publication Data

Transforming philosophy and religion : love's wisdom / edited
by Norman Wirzba and Bruce Ellis Benson.
    p. cm. — (Indiana series in the philosophy of religion)
    Includes bibliographical references and index.
    ISBN-13: 978-0-253-35073-2 (cloth : alk. paper)
ISBN-13: 978-0-253-21958-9 (pbk. : alk. paper) 1. Love.
2. Philosophy. 3. Religion—Philosophy. 4. Love—Religious
aspects—Christianity. I. Wirzba, Norman. II. Benson, Bruce
Ellis, date
    BD436.T73 2008
    190—dc22
                                        2007036772

1 2 3 4 5   13 12 11 10 09 08

Contents

Acknowledgments / vii

Introduction   *Norman Wirzba and Bruce Ellis Benson* / 1

PART 1. The Nature of the Quest

1. The Primacy of Love
   Norman Wirzba / 15

2. The Economies of Knowledge and Love in Paul
   Bruce Ellis Benson / 28

3. Love, This Lenient Interpreter: On the Complexity of a Life
   Edward F. Mooney / 42

PART 2. Justice

4. A Love as Strong as Death: Ricoeur's Reading of the Song of Songs
   Mark Gedney / 63

5. Paul Ricoeur and the Possibility of Just Love
   Christopher Watkin / 73

6. Why There Is No Either/Or in *Works of Love*:
   A Kantian Defense of Kierkegaardian (Christian) Unconditional Love
   Bertha Alvarez Manninen / 84

7. Living by Love: A Quasi-Apostolic *carte postale* on Love in Itself,
   If There Is Such a Thing
   John D. Caputo / 103

PART 3. The Sacred

8. A Love that B(l)inds: Reflections on an Agapic Agnosticism
   B. Keith Putt / 121

9. Absence Makes the Heart Grow Fonder
   Brian Treanor / 142

10. Creatio Ex Amore
    James H. Olthuis / 155

11. Militant Love: Zizek and the Christian Legacy
    Tyler Roberts / 171

12. Love as a Declaration of War? On the Absolute Character of
    Love in Jean-Luc Marion's Phenomenology of Eros
    Christina M. Gschwandtner / 185

Contents

PART 4. Rethinking Humanity

13. Liberating Love's Capabilities: On the Wisdom of Love
Pamela Sue Anderson / 201

14. The Genesis of Love: An Irigarayan Reading
Ruthanne S. Pierson Crápo / 227

15. You'd Better Find Somebody to Love:
Toward a Kierkegaardian Bioethic
Amy Laura Hall / 239

List of Contributors / 257
Index / 259

Acknowledgments

Bruce Ellis Benson's essay (chapter 2) appeared in a somewhat different form as "Paul and the Knowledge that Puffs Up: A Taste for Idolatry," in *Journal of Philosophy and Scripture* 2:2 (2005): 11–22.

The editors would like to thank Trent Koutsoubos for his work on the index.

Introduction

NORMAN WIRZBA and BRUCE ELLIS BENSON

There are many books on the morality of love. In studies of that sort, philosophers and theologians turn their analytical skills to an examination of love's nature and extent[1] as well as its inspiration and concrete expression. They consider, for instance, how a particular conception of love has practical or applied implications in domains as diverse as politics,[2] health care,[3] gender relations,[4] and education.[5] In these various cases, a version of love is philosophically or theologically defined and defended, and then "tested in the field" for its transformative potential and usefulness. Such work is very important and sometimes also very good. It certainly needs to continue.

The essays gathered in this volume, however, are focused on something substantially different: *describing how various expressions of philosophical and theological reflection are transformed by the discipline of love*. Rather than turning attention immediately to how reflection on love engages and transforms our world, this book focuses on how the practice of love engages and transforms our reflection. Though it is fairly common for people to consider how love changes the way we think about "x," the "x" under consideration is rarely philosophical or theological reflection itself. So why this different and unique emphasis?

The contributors to this volume are convinced that to practice philosophy is always already to be implicated in the ways of love. It isn't simply that philosophers can choose from time to time to turn their analytical tools specifically to the various expressions of love. Rather, the matter goes much deeper, because the very attainment of wisdom (*sophia*)—as the etymology of the word "philosophy" suggests—requires that we practice love (*phileo*) in some form. In this sense, philosophers not only study love as an optional affair, but their study itself becomes the conceptual expression of a more fundamental disposition or set of practices that goes by the name "love." The character of our purported wisdom will itself be a reflection of our ability or inability to love, *whether we know it or not.* Given that our thinking invariably colors and shapes the way we receive and engage each other, what is ultimately at issue here is not only the way we characterize wisdom but also how we characterize humanity, the world, and God.[6]

Of course, this is a curious state of affairs. For if such a thesis is correct, it would seem that philosophers—in order to be authentic and at their best—must first be lovers *before* they can truly practice their art. They must, as Plato suggested in the *Symposium*, be consumed with *eros*, that passionate movement that draws the seeker out of him- or herself so that the world outside can be embraced and understood. Insofar as philosophers are incapable of exercising love, they are rendered simply "unphilosophical." If Socrates is right, such philosophers (and thinkers more generally) are little more than sophists who are skilled in the artful and persuasive manipulation of words. Though they may teach a lucrative skill, these "teachers for hire" or "word slayers" must not be mistaken for genuine philosophers.

Given this philosophical predicament, it is striking how little time and energy philosophers and theologians have devoted to the careful examination of love's determinative influence in wisdom's pursuit. How does the disposition and discipline of love alter the way we read, or change the questions we ask, or transform the methods and scope of our inquiry? Does philosophical argument take the same shape and have the same force in the face of love? Does the claim to knowledge itself change when it is preceded and permeated by the commitment to love? Do our conceptions of major ideas like justice and morality, faith and doubt, self and other undergo significant adjustment when informed by practices of love? Must not the limits of thought itself be redrawn in a context of love? These questions alert us to the fact that philosophical and theological reflections are never innocent or neutral. They occur, as phenomenologists would put it, within a horizon that can be more or less formed and colored by the dispositions of love.

Another way to put this is to say that philosophical reflection always runs the risk of being reduced to instrumental reason, a merely economic or technical skill whereby we become more adept at controlling and manipulating the world to our own ends. Instrumental thinking leaves us as thinkers unaltered and unmoved—perhaps even unquestioned—because the world is remade or refashioned to suit our tastes. Instead of allowing our thoughts (and ourselves) to be changed so that we more adequately represent and respond to the world as it is, we change (often violently) our surroundings. What is lost is the sense of the philosopher as someone who undergoes a profound personal transformation as a result of entering patiently and deeply into a conversation with reality. The sense for the wonder of existence and the world evaporates. As long as we think, using instrumental reason, there is no need for the philosopher to excel in virtues—such as love and fidelity—that make true thinking possible.

If we genuinely wish to understand others and the world, then we need the virtue of love, because love (in its most basic orientation) entails an honest and faithful engagement with others. If love is absent from the pursuit of understanding, then that understanding can become corrupt—even to the point of being dangerous—as we now produce minds capable of unleashing domination and destruction upon the world. Love is central and primary because it is the fountainhead of the practical and philosophical virtues. As Norman Wirzba puts it in his essay "The Primacy of Love," love is the indispensable prerequisite for wisdom because it opens our hearts and minds to the wide and mysterious depths of reality. Love inspires, guides, and corrects our reflective paths so that they can be faithful and true. It also takes us to the heart of a religious life, for as Timothy Jackson has well argued, "Charity is a participation in the very life of God and, as such, the foundation of all virtues for those made in the Image of God."[7] To pursue the "wisdom of love" is to recover the more ancient conception of philosophical practice as a "spiritual exercise" in which personal transformation and the creation of a good life and just social order are primary. The result is a wisdom that equips us to assume a more humble and just position within the world, one that makes us more available to and responsible for the grace of life.

As Bruce Ellis Benson shows in his essay "The Economies of Knowledge and Love in Paul," when the wisdom of love is rigorously pursued, the very character of our knowing undergoes transformation. By examining Paul's letter to the Corinthian church, Benson shows how knowledge can be used as a way to build oneself up at another's expense or to make claims that are injurious. The practice of love as Paul describes it, however, leads to a different "economy" of exchange. Whereas knowledge "puffs up," love builds up; whereas knowledge claims lead to arrogance and insistence on one's "rights," love leads to servanthood. Moreover, Paul connects the claims of knowledge to idolatry: precisely insofar as the Corinthians think they "know," they have given in to idolatrous practices. As a corrective, Paul shows how love is of a completely different order. Instead of putting the self first, the economy of love puts the other first. Instead of *hybris*, the economy of love is characterized by humility. One is only truly wise when love grounds knowledge.

This inextricable bond between the practice of love and the attainment of wisdom has not received nearly the sustained attention it deserves. Indeed, we do not need to go deep into the histories of philosophy, even at their key moments, to discover that love is derided and dismissed rather than given an exalted status. Of course, it is easy to see why this might be the case, particularly if the philosophical task is conceived to be the objective, impersonal knowledge of the world as it is by itself. On this view, love would deflect philosophical inquiry precisely because it introduces personal and interpersonal passions that invariably distort or dissimulate the reality that lies before us. Moreover, love is not easily controlled or ordered, since it is so attuned to personal ambition, fear, pride, and anxiety. In sum, we should be suspicious of love—so the story goes—because it effectively renders our judgments cloudy and subjective, making us blind to the truth of the world as it really is. Indeed, such was the verdict of modernity.

Is it not possible, however, that love might be the expression of a more faithful attunement to a world of others? From this perspective, it turns out that the very desire for indifferent and impersonal knowing prevents us from seeing others in their full, mysterious depth. The distant, dispassionate stance of the knower, while it may render our judgments more precise or unclouded, may also miss the complexity and interconnectedness of the world that a charitable stance and vision—coupled perhaps with a measure of personal suffering—is able to see and understand. Love is vital because it entails the patience, attention, long-suffering, and kindness that enable care-full vision and sustained self-inspection. On this view, love becomes the means whereby the distortions caused by the anxious ego can be brought to light and corrected, both because we have now made ourselves more vulnerable to being known by others and because we see in a different way.

The distortions we live with often run deep, extending all the way to practices as (seemingly) simple as reading. As Ed Mooney puts it in his essay "Love, This Lenient Interpreter," we cannot become good interpreters of the world if we have not first learned to "read" differently. To this end, he reflects on two recent biographies of Søren Kierkegaard, one of which is written in the mode of suspicion—with an eye to revealing character flaws—while the other is written from a viewpoint of charity—with the intention of opening new perspectives on a complex life. Mooney demonstrates how the charitable reading actually enables us to observe that a life takes shape through many twists and turns, has many forms, and is fluid and open to change as it responds to the plasticity of the world. In contrast, the reading of Kierkegaard that uses the rigid and scientific standard of "consistency" simply gets Kierkegaard "wrong." Thus, a lack of charity in this second case leads to a lack of true understanding. By attending to the pseudonyms and masks of Kierkegaard in a *charitable* fashion, one discovers that they are actually revelatory.

The majority of the essays in this book are in conversation with European or Continental traditions. To a considerable extent, this is because these traditions, perhaps more than others, have been relentless in their questioning of philosophy itself. Thinkers as diverse as Kierkegaard, Husserl, Heidegger, Levinas, Ricoeur, Derrida, Marion, Zizek, Irigaray, and Le Doeuff have compelled us to rethink the nature of knowledge, the limits of thought, and the inspirations and contexts of reason. Often, in good phenomenological fashion, they have offered powerful descriptions of the thought process itself, exploring its narrative, symbolic, social, and sometimes subterranean dimensions. This book's writers continue that work of philosophical description. However, they add a new, though crucial, dimension. Attuned as they are to the complexity of love and the diversity of its manifestations, each author considers how love makes possible a more honest and faithful encounter with the world. They ask us to rethink philosophical and theological categories and methods by examining issues as diverse as social justice, the role of faith, gender, creation, political action, and bioethics.

Consider our thinking about justice. According to several accounts, it would not seem that love has much to do with justice, particularly if justice is about the equal distribution of goods or the establishment of a contract in which fairness or personal freedoms are the primary goal. The rational principles that guide our thinking about justice, we might assume, would be distorted by the priorities and manners of love. But both Mark Gedney and Chris Watkin argue that exactly the opposite is the case. In "A Love as Strong as Death," Gedney considers Paul Ricoeur's idea of a "third way" between love and justice. Following Ricoeur, he argues that these two can indeed exist together, and in a way that makes possible a more responsible human life. On the basis of a reading of the biblical creation story and the Song of Songs, Ricoeur understands love to be at the heart of the created world. It *opens up the space* where we can meet each other and join together in relationship. The distance between two people, in other words, makes love possible. Love is also the medium of exchange that can exist between them, so that their living together goes beyond the level of command (or law). While law is a necessary restraint against that which destroys relationships, love is a gift that goes beyond law and sustains the law. So love ultimately comes *before* justice and *makes justice possible.*

In "Paul Ricoeur and the Possibility of Just Love," Watkin challenges Emmanuel Levinas's suggestion that love and justice are incommensurable. Again, love turns out to be central. According to Ricoeur, love amounts to the intensification of justice, to justice in a festive mode, all based on the acknowledgment of creation as a primordial gift. Thus, both calculating and uncalculating love co-exist in a "living tension"—one that cannot be resolved through a collapse to one pole. Yet it is this tension that makes possible (as Ricoeur puts it) "a supplementary degree of compassion and generosity in all of our codes." For Ricoeur, even the Golden Rule must be interpreted, not as calculation, but as generosity. And unlike Jacques Derrida, Ricoeur thinks that gifts truly can be given without falling back into an economy of exchange.

One of the hallmark notions of justice is that it be impartial. Fairness seems to dictate that we not show preferential treatment. How, then, are we to think of Jesus' commandment that we should love one another? Does love fall within the legal parameters of a command, or must it include an affective dimension that is in some sense beyond the realm of law and command? How does our idea of law itself change in the face of the command to love? Bertha Alvarez Manninen, in "Why There Is No Either/Or in *Works of Love*," uses the ethics of Immanuel Kant to clarify Kierkegaard's calling us to choose between unconditional love (to all people) and personal relationships. The problem with what Kierkegaard calls "preferential love" is that at any moment it can evaporate. Unconditional love, on the other hand, is love that literally has no (even legal) "conditions." Yet, if unconditional love is superior to preferential love (and if preferential love often *hinders* unconditional love), can there still be room—or is it even still *moral*—to have feelings of preference? Manninen concludes that, since moral actions can be "overdetermined," one could feel an inclination yet act on the basis of duty alone. In the same way, one could act out of unconditional love yet still have feelings of preference. Here, as in the two studies of Ricoeur mentioned above, we see that the practice of love changes the way we think about justice in a profound way.

In "Living by Love," John D. Caputo develops this tension by examining the difference—or *différance*—between love and the economy of the law. Here the concern is not so much over the legality of social institutions and practices as, more broadly (and religiously), the order that leads to our ultimate good and salvation. Caputo notes that according to Paul's writings in scripture, and phenomenologically speaking, love needs the law, for law provides something for love to exceed. By its very nature, love is excessive. Moreover, what was needed to overcome the rule of law (which is the rule of death) was the ultimate act of love: Christ's death. Still, whereas the law was a limiting factor in that no one could fulfill it, now the fact that not everyone has heard (and accepted) the gospel becomes the limiting factor. Paul could unite Jew and Greek, slave and free, male and female—but not "those who accept the gospel" and "those who do not." Caputo rejects a strong theology that would insist on such a distinction. This option, however, presents a different problem for Caputo, namely, the fact that Jesus does not merely *suggest* love as a nice idea but actually *commands* it. Can love still be love if it's commanded? Does not this then mean that love is "tainted" by law? To this problem Caputo replies that law is deconstructible, while love is not. Of course, its undeconstructible status *also* means that love is impossible—not *simply* impossible but *the* impossible. Love, then, is not against the law or even beyond the law; rather, it is situated *within* the law, constantly haunting, loosening, and challenging the law. Without love, the law would not be "just." So once again love turns out to be a possibility condition of justice.

Throughout much of its history, philosophy has been tuned to a religious impulse. In part, this is because thinking about life eventually leads us to questions about its ultimate value. But in thinking about the ultimate, we must at the same time consider the limits of thought and examine reason's capacity to plumb the depth and extent of the sacred. As the essays by Brian Treanor, B. Keith Putt, and James H. Olthuis make clear, it is hardly enough to set up a faith/reason dichotomy and assume that we have therefore been truthful about the complexity of the human/divine relationship. Does the practice of love change the character of our relationships, and if so, how? Here questions about our naming of God, of our relationship to God, and of God's relationship to the world come to the fore.

In "A Love that B(l)inds," Putt investigates Shakespeare's famous claim that "love is blind" by way of a careful consideration of Derrida and Jean-Luc Marion. Love ends up being not only a kind of unknowing but also a faith without sight. Following Caputo, he describes the act of love as one that moves from a passion *for* the impossible to a movement *by* the impossible and in terms of it. Love is what limits experience of the dark night where we become completely dependent on the other, having forsaken every gnosis, since all our attempts to know would result in the reduction of the other in terms of the mastery of self-presence. At the end, I do not *know* what I love when I love my God. Instead, I love by faith, not by sight.

This question of not knowing—of not being able to identity the other—is likewise taken up by Treanor in "Absence Makes the Heart Grow Fonder," though he comes to a different conclusion. On the one hand, Treanor is sympathetic to the Levinasian and Derridian point that the other cannot be properly identified (and still remain other). Deconstructors are to be commended for their caution. On the other hand, Treanor argues that—in the name of wishing to avoid violence—deconstruction refuses to love. It *talks* about love a great deal but is afraid to *practice* love. For loving requires that I love *someone*, a neighbor who has some *identity* and who is not completely different from me. Treanor concludes that one can take the otherness of the other seriously without lapsing into a hyperbolic account of absolute otherness. Indeed, only an otherness that has some sense of similarity can ever be recognized or treated ethically. It is not a question of choosing between alterity and similitude: both are present and intermingled.

The great faith traditions of the Western world have often maintained that the ultimate value of the world is a feature of reality finding its origin and purpose in a Creator God. But what if the God who creates "is love," as the letter of John suggests? James Olthuis argues that the traditional doctrine of creation *ex nihilo* ("from nothing") rests far too much on an understanding of God as a distant, all-powerful, controlling divinity not passionately involved in the fate of all created beings. He proposes that we revise this teaching to read creation *ex amore, cum amore,* and *ad amorem* ("from love," "with love," and "to love"), since this would more faithfully reflect what we know about God as the one who intimately and patiently enters into creation, suffers with it, and longs to redeem it. Love is the active, vivifying, and healing force that acts as the glue that holds all of reality together. Love reflects God's omnipotence, not as a coercive or violent power over another, but as the steady, caring presence that "keeps on coming" no matter what. If love is the heart of the world as its origin and end, then the ways in which we interact with each other, the world, and God undergo a profound transformation.

For instance, how does love affect the social order? The history of politics demonstrates that love has not very often been the model for ordering our social relationships and institutions. The question then becomes: What bearing does love have for the way we order our relationships? What should the

7

basis for political action be? Tyler Roberts argues in "Militant Love," following the contemporary theorist Slavoj Zizek, that the Christian legacy is important precisely because it has bequeathed love, a conception that provides a basic principle for structuring human collectivities. For Zizek, love is affirming the other on behalf of the other. What Christianity accomplishes—through Paul—is the movement from desire to love. Yet for Zizek, Christianity can only complete itself by following its own logic and sacrificing itself. Christianity thus provides a model of true commitment: one believes, not in something "real," but in what Zizek terms "the fragile absolute." According to Zizek, Christian love is "violent" in its rupture with its Jewish past and its insistence on sacrificing self and relationships. Yet the question is whether Christianity truly provides the "militant model" that Zizek seeks and whether he fails to pay close enough attention to Jesus' own model of love.

Christina M. Gschwandtner continues the discussion on love's possible militancy in "Love as a Declaration of War?" Precisely because of her recognition that love should affect our knowledge of and relationship to the other, she finds it troubling that Marion—in key passages of *Le phénomène érotique*—resorts to the metaphor of *war* to provide a phenomenological account of eros. This results in a number of seemingly strange features of erotic love. First, for Marion, the lover advances toward the beloved in a way that makes the advance of the lover virtually impossible to resist. Moreover, since the lover sets the conditions for love, the beloved is completely passive. Indeed, Marion thinks that love is complete even without the return of love from the beloved. Second, since the lover is the possibility condition for the beloved, the lover seems to have a kind of control over the beloved. Gschwandtner argues that the lover—on this account—seems almost like God. Third, Marion insists that the only appropriate way to speak of eros is in terms of mystical theology. But why, Gschwandtner asks, must eros be thematized in theological terms? Moreover, are theological terms even the appropriate ones for speaking of eros? Fourth, Marion insists that all love—whether romantic love or friendship—ends up being the same. Simply from a phenomenological point of view, such a description seems inadequate to describe the various types of relations in which some form of love plays a role. Finally, Marion makes yet another questionable move in asserting that erotic love is ultimately divine *agape*. Gschwandtner argues that, even if this move were to work theologically, it is certainly open to question phenomenologically. Note that these criticisms raised by Gschwandtner assume that the economy of love should be radically *different* from what Marion is describing.

In "Liberating Love's Capabilities," Pamela Sue Anderson makes surprisingly similar criticisms to those of Gschwandtner, but regarding the very Western philosophical imaginary itself. Unfortunately, that imaginary is dominated through and through by conceptions of love as a kind of bondage (and Marion is simply another example of this tendency). The history of patriarchy reveals that women have been placed (sometimes violently) in the uncomfortable position of being unable to love in terms unique to themselves. On the one hand, women have been demonized as the originators of evil and thus not worthy of love or incapable of expressing love. On the other hand, they have simply been subsumed within the world of men and so denied the opportunity to develop patterns and symbols—what we might call a language and grammar —of love unique to their own experience.

This construal of love has been particularly damaging to women who are denied the freedom and ability to discover themselves and contribute to the world. When our notions of love are released from the bondage of patriarchal myths, not only are new conceptions of personhood opened up, *but the very sense of wisdom changes*. Liberated love makes possible new kinds of thinking that are permeated by tenderness and attention. When people, both women and men, are liberated by love to be themselves, the possibility for new attachments to each other, the world, and God emerges in such a way that members are no longer fused or subsumed into each other (as when women are alternately yoked to the demonic or the divine).

The concern with the absorption of one gender into another continues in Ruthanne Crápo's essay "The Genesis of Love." Working with Luce Irigaray, Crápo argues that our cultural and mythic past has contributed to the silencing and virtual obliteration of the female sex. The feminine has no desire or language because, and as the story of Electra makes clear, she is presumed to be but a variation on the male. Patriarchy and misogyny mean that we have a language of sameness. In other words, the feminine has been absorbed into the masculine self—and this has had a profound effect on women's ways of knowing. Through a reading of Genesis, however, Crápo constructs an alternative story, one in which male and female are not absorbed into, but rather complement, each other. She envisions a world in which we can be "two and together," a world in which the two genders do not fuse but grow, flourish, and dance with each other.

The question of love—and its relation to human ways of being—extends even into recent developments in biotechnology and genetic engineering, for such developments call into question the very nature of what it is to be human and what it means to love. Rather than women being subsumed within the world of men, humanity itself runs the risk of being absorbed into the manufactured and arbitrary world of economic efficiency and personal style. What is it to be a human being in a world where the options to change or reconstruct people and infants are multiplying? Does love have anything to say about the heart of our humanity? Amy Laura Hall, in "You'd Better Find Somebody to Love," offers a trenchant criticism of the burgeoning field of bioethics. She argues that for the most part love is absent from bioethical decision making as ethicists and scientists have succumbed to dehumanizing and thoroughly utilitarian/economic modes of reflection. What does it mean to be human in a world of gene therapy and eugenics, where researchers and engineers now promise "No more stupid or ugly or short—or in any other way 'deficient'— babies"? As Hall argues, it is by no means a simple thing to say what "being human" is, particularly when we remember that varying cultures at different times characterize domestic, social, and personal existence in different ways. In the face of this confusion, Hall interjects a Kierkegaardian voice on love, a voice that finds its poignant expression in the love of the suffering, vulnerable Christ. It is this divine love that makes it possible for us to welcome each other as unique gifts of grace, as ones befitting every ounce of our care, rather than as always imperfect marks in the vastly profitable web of reproductive and ge- netic technologies.

* * *

Together, these essays offer multiple and varying ways of demonstrating just how central love is to true wisdom. As they aptly show, love is not just an "add-on" to wisdom but a central *feature* of being wise. Thus, these essays do something that so desperately needs to be done: they call our attention back to the fundamental role that love plays in being wise. These essays consider some of the most significant questions of philosophy: How does philosophy contrib- ute to a good life and a just world? Does it matter what kind of philosophy we practice? How is philosophy different from sophistry or rational technique? But these questions are asked from the perspective of love's relation to life and wisdom, rather than simply as open-ended general questions. These questions have to do with the wide range of epistemological, metaphysical, and ethical concerns that otherwise animate philosophers. And what these essays show is just how deeply love affects our thinking. One cannot read these essays with- out being truly challenged to pursue philosophical questions *from the stand- point of love*. And the effects of that change in standpoint are bound to be remarkable.

NOTES

1. See the three-volume philosophical (and encyclopedic) treatment by Irving Singer, *The Nature of Love* (Chicago: University of Chicago Press, 1984–87). On the theological side, see Gene Outka's *Agape: An Ethical Analysis* (New Haven, Conn.: Yale University Press, 1972), and more recently, Timothy P. Jackson's *Love Disconsoled: Meditations on Christian Charity* (Cambridge: Cambridge University Press, 1999) and Oliver Davies's *A Theology of Compassion* (Grand Rapids, Mich.: Wm. B. Eerdmans, 2001).

2. See Paul Tillich's *Love, Power, and Justice: Ontological Analysis and Ethical Applications* (New York: Oxford University Press, 1961) and more recently the work of Michel Foucault, particularly the collection *Politics, Philosophy, Culture* (New York: Routledge, 1990).

3. See Norman Daniels's *Just Health Care* (Cambridge: Cambridge University

Press, 1985) and the essays in *Medicine and Social Justice*, ed. Rosamond Rhodes, Margaret Battin, and Anita Silvers (New York: Oxford University Press, 2002).

4. See Eva Feder Kittay's *Love's Labor: Essays on Women, Equality, and Dependency* (New York: Routledge, 1999) and the collection of essays edited by Mary Jeanne Larrabee, *An Ethic of Care: Feminist and Interdisciplinary Perspectives* (New York: Routledge, 1993).

5. See the very influential work of Parker Palmer, especially *To Know as We are Known* (San Francisco: Harper, 1983, reprint 1993), and more recently Jing Lin's *Love, Peace, and Wisdom in Education: A Vision for Education in the 21st Century* (New York: Rowman & Littlefield, 2006).

6. For a powerful redrawing of what it is to be human in the twin contexts of personal frailty and love, see Jean Vanier's 1998 Massey Lectures, *Becoming Human* (New York: Paulist, 1998). Vanier argues that the dominant conceptions of human nature and morality are based on the Greek conception of a well-equipped, fully functioning person. But where does this leave the vulnerable, the handicapped, and the chronically ill among us? True maturity, Vanier claims, follows from a compassionate heart. Without love, we are stunted in our development, unable to fully and faithfully receive each other and the world.

7. Timothy P. Jackson, *The Priority of Love: Christian Charity and Social Justice* (Princeton, N.J.: Princeton University Press, 2003), 14.

PART 1.
THE NATURE OF THE QUEST

1

The Primacy of Love

NORMAN WIRZBA

Philosophy is the wisdom of love at the service of love.

—Emmanuel Levinas

It is misleading, even if it is etymologically correct, to define philosophy as the "love of wisdom." As a definition it assumes too much. Do we know what we mean when we utter the word *wisdom*, especially in a time dominated by the "end of philosophy?"[1] Do we fully appreciate the significance and the complexity of the *relation* between the work of love and the realization of wisdom? Moreover, how does the practice or character of our *love*, especially given the precarious, flexible, and fluid nature of contemporary social bonding, determine the shape of our wisdom?[2] If we attend to these questions, it should become clear that the pursuit of wisdom entails much more than the mere accumulation of knowledge or information. Indeed, the mass production and consumption of data that characterizes our "information age" may actually be an impediment to the realization of those forms and habits of love that promote genuine wisdom.

Put differently, the pursuit of wisdom requires that we be as attentive to the manner of our pursuit as we are to the goal of it. We need to ask about the very practical conditions—our skills and work environments, cultural assumptions and goals, personal dispositions and aspirations—that inspire and propel any and all pursuits. Are there forms of life that better ignite and fuel a genuine love of wisdom? Conversely, are there personal, social, or institutional contexts that, because of their flow and aim, work against the development of an affectionate, charitable, understanding stance in the world? When we consider these sorts of questions, the issue of primary importance is whether or not we have developed the capacity to love. Love, as this essay will argue, is the indispensable prerequisite for wisdom. If we do not exhibit appropriate forms of love, our access to wisdom will be seriously impaired if not altogether denied.

What love itself is, of course, is not easily or simply determined. This is especially apparent when we consider how other languages, Latin for instance, employ several terms to reference love: *amor, caritas, pietas, dilectio, affectio,* and *studium.* The diversity of these terms, their meanings but also the practical contexts in which they would appear, indicate that love is a varied and complex phenomenon that should not be narrowly or quickly reduced to one thing. It may be more appropriate to cast love as being an essential ingredient in the several dimensions of human existence and practice that bind us to each other, to the world, and ultimately to God. On this view, familiar and unfamiliar human relationships, the work of devotion and attention, our response to suffering, and our handling of the material world are at their best when they are permeated by a disposition to love. Love begins in our opening to and welcome of others, and grows as we attend to them in their integrity and wholeness.

Though love flowers into many different forms, at root a loving disposition is one that acknowledges, affirms, and nurtures (human and nonhuman) others in their ability to be. Love cherishes and exults in the independence and interdependence of another. The prototype for this sort of affirmation is to be seen in God's own creative, loving act that keeps and brings the whole world into existence (remembering here the theological link between creation's affirmation as "very good" [Genesis 1:31] and the view that "God is love" [1 John 4:8]). God loves primordially and concretely by "making room" for others "to be" and to flourish.[3] Creation is, in the first instance, a *given* reality and thus a reflection of the divine life as giving-ness itself.[4] Because creation did not need to exist (it does not contain the principle of its existence within itself or hold it as an intrinsic property), the fact of its existence must be understood as a reflection of divine love.

If we are to become acquainted with this world and truly know and understand it, we must also become acquainted with—and *learn to practice*—the divine love that inspires and sustains it. Having wisdom would require us to understand the world and God *together,* since the former finds its bearing in the latter, that is, the meaning of the world is tied to its origin in the mystery of divine love. Wisdom's pursuit would also require us to proceed along the paths of love, since love is the root of our and all being. The various blossoming forms of human love—as revealed in our relationships, economies, art, work, and philosophical reflection—must tap into this primordial divine love if they are to be considered true or authentic. What this means is that wisdom does not have its origin or goal in us, for whatever finite power we possess would have the characteristic of making others dependent upon us. When our inspiration and focus is ourselves, our contact with others is rendered oblique and distorted, since who or what they are is always mediated by our desires, fears, anxieties, and needs. This is why John insists that "Whoever does not love does not know God, for God is love" (1 John 4:8). Only love makes it possible for us to meet another as genuinely other (and not a projection of our needs or desires).

The practical pattern for this love, John continues, is the life of God's own son Jesus Christ: "God's love was revealed among us in this way: God sent his Son into the world so that we might live through him" (v. 9). From a Christian point of view, if we want to truly know the world, we must approach all of it with a Christ-like disposition and perspective. Sensing how the Christian "way" leads to new patterns of relating to others and to the world, early Christians thought it entirely appropriate to speak about Jesus as the "true and complete philosopher" and to claim a "philosophy according to Christ."[5] We cannot have wisdom of the world if we have not first firmly committed ourselves to loving it in ways modeled for us by Christ, which means that we have put to death sinful patterns of relating that dissimulate, distort, disfigure, and destroy.

Not surprisingly, given this Creator/creation/Christic starting point, an emphasis on the primacy of love is fairly common within mystical literature. Here the anonymous fourteenth-century text *The Cloud of Unknowing* can be seen as representative: "Thought cannot comprehend God. And so, I prefer to abandon all I can know, choosing rather to love him whom I cannot know. Though we cannot know him we can love him. By love he may be touched and embraced, never by thought."[6] A primary problem with thought is that it seeks comprehension, whereas God is in principle incomprehensible. The capacity of thinking is simply too small for the grandeur of God. Moreover, the faculty of thought is itself constantly constrained by the power of sin: anger, envy, sloth, pride, covetousness, gluttony, and lust. The merit of love, however, is that it "heals the root of sin" and nurtures practical goodness, making us more sensitive and responsive to God's grace at work in the world. Whereas the drive toward knowledge lends itself to personal conceit—a separation from the love of God—the work of love promotes humility, a form of self-forgetting that makes room for the truth of the world and the glory of God to appear.

But what does mysticism of this sort have to do with philosophy? Should not philosophers be dedicated to the scientific, objective, disinterested pursuit of knowledge, and thus shun such mystical talk? Clearly, it would be a mistake to advocate the mass conversion of philosophers into mystics. Nonetheless, it will be my claim that the primacy of love that mystics advocate is of crucial significance for philosophical work. We cannot have anything like an honest, detailed, clear look at reality if our sight and our sensitivity have been tainted or clouded by a knower's ambition or desire for mastery and control. *Love is central to the philosophical task because it keeps our focus off ourselves, and directs our energy and discipline to the expansion of our sympathies and the clarification of our vision so that we can better attune our lives to the complexity and depth of the world.* Love makes it possible for us to receive the world as it is rather than as we want or wish it to be. Love enables us to resist the (often violent) integration of others into the sameness and comfort of the thinker's world.[7] It acknowledges in a way that no other disposition or activity can the integrity and the mystery of existence.

Philosophy, in other words, needs to be a practical discipline in which the expansion of our sympathies and the clarity of our vision assume first importance. If these disciplines are lacking, perhaps because they do not have sufficient social or cultural support or because the material conditions of our economic and practical life militate against them—consider here the speed, ephemerality, and transience of global culture—then it is safe to say that our perception and understanding will have been compromised. It isn't that we will fail to perceive altogether. More likely we will see and feel differently, with more superficiality and less insight. The irony, of course, is that a problem of perception is rarely "perceived" to be a problem. More than we care to admit, we are like Plato's prisoners, stuck in the bottom of our self-assured caves, convinced that reality is as we take or make it.

Our movement toward true enlightenment (which is not to be confused with modern Enlightenment ideas of "progress")—remembering here the long-standing affinity between love and light—has been hampered by the confusion between knowledge and genuine understanding or wisdom. In modernity this confusion reached a fevered pitch as the quest for scientific knowledge took center stage. In part, this happened because technical knowledge enabled the newly autonomous individual to better control or master the world. In this context, philosophical training lost its earlier focus on wisdom so that it could become the handmaiden and legitimating support of economic, political, and social practices that would maximize human ambition and success (often at the expense of each other and the world). The only knowledge that was prized was of the instrumental or pragmatic sort that we could easily possess or wield as an instrument with the aim of exercising possession or power.

Wisdom, however, is not a possession or a tool in the service of controlling the world. Consider here the words of Henry Bugbee:

> Wisdom is not a form of knowledge which we can be strictly said to *possess*. Wisdom may better be conceived as giving us the strength and courage to be equal to our situation than as knowledge giving us command of it. To the extent that human well-being and capacity for acting well ultimately turn upon understanding (I will not say knowledge), the understanding in question is going to have to be distinguished from powers we can be said to wield, including such knowledge as we *acquire* and might employ as an acquisition.[8]

Bugbee is alerting us to a long tradition of philosophical practice that appreciates wisdom as fidelity and attunement to the world. Wisdom cannot be reduced to knowledge, nor should knowledge invariably be understood as a sufficient condition for understanding. We can see this because at precisely the time when we have the greatest amount of data or information in the natural and social sciences, we are also witnessing human communities and natural habitats everywhere in decline or under assault. Social and personal life are beset by anxiety, worry, boredom, stress, loneliness, violence, and fear. Biological life is compromised by soil erosion and toxification, water and air pollution, unprecedented rates of species extinction, deforestation and desertification, and uncontrolled suburban sprawl. Apparently what we "know" has not translated into the sort of understanding that would enable us to affirm others in their integrity and equip us to live well or in a manner that facilitates mutual flourishing.

Knowledge without understanding unleashes destructive potential because it is knowledge without sense or purpose, knowledge without an appreciation for what our "knowing" is ultimately for. Put differently, when our knowledge is merely *about* the world or others, it becomes abstract and simplistic because it is not forged *through* a sympathetic and practical engagement with them. What is missing is an appreciation for the complex requirements and responsibilities that follow from our living with others—fertile soil, clean water, healthy organisms, vibrant farming communities, sustainable production practices, a just distribution of goods, meaningful work, face-to-face encounters/conversations, nurturing friendships, and grateful consumption. The modern disenchantment with the world reflects a failure to understand how our living is supported by others and in turn affects others, a failure that is repeated again and again in the ways we shop, work, and consume. Our cultural malpractice prevents us from living lives that are healthy and whole. In too many cases our practical living is without art and without love. It is no accident that the gradual disappearance of wisdom should go hand in hand with a gradual loss of the sense that we belong to the world and are deeply implicated in its well-being.[9]

The difference between knowledge and understanding is decisive. Though the discovery and production of knowledge can be difficult enough, the process of understanding entails a much more intimate, and thus also more complex, involvement and participation in what is understood. As we enter the domain of understanding, we move past a description of things (the surface perception of them) to their explanation, the discovery of the workings of things, their sense, direction, integrity, and purpose as well as their connectedness with others.[10] At a bare minimum, understanding requires our interaction with and participation in things in a way that knowing about them simply does not. Wisdom reflects this patient, educative experience and practice informed by basic care and affection. It manifests itself in persons who understand who they are in relation to the many others that inform and intersect their living. It results in a life of propriety, a life in which the patterns of individual existing resonate and harmonize with the existence of others.

We attain a level of understanding insofar as our thinking and acting acknowledge and are informed by the many bonds that connect us to others. We should ask: Are these bonds inspired and directed by love? The character and extent of our connections to reality are crucial. The sense (direction) or purpose of our own living as well as the meaning of things around us depend on whether we can perceive the complex flows of life going on around us and then learn how to adjust our lives accordingly so that they fit or harmonize.[11] Without this fundamental level of perception or sympathy, something like a moral or religious sensibility risks becoming artificial or disingenuous, a feigned piety that relies more on changeable emotional states than it does on a faithful accountability to others and the world. As we engage the world around us, not with an eye to understanding it, but rather with the goal of turning it to our own advantage, we falsify and destroy it. "He who has his mind on taking, no longer has it on what he has taken."[12]

Reflection on the distinction between knowledge and understanding, between information and wisdom, helps us appreciate how and where practices of love assume such significance in our philosophical work. Put simply, love makes possible an attentive regard for others. It creates the space in which another can appear and shine as the one it uniquely is. Jean-Luc Marion has put it this way: "Only charity . . . opens the space where the gaze of the other can shine forth. The other appears only if I gratuitously give him the space in which to appear."[13] Marion's concern is that the machinations of consciousness normally reduce experience of others to what any particular consciousness allows or utilitarian intent demands. From a phenomenological point of view, even though we would think that the intentionality of consciousness would direct us beyond ourselves, the net effect of our reaching is to draw others into horizons of meaning and significance that we have predetermined. If love of another is not to devolve into self-love, a kind of self-idolatry in which I see in others always versions of myself, then there must be a transcending of intentional consciousness. For Marion, as for Emmanuel Levinas,[14] this occurs in the destabilizing gaze or "face" of another person who calls into question the conclusions of our intentional aim.

Another way to put this is to say that love makes possible a responsible engagement with the world. Though it is tempting to reduce responsibility into a decidedly moral description, as when we say that it is important for people to accept responsibility for their actions, responsibility's more fundamental meaning emerges as we demonstrate the patient, honest, non-evasive regard for and acceptance of what is before us. To be responsible is to be open to the sanctity of others and to sense the questionableness of the strategies we normally employ for comprehending them. To be irresponsible is to exhibit the basic impropriety in which the alterity and integrity of others does not register or does not count. It is to assume that we can understand ourselves and the world through and from ourselves alone.

It doesn't take much honest reflection to conclude that this assumption is false, because rather than our possessing or mastering life, life encompasses us. In its wholeness we are but one part. More fundamental to our living than our acting or planning, our choosing and deciding, is the fact that even before we are born we are receiving and appropriating the gifts of those around us. As Jean-Louis Chrétien would remind us, "Whatever we do, or do not do for that matter, wherever we are, we are always already called and requested, and our first utterance, like our first glance, is already an answer to the request wherein it emerges."[15] This means that we cannot consider ourselves to be autonomous or autarchic: "Before I can ask 'what should I do?' or 'how should I live?' I have already been addressed by a voice that positions me as a respondent. Its summons makes me a 'you' before I can establish myself as an 'I.' As responsivity, morality follows an address."[16] As one addressed by the world and thus called to respond to it, I am not without freedom altogether. Rather, the character or shape of our freedom develops as we move care-fully and responsively *within* the world instead of *apart* from it. Being truly within the world means that another can enter into our subjectivity and inspire us: "I exist through the other and for the other, but without this being alienation: I am inspired. This inspiration is the psyche."[17]

We are always dependent on others for our living, so the key distinction is not between freedom or unfreedom but between responsible or irresponsible dependence, between loving or non-loving engagement. Our living, in other words, is always conditioned by the limits and possibilities at work in the particular social and natural contexts we find ourselves in. If we deny these limits or think we can escape or surpass them, we will invariably, as history clearly shows, abuse the very contexts on which we depend. But if we respect these limits and accept our partiality—consider and attend to the distance and interdependence that characterize all of life—we position ourselves to develop an understanding that will make the world healthy and whole.[18]

Love is an exacting discipline that is vital to philosophical reflection because it is centrally about how we position ourselves in the world. Is our stance one that enables us to possess, control, manipulate, or predict (with an eye to subsequent control or manipulation)? If it is, then it is likely that we will not meet another as genuinely other, and will thus render ourselves incapable of affirming and nurturing others in their ability to be. We will not receive or engage others in their integrity or depth, but will instead only be dealing with reduced others, with others that conform to (and thus do not unsettle) the expectations or desires of a strictly pragmatic or self-serving consciousness. We will mistake what we wish another to be for what it in reality is.

For this very reason, the earliest vocation of the philosopher was essentially tied to the work of self-purification. In this work, what happens is that the ego learns to cleanse itself of the fantasies and arrogance that so readily distort its approach to the world. To be a genuine philosopher is to practice forms of philosophical detachment so that we can be truly open to the world and let it inform and inspire us. In significant measure, this is how we must understand the figure of Socrates, Western philosophy's prototypical philosopher. The piety of (unrelenting) questioning, but also the admission of our own ignorance, has everything to do with the destabilizing of egos determined to grasp and use others for their own wills.

Pierre Hadot has done a superb job drawing out this side of ancient philosophical practice. Referring to Socratic questioning, he observes that its purpose was not to bring an interlocutor to some conclusive result. It was rather to confront him or her with the vanity of their presumed knowledge. In exposing this vanity an important discovery becomes possible: the questionability of the knowledge seeker. "In the Socratic dialogue, the real question is less what is being talked about than who is doing the talking."[19] Or more specifically, what comes into view (and is thus made available for inspection) is the manner of life of the one doing the talking. For Socrates, the focus is not on what we know but on how we practically live and who we are. Are we living in pursuit of the good? Are we open and faithful to reality in its fundamental depth and complexity? The measure of our moral excellence, but also of our rationality, is a feature of such honest openness.

What Socrates initiated was a conception of philosophy rooted in "metanoetic consciousness," a way of thinking that is confessional and self-searching to the core. In an important sense, philosophizing must have as a recurring theme the acknowledgment of failures and sin (most notably pride). It must continually go through repentance (from the Greek *metanoia*, a change in the direction of one's mind and heart), the perpetual transformation of mind, so that the philosopher might be conformed to the good that he or she so much desires.[20] Genuine philosophizing takes the philosopher beyond his or her own fears, predispositions, or securities so that a more faithful and true embrace of the world becomes possible. The great philosophical error and perennial temptation, however, is to think that a genuinely philosophical life could proceed without attention to these practical disciplines of detachment and self-purification.

It is the merit of Martin Heidegger to have shown that one of the longstanding devices for avoiding this self-purification is the giving of reasons. When we give a reason for something, what we are finally doing is securing the position of it, placing (grounding) it in a context where it can be meaningful within a rational paradigm. As part of a rational order, it can then be "taken up" by a rational agent and "dealt with" in a variety of ways.[21] The reasons we give, therefore, and how we represent the world to others and ourselves are of profound moral and practical significance because it is as we represent the world according to this or that rational schema that we at the same time legitimate our practices. In other words, the philosophical work of giving reasons can become a means whereby thinkers justify or facilitate self-chosen aims, desires, or fears. Rather than being an opening to genuine understanding of the world, an understanding that acknowledges and affirms the alterity and integrity of others, philosophical *ratio* may turn out to be little more than the technical support for an industrial or technological program.

It is significant that Heidegger came to this realization through his reading of the mystics. *Gelassenheit*, Heidegger's term for letting others be what they are, presupposes an inward transformation such that thinking does not become an imposition of the ego upon another. Practically speaking, this means that the thinker must overcome a narrow self-love, the disposition that reduces others to the fulfillment of self-chosen aims, so that the integrity and sanctity of others can be acknowledged and affirmed. Because undue care for self—the strategies we employ to secure our position or advantage over and against that of others—has been overcome, we now become freed to encounter the other on its own terms.

Meister Eckhart, but also Angelus Silesius, were foremost in Heidegger's mind when he developed this position. According to Eckhart, the soul that is genuinely attuned to God must strive for nothing for fear that some vestige of the ego will be animating it. The soul must become completely available to God, and it does this by not caring for itself, by not trying to legitimate itself through some act of reason-giving. It must become, according to Silesius, like a rose that is "without why," a rose that simply blooms without need for an agenda or justification. It simply grows into the grace of God because it is animated by nothing but that grace. The rose has, in a sense, become a "clearing" in which God's givingness can take hold and shine. Its beauty resides in and is an unblemished display of the love of God at work within it. When the soul resembles the rose, it has stripped the ego of its controlling grip and thus made itself open and available to the grace of God. "The soul is the place of God, as God is the place of the soul. The ground of the soul is a 'place' among creatures into which God may come, a 'clearing' for God's advent into the world. An 'event'—God's coming—can happen in the soul because the soul has 'cleared' a place in which it may take place."[22]

To live "without why" or without the need to give self-justifying reasons is to live in a loving manner because now one has genuinely been opened to the mystery and wonder of the world. The soul is now detached and available so that others can inform and inspire its living. What becomes possible is a repositioning of the self so that it can be in harmonious and sympathetic alignment with the ways of the world. Rather than engaging others in terms of a calculating or controlling intelligence, an intelligence we see to be wreaking havoc and destruction in our social and biophysical neighborhoods, we learn instead to welcome and embrace the world as it is.

But is it possible, practically speaking, for us to live like a rose? After all, is it not naïve or rash to suppose that we can do away with reasons altogether? My point has not been to demolish all kinds of reasoning, since we can readily observe forms of reasoning that would highlight or amplify the integrity of others or that would draw out the complexity and depth of relationships that bind us together. Our goal should be to guard against the forms of reasoning that dissimulate or violently assimilate and that cloud the extent of our interdependence or the distance between ourselves and others. What we need to develop are practices of philosophical reflection that open us to the wonder and the sanctity of the world, practices that more humbly and responsibly position us in the world.

For this, we have models to help us. Consider here the ancient estimation that philosophical skill is analogous to the skill of a craftsperson. The successful execution of a craft depends on a craftsperson's first having undergone an apprenticeship to reality. What I mean by this "apprenticeship" is that the craftsperson never simply imposes his or her will on the world. Rather, what happens is that the apprentice learns to see cues that inspire and guide the design and work, cues that have their origin in the world itself. What makes a craftsperson excellent is that he or she has learned to be attentive to the needs, limits, possibilities, and desires of the social and natural world in which he or she moves, and has developed the skill to turn possibilities into realities that are pleasing, useful, enduring, and beautiful.[23]

On this view, true skill is a measure of how faithfully, honestly, and creatively one can respond to the potential that is the world. Such skill takes considerable time and discipline. It also requires repentance or *metanoia* as we learn to see our mistakes and correct them. The overall goal, however, is for the craftsperson to come into clearer alignment with the world. This aligning process is something like a conversation in which we offer our thoughts and plans to be tested in experience, knowing that we will be spoken to through the effects of our work (a failed or destructive result "calls" for a reevaluation of our entire plan and thought process). The master craftsperson is thus someone who puts him- or herself at the disposal of the craft. Building on the hermeneutical theory of Hans-Georg Gadamer, Joseph Dunne has put it this way: "A conversation really has a life of its own, and is most fruitful when the partners surrender to this life—a surrender that is accomplished, of course, only through the intense 'activity' of remaining open and responsive to the to and fro movement of the questioning."[24] Surrendering is a form of detachment in which the craftsperson submits to the demands of an art or skill. He or she becomes a "master" of a discipline insofar as his or her personal will is held in check. Of people such as these it is possible to say they are lovers of, rather than rulers over, their art.

The history of Western culture demonstrates that philosophers have wanted to be rulers far more than they have wanted to be lovers. Rather than offering ourselves up in a loving response to the world—in ways that would promote mutual flourishing—we have instead sought to bring others within our control. The result has been the world's and our own destruction or disfigurement. More than ever before, what we need is a transformation of philosophical practice so that an affirmation of others in their integrity can take place. But we cannot do this until we learn to encourage and practice those forms of love—affection, kindness, charity, mercy, delight, self-forgetting, and humility—that promote the expansion of our sympathies and the clarity of our vision. As we do this, we participate in the divine creative love that first brought and affirmed the world into being.

NOTES

1. Consider here Martin Heidegger's influential 1964 essay, "The End of Philosophy and the Task of Thinking," in *On Time and Being* (New York: Harper & Row, 1972), where the "end" refers to the realization of philosophy's "most extreme possibility." That possibility is modern technological culture, the scientific ordering of the world in terms of a utilitarian calculus. In our drive to manipulate the world for our own benefit, the "opening" or "unconcealing" (*aletheia*) of the world itself, what we might call its sacred dimension and its capacity to inspire wonder in us, is lost.

2. For a wide-ranging sociological analysis of our current situation, see Zygmunt Bauman's *Liquid Love: On the Frailty of Human Bonds* (Cambridge: Polity, 2003). The advent of "virtual proximity" and the dominance of free-market global economics have rendered all forms of social bonding more ambivalent and tenuous. In Bauman's view, the "skills of sociality" as well as care and affection are simply crumbling away.

3. In his *Journals and Papers* (ed. and trans. Howard V. Hong and Edna H. Hong [Bloomington: Indiana University Press, 1970], entry #1251) Søren Kierkegaard casts God's goodness and omnipotence in the following way: "All finite power makes [a being] dependent; only omnipotence can make [a being] independent, can form from nothing something which has its continuity in itself through the continual withdrawing of omnipotence" (2:62). My thanks to Merold Westphal for alerting me to this passage.

4. Jean-Luc Marion argues that we should understand God as "being-as-given" without restriction, reservation, or restraint. As such, God does not simply stand behind creation as its efficient cause. God ecstatically, lovingly "disseminates" Godself in creating a world that is not itself divine. This divine dissemination gives to creatures their character as saturated beings, beings that witness to "donation without reserve." See his essay "Metaphysics and Phenomenology: A Summary for Theologians," in *The Postmodern God: A Theological Reader*, ed. Graham Ward (Oxford: Blackwell, 1997), 279–96.

5. See Pierre Hadot's essay "Ancient Spiritual Exercises and 'Christian Philosophy'," in *Philosophy as a Way of Life*, ed. Arnold I. Davidson (Oxford: Blackwell, 1995), 126–44.

6. *The Cloud of Unknowing*, ed. William Johnston (New York: Doubleday, 1973), 54.

7. Simone Weil writes: "To love purely is to consent to distance, it is to adore the distance between ourselves and that which we love" (*Gravity and Grace* [London: Routledge, 1963], 58). This is why she also notes that love is the only real organ for genuine contact with existence (57).

8. Henry Bugbee, *The Inward Morning: A Philosophical Exploration in Journal Form* (Athens: University of Georgia Press, 1999), 65.

9. I am thinking here of the general homelessness and disembeddedness that characterize modern life. See the sociologist Anthony Giddens's work for an elabora-

tion of these themes, especially *The Consequences of Modernity* (Stanford, Calif.: Stanford University Press, 1990) and *Modernity and Self-Identity: Self and Society in the Late Modern Age* (Stanford, Calif.: Stanford University Press, 1991), and Erazim Kohák's *The Embers and the Stars: A Philosophical Inquiry into the Moral Sense of Nature* (Chicago: University of Chicago Press, 1984) for a particularly insightful account of the loss of wisdom in the context of homelessness. Kohák writes: "The bond of belonging that grows up over years of life, love, and labor is the most basic truth of being human in a world. . . . The distinction between possessing and belonging is crucial. Though humans may need to formalize having as possessing, the living truth of having is belonging, the bond of love and respect which grows between one being and another in the course of the seasons. The claim to having is as strong as all the love and care a person gives, and only that strong. It is crucial to have no more than we can love, for without love the claim to having becomes void. Loveless having, possessing in the purest sense, remains illegitimate, a theft" (107–108).

10. As Aristotle says (*Metaphysics* 981b10–13), sensory experience by itself is not wisdom because it does not tell us the "why" of things. Though the senses may be able to tell us that a particular thing is hot or of this or that composition or shape, they do not tell us why a thing is the way that it is, how it came to be this way, or what purpose its being serves. The analyses of the four causes (material, formal, efficient, and final) move us beyond the level of description to the deeper appreciation called understanding.

11. "It seems that there is a stream of limitless meaning flowing into the life of a man if he can but patiently entrust himself to it. There is no hurry, only the need to be true to what comes to mind, and to explore the current carefully in which one moves" (Bugbee, *Inward Morning*, 83). In a time of hyper-reality, of course, we are all hurried all of the time and thus do not have the time or patience to explore currents.

12. Michel de Montaigne, "Of Coaches," III:6 in *Essays*, trans. Donald Frame (Everyman Edition, New York: Alfred A. Knopf, 2003), 837.

13. Jean-Luc Marion, *Prolegomena to Charity*, trans. Stephen E. Lewis (New York: Fordham University Press, 2002), 166. Marion further compares our "making room" for another with God's original creative hospitality that makes room for creatures to be (167). In this respect, authentic human love is patterned upon God's love.

14. "The presence of the Other is equivalent to this calling into question of my joyous possession of the world" (Emmanuel Levinas, *Totality and Infinity: An Essay on Exteriority*, trans. Alphonso Lingis [Pittsburgh: Duquesne University Press, 1969], 75–76). For a description of the significance of the "face-to-face" encounter for philosophical work, see my essay "From Maieutics to Metanoia: Levinas's Understanding of the Philosophical Task" (*Man and World* 28 [1995]: 129–44).

15. Jean-Louis Chrétien, *The Call and the Response*, trans. Anne A. Davenport (New York: Fordham University Press, 2004), 14–15. In the face of our continually being called, Chrétien suggests, much like Bugbee, that "our task is not to give an answer that would in some sense erase the initial provocation by corresponding to it, but to offer ourselves up as such in response, without assigning in advance any limit to the gift" (13).

16. Adriaan Peperzak, *Elements of Ethics* (Stanford, Calif.: Stanford University Press, 2004), 54–55.

17. Emmanuel Levinas, *Otherwise than Being, Or Beyond Essence*, trans. Alphonso Lingis (The Hague: Martinus Nijhoff Publishers, 1981), 114.

18. For a careful description of the relation between wholeness and the acceptance of limits, see Wendell Berry's *The Unsettling of America: Culture and Agriculture*,

3rd ed. (San Francisco: Sierra Club Books, 1996), esp. chaps. 6 and 7. "A healthy culture is a communal order of memory, insight, value, work, conviviality, reverence, aspiration. It reveals the human necessities and the human limits. It clarifies our inescapable bonds to the earth and to each other. It assures that the necessary restraints are observed, that the necessary work is done, and that it is done well" (43). We simply cannot thrive for long at the expense of those on whom we depend. Our current environmental crises make this point very well; it is a fundamental error to think we can ignore or override biological limits and possibilities.

19. Pierre Hadot, *What is Ancient Philosophy?* trans. Michael Chase (Cambridge, Mass.: Harvard University Press, 2002), 28.

20. For a wide-ranging discussion of "metanoetic consciousness" in ethical and spiritual development, see Michael McGhee's *Transformations of Mind: Philosophy as Spiritual Practice* (Cambridge: Cambridge University Press, 2000), and the extensive study by Tanabe Hajime, *Philosophy as Metanoetics,* trans. Takeuchi Yoshinori (Berkeley: University of California Press, 1986). For Hajime, philosophical reflection reaches its most authentic pitch as the self moves beyond itself (as a self-standing being) and identifies with the being of the world: "'Meta-noetics' means transcending the contemplative or speculative philosophy of intellectual intuition as it is usually found in the realms of thought based on reason . . . it is not a philosophy founded on the intuitive reason of *jiriki* (self-power), but rather a philosophy founded on action-faith-witness (*gyō-shin-shō*) mediated by the transformative power of *tariki* (Other-power)" (2–3). What Hajime is describing is a submission to the world and the testing and correcting of one's thought and speech made possible by that submission.

21. Martin Heidegger, *The Principle of Reason,* trans. Reginald Lilly (Bloomington: Indiana University Press, 1991).

22. John D. Caputo, *The Mystical Element in Heidegger's Thought* (Athens: Ohio University Press, 1978), 113. In this excellent study, Caputo demonstrates convincingly the theological parallels in Heidegger's philosophical work. Of course, this is not to turn Heidegger into a theologian. Caputo summarizes: "Eckhart's life without why is a life of perfect love and perfect unity with God, which allows God to enter the soul and become the principle of life. Heidegger's life without why is the renunciation of concepts and representations, of propositions and ratiocinations about Being; it lets Being be Being" (191).

23. The forms of attention that are here essential have become much harder to realize in the context of global economic life. Promising alternatives, alternatives that can help restore social and natural health and wholeness, are to be found in emerging "local economies" and the encouragement of "focal practices." For accounts of the former, see *The Case Against the Global Economy: And a Turn Toward the Local,* ed. Jerry Mander and Edward Goldsmith (San Francisco: Sierra Club Books, 1996) and Bill McKibben's *Deep Economy* (New York: Times Books, 2007), and for the latter, Albert Borgmann's *Crossing the Postmodern Divide* (Chicago: University of Chicago Press, 1992).

24. Joseph Dunne, *Back to the Rough Ground: 'Phronesis' and 'Techne' in Modern Philosophy and in Aristotle* (Notre Dame: University of Notre Dame Press, 1993), 136.

2

The Economies of Knowledge and Love in Paul

BRUCE ELLIS BENSON

The entire pericope of 1 Corinthians 8–10 can be situated between the strange juxtaposition of two phrases that we find at the beginning of chapter 8: *"Peri de tôn eidôlothutôn"* [now concerning food sacrificed to idols] and *"oidamen hoti pantes gnôsin exomen"* [we know that 'all of us possess knowledge'].[1] While it might seem as if Paul turns to idolatry only to be immediately distracted by one of the chief claims of the Corinthians—that they "know"— the linking of idolatry and knowledge is crucial to Paul's argument.[2] Since knowledge claims and idolatry often go together, Paul actually addresses what turn out to be variants of a well-established pattern.

In what follows, I will argue that Paul in effect lays out two economies, that of a particular sort of knowledge (rather than simply knowledge per se) and that of love. These economies are in turn defined by a series of dichotomies—puffing up and building up, the strong and the weak, and exercising one's freedom versus being a servant and a steward. All of these categories have a connection to idolatry. As we will see, for Paul idolatry is very closely connected to knowledge claims that Paul thinks one simply isn't entitled to make. And making those claims means that one is part of the economy of knowledge, not love.

The Economy of Knowledge

That Paul thinks knowledge and love are dichotomous is clear from the way he contrasts them already in the first verse. "Knowledge puffs up," he says, "but love builds up" (8:1). *Gnôsis phusioi, agapê oikodomei.* This puffing up versus building up is not merely a feature of English translation. Each verb carries the idea of "constructing," though the two constructions are remarkably different in nature. *Phusioô* literally means "to inflate" (from the term for bellows, *phusa*). Yet Paul always uses the term metaphorically (and negatively) for the pride that inflates one's ego. *Oikodomeô* is literally "the building of a house," an *oikos*. For instance, Matthew uses the term in that well-known parable of two persons who build houses, one on the rock and the other on the sand (Matt 7:24). Yet the term is used both literally and metaphorically for building in general.

Although Paul doesn't explicitly "build" his argument on the root of *oikodomeô*, I read him as setting out—both in this verse and throughout the letter—two conflicting economies. The economy of love is an *oikonomia* that is focused on an *oikos*, not a house in this case, but the household of faith. But as we will see, it is also a "stewardship" of that with which one has been entrusted—the right use of something that comes as a gift. Paul clearly would have been aware of the etymological connections between *oikodomeô* and *oikonomia*, though whether he is thinking in terms of two economies per se would be hard to argue. Thus, my argument is merely that this is effectively what he does, rather than that this is what he had (so to speak) "in mind."

Given that Paul begins chapter 7 by saying "Now concerning the matters about which you wrote," commentators generally agree that Paul is responding to a letter or series of letters from the Corinthians.[3] His use of the locution *peri de* here and elsewhere in this text indicates that he is responding to a concern raised by the Corinthians. Moreover, Paul appears to be quoting from the Corinthians' letter(s) and responding to each point. What makes Paul's use of quotations complicated is that the degree to which he agrees with what the Corinthians write is not always clear (nor is it clear what is part of the quotation and what is Paul's addition). As will become evident, my own view is that Paul's use of quotation in the text is often both ironic and critical.

Certainly the first quotation of chapter 8 fits that description. Paul quotes back to the Corinthians something that seems to have been a kind of motto of theirs: "We all know" [*pantes gnôsin exomen*]. But more than that, he prefaces that motto with the phrase "*oidamen hoti.*" Taken together, the entire phrase "*oidamen hoti pantes gnôsin exomen*" is a meta-epistemological claim: "We know that we know."[4] Although we could explore exactly how *gnôsis* functions here (for instance, does it denote some esoteric knowledge regarding the true nature of the physical and spiritual realms?), I'll leave that question aside. Whatever this *gnôsis* may be, the Corinthians clearly think it empowers them —and *that* is what disturbs Paul.[5] Rather than reading Paul as including himself in the "we know that,"[6] I read Paul as describing the attitude of the Corinthians.

That the problem here is not simply "knowing" but a kind of "knowing that one knows" becomes clear in verse 2. Paul says: "Anyone who claims to know something does not yet have the necessary knowledge." The key word here is *dokeô*, which means "to suppose or think something." In effect, Paul says that, at the very moment you think you "know," you don't actually know as you ought to know—which is to say, you don't really "know." Here we have Paul at his enigmatic best. But he is certainly not without precedent in making such a puzzling claim. One cannot help but think of the similarly enigmatic remark Jesus makes to the Pharisees. They say to him: "Surely we are not blind, are we?" He responds: "If you were blind, you would have no sin. But now that you say, 'We see,' your sin remains" (John 9:40–41).[7] It is not the moment of knowing (or seeing) but the moment of claiming knowledge that is problematic. Not only is the claim disproportional to the actual knowledge they possess, but also *how* they make the claim troubles Paul.

Let us first turn to the "disproportionality" of the claim. At issue here is the status of their knowledge claims—or, put more pointedly, the status they *claim* for those claims. If one says *"oidamen hoti pantes gnôsin exomen,"* then one is making a very strong claim indeed. The verb *oida* (to know) comes from the root **eidô* (to see). In Plato's philosophy, for instance, knowing the *eidos* (usually translated as 'form' or 'idea') of something means that one has grasped it perfectly. To know the *eidos* is not merely to know the "outward form" of something but to know its "true reality." When comparing his knowledge of the Father to that of the Pharisees, Jesus claims, "You have never heard his voice or seen his form [*eidos*]" (John 5:37). In other words, they don't really "know" the Father. The kind of knowledge that *oida* provides is "comprehension," as opposed to "apprehension." Whereas comprehension is to "conceive fully or adequately,"[8] apprehension suggests incompleteness. "Adequately" here does not mean "good enough" but "adequation" in the sense of the medieval phrase *adaequatio intellectus et rei*—a perfect one-to-one correspondence between the mind and the object of thought. *Oida* is often used in this sense of knowing perfectly or fully in the New Testament. Again, in rebuking the Pharisees, Jesus contrasts his knowledge of the Father with theirs by claiming that his is on the order of *oida* (John 8:55). That Paul uses the term *dokeô* in the phrase "anyone who claims to know" [*dokei egnôkenai*] shows that he thinks their knowledge claim is no more than an opinion—and a bad one at that.

But there is a second, even if closely related aspect at stake: *how* those claims are made. It is a common interpretation to suggest that Paul contrasts knowledge and love in verse 1 with the intention of saying that love needs to temper or inform knowledge. For instance, Augustine says:

> Now the Apostle, under the inspiration of the Holy Spirit, says, "Knowledge inflates; but love edifies." The only correct interpretation of this saying is that knowledge is valuable when charity informs it. Without charity, knowledge inflates; that is, it exalts man to arrogance which is nothing but a kind of windy emptiness.[9]

At the risk of going against "the only correct interpretation," I want to argue for a distinction between the economy of knowledge and the economy of love. The difference between the two is where each begins, which is to say their respective *grounds*. Whereas the economy of knowledge begins with me, the economy of love begins with the other. Or to put it another way, while knowledge is something that *I* ground, love is that which the *other* grounds. In the economy of knowledge, I maintain that *I* am able to give sufficient reasons for whatever it is I take to be true.

Precisely that difference explains another strange transition, the one that occurs between verses 2 and 3. In verse 2, Paul speaks from the active perspective of the knower. Yet in verse 3, he suddenly reverses perspectives: he now talks (passively) about *being known* by God: "But anyone who loves God is known by him." Furthermore, it is here that knowledge and love are connected, not in the sense that love "informs" knowledge (*pace* Augustine), but in the sense that love proves to be the possibility condition for knowledge. So there is still knowledge, but two significant changes have taken place: first, one only obtains knowledge by way of love; and second, knowledge is fundamentally not about *what I do* but about *what God does*. Love is put in first place, with knowledge taking second place. Moreover, God is put in first place, with me taking second place.

That Paul thinks there is a distinct difference between the economy of knowledge and the economy of love is already clear from the first chapter of his letter, where he asks (rhetorically): "Has not God made foolish the wisdom of the world?" (1:20). Although Paul does distinguish between "wisdom" and "knowledge" (most notably in 1 Corinthians 12:8, in which they are listed as separate gifts of the Spirit), that distinction is irrelevant for the point I am making here. For both the "wisdom" and the "knowledge" that Paul criticizes in 1 Corinthians have a *human* basis, meaning that they are grounded on the self. But this is precisely what Paul takes to be impossible. Moreover, such "justification" likewise provides license for sinful practices.[10] For Paul, the "wisdom of the world" [*sophia tou kosmou*] includes both the Jewish demand for signs [*sêmeia*] and the Greek search for wisdom [*sophia*] (1:22). In their place is put a new *logos*, "*ho logos ho tou staurou*" [the *logos* of the cross] (1:18).[11] As Stanislas Breton notes, with the adoption of this new *logos* "we have left the home of Israel just as we have left the home of Greece," the result being that "the Western thinker is divided from *within*."[12] Leaving Jerusalem means that we can no longer demand a sign as the requirement of our belief. Leaving Athens means that we give up the demand of *logon didonai*—giving reasons. From the standpoint of the economy of knowledge, then, the *logos* of the cross is truly foolishness. Indeed, the very connection of *logos* with *stauros* [cross] can only be reckoned as folly [*môria*]. Yet that folly, which has at its heart the kenotic self-emptying of Godself, demonstrates its own sort of strength in that it "shatters the idol of power."[13] In place of the wisdom of the world is put God's wisdom, which is "secret and hidden" and "decreed before the ages" (2:7). Such wisdom cannot be "owned" or "mastered." It is beyond our comprehension.

A Taste for Idolatry

The strange series of reversals that we noted in verses 1–3 of chapter 8 takes place within the context of idolatry—more specifically, food sacrificed to idols. And that is not purely coincidental, for there is an important connection between Paul's claims regarding knowledge and the topic of idolatry. Earlier we noted the connection between *oida* and **eidô*, in which seeing for the Greeks is equated with knowing. The word for *idol* in Greek—*eidôlon*—is linked to both of those terms. Unlike God, the idol is something we both see and are truly able to grasp (to *comprehend*), for the simple reason that we are its creators. As Jean-Luc Marion puts it, "The idol presents itself to man's gaze in order that representation, and hence knowledge, can seize hold of it."[14] Yet, claiming that the idol is in reality "nothing," the Corinthians feel confident enough to write, "We know that 'no idol in the world really exists'" and "'There is no God but one'" (8:4). In one sense, the Corinthians are correct. But it is in both the Corinthians' actual claim and the *way* it is made that Paul detects the threat of two sorts of idolatry. The first sort is the obvious one of partaking (either directly or indirectly) in pagan rites. We'll turn to that momentarily. But it is the other sort of idolatry—what we might call the idolatry of knowledge or "conceptual idolatry"—that we turn to first. In such idolatry, not only are human claims made too strongly, but those claims foster an arrogance that can lead one to idolatry. *This* sort of idolatry—rather than that of creating or bowing down to graven images—is actually the first recorded in Scripture.

Dietrich Bonhoeffer points out that in Genesis 3 we have "the first conversation *about* God, the first religious, theological conversation."[15] Like all theological conversations, this one depends upon a particular *conception* of God, for there can be no theology without a "*logy*" or a *logos*. It is here that we find the first *mis*conceptions of God. But it is also here that human beings develop a *taste* for idolatry—and this taste is closely connected to knowledge.

Consider the opening salvo of the serpent's seduction of the woman. "Did God ['elôhim] say, 'You shall not eat from any tree in the garden?'" (Gen 3:1). The serpent's subtle rhetorical twist turns the focus from God's gracious permission ("You may freely eat of every tree of the garden," 2:16) to the one and only prohibition placed on Adam and Eve's liberty ("but of the tree of the knowledge of good and evil you shall not eat," 2:18).[16] Given the serpent's characterization, God's nature has already been distorted—a false image of God, as one who prohibits rather than enables, has been put in God's place. To this distortion, the woman responds: "We may eat of the fruit of the trees in the garden; but God said: 'You shall not eat of the fruit of the tree that is in the middle of the garden, nor shall you touch it, or you shall die'" (3:2). The woman rightly rejects the image of God presented by the serpent, even if she also slightly distorts what God has said by adding "touching" to God's more simple command of "eating" (2:17).[17] In response to the woman's correction, the serpent simply provides a *different* distorted image of God. For the serpent now says: "You will not die; for God knows that when you eat of it your eyes will be opened, and you will be like God, knowing good and evil" (3:4–5). Here we have not merely an image of God as liar but also one that actually reflects the serpent's deceitfulness. Yet this should come as no surprise, for Marion reminds us that the idol always serves "as a mirror, not as a portrait; a mirror that reflects the gaze's image."[18] That is exactly what we get from the serpent: a "portrait" of God that is a mirror image of the serpent. Such is the nature of all idolatry, according to Marion:

> The idol reflects back to us, in the face of a god, our own experience of the divine. The idol does not resemble us, but it resembles the divinity that we experience, and it gathers it in a god in order that we might see it.[19]

Thus, the nature of the conceptual idol is always based on the nature of the viewer. What we get in idolatry is a "picture" of God that reflects our distorted experience of God. Yet the idolatry does not stop there, for the serpent in effect claims to be able to get into the mind of God and postulate *why* God has made this command. Not only does this theory regarding God's motives presume knowledge the serpent cannot have (resulting in its being *ungrounded*), it also makes God out to be both petty and envious.

Up until this point, only the serpent is engaged in idolatry. But the hook that draws the woman in is the claim that she "will be like God." It is here that the taste for idolatry—perhaps already latent—is cultivated. Jacques Derrida speaks of his "taste" for the secret, for whatever can "never be broached/breached."[20] We have a taste for that which is secret precisely because it stands at the edge of our limits. It is the "absolute," that which language cannot express or human reason fathom.[21] We want to invert the order of things, taking ourselves beyond our natural limits. It is *this* taste that the woman has. At the moment that she lusts after the fruit, she has developed a taste for idolatry. She seeks the transcendence of human limitations, enabling her to become like God. Gerhard von Rad describes that desire as follows:

> What the serpent's insinuation means is the possibility of an extension of human existence beyond the limits set for it by God at creation, an increase in life not only in the sense of pure intellectual enrichment but also familiarity with, and power over, mysteries that lie beyond man.[22]

Exactly what this God-like "knowing" [*yd'*] involves is certainly open to debate,[23] but it is instructive that the woman sees the tree as (1) "good for food," (2) "a delight to the eyes," and (3) "desired to make one wise." Here we have the combination of taste, sight, and knowledge. Eve clearly has a taste for that knowledge (whether *yd'* or *oida*) that constitutes idolatry. For the delight that Eve experiences is primarily the delight of inverting the proper order of creator and creature and usurping God's place. She lusts after the knowledge that puffs up. The eating of the fruit is merely the satisfaction of that desire. Yet the result of that "puffing up" is a broken fellowship. What had been a perfect relationship between human and divine being is broken at the very moment that the human wants to become divine. So idolatry begins with a distorted image of God and ends with wanting to *be* God.

The Corinthians likewise have a taste for idolatry, in at least two different (though not unrelated) senses. The most obvious aspect of that taste is the literal taste that appears not to be "idolatrous" at all. Although commentators have often taken the issue in these chapters to be simply about buying idol meat in the market or the possibility of being served it while dining with friends, the situation faced by the Corinthians was far more complicated than that. For the Corinthians were literally *surrounded* by pagan practices. Imagine an atheist living in the Bible Belt in the 1950s, and you begin to get a kind of reverse perspective. There were all sorts of social occasions—weddings, birthdays, thanksgiving dinners, funerals, holidays—that would have included sacrificial rites or at least prayers as part of the celebration. Moreover, meals were served both in temples as part of pagan ritual and likely also just as "regular" meals.[24] Given that environment, if one wanted to take part in Corinthian social life, one had to make some concessions to pagan practices. And how could one turn down all of those invitations to lavish parties and dinners given by one's pagan friends who served such tasty fare, especially if one wanted to get ahead in life? Just as in our society, in the Greco-Roman world one's status was measured by the company one kept and the people with whom one dined. The Romans actually had a word for a "social climber" who advanced by getting dinner invitations from important persons—*parasitus*.[25] But the Corinthians rationalize that they can continue social life as usual just by thinking "no idol in the world really exists." Going back to my earlier comparison, it would be like an atheist attending a Thanksgiving dinner at the home of Christian friends who begin the meal with a prayer in which they asked God's blessing on the food. The atheist thinks: "There's no god, so the prayer is just meaningless." Likewise, the Corinthians insist that, since idols don't really exist, eating idol food shouldn't be a problem.

While it might appear (from chapter 8) that Paul agrees with them, his argument in chapter 10 makes it clear that he has been parroting back their own beliefs, not necessarily agreeing with them.[26] For in chapter 10, he claims that "what pagans sacrifice, they sacrifice to demons [*daimoniôn*] and not to God" (10:20). In other words, it is too simple to say that idols are just "nothing." Although an idol does not truly "exist," Paul thinks that taking part in pagan rites (including meals associated with them) means partaking in "the table of demons" (10:21). That Paul thinks they are in danger of idolatry is clear from his warnings in the first part of chapter 10, where he draws a parallel between the ways the Israelites continually "tested" God and the ways the Corinthians are testing God by their behavior. "We must not put Christ to the test," warns Paul in 10:9, and he asks, "Are we provoking the Lord to jealousy?" (10:22). Paul thinks the Corinthians' arrogance has caused them to be so bold as to put God to the test, which is itself idolatrous.

Yet the Corinthians test God in another sense. Their arrogance does not merely lead to this literal sort of idolatry. It likewise leads to one of a much subtler sort, one that might not even seem to be idolatry at first glance. For the Corinthians have a taste for pushing things to the limits, for seeing just how far they can really go. Again, the taste is for a kind of transcendence. In the same way that "We all know" was one motto for the Corinthians, "All things are lawful" (6:12 and 10:23) was another. Literally, this could be rendered "I am free to do anything" [*panta moi exestiv*], but we might better capture the *force* of the claim if we translated it—in keeping with current usage—as "We have our rights!" What is at stake here is not merely the Corinthians' *exousia* (right) and *eleutheria* (freedom) but also their absolute *insistence* on being able to exercise those rights without hindrance. That haughty insistence stands behind Paul's entire discourse in chapters 6 through 10.

While Paul himself preached a message of freedom from the law when he had been in their midst, he clearly thinks they are abusing it in selfish—and even idolatrous—ways. Once again, Paul takes on an ironic posture, much like that which he exhibits in 4:10 where he says, "We are fools for the sake of Christ, but you are wise in Christ. We are weak, but you are strong. You are held in honor, but we in disrepute." That passage almost drips with sarcasm. Paul's move is first and foremost deflationary. When he writes, "It is not everyone, however, who has this knowledge" (8:7), it is an inversion of what he had said only a few verses before—*oidamen hoti pantes gnôsin exomen*. As it turns out, we *don't* all possess knowledge—and that "we" can easily be taken to include the seemingly "strong." In other words, Paul can be read as suggesting that the Corinthians are not necessarily so strong after all. With that in mind, Paul's famous warning in chapter 10—"So if you think you are standing, watch out that you do not fall" (10:12)—should be taken as a rebuke to those who *think* they are strong. The message is clear: your pretensions to strength may well prove your undoing.

But Paul does not stop with merely undercutting their arrogant claims to "knowledge," to "knowing the secret." To correct the abuse of their *exousia* and *eleutheria*, Paul articulates a guideline by invoking a fictitious entity—the so-called "weak." There is no textual evidence to suggest the existence of any "party" of weaker believers in Corinth, so it is hard to maintain the usual view of this passage: that there were "weak" and "strong" factions in the church at Corinth.[27] If anything, it seems that the Corinthians uniformly consider themselves "strong." So the example of the weak is not an *actual* case but a *test* case invoked as a kind of guiding principle designed not only to call the Corinthians up short but also to demonstrate what the proper exercise of Christian liberty looks like in practice. By turning to the weak, Paul shows that one's freedom is not curbed by some law but rather by other members of the body.

Here one cannot help but think of the way Emmanuel Levinas argues that it is the *other* who curbs my freedom. "Autonomy or heteronomy?" asks Levinas. "The choice of Western philosophy has most often been on the side of freedom."[28] Such has certainly been the choice of the Corinthians, who are insisting on their autonomy. To act with autonomy is literally to be one's own [*auto*] law [*nomos*]. Yet Levinas calls us to "heteronomous" acting, in which concern for the other curbs our freedom. There is a good reason why Levinas speaks of being "traumatized" by the other in *Otherwise than Being,* for the other's appearance radically disturbs my egoism and calls my vaunted autonomy into question.[29] In effect, Levinas distinguishes between a natural self, one defined by its egoism of enjoyment, and an ethical self that takes the other into account.[30] In order to become an ethical self, I must become a self that is directed toward the other, and this requires a radical rethinking of who I am. Levinas says: "The word *I* means *here I am,* answering for everything and everyone."[31] Thus, the subject for Levinas is truly a "subject" in the sense of *being subject* to another.[32] And the paradigmatic figures to whom the subject is "subject" are precisely the lowest in terms of strength. "The Other who dominates me in his transcendence is thus the stranger, the widow, and the orphan, to whom I am obligated."[33] In this, as in so many other ways, the economy of love demands that the "first will be last" (Mark 10:31). The result is that "I *am no longer able to have power*: the structure of my freedom is . . . completely reversed."[34] "Before the Other, the I is infinitely responsible."[35] What Levinas means by this "infinity" of responsibility is (among other things) that there is no point at which I can draw the line and say: "I'm no longer responsible for you. I've done enough." Instead, my responsibility extends indefinitely, in the same way that Jesus makes clear in the parable of the so-called good Samaritan (Luke 10:29–37) that our responsibility to the neighbor has no clear boundaries or limits. I say "so-called good," because Jesus makes it clear that the Samaritan, while "good," does nothing extraordinary or even particularly commendable. Rather, he simply does what any good neighbor would do.

In invoking the weak, Paul is telling a story of what true neighborliness looks like—which is to say, a proper exercise of *exousia* and *eleutheria*. And evidently Paul had read his Levinas. For he makes it clear that, given the choice of autonomy or heteronomy, I am compelled to choose heteronomy. My responsibility is fundamentally to my neighbor. It is not that I am not free or that I do not have any rights; rather, it is that the boundaries of my freedom and rights are drawn by the mere existence of my neighbor. Moreover, not just *any* members of the body have this effect on us: the *weakest* ones turn out to have the *strongest* claim on us. No doubt the Corinthians—if they took Paul's letter seriously, which is certainly open to question—would have found his claim traumatizing. "I have to turn down those important social invitations *just because* my eating affects someone else?" Paul's answer to any such objections takes up all of chapter 9. There Paul details his reasons why he could—if he so chose—exercise his rights, not just as a Christian but as an apostle who has seen the risen Lord (9:1). Paul's argument is that it is not his *rights* that compel him to act as he does, but his responsibility. He says: "An obligation is laid on me" and "I am entrusted with a commission" (9:16–17). It is in light of that responsibility that Paul talks about becoming all things to all people. But, of course, such is the truly neighborly thing to do.[36]

What, though, does all of this have to do with idolatry? Paul makes it clear that, in improperly exercising one's liberty, one sins not merely against one's neighbor but also "against Christ" (8:12). To say that such believers sin against Christ is really to say that they are guilty of idolatry, because they have allowed themselves a freedom that they simply are not allowed to have. In effect, such persons make themselves out to be "God" by elevating themselves above others. It is the same desire for transcendence found already in Genesis 3.

In response to their supercilious claims of "knowledge" and insistence on their *exousia* and *eleutheria*, Paul provides an account of the economy of love, which overcomes knowledge and has its own kind of "wisdom."

The Wisdom of Love

Inverting the literal meaning of "philosophy" [the love of wisdom], Levinas speaks of "the wisdom of love." What distinguishes this "wisdom" is that it is "at the service of love."[37] Here Levinas follows the same kind of inversion that we saw earlier in Paul: love takes the place of knowledge in the sense that it both *founds* knowledge (and founds *us*) and *transcends* knowledge. "Knowledge puffs up," says Paul, maybe not always but often. In contrast, love edifies, for love partakes of an entirely different economy than that of knowledge.

The economy of love is the economy of the gift, which is to say an economy that does not begin with us and is in reality no economy at all (in the sense that it does not operate by the usual structure of reciprocity).[38] Earlier we noted the strange reversal between verses 2 and 3 of chapter 8, in which Paul suddenly shifts from our knowing to our being known. That formula of being known by God as preceding our knowledge of God is common in Paul. For instance, in Galatians 4:9 Paul begins by saying, "Now, however, that you have come to know God," but then he quickly corrects himself by adding "or rather to be known by God." We think in terms of our "knowing God," but that—to use Heideggerian language—is a "founded" mode of knowing. Properly speaking, the ground of our knowing is our *being known* by God. In speaking of one day knowing "fully" (whatever that means exactly), Paul describes this state with the phrase "even as I have been fully known" (13:12).[39] But this shift of standpoint from us to God is not just found in Paul's comments about knowing: it applies universally. Paul says to the Corinthians, "All things are yours," but immediately qualifies that claim by saying "and you belong to Christ" (3:23). In short, both our knowing and our having begin with God's knowing and having. That we have anything at all is purely a gift.

Much like Levinas, Marion speaks of the other's claim on me. Yet this "other" turns out to be the ultimate "Other." In language clearly reminiscent of that of Levinas, Marion says that we are held in *God's* gaze, which means that we are "deposed from any autarchy and taken by surprise."[40] In effect, God's call displaces me from being the center of my world. Since the call (vocative) is to *me* (dative), there is no longer an *I* but a *me*. The "I" is no longer the source of reason or even my identity, which "can be proclaimed only when called—by the call of the other."[41] In *Reduction and Givenness*, Marion refers to the one called as the *"interloqué."* But, in *Being Given*, he speaks of the *adonné*, "the gifted." There he says that the "gift happens to *me* because it precedes *me* originarily in such a way that I must recognize that I proceed from it."[42] In keeping with what Paul says about knowledge (i.e., that it is a gift, 12:8), Marion says that "the gifted [*adonné*] does not have language or *logos* as its property, but it finds itself endowed with them."[43]

The logic of love is that we are first loved. And the love bestowed on us is the possibility condition of our showing love to others. Thus far, the logic of love makes sense. But at its very core, it is inscrutable. For the logic of love is the logic of a gamble, of a loss without any assurances of a possible gain, a kenosis. As Marion puts it, "The logic of love . . . does not rely upon an assurance."[44] And yet love persists. The *oikonomia* that constitutes the *oikodomeô* of love that Paul describes is remarkable in its tenacity. In what is clearly a stinging rebuke of the Corinthians, Paul describes precisely how they have *not* been acting:

> Love is patient; love is kind; love is not envious or boastful or arrogant or rude. It does not insist on its own way; it is not irritable or resentful; it does not rejoice in wrongdoing, but rejoices in the truth. It bears all things, believes all things, hopes all things, endures all things (13:4–7).

That love "bears," "believes," "hopes," and "endures" *all things* is precisely why Marion calls it an "unconditional surrender," a surrender that certainly also requires *faith*.[45] No better illustration of the sheer inexplicability of love is that Christ gave himself despite the fact that "his own received him not" (John 1:11, KJV). Yet such is the nature of *agapê* that "surpasses all knowledge, with a hyperbole that defines it and, indissolubly, prohibits access to it."[46] How could one make sense of that which bears and believes and hopes and endures all things? Love utterly confounds the wisdom of the world. It is no wonder, then, that Heidegger asks: "Will Christian theology one day resolve to take seriously the word of the apostle and thus also the conception of philosophy as foolishness?"[47]

What could be more at odds with the Corinthians' pretensions to "knowledge" and their insistence upon their *exousia* and *eleutheria* than love? Precisely in *not* being "envious or boastful or arrogant or rude" and in refusing to "insist on its own way," love does not puff up but edifies. Yet it also escapes idolatry. Whereas the economy of knowledge, with its certainty and insistence upon its *exousia* and *eleutheria*, naturally leads to idolatry, the economy of love leads in the other direction. For the one who loves neither makes boastful claims about his "knowledge" nor seeks to be elevated to a higher station. The one who loves is instead content to be held in God's loving gaze, not clinging tightly to a knowledge that "will come to an end" but instead basking in the gaze of a love that "never ends" (13:8). And that love that comes from God naturally and spontaneously overflows to one's neighbor, without measure or thought of repayment.

NOTES

1. All biblical citations are from the *New Revised Standard Version* unless otherwise indicated.

2. Gordon Fee claims that the entire passage seems to be a non sequitur. But the non sequitur actually occurs between the first and second part of verse 1. Verses 2 and 3 follow Paul's switch to the theme of knowledge, while verses 4 through 6 return us to the original theme of food sacrificed to idols. See Gordon D. Fee, "*Eidolothuta* Once Again: An Interpretation of 1 Corinthians 8–10," *Biblica* 16 (1980): 172.

3. For some possible hypotheses on the exact sequence of exchange of letters, see Hans Conzelmann, *1 Corinthians: A Commentary on the First Epistle to the Corinthians*, trans. James W. Leitch (Philadelphia: Fortress, 1975), 3–4. For an attempt to reconstruct the exchanges, see John C. Hurd Jr., *The Origin of 1 Corinthians* (New York: Seabury, 1965), 290–93.

4. It is quite possible that the entire phrase—"*oidamen hoti pantes gnôsin exomen*" [we know that we know]—is from the Corinthians. If so, that would further strengthen my case. But in order to make my point I only need to claim that it represents what the Corinthians think about themselves.

5. While Paul often uses *gnôsis* positively (e.g., in 1 Cor 1:5), here he thinks that it is problematic.

6. Such is Conzelmann's reading, for example.

7. This strange saying is preceded by yet another. Right before the Pharisees ask their question, Jesus says, "I came into this world for judgment so that those who do not see may see, and those who do see may become blind" (John 9:39). It is in response to *that* statement that the Pharisees pose their question.

8. *The Oxford English Dictionary*, 2nd ed. (Oxford: Oxford University Press, 1999), s.v. "comprehend."

9. Saint Augustine, *City of God*, trans. Henry Bettenson (London: Penguin, 1972), 9.20.

10. Wisdom and knowledge are woven together in Paul's discussion in 2:6–16. For more on the relation of wisdom and knowledge in 1 Corinthians, see Michael D. Goulder, *Paul and the Competing Mission in Corinth* (Peabody, Mass.: Hendrickson, 2001), 92–103.

11. Louis Martyn notes that "the cross is and remains *the* epistemological crisis." See his chapter titled "Epistemology at the Turn of the Ages: 2 Cor. 5:16," in *Christian History and Interpretation: Studies Presented to John Knox,* ed. W. R. Farmer, C. F. D. Moule, and R. R. Niebuhr (Cambridge: Cambridge University Press, 1967), 285.

12. Stanislas Breton, *The Word and the Cross,* trans. Jacquelyn Porter (New York: Fordham University Press, 2002), 132.

13. Ibid., 98

14. Jean-Luc Marion, *God without Being,* trans. Thomas A. Carlson (Chicago: University of Chicago Press, 1991), 9–10.

15. Dietrich Bonhoeffer, *Creation and Fall: A Theological Exposition of Genesis 1–3,* trans. and ed. Martin Rüter and Ilse Tödt (Minneapolis: Fortress Press, 1997), 111.

16. Walter Brueggemann points out that the story of the garden is one in which God gives human beings a vocation, permission, and a prohibition. By deliberately focusing on the prohibition, the serpent distorts what God has said (and thus—I would add—*who* God is). See Walter Brueggemann, *Genesis: A Bible Commentary for Teaching and Preaching* (Atlanta: John Knox, 1982), 46.

17. Of course, some commentators assume that "touching" is implied by "eating."

18. Marion, *God without Being,* 12.

19. Jean-Luc Marion, *The Idol and Distance: Five Studies,* trans. Thomas A. Carlson (New York: Fordham University Press, 2001), 6.

20. Jacques Derrida and Maurizio Ferraris, *A Taste for the Secret,* trans. Giacomo Donis (Cambridge: Polity, 2001), 57.

21. It is not accidental that the Latin term *sapiential* also connotes "taste."

22. Gerhard von Rad, *Genesis: A Commentary,* rev. ed., trans. John H. Marks (Philadelphia: Westminster, 1972), 89.

23. See E. A. Speiser's discussion in his *Genesis* (New York: Doubleday, 1982), 26. He claims that *yd'* means not merely "know" but the entire process of coming to know. Lyn M. Bechtel, no doubt influenced by structuralism, claims that this knowing is "the capacity to discern the binary oppositions of life." See her "Rethinking the Interpretation of Genesis 2.4b–3.24," in *A Feminist Companion to Genesis,* ed. Athalya Brenner (Sheffield, U.K.: Sheffield Academic Press, 1993), 88.

24. Here I am particularly indebted to Peter D. Gooch, *Dangerous Food: 1 Corinthians 8–10 in Its Context* (Waterloo, Ont.: Wilfrid Laurier University Press, 1993). Gooch argues that Paul is not primarily addressing sacrificial meat sold in the market. Instead, Paul is concerned with partaking in meals connected to pagan rites. Note that the question is not just one of "meat" (*krea*), since Paul also uses the generic term for food (*brôma*) in 8:13.

25. See the discussion in Gooch, *Dangerous Food,* 40–45.

26. In 8:4, Paul repeats the Corinthian claim that "no idol in the world really exists," but he does not necessarily *affirm* it.

27. Both Hurd and Fee (following Hurd) take this view, and I find their arguments convincing. See Hurd, *The Origin of 1 Corinthians,* 124–25, and Fee, "*Eidolothuta* Once Again," 176.

28. Emmanuel Levinas, "Philosophy and the Idea of Infinity," in *Collected Philosophical Papers* (Dordrecht: Kluwer, 1987), 48.

29. Emmanuel Levinas, *Otherwise than Being,* trans. Alphonso Lingis (Dordrecht: Kluwer, 1991), 111.

30. Emmanuel Levinas, *Totality and Infinity,* trans. Alphonso Lingis (Dordrecht: Kluwer, 1979), 175.

31. Levinas, *Otherwise than Being*, 114.

32. Simon Critchley makes this point in *Ethics, Politics, Subjectivity* (New York: Verso, 1999), 51.

33. Levinas, *Totality and Infinity*, 215.

34. Levinas, "Philosophy and the Idea of Infinity," 55.

35. Emmanuel Levinas, "Transcendence and Height," in *Basic Philosophical Writings*, ed. Adriaan T. Peperzak, Simon Critchley, and Robert Bernasconi (Bloomington: Indiana University Press, 1996), 18.

36. I should note that there *is* one thing Paul says that *might* be taken to support the Corinthians' free exercise of their *exousia* and *eleutheria*. In 10:29 he writes: "For why should my liberty be subject to the judgment of someone else's conscience?" Yet if that question is set in context, it becomes clear that Paul merely means that our own respective consciences should normally be our guide—*except* when following my conscience does another harm.

37. Levinas, *Otherwise than Being*, 162.

38. Whether a gift can truly be "given" has been the subject of heated controversy. Derrida insists that the gift is "the very figure of the impossible," which is why we want it all the more. See Jacques Derrida, *Given Time I: Counterfeit Money*, trans. Peggy Kamuf (Chicago: University of Chicago Press, 1992), 7. Marion responds by refiguring the gift in *Being Given: Toward a Phenomenology of Givenness*, trans. Jeffrey L. Koskey (Stanford, Calif.: Stanford University Press, 2002) and *In Excess: Studies of Saturated Phenomena*, trans. Robyn Horner and Vincent Berraud (New York: Fordham University Press, 2002), particularly chapter 6. John Milbank has attempted to argue for the possibility of gift giving *with* reciprocity as a component by refiguring the notion of reciprocity. See his "Can a Gift Be Given? Prolegomena to a Trinitarian Metaphysic," *Modern Theology* 11 (1995): 119–61; "The Soul of Reciprocity Part One: Reciprocity Refused," *Modern Theology* 17 (2001): 335–91; and "The Soul of Reciprocity Part Two: Reciprocity Granted," *Modern Theology* 17 (2001): 485–507. Here I will assume that, while gift giving is a rather complicated enterprise, gifts truly can be given. But it is beyond the scope of this paper to provide an argument for that stance.

39. For an interesting attempt to make sense of Paul's claim "For we only know in part, and we prophesy in part; but when the complete comes, the partial will come to an end" (13:9–10), see Paul W. Gooch, *Partial Knowledge: Philosophical Studies in Paul* (Notre Dame, Ind.: University of Notre Dame Press, 1987), particularly chapter 7.

40. Jean-Luc Marion, *Reduction and Givenness: Investigations of Husserl, Heidegger, and Phenomenology*, trans. Thomas A. Carlson (Evanston, Ill.: Northwestern University Press, 1998), 201.

41. Ibid. Whereas one of Marion's strategies for making sure the gift remains truly a gift is by making sure the call remains unidentified (particularly in chapter 6 of *In Excess*), Scripture identifies God—though on God's own terms.

42. Marion, *Being Given*, 270.

43. Ibid., 288.

44. Marion, *God without Being*, 194.

45. Jean-Luc Marion, *Prolegomena to Charity*, trans. Stephen Lewis (New York: Fordham University Press, 2002), 101.

46. Marion, *God without Being*, 108.

47. Martin Heidegger, "Introduction to 'What is Metaphysics?'," in *Pathmarks*, ed. William McNeill (Cambridge: Cambridge University Press, 1998), 288.

3

Love, This Lenient Interpreter

On the Complexity of a Life

EDWARD F. MOONEY

If there is a correct blindness, only love has it.

—Stanley Cavell

Why read a writer's work or life? We might read for love, for love of wisdom or of God, for love of the Unknown or love of this particular writer whose life and work lies here before us. Reading for love of a writer's life and work, we'd be warmly disposed, we'd be ready to have words lift our spirits (even though, in other moods, from different lives, those words might strike us differently). Reading for love, strange to say, might also be "hiding a multitude of sins," or if not hiding them, then showing them mercy rather than submitting them to the full brunt of the law.[1]

Kierkegaard has a *Discourse* on this biblical reminder that love is forgiving of sins, or even hides them, and he makes the hermeneutical connection, calling love "this lenient interpreter."[2] Reading in the name of love or charity lets certain aspects of a life or work fall out of sight. Apart from some good end, apart from a larger generous aim, raising suspicions, aversions, or marks of failure is, in fact, a morally suspect enterprise. Exposing fault or failure for the very pleasure of it shows a heart askew. An exposé, or "revelation," as we say, should answer to a larger purpose—for instance, healing us by putting us in closer touch with a fact or circumstance that might help us through a rough patch of life. Exposing someone's failure can mark mere spite or vengeance. Bringing out failure in a tender, loving way can convey sympathy or sadness and can testify to the need to preserve love. Reading from love does not mean papering over the fissures or faults of a life. But bringing out the cracks and fissures should be a prelude to a "lenient" care and receptivity—that is, if we read from a generosity of spirit.

Charity and Suspicion

There's nearly infinite scope for a hermeneutics of suspicion. I read my daily politics that way, through a lens of caution—and often, of great mistrust. But it's a lens I drop, turning to last night's Fenway Park festivities. Kierkegaard reads his Christendom suspiciously in an ideology critique that bears comparison with those of Marx or Freud or Nietzsche.[3] But somewhat paradoxically, a hermeneutics of charity, love, or affirmation can live side by side with a hermeneutics of suspicion.[4] Uncovering a covey of sin might result from a proper dose of suspicion, but that's compatible with a caring uncovering, whose aim is to help love prosper. Releasing shames into a recuperative light can stem their tendency to multiply and fester while in the dark. Love needn't hide *every* multitude of sin, nor hide every sin completely. The grand unmasking narratives of Kierkegaard or Freud expose human failing *to some good end*, and thus free us to move on affirmatively. Then we have, not just suspicion, but a concomitant hermeneutics of trust, love, or affirmation.[5]

If the amplitude of affirmation, trust, or generosity is curbed, then the swing of *ennui* and cynicism is given greater scope. At one end of a spectrum are those who hanker after scandal, sleaze, or evil just because it's there, or who gloat as the high and mighty fall, or who seek twisted pleasure in bringing others down, or who deflate innocence just for sport. In some academic quarters, a hermeneutics of suspicion occupies the high ground, so to speak. The assumption is that a trusting hermeneutics is not properly hard-headed. It betrays a naïve premodern faith in the good in an age whose maturity is to applaud the armies of doubt.[6] Later on, I make the case for the *primacy* of trust. Why should doubt or suspicion be given priority?

Mistrust can be overrated and seem like childish stalling, or it can betray false expectations, as if one should have a Rule to tell us when it's best to *bet* on trust, or as if one should have an epistemologically registered chaperon to cover all our risks. Mistrust can get rationalized as cautious prudence, or more deeply still, as fear of bloating up the world with illusory value—as if values that were run out of town by Marx, Schopenhauer, Nietzsche, or Freud might be working their way back in. Love's hermeneutics is drowned out, dead at the gate, if there's no place for praising trust, charity, or generosity. Teachers like Harold Bloom, Martha Nussbaum, or Stanley Cavell keep a hermeneutics of trust alive. They show how our ambient traditions hold an unsuspected surplus of things fit for our concern and praise. That's not to promote anything as cosmic or empty as a general optimism. Their pens are fixed on less general matters—on local sites, miniatures, poems; or on novels, dramas, films, or essays; and occasionally on larger works.

I have an extended example of the push and pull between a hermeneutics of suspicion or mistrust and love's lenient hermeneutics. Starting at a local site, I take up a large and celebrated biography of Kierkegaard that displays the dangers of a hermeneutics of suspicion. I'll try to neutralize the fallout of suspicion by recasting aspects of the biography under the aegis of a hermeneutics of trust or generosity. Within the present terrain, the harvest of charity is wisdom, while the spoils of suspicion are empty trifles.[7]

Reading Kierkegaard

During a recent August I found myself caught up in two newly published, impressively intelligent biographies of Kierkegaard. The author of the first, from Oslo, held the life and works in expert care, turning a Kierkegaard text or life-episode slowly to find the most appreciative light, tendering events and struggles and textual themes an alert, open, respectful embrace. This was a hermeneutics of care, if not of love, a reading stance of trust or affirmation. The author of the second was from Copenhagen. More often than I wished, I found him all too ready to catch Kierkegaard in authorial deceptions, moral blunders, or personal indignities. His hermeneutics of suspicion, I learned, was a conscious strategy. He opens his quite attractively presented book with a frank revelation.[8] "*My aim,*" he confides, "*is to uncover the cracks in the granite of genius.*"[9]

Let's work through the dubious assumptions that travel with this frank announcement of his mission.

1. Why should we assume that genius pretends to indestructible hardness ("the *granite* of genius")? Isn't it possible that genius might be pliant or supple? Does genius aspire always to an indestructible immortality? Might Kierkegaard's genius be fragile, insecure, all too aware of the finite and fragmentary? Our contemporary Copenhagen author stacks the deck against such reading by assuming that the genius who lived in the streets of Copenhagen from 1813 to 1856 pretended to the hardness of granite.
2. Suspicion lurks in the author's self-assigned task of *uncovering cracks*: are we assuming an adversarial relation between genius and biographer, the latter heroically testing *his* strength, against a granite resistance?
3. Why assume that granite—genius—is always *flawed*? We're finite; but does that make our talent, our genius, our inspiration inevitably flawed?
4. The impulse to hide a flaw, if there be one, is not necessarily dominant. If genius can wear its cracked vulnerability on its sleeve, it needn't be *uncovered.*

5. Why should we *expose* fragility or fault? Is tracking down someone's weakness a *duty*? Is it just the critic's *pleasure*? The hunt for fragility locks us in a primal predator-prey scenario. Must we sign on?

To work at *"uncovering the cracks in the granite of genius"* exemplifies an uncharitable lack of trust. And if truth be told, the stain of this approach runs even deeper.

Extending the implications of this mission to expose cracks leads us to an unexpected but persuasive conclusion. Uncovering fissures is exposing lines of weakness. Can we avoid the conclusion that the reason our author seeks cracks in the granite of genius is not just to expose flaws but to have a target for some well-aimed blows? Our Copenhagen biographer quite frankly aims to *shatter* the genius of Kierkegaard. The rock will break along its cracks. But why announce this destructive aim? I suppose the plot of patricide is as attractive as the plot of love. Yet a different disposition might speak of the fissures of a genius as wounds crying for attention, pleading to be healed or to be discretely covered by a scarf.

Without some good purpose in mind, it can seem to be a waste of good intelligence for a writer to marshal creative energies to exposing *"cracks in the granite of genius."* And there's a lesson here for me to take to heart. Do I have some good purpose as I set about exposing cracks in the accounts that flow from the mistrusts that our Copenhagen biographer harbors? Of course the *aperçu* that love won't spotlight sin doesn't say we should be blind to sin, or always turn the other way, or automatically forgive. Yet there's something morally distasteful in approaching Kierkegaard's life and works always on the lookout for scandal, deception, hard-heartedness, or hypocrisy, and bloating their presence, if they're present, out of all proportion.

Now taking in my own lesson, that a generous hermeneutics should not be trumped by the undeniable allure of suspicion, let me check my impulse to merely make a trumpeting polemic of the infelicities of suspicion in the present case. There is a need to bring out alternative construals of the life and work, to lay out interpretative options that otherwise get buried by an onslaught of suspicion. In this constructive and affirmative vein, let me try to place the offending aphorism from the preface to this biography, *Seek cracks in the granite of genius!* in a better light, and in a register quite opposite to the intent of our Copenhagen biographer. That striking aphorism can be brought to a more charitable site where a beam of love can shine through. Reading through "love, that lenient interpreter" should yield a more interesting, attractive, and profound thinker and writer than is available when we set out to shatter him.

Cracks might be slots or windows, windows in the hardened case of genius through which we glimpse a soul. Of course, this search might still be tainted. It might be just a chance to peep and leer at someone else's mess. But windows might work differently. The ancient Silenos figure—so like Socrates—may have a hard, repellant exterior. But Silenos also gave a glimpse of gods secreted within.[10] We could do worse than hope for such a sight through "cracks" in Kierkegaard's exterior.

Trusting Contact

As an occasional visitor to the magnificent and humbling Yosemite Valley, I often watch, mesmerized, as climbers ascend the massive granite face of El Capitan alone, finding their route by hand and foot and rope along tiny cracks and fissures. The cracks and fissures are neither signs of vulnerability nor narrow windows to an interior. They mark a pathway for an intimate, loving kind of knowledge, a wisdom and final satisfaction (as final as can be), a knowing that's more than factual or theoretical or prudential (though each of these may play a necessary part). It's an Old Testament hands-on intimacy, a contact and connection with a world or a surface or a face, an intimacy that can be frightful or reassuring or both.

Of course, a full taxonomy of knowledge would go beyond the fourfold "factual, theoretical, prudential, and 'tactile' or 'intimate'" that I suggest here. There's also "know-how," and perhaps "knowing one's way about" would fig-ure in as well. Bertrand Russell distinguished knowledge by description from knowledge by acquaintance, but "acquaintance" strikes far too low a key for the cognitive impact of my witness of a powerful scene from Shakespeare, my knowing of a thunderclap in the hearing of it, or my knowing of an ocean swell in the rowing of it.[11] Henry Bugbee explores a kind of 'tactile wisdom" or intimacy with one's surround that he calls "immersion."[12] To know the world one is immersed in is to have immediate visceral access. There's cognition in being caught up imaginatively and affectively in making or composing but also in undergoing or suffering a passion. Giving birth creatively is both a making and an undergoing, a suffering and a doing. Such knowing as one undergoes or suffers in the process is not a matter of "mere acquaintance," nor is it knowing how to negotiate or cope, nor is it factual or theoretical.

I think of "tactile wisdom" as the knowledge the rock climber has of the wall, or that a lover has of a face, or that a mother has of her child's pain.[13] It's not cerebral, or not only that, though it requires intelligence, even "bodily intelligence," and it may involve the kind of emotional self-knowledge that allows one to gauge one's fear and excitement as cues to what's happening and what comes next. It might resemble the immediate, often awe-filled Old Testa-ment carnal knowledge between mortals, but it also resembles knowing God in wrestling him, or knowing him in something like the musical theophany at the end of the biblical book of Job. In Job, intimate knowledge is more than immersion; it's invasive, a sublime overwhelming. With intimate (or tactile) wisdom, we pull toward what Kierkegaard might call essential or saving knowledge. In such intimacy, one is enmeshed, reticulated with the rock, the river, the lover, the great divine song in Job.[14] It's a knowing that requires the great risks of faith or care or trust.[15]

This image of tactile knowing clears the way for a generous way of reading. It invites us to inch along the weathered and more recent wrinkles in the face of genius, vulnerable and hanging over 70,000 fathoms, in something close to tenuous embrace. It's an image for a stint with Kierkegaard, approaching the writer and his work daringly, receptively, tactilely, taking in wonders and redemptions not otherwise accessible.

Initiating Images

Hermeneutics can focus on an image, say the image of negotiating a crack in granite; or on a passage; or an indefinitely large number of images, phrases, and passages—not to mention a life—the actions, needs, and projects that carry passages and texts along. Interpreting a life and writing starts *somewhere*. What *is* this "life," this "work"? Where, and on what, does the hermeneutic impulse get its grip?

There's an "undecidability" lurking in this query. Start with the texts? The life? When in the life? Where, in which text? And this uncertainty is also a moment to be decisively alive to the mystery of this other, this life and work—chilled, awed, humbled by its unmanageability, its unfathomability. Then some obscure force gathers welter into focus. We say (or think), "*This* is Kierkegaard!—*Here's* where he stands!" We know it's a place we can stand with him to begin to sketch this figure, still strange but familiar enough to begin to know. Some of the whirl recedes. But what *authorizes* the ready declaration, "This is Kierkegaard! This is where he stands"? What authorizes starting with Kierkegaard as strolling citizen, or as Copenhagen's Socrates? As Regine's absent lover or as the Bishop's bitter enemy or as his father's wayward son? What authorizes starting with him as Sibbern's brilliant student? Among the endless possibilities a figure snaps into semi-focus under an aspect of familiarity that allows us to begin.

We still ask, what authorizes us to begin just where we do? Perhaps the question is a little off-key. Scanning the pond, what authorizes our simple declaration, "That's a duck!"—or, to complicate matters, what authorizes our declaration "That's a duck!" when it's the reversible duck-rabbit figure that comes into view? Or "That's a rabbit!"—or, since we're getting into it, "That's a duck-rabbit!"—or even, dismissively, "That's just random lines on paper!"? It happens things *jell* a certain way. It *happens*, pure and simple, without august, articulate authority.[16]

"*This* is Kierkegaard!" we say, as he clicks into view, and a series of alternatives (a differently figured Kierkegaard, or the Kierkegaard not yet there for me) clicks decisively off screen. In fact, there's no deep authorization here. It wouldn't help to find a reassuring signature, "Made by SK" affixed to swirling shards, for we still can ask, "Why make that signature definitive? What, after all, *is* an SK signature?" It might lie or deflect or show up accidentally, with neither rhyme nor reason. Of course Kierkegaard is hydra-headed, a monstrous whirl of tendencies and themes, passages and tomes, engagements and attacks, prayers and idle walks. But still, we say—"This is Kierkegaard!" And find our feet with him, and stay with him to enter the alluring labyrinth awaiting us, now called "Kierkegaard." And in the tangle of his life and texts, we latch on to a guiding image around which things jell.[17]

Consider three images that we find in the frontispiece to Alastair Hannay's 1982 Kierkegaard book: Socrates, Satan, and Saint.[18] This trio invites divergent outlines for a reading. Socrates, Saint, Satan—each face gives us footing in an otherwise unmanageable whirl. A script might appear under the aspect of Socrates, which would bring out the irritating, ironic, yet brilliantly intelligent interrogator—and one who's steadfastly loyal to the good. A script could show us Kierkegaard as Mephistopheles, full of devilish guile, rebellion, and seduction. It could script Kierkegaard as a saintly martyr, show his devotion as dying to the world. The tangle we so confidently label "Kierkegaard" can be tamed by images rich enough to be drawn out in a scripted narrative expression.

There's a possibility that Kierkegaard might be all three—Satan, Saint, and Socrates. It wouldn't be as if he were simultaneously carrot-like, oak-like, and tulip-like. It would be more as if he were sometimes Satanic, sometimes saintly, sometimes Socratic. It might be preferable to have a single mold into which to pour a life's complexity, and some lives may in fact fit a single mold without distorting much detail. But I suspect that most lives have no single shape, or better put, something is lost the minute we cast the tangle of a life into a single mold. Rather than reduce a life to an image or set of images, we might expand a life as variegated as Kierkegaard's so that it includes what he accomplished, which was to write strange books of endless variety, and have that life include what those books accomplished in his name. It then becomes a fantasy to seek a single mold. Far better to settle pretty early in the casting for an indefinite variety of molds—far more than three or four, and as apparently opposed (yet strangely congruent) as Satan, Saint, or Socrates.

Hermeneutical Tilt

Does a guiding image boost one sort of hermeneutics rather than another? Casting Kierkegaard as Satan colors him suspiciously, reflecting and instigating fear and mistrust. But our imaginations may just be shallow here. Some devils might be endearing.[19] *Affection* for Mephisto might yield a kind of wisdom. Perhaps he's a lovable imp, and so quite forgivable. Casting Kierkegaard as Socrates colors him affirmatively, reflecting and instigating charity in interpretation—but then, the gadfly might turn out to be an argumentative snob. Casting Kierkegaard as Saint reflects and furthers charity in interpretation—but then, Saints can be insufferable. Even as a guiding image falls in place, how it's taken isn't settled. Interpretative options exist all along the way. An image grips—happens, strikes—and then, in the aftermath, we read it out along one of several plausible expressive paths. We can't tell off the bat if an initiating image betokens a generous spirit or a cramped and choking one.

The initiating image can be dramatically suggestive, but we discover what it suggests only as we join up and follow one of its plausible trajectories, only as we set out as readers (or writers) on the interpretative path we hew but also find. Accepting the bestowal of an image and following it out requires trust. This is the fertile kernel of a somewhat Kantian transcendental deduction of the *priority of trust*.

Say interpretation goes "all the way down." To start up, it has to bottom out. If we don't touch bottom, then there's no interpretation. We start with that unauthorized immediate sense, "*This* is Kierkegaard!" or amidst a whirl, "*This* is *Socrates*-Kierkegaard!" That's the *given* there to work with. Of course, we can take a step back from the task of interpretation and observe that what we take as bottom is theoretically contingent, and that we take something *as* bottom, so that what strikes us as inescapably bottom in fact is a tacit piece of interpretation. But if anything like an explicit interpretation is to get going, it has to start with the sense of givenness, that *this* is where we start.

Ending Upbeat

The given is not theoretically secure, but it's given, nonetheless. It's practically necessary and forcefully evident experientially, imaginatively, as that which *strikes* us. That's Socrates! Ah! It's a *duck-rabbit!* The bottom that gives us footing, purchase, might have been otherwise, might not hold. There might *be* no bottom (if I went probing). Cavell says that the one permissible (or "correct") blindness is the blindness of love, of falling in love with the world.[20] Of course, we might have loved a different world, or never loved at all. So if we venture the skeptical step back, skepticism will no doubt find a foothold. But to venture down this backward stepping road gives theory and the rational demand for footing the upper hand and leaves us hamstrung. It dissolves—often for no good reason at all—the certitudes of contact. The sense of needing to get off that road of skeptical possibility can obtrude, for one traveling unwillingly on it, and thankfully it does, and a forward path of gifted groundedness can supervene to save us. We let a practical, imaginative imperative supervene. We just let the inescapable draw of a Kierkegaard-*Socrates* have its way with us— take over. The theoretical possibility of traveling a different path isn't refuted (theoretically). It's replaced by that which calls on us, here and now, with immediate necessity. Then the space of *actual interpretation* supervenes. We find ourselves already in the venture of interpretation, which means a sense of felt rock bottom will have appeared with the simultaneous sense that an unfolding job of reading has begun. Socrates is gift and task. Love of life and works is gift and task. We're already knee-deep in Kierkegaard interpretation. Someone else can second-guess, unsettle footings. So here's the quasi-Kantian transcendental formulation for the priority of trust: *If interpretative reading is underway and so exists, its condition is that interpretation is not free-floating, that it touches bottom, that it builds on something that in that local context is basic. If our interpretation runs full tilt ahead, then it's a practical necessity that we have trust in that.*[21]

Concealing and Revealing

Kierkegaard provides a surplus of partially competing open-ended stories of his life and works. This creates a worry for charitable readings. When versions differ, which do we affirm? Perhaps conflicting motives (and proliferating pseudonyms) are meant to throw us off track. With our Copenhagen biographer, we can suspect a penchant for uncovering prevarication, pretense, or hidden shames. That's the hermeneutics of suspicion. Yet as a general matter, revising or reshaping self-interpretations isn't necessarily suspect. A change of story doesn't always indicate deception or dishonesty. After all, it's not a courtroom or a bookstore credit identity that's at issue. It's an identity more intimate and elusive, whose "true shape" depends in large measure on the way a person —in this case Kierkegaard—hews, discovers, articulates it. Should the self-portrait be Heroic-Epic? Faustian? Socratic? Should we switch guiding images mid-stream? Should *he* switch images?

As we'd expect, Kierkegaard experiments. Putting *this* in focus blurs *that*— or puts it out of range. Experiments are needed, for one can't know *if,* or how *well,* a shoe will fit until one puts it on. And experiments will be ongoing. Both life and its expressive accounts will wear with time and often beg for alteration, if not major overhaul. Honesty doesn't deliver a *single* "state of the self" account. It just delivers an account as truthful as can be—as one lives out and through a plurality of versions, each always painfully, promisingly fragmentary.

Kierkegaard leaves us the preliminary studies to sort through, and if truth be told, nothing *but* preliminaries. This, in part, just goes with the territory. We might say that no life has a final version. But in part it is precisely Kierkegaard's exploratory venture to *show* us the inescapable variability of self-portraiture, each effort bound to be seen, in retrospect and with time, as preliminary. He portrays himself now as jesting, now as offensive, now as purely yearning; now as Faust, now as Socrates, now as would-be Christian. Each expression tunes him to a local setting and is offered as a try for the truth of that episode in the life unfolding; what it is at present includes its promise for tomorrow. This reminds us that we're dealing here with narrative *truths* (plural), not the chimera of a sole timeless truth of the matter. A courtroom demand for *all the truth and nothing but the truth* is at cross-purposes with honest growth and is, in any case, impossible. This deflates the charge, barely disguised in the recent Copenhagen biography, that Kierkegaard in his multiplicities deceives, is even the arch deceiver, out to engineer cover-ups, here or there or even everywhere.

Closer to the Text

"Hilarius Bookbinder," a lesser pseudonym, offers the public something our biographer calls a "counterfeit."[22] The charge is that at the last moment Kierkegaard brings two previously independent books together, thereby tricking us. At the shop, we assume that what we buy is, and was "all along," a single work. But why assume this? Its "author," after all, is (eponymously) one who stitches books together. That's a revelation (for those with eyes to see), not a deception. And even if Kierkegaard weren't so forthright, there'd be nothing deceptively counterfeit in his practice. At the eleventh hour an artist can join two canvases at first taken to be separate—without moral culpability. Kierkegaard presents the printer with what he declares to be a single book, and that declaration *makes* it single. The presentation is a performative truth-maker that can trump alternative construals, including any Kierkegaard may have previously made. This charitable reading highlights Kierkegaard's creative inventiveness and allows wisdom to accrue. And in any case, the writer at the printer's shop with *Stages on Life's Way* was himself book *binder*.

Kierkegaard attaches a pseudonym to a manuscript en route to the printer, one that *reveals*. There's no sin here for love to hide or to forgive. He shows our inner lives as subject to continual couplings and uncouplings, bindings and unbindings. My inner story depends on how I couple story bits together—and uncouple other bits. Rembrandt can touch up a self-portrait years after its first rendition. This is not a shady business.

Anxiety in the face of fragmentation is a mark of modern life. Traditional roles and authorities for settling identity slowly fall apart. Kierkegaard accentuates this unsettling dynamic by taking up a polemical relationship to his own writing and identity. This keeps both in motion. He's unafraid to hear a change of tune—or to *change* his tune. Far from being fickle or a deceiver, even a godly one, as some hold, he's quite frank in laying bare the struggles, the feints and parries, that constitute conflicting contours inevitable in formation of a modern (or postmodern) self.[23]

How Masks Reveal

"Masks are masks," you say, *"devices for concealment if not deception."* Yes, they *can* deceive, and partially conceal. But they also can reveal, which can be a helpful and charitable view. Playing Hamlet, I show a side of myself not

otherwise available. If I pretend to be a bear, I growl and show myself in unexpected ways. There's no necessary deception in play, and quite a bit of revelation.

Furthermore, the very task of self-revelation requires a phase of trying out a role, trying on a persona, experimenting with what we could call a mask. We're apt to think that honesty requires casting off the masks, and there's some truth in that—we try to get beneath affectations. But self-articulation is often as much taking *on* a mask as removing one. I pull myself together to look brave because I need to here—and that itself, putting on a brave face, can affirm my capacity to *be* brave. Covers can be exploratory or mandatory, and in either case, not necessarily an affectation or deception. I display my game face; my doctor comes to look the part he is as he enters the surgery theater. My visage is gentleness pleading for expression; my countenance is masked in grief. These crucial moments of self-revelation require a face—a face that we in some sense don. There's no crime in that.

Owning and disowning masks is the way every child grows, and even as adults, growth means owning and disowning. Of course, we inhabit, or have access to, a far wider range of expressions, of covers, than could ever be lined up for *explicit* owning and disowning. Much of this occurs behind our backs. It's not a matter of a preexisting self-essence getting pressed out into view. A self-expressive visage is just an expression *than which there is nothing deeper at the moment.* It's not put on or delivered by something "deeper" that exists "earlier" than the delivery.[24] Masks seem intrinsically dishonest in robberies. But that can be taken as a special, not a paradigmatic, case.

Richard Burton puts on his Hamlet face. That's not dishonest. A deep and misleading picture is at work, even when we imagine Burton non-deceptively becoming Hamlet. We imagine the self as a fixed glassy essence that a mask unfortunately (or fortunately) hides. But surely we know more about Kierkegaard by *seeing* the mask, seeing the signature "Johannes Climacus" or "Johannes de silentio." And this does not require seeing any essence. We know more about Burton and Hamlet as the actor dons the mask, not less, and we never see the glassy prior essence of either Hamlet or Burton. There's mutual revelation here. We know more about Kierkegaard (or Burton or Hamlet) *through and because of the mask*—there's revelation without our having to assume something deeply hidden of which the performance is an expression. In this light, Kierkegaard's tactic of proliferating pseudonyms is not a device to hide a deep and secret self but a way to display his inventiveness, the plasticity of the world, and the variety of his faces-to-the-world.

A hermeneutics of suspicion, in league with Freud, Marx, and Nietzsche (and perhaps Foucault) has had a good run at unmasking, at doubting the very idea of self-revelation. But we needn't make a fetish of unmasking. An actor trying on fictive roles is not promulgating fictions. Someone floating many stories of who he is, is not necessarily hiding something. Writing out identity through revisable experiments may be the inescapable modern fate. Changing faces, donning masks, finding new worlds to which we are receptive, may be no more culpable than switching (or being switched) from parenting to brokering, from weekend tennis to a transforming museum moment before a Goya nightmare. Are we importantly the *same* through all these changes? Where is the glassy essence the skeptic thinks we hide or cover up?

I don't pretend that I've made much decisive headway in settling fundamental debates in contemporary metaphysics of the self.[25] But I do hope to have given life to the idea that Kierkegaard puts his signature on the age by writing out, living out, a theater of ever-shifting lines, parts, crises, and resolutions that are lasting revelations.

Hiding Meaning in the Texts

Mistrust hides what's profound about pseudonyms or masks—that they don't just hide, but can also reveal. In the case of our Copenhagen biographer, the hermeneutics of suspicion or mistrust leads to the suppression of some of Kierkegaard's most important texts. "Soap Cellars," an unpublished Kierkegaardian miniature, gets more pages in this new biography than the giant and massively important *Concluding Unscientific Postscript*. Reading between the lines, "Soap Cellars" lets us see the people Kierkegaard likes to parody or mock in the cultural circles he traveled in. He "hides" the true objects of his amusement, we might say. But if no attempt is made to wrestle with the *Postscript*, how can we appreciate the reception of Kierkegaard by generations of philosophers and theologians—by Bultmann, Heidegger, Tillich, or Wittgenstein, for example? After all, it's *Postscript*, not "Soap Cellars," that argues directly about what's central to a self, about truth and subjectivity, about "objective uncertainty" and faith, about the relevance of history to personal identity, about irony and humor and the paradox of Christ—and so on. To spend so little time with *Postscript*, or *Fragments*, as this contemporary biographer does, is something like presenting Lance Armstrong without the Tour de France, or Beethoven without the Late Quartets. My own suspicion is that *Postscript* floats its own dialectic of trust and mistrust, a dialectic powerful enough to bite someone looking for an easy unmasking of it.[26]

Our biographer's hermeneutics of suspicion feeds appetites for scandal, which means he misses richness even in the particular texts he covers at some length. He links *Fear and Trembling*, which depicts Abraham's near-sacrifice of Isaac, to Kierkegaard's supposed culpability in breaking his engagement to Regine. He reads the four opening Abraham scenarios as a simple progress in deception. This makes the central event on Moriah the fact of Abraham *deceiving* Isaac—and nothing worse! As if telling the truth—telling Isaac what he was about to do—would have made everything all right (at least between Abraham and his son). But that would hardly fix his dilemma on Moriah. For a reader fixated on suspicion and a fascination with Kierkegaard-the-deceiver, the story of Moriah becomes hopelessly truncated and thus distorted.

Although a reading needn't, and probably shouldn't, start with Kierkegaard's infamous broken engagement, it's worthwhile seeing what a hermeneutics of charity might make of that traumatic episode in his life. With charity, we might picture Kierkegaard with two life-defining relationships at stake—one to his writing (intermixed with religious passion), one to Regina (intermixed with worldly expectations). The perceived total, exclusive, and exhaustive demands of each—his commitment to writing (religiously) seems every bit as all-consuming as his commitment to his fiancée—force a terrible question. Which, we ask, should be abandoned? Let's say that a compromise, splitting the difference, being half-writer, half-husband, is out of the question. We then have a major crisis of identity that Kierkegaard must undergo. But an unmasking hermeneutics, bent on seeing only deception, cannot see or formulate this crisis.

To be sure, on a generous, charitable view, it's still terrible to sacrifice one's beloved to one's vocation; but then it must be terrible, too, to sacrifice one's vocation! We needn't say Kierkegaard was *right* to abandon Regine. But neither can we say it would have been right to abandon a writerly or religious vocation for her sake. It might be plain wrong to break the engagement and be plain wrong to let the engagement stand. If so, then the theme of the Abraham scenarios is not the web of culpable deceptions so attractive to our suspicious biographer. Instead, those scenarios convey an imponderable and terrifying question. How is one to proceed gracefully (if that's at all possible), or even to survive, when incompatible identity-constituting commitments bear down killingly? This is at the heart of Kierkegaard's dilemma, and Abraham's too, for Abraham faces the terror of abandoning a call from God or abandoning a call from son and wife.

Once we set aside a blinding fixation on deception, we can see *the* central, twisting conflict of the text. And we can also see thereby the impossible redemption it proposes. It's hardly a possibility available to practical common sense, but the narrative proposes it anyway. Abraham must know that his situation is impossible (he can't live without abandoning one of his identity-constituting commitments). And yet he knows that since God is the *dominant* factor in his situation, then perhaps his situation is *not* impossible—that for God, all things are possible, so God can ask for Isaac and yet keep his promise that Isaac will continue Abraham's seed.

God can handle impossibilities, as it were. He can handle the weight of abiding by the general moral injunction that a father love and protect his son— *along with* the weight of having made a particular demand that Isaac, his son, must die by his father's hand—*along with* the weight of having made a particular promise that the son-to-be-killed *won't* die but will carry a seed into an endless future. Carrying this threefold weight with its radically divergent, even incompatible, implications is impressive, to say the least. Yet I'd think that lurking somewhere in this dramatic interchange between God and Abraham must be the thought that God's capacity to live with and in this field of wrenching conflict (impossibilities *are* possible for him) is at the same time an aspect of Abraham's capacity to live with and in this field of wrenching conflict (impossibilities *might* be possible for him).[27] It's as if we're meant to think that what's possible for God (despite a seeming impossibility) might also perforce be possible for an individual (despite a seeming impossibility). And it's as if we're meant to think that *God's* weathering the impossible helps *us* to weather the impossible, or to see our way in that direction. Abraham's trust or faith that God will give him Isaac back is akin to God's "trust or faith" that ordering Isaac to be sacrificed is compatible with expecting Abraham to keep loving Isaac— and compatible with expecting Abraham to keep believing in the promise that Isaac's seed will not perish, that he'll get Isaac back. How can God not see the obvious *incompatibilities*—the *impossibilities*—here?[28]

The parallel with Kierkegaard's quandary is straightforward and exact. If he *had* had faith (he confesses that he didn't), Kierkegaard would have married Regine in the trust or faith that God "impossibly" would provide for his religiously writerly existence. Or alternatively, in opting for a religiously writerly existence, in a suspension of the ethical requirement that he honor his engagement to Regine, he would have maintained the "impossible" faith and hope that he would get her back.[29] Yet do we fault Kierkegaard for falling short of such unbelievable faith?

The Allure of Undersides

There's no good reason to think that, as a general matter, a hermeneutics of mistrust trumps a hermeneutics of love. And in any case, we can show that the hermeneutics of love shows us parts of a writer's life and works that are blotted out by a hermeneutics of suspicion. Taking the path of "love, that lenient interpreter" provides a helpful and hospitable welcome and receptivity to the non-debunking idea that Kierkegaard's masks and pseudonyms not only hide but also reveal. Charity helps that thought along. Furthermore, we've seen that suspicion blots out the central theme of a central text, *Fear and Trembling*. And on a more general front, beyond the reading or misreading of particular texts, a charitable reading of Kierkegaard's life and works has no need to leap headlong, as our present biographer does, into unmasking a purportedly pervasive sexual subtext.

Unfortunately, this new biography loses credit through recurrent digressions along sexual paths that do little to illuminate the life and even less to illuminate the texts. There are more than a dozen pages on a confessedly undocumented bordello incident, on fear of syphilis, and on the criminality of masturbation in the culture's imagination. All this makes for "interesting" reading, as Kierkegaard might say. It tells us something about cultural sensibilities and fears in Copenhagen (and elsewhere) in nineteenth-century Europe.

A hermeneutics of suspicion too easily unearths this otherwise buried material. But how does it bear on the life and works at hand? Are we to suppose that fear of syphilis or masturbation had an *especially* powerful effect on Kierkegaard's life and works—an effect decidedly in *excess* of the part that these factors might play in the most commonplace of lives, and so perhaps determinative of the shape of this most extraordinary life and work? Why do we assume that these fears had greater effect than his love of expensive meals or chatting with town folk, or surveying the sea—or perhaps more to the point, his passion for Shakespeare, Mozart, and Socrates? The general rule, from the standpoint of a hermeneutics of charity, is that even documented shames or scandals are worth retelling only if their revelation serves a charitable end. Otherwise, what is gained by our exposure to these revelations? Perhaps they're included just to feed a voyeuristic disposition.

Our author traces echoes of masturbation resurfacing in the repetitions of writing—and in the formal concept "repetition." He doesn't explicitly claim that Job's repetition—his being "blown away" by an overpowering storm that both empties him and brings him exquisitely alive—is a sexual *ekstasis*. But the dots seem to point that way. He catches Kierkegaard repetitively recycling favorite passages through his writing in a kind of pleasurable self-plagiarism.[30] But why is this a sin—as opposed to a fairly common process for creative minds? Self-citation is common enough in film and music, but not thereby an evident sin or defect.

Some of the "interesting" interpretations provided by our biographer are spell-binding, informative, and laid out with enviable flair and sustained suspense. But the question remains whether what purports to be a major biography of a figure whose footprint on contemporary culture is immense, whose works shape it through and through, should spend so much time with material that does little more than feed the thrill of peeking and being in on nasty secrets. Our biographer sketches what he calls "a Kierkegaard complex." The non-stop obsessive scribbling is seen as a compensatory tactic exploited by a wounded ego unable to negotiate a sexually healthy existence. That takes Kierkegaard *down* a notch. At last we're meant to think that the fissured granite of this genius has been shattered under another writer's sustained, sophisticated, but ultimately condescending hammer tap.

A more generous look would marvel at the dazzling transformation Kierkegaard effects in turning so many pedestrian things toward surpassing religio-poetic affirmations. That raises Kierkegaard *up* a notch. His life and work are made to make life richer all around. As we read, so we will be read; and as we would be read, so we *should* read.[31] Here we have the labile face of this astonishing Copenhagen citizen. We seek the lines in which the weathered beauty of a life are etched and then, as a climber might, trace in them the pathways for a gentle, tactile knowledge of the writer and his texts.

NOTES

1. This is a place to notice that a teleological suspension of ethics has to include the suspension of the law we see in forgiveness and mercy.

2. Søren Kierkegaard, "Love Hides A Multitude of Sins," in *Works of Love*, ed. and trans. Howard V. Hong and Edna H. Hong (Princeton, N.J.: Princeton University Press, 1995), 280–99. The phrase "love, this lenient interpreter" appears on p. 294. I thank John Lippitt for alerting me to this phrase.

3. Merold Westphal reads Kierkegaard's *Concluding Unscientific Postscript* as ideology critique, and more generally, he shows that the "masters of suspicion"—Freud, Marx, Nietzsche—have much to teach religion and theology. See Merold Westphal, *Suspicion and Faith: The Religious Uses of Modern Atheism* (New York: Fordham University Press, 1998), and *Kierkegaard's Critique of Reason and Society* (Macon, Ga.: Mercer University Press, 1987). The Frankfort School's Marcuse takes Kierkegaard's critique of Christendom as an important supplement to a broadly Marxist critique of contemporary life. See Herbert Marcuse, *Reason and Revolution: Hegel and the Rise of Social Theory* (New York: Humanity Books, 1999).

4. For the classic statement of a hermeneutics of suspicion, see Paul Ricoeur, *The Conflict of Interpretations: Essays in Hermeneutics* (Evanston, Ill.: Northwestern University Press, 1974). See also Richard Kearney, *On Paul Ricoeur: The Owl of Minerva* (Burlington, Vt.: Ashgate, 2004).

5. For a reading of Nietzsche as a "master of suspicion" who is also a "master of affirmation," see Tyler Roberts, *Contesting Spirit: Nietzsche, Affirmation, Religion* (Princeton, N.J.: Princeton University Press, 1998).

6. I discuss the primacy of trust in *Selves in Discord and Resolve: Kierkegaard's Moral-Religious Psychology* (New York: Routledge, 1996), 72ff. and 86ff.

7. I draw no global lessons from this exercise, but I don't exclude such lessons either.

8. See Joakim Garff, *Søren Kierkegaard, a Biography*, trans. Bruce Kirmmse (Princeton, N.J.: Princeton University Press, 2005). For the non-Danish, "Oslo" biography, see Alastair Hannay, *Kierkegaard, a Biography* (Cambridge: Cambridge University Press, 2001).

9. If my aim were to give a full review, I would cite the book's often charitable and sympathetic strands. To his credit, Garff often fails to follow the tainted practice promised in his preface. My goal is limited to bringing out a prominent strand of mistrust and showing the consequence of that mistrust. The condescension implicit in his search for "cracks in the granite of genius" is continued when he names the personal Kierkegaard configuration he sets out to explore "the Kierkegaard complex."

10. I thank David L. Miller for reminding me of this ancient figure.

11. Rick Furtak talks of a sort of intimate knowing he calls "emotional knowing" in "Skepticism and Perceptual Faith: Thoreau and Cavell on Seeing and Believing" (forthcoming). Somewhere in this taxonomy we should note the parallels and differences between "knowledge of the sublime," when we confront and are overtaken by a vista of raging sea, and "knowledge of pain," which is certainly not a matter of observation or theory and which escapes representation in something like the way the raging sea escapes representation. In pain, we can lack concepts altogether and have to rest content with metaphor—"a stabbing pain, a burning pain." In the sublime, we suffer, in a way, with an excess of concepts and representations, perspectives and thematics, all in a rage. Emily Dickinson tells us *"Pain—has an Element of Blank—/ It cannot recollect /*

When it begun—or if there were / A time when it was not—/ It has no Future—but itself—/ Its Infinite contain / Its past—enlightened to perceive / New Periods—of Pain" (1862).

12. See Henry Bugbee, *The Inward Morning: A Philosophical Exploration in Journal Form* (Athens: University of Georgia Press, 1999).

13. See note 11, above.

14. For Thoreau on contact, see the final paragraphs in *The Maine Woods* detailing his descent from Katahdin.

15. "Acknowledgment" is a term of art central to the writing of Stanley Cavell, a way of contact with oneself, others, and the world that is not, in the classic sense, a matter of knowing.

16. In the background, I hear Jack Caputo's "obligation happens." See John D. Caputo, *Against Ethics* (Bloomington: Indiana University Press, 1993). Identification of particulars as the particulars they are, we might say, in the ordinary course of things "just happens." We neither have nor need, as a rule, authorization for declaring "I'm obliged (here)!" or "That's a rabbit!" or *"This* (pointing to the shelf of books) is Kierkegaard!"

17. *On Søren Kierkegaard: Dialogue, Polemic, Lost Intimacy, and Time* (Burlington, Vt.: Ashgate, 2007), chap. 10, in which I characterize the swirl of moral views as "the ethical sublime."

18. Alastair Hannay, *Kierkegaard: The Arguments of the Philosophers* (New York: Routledge, 1982).

19. The Satan of the book of Job and Ivan Karamazov's Satan, not to mention Faust's, have admirable qualities. In some sense we learn to like them. They needn't be inhuman beasts. Ivan's is a "harmless" scholar.

20. Stanley Cavell calls this sort of yielding to (or trust in) the given, despite the persistence of possible skeptical retorts, "falling in love with the world," the only "correct blindness" as he puts it, that there is (Cavell, *The Claim of Reason* [New York: Oxford University Press, 1979], 431). This is a theme I discuss at length in "Acknowledgment, Suffering, and Praise: Stanley Cavell as Religious Continental Thinker," *Soundings* 88, no. 3–4 (Fall/Winter 2005): 393–411, and in "J. Glenn Gray and Hannah Arendt: Poetry in a Time of War," in *American Intimates* (Scranton, Pa.: University of Scranton Press, 2008).

21. This embryonic transcendental deduction of "the given," I suggest, resembles Ricoeur's recognition of the necessity of a "second naiveté," and Kierkegaard calls it a "second immediacy." From an apparently different camp, consider Bernard Williams: "I must deliberate from where I am. Truthfulness requires trust in that, and not the obsessional and doomed drive to eliminate it" (*Ethics and the Limits of Philosophy* [Cambridge, Mass.: Harvard University Press, 1985], 200). See too, my *Selves in Discord and Resolve,* 72ff. and 86ff.

22. Garff, *Kierkegaard,* 340.

23. For another account that finds pervasive deception in Kierkegaard's authorship, see M. Holmes Hartshorne, *Kierkegaard: Godly Deceiver* (New York: Columbia University Press, 1990).

24. "Behold the dawn! The face of things is changed by it!" Here Job's Whirlwind Voice unveils an expressive world with no "essential world" behind it of which it is the expression. Embracing an expressive self is not embracing the picture of an essential self that "pushes itself out" in expressions. For a helpful discussion, see Anthony Rudd, *Expressing the World: Skepticism, Wittgenstein, and Heidegger* (Chicago: Open Court, 2003).

25. There are a number of critiques of a "narrative unity" view of the self as well as

of the view that this "unity" is no more than my present identification with an immediately preceding self. See Derek Parfit, *Reasons and Persons* (Oxford: Oxford University Press, 1986), and *Kierkegaard After MacIntyre: Essays on Freedom, Narrative, and Virtue*, eds. John J. Davenport and Anthony Rudd (Chicago: Open Court Press, 2001).

26. See my *On Søren Kierkegaard*, chap. 12.

27. A discussion with Clark West about Spinoza's striking claim that the intellectual love of God is God's love of God has been of help here. One could see Abraham's struggle with God as a reflection of God's internal struggle with himself as a variation on Spinoza's claim. The formula corresponding to Spinoza's might be, "A person's struggles with God are God's struggle with God."

28. My reading of the "impossibilities" that Abraham faces is at variance with the picture Derrida paints in *The Gift of Death*, trans. David Wills (Chicago: University of Chicago Press, 1995), 70–71. Kierkegaard would protest that Derrida is making out Abraham to be "only" a tragic hero, still within the ethical, not within the deeper crisis of a knight of faith. I discuss Derrida's missteps in *On Søren Kierkegaard*, chap. 5, pp. 102ff.

29. For a fuller treatment of these issues, see my *Knights of Faith and Resignation: Reading Kierkegaard's Fear and Trembling* (Albany: State University of New York Press, 1991).

30. Does this recycling of passages make Kierkegaard only a kid rearranging blocks —and "playing with himself" to boot?

31. *Kierkegaard's Papers and Journals, a Selection*, ed. and trans. Alastair Hannay (New York: Penguin Books, 1996), 48 IX A 438.

PART 2.
JUSTICE

4

A Love as Strong as Death

Ricoeur's Reading of the Song of Songs

MARK GEDNEY

The struggle against claims of absolute com-prehension and totaliz-ing theory was one of the hallmarks of the work of Paul Ricoeur. One of these areas of struggle was his longstanding attempt to keep philosophical analysis and religious investigation independent of one another. Over the last decade or so of his life, however, as he integrated the concept of the command of love—following an interpretation of the Song of Songs by Franz Rosenzweig— into his philosophical discussion of self-identity and justice, he came to reject such an absolute "conceptual asceticism."[1] This move was not a simple ac-commodation, but rather it represented a recognition of certain aporias that arise in any attempt to maintain absolute philosophical purity. In terms of the opposition between love and justice, Ricoeur argued: "Rather than confusing them or setting up a pure and simple dichotomy between love and justice, I think a third, difficult way has to be explored, one in which the tension between the two distinct and sometimes opposed claims may be maintained and may even be the occasion for the invention of responsible forms of be-havior."[2] The necessity of such a third way came increasingly to the fore in Ricoeur's account of what it meant to be just to oneself, to the other, and to the collective history of ourselves. In particular, Ricoeur saw this problematic in light of the question of forgiveness. Echoing Derrida's discussions about the impossibility of forgiveness, Ricoeur developed an account of love and justice that recognized the aporias of forgiveness while resisting the absolute claim that forgiveness is impossible.[3] We shall begin with Ricoeur's account of love in his essay on the Song of Songs before concluding with a brief look at how he used these insights to develop a particular reading of the relationship(s) be-tween love, justice, gift, and gratitude.

If one of the hallmarks of Ricoeur's work was the rejection of the possibility of human beings' comprehending themselves, God, or the cosmos as a complete system, this rejection in no way implied that any relation between God and self is impossible.[4] On the contrary, Ricoeur defended a relationship between God and the singular human person made possible by the command to love, specifically as articulated in the dual command to love God and neighbor, a possibility that we find given special attention in his reading of the Song of Songs. Ricoeur begins his discussion of the Song of Songs by pointing out how this text resists in a special way any absolute theoretical reinscription or reduction,[5] insofar as identifiable authorities and social structures are dismissed, manipulated, and reinterpreted for the sake of the singular love of the two lovers. The brothers, the mother, the daughters of Jerusalem, Solomon, and even the typical religious paradigms and customs of the day are all there in the story, but these realities are noted precisely so as to be put aside; their traditional value challenged (even if not absolutely).[6] It is precisely this power to resist our urge to systematize or neutralize the particularity of the lovers' relationship that makes this text so important,[7] and it is precisely this power that allows Ricoeur to relate the poem to the inaugural story of God's love in Genesis. For Ricoeur, we need to see how God's love, which is ultimately as strong as death, is introduced "in the beginning," before it is taken up as the love that brings about redemption. Ricoeur brings Genesis 2:23 and the Song of Songs together in order to highlight three features about creation and love: (1) the central and positive character of a form of *eros* that must be seen as a fundamental dynamic of human being; (2) the innocent joy of this *eros* that prefigures and underlies the drama of sin and redemption; and finally (3) the fact that this powerful poem of joyful human love cannot be understood apart from the love of God found implicitly and explicitly in the very notion of creation. We shall examine these points in order.

First of all, it is in Genesis that the value of individuals as individuals and a new conception of temporality are established. Adam named the animals according to their type, but in this catalogue something was missing. It cannot be simply gender, for it seems as though the animal and plant kingdoms were created fully functional in terms of the mere perpetuation of the various species. The story of Eve's creation in the second chapter of Genesis must point to a more fundamental lack, namely, the other as other person (not just as other gender). It is "this one here" that fills what is lacking. As Ricoeur points out, "Before the creation of the woman, language is certainly there, but simply as a system of signs [*langue*], that is, as a simple repertoire of appropriate words assigned to other living creatures. It is only with the woman that language comes to be once and for all a living or spoken language [*parole*], or, to be more precise, as sentences filled with deictic terms ('this here'—expressly repeated two times and 'this time here')."[8] The fullness of this language is found more perfectly in the Song of Songs for Ricoeur, but before turning to this text we must first attend to this initial appearance of communication "at the beginning."

This originary goodness of the need for other people and thus of the appropriateness of an *eros* that arises between persons indicates the innocent character of the joy in the beloved. As Ricoeur notes, however, we often miss this in our rush to move on in the narrative.

> The innocence of *eros* is thus wrapped in divine approval. It is a creaturely innocence, where "creature" means created by God. It is true that the break is next. If we, however, see this story of the creation of the woman in the larger context of the complete "story" [*histoire*] of beginnings, this birth and the word that welcomes it comes into being in a significant interval between the position of the prohibition—"You shall not eat. . . ." (Gen 2:14)—and the act of its transgression (Gen 3). However, this interval does not constitute a simple narrative transition to be rapidly passed through but rather a powerful time in the *story* of origins, a story that absolutely affirms the stature of the creature as good. The cry of jubilation of the man puts the erotic before good and evil, because it exists before this distinction. Could we not say, then, that the Song of Songs re-opens this enclave of innocence and gives it all the space that the autonomy of a complete poem allows?[9]

This originary space of *eros* and the necessity of the human other even before the rupture of the Fall points, however, to the more primordial character of God's love.[10]

As we have seen, the distance/difference inaugurated by the introduction of the beloved, Eve, and the longing made possible because of it, is not due to the Fall, but rather is the precondition for their relationship. As such, this distance/difference is good and arises from the primordial or *agapic* love of God that springs *ex nihilo* and inaugurates their relationship and longing.[11] Thus, human longing for God (like Adam's desire for Eve) is a central part of our being. Longing for God is not the result of the rupture of some immediate unity of God and Adam and Eve due to some mysterious event. In fact, one might argue that it is precisely a failure to desire or long for God that instigates the Fall. In other words, it is the failure of fidelity to God, a failure to absolutely love God as he loved them, that led to the actual eating of the forbidden fruit; and the breaking of the commandment is more fundamentally the refusal to love fully and absolutely. This originary longing is not the desire to dominate or possess the erotic object,[12] but rather a recognition of a necessary distance that impels action. This drama, before infidelity, is captured powerfully in the Song of Songs. One can see it as a play of call and response that echoes divine love. In the Song of Songs the lovers call out to one another in the expectation that love will prove as strong as the barriers in place against it.

Here, perhaps, is a response to the tendency of many to find in this originary distance a sign of an "original sin," which, because of the impossibility of a pure speaking to the other that would finally and completely close the distance/difference between oneself and another and thus once and for all eliminate the possibility of foreswearing or being unfaithful, stains us all. If this is so, then what seems to be a fundamental aspect of our selfhood—the distance/difference between two persons (and for that matter the distance/difference between what one desires for oneself and one's current character as Ricoeur points out in *Oneself as Another*[13]—is seen as the very root of evil.[14] Against this view, Ricoeur argues for the primordially productive character of this distance; for it is in this very distance that the possibility of loving arises. It is only because of this distance that faithfulness is possible. This possibility of fidelity, does, however, bring about the possibility of infidelity.

The story found in the second chapter of Genesis has its unfortunate counterpoint in the story of the Fall, where the tempter is heeded rather than the beloved. Using the Song of Songs as a clue, we may argue that it is Adam and Eve's hiding that is the true sign of their sin. If it were simply a matter of breaking a rule, then their punishment could have been meted out, as in many myths of violation, by a magical and immediate consequence. One touches the forbidden object and is immediately consumed or turned to stone, for example. The eating of the fruit, however, is run through fairly straightforwardly, and the story only comes alive again when God calls out. If they have violated a command, it is not because they are distant or different than God, but rather because they are unfaithful to God in their failing to truly long for and continually move after their lover. It is this failure that earns for them the "natural" consequence of their infidelity, namely, the return to dust and to a natural self that dies and is replaceable. In order to better understand how this sin, even "original sin," may be overcome, we must re-examine a typical reading of the drama of the Fall that Ricoeur's account is meant to overcome.

This story is often told in terms of a power struggle, where the major concern is with which party will have its desires or commandments obeyed. As such, it has been recast in modern Western philosophy as a question of recognition or sovereignty: Either you accept God's command and thereby mirror his will, or you maintain yourself against God's will and choose something else.[15] Recognition, on this view, is a battle between wills. Hegel's famous solution to this battle, which attempts to avoid the reduction of God to human desires (one form of unity) or human desires directly to God's (to the point where the person becomes a mere replica of God), is mutual recognition. This solution, however, seems either to place a third thing between the two wills, something to which they mutually conform their will, or it seems to return to the problem just stated, namely, one of the members of the battle imposes his or her will on the other. In other words, if it is resolved according to a third thing (the "Concept" for Hegel), then it seems that we either label this *God* (or, in Hegel's case, "Spirit" or *Geist*) and thus raise questions about the God that was originally one of the members of the battle, or we simply label it the ultimate universal, which is beyond the relationships that led to the struggle for recognition. This latter option seems merely to re-instate the dilemma of the universal and singular (or particular) once again. Ricoeur, noting the influence of the biblical notion of love, especially as characterized in the Song of Songs, holds out for the possibility of a peaceful process of recognition in his last published work, *Parcours de la reconnaissance*, in which the exchange between the two members is not based on conflict, but rather on the command (gift) of love.[16]

It is precisely this mutuality of peaceful recognition that characterizes the initial "innocent" exchanges between Adam and Eve and between this couple and God articulated in the command of love: "You, (Eve/Adam), love me, (God)." This command, this "ought," is not opposed to the "is"; it is not a simple denial of what the other is, but rather the command opens up a space for the other to be other. Eve is, in fact, the beloved because God, in fact, does love her (freely, as an initial *agape* that comes from an absolute beginning). In being faithful and responding to this command, she is not in principle called to be other than she is (though this love will transform who she is, but this becomes a product of what she already is, that is, beloved). In being faithful to this call, she testifies to her nature as the beloved. She comes to recognize herself in a compressed "temporal" moment that echoes the *anamnesis* or recollection of Plato, but this echo is not bound to the theory of forms and the preexistence of the soul. The one commanded to love, miracle of miracles, recognizes herself in this "new" self-perception as what she is in fact—beloved.

After the Fall, however, we do not see ourselves as what we wish to be, namely, worthy of absolute love. For Ricoeur, it is not a question of our being absolutely depraved and incapable of any relationship, for such a condition would make love impossible. Lévinas, who worried that any form of recognition of the rightness of God's commands or the demands of others risked reducing God and others to one's own selfish agenda or will, often seems to argue for an absolutely exterior command that shatters the integrity of the ego without reserve. Ricoeur, however, defends the essential goodness of our desire to be a person, to be a person who matters and who is able to legitimately recognize this value.[17] We are not called to substitute our personhood for the sake of the other, but rather to testify to this gift of love from the other that in fact grants to me my status as a unique being or person, precisely because I am loved.

Of course, the fact is that we are unfaithful, and the relationship between the lover and the beloved is fractured and appears as a duty that I have not met and a self that I am not yet. The things that I would do for the beloved have become stumbling blocks, that is, things that I have failed to do. It is the violation of this originary eros, an eros prompted by the anarchic *agape* of creation, that leads to sin and death. Our final question, therefore, must concern the power of a love that is as strong as death in which we come to recognize ourselves in a new way, namely, as forgiven.

If faithlessness is the true root of evil, then violation or transgression is always the breaking of a relationship—a hiding when called. As such, there is a sense that all moral evil is inexpiable in terms of a calculation on the part of the sinner. There is no act of contrition or propitiation that can be performed by the sinner that can logically guarantee the return of love. Rather, according to Ricoeur, and here he is also relying on Hannah Arendt, if we understand the dynamics of success and failure, faithfulness and unfaithfulness, good and evil in light of the demands of the one who calls me to myself and to whom I must be faithful, then we can understand that the failure of my action, my un-faithfulness, which is unredeemable on my part, may be redeemed by a new call from the one betrayed. A self may be disassociated from any particular evil, not because of some bootstrap operation, for example, by a conscience that calls itself out of complacency and desires Being (as perhaps in Heidegger),[18] but rather because this self may be reborn in the renewed call of the lover. Ricoeur argues that this "intimate disassociation signifies that the capacity of the moral subject to be engaged is not exhausted by these diverse inscriptions in world events. This disassociation presents an act of faith, a credit that points to the resources of regeneration in the self."[19]

This is no antinomianism, for the laws of justice, while inadequate to express the absolute commitment to the beloved, are a necessary (at least in this world) restraint against the forgetfulness, self-absorption, and hate that destroys relationships. As finite creatures who also suffer under sin and whose impulse to love the other—the one who is next to me (the neighbor)—falters, our love must be measured against the law that arises out of the various prom-ises made to the beloved. This said, however, one must not mistake these necessary "legal" products for the concern for the other in her or his sin-gularity.[20]

The question that follows naturally here concerns the possibility of a forgiveness that in one sense violates justice and in another sense is the answer to justice. As Ricoeur notes: "The person of *agape* . . . finds herself or himself lost in the world of calculation and equivalences, where she or he is incapable of giving an account."[21] In order to truly understand the radical character of forgiveness, we must turn here to the question of a divine love that is experi-enced directly in the life of the solitary believer and spills out into love of neighbor and returns again as the love that inspires hope—hope for the re-demption of the world. It is God who so loved the world that he made love possible for humankind in the immemorial call to Adam and Eve, who makes love possible in the perennial call to his creatures in the present, and who will make love possible in the eternal kingdom insofar as his call is sufficient to call out even the dead—for is not love as strong as death?[22] Of course, this is no strict proof, but rather it is a concrete experience that makes me capable of acting anew. It is the experience of a love that comes as a true gift. This experience is developed in Ricoeur's final thoughts on the relationship of love, justice, and forgiveness as it relates to the possibility or impossibility of such a gift.

Ricoeur agrees with Derrida and others that there is always a danger that the giving and receiving of gifts (especially the gift of forgiveness) will fall back into an economic exchange,[23] but he argues that the desire to give back in recognition of the gift may be of a different sort than the desire that promotes the economic cycle of exchange or the balancing of the accounts of justice. With the offering of the gift, one finds that

> [i]n place of the obligation to give back, it is necessary to speak, under the sign of *agape*, of a response to a call issuing from this initial generosity of the gift. Following this same line of thought, is it not necessary to put a particular accent on the second moment of the triad—giving-receiving-giving back? Receiving thus becomes the pivotal category in that the manner by which the gift is accepted decides the manner in which the receiver feels obligated to give back. A word that was noted earlier in passing shares this spirit, namely, "gratitude." Now it is the case that the French language is one in which "recognition" [*reconnaissance*] may be used instead of "gratitude." Gratitude lightens the weight of obligation to give back and orients this obligation towards a generosity equal to that which called forth the original gift.[24]

Rather than an economy of exchange, where the desires of the individuals are to be calculated and inspected, the illogic of giving points toward the source of the generosity that inspires and calls us out. We give a gift in the name of generosity, and thus love, and we receive a return in that name as well.[25] Though Ricoeur does not speak specifically of it here, one might see this peaceful enjoyment of one another as a species of friendship, of *philia*; a love that arises out of the initial uncalled-for love as *agape*, is developed in the love or *eros* for this lover, and culminates in a mutual recognition of each in community. Ricoeur speaks of this community as typified by celebrations and festivals, where the exchange of gifts is an affirmation of love and gratitude for which the proper response is praise and rejoicing. "The festive, which can be a part of the rituals of the art of love, in its erotic, familial, and social forms, shares in the same spiritual lineage as the gestures for asking for forgiveness. Even more, the festive character of the gift is, in terms of the repertoire of gesturing, that which is elsewhere on the level of hymns. What comes together here is a series of expressions that I like to put under the auspices of the optative mood in grammar, the mood which is neither descriptive nor normative."[26]

In his account of the Song of Songs, Rosenzweig connects his account of the joy of the lovers with David's dancing before the Ark.[27] For Ricoeur, the lovers' joy is connected to the joy of Adam at the appearance of Eve. Neither denied that this joy often becomes ashes in our mouths in the face of the assassins both great and small that inhabit the earth, but both reminded us and continue to remind us even in death that the power to speak out in the name of justice is grounded in a temporality that points back to a primordial having been loved that sustains us through the present and that reaches out in the hope that the primordial love that lies before all hatred will fulfill itself in an eschaton where love is truly seen to be as strong as death and where one can repeat in joy the words addressed to the young woman:

> Arise, my love, my fair one, and come away:
> For now the winter is past,
> The rain is over and gone.
> The flowers appear on the earth;
> The time for singing has come. . . .
> (Song of Songs 2:10–12)

NOTES

1. This phrase comes from a recent interview with Ricoeur by Richard Kearney, *On Paul Ricoeur: The Owl of Minerva* (Aldershot: Ashgate, 2004), 169.

2. "Love and Justice," in *Figuring the Sacred: Religion, Narrative, and Imagination* (Minneapolis: Fortress Press, 1995), 324. See also my "Jaspers and Ricoeur on the Self and the Other," *Philosophy Today* (Winter 2004): 331–41.

3. Ricoeur speaks of this difficult forgiveness in the Epilogue of *La mémoire, l'histoire, l'oubli*, entitled, "Le pardon difficile" (Paris: Éditions du Seuil, 2000) 593–656. *Memory, History, Forgetting*, trans. Kathleen Blamey and David Pellauer (Chicago: University of Chicago Press, 2004), 457–506.

4. For Ricoeur, as for many of his contemporaries, Hegel's philosophy represents just such a system. See "Should We Renounce Hegel?" in volume 3 of *Time and Narrative*, trans. Kathleen Blamey and David Pellauer (Chicago: University of Chicago Press, 1988), 193–206; *Temps et récit*, tome III (Paris: Édition du Seuil, 1984), 349–72. This is also one of the points at which Ricoeur's analysis joins common cause with Rosenzweig's work in the *Star of Redemption*. Rosenzweig develops his account of the command of love precisely in order to re-establish a relationship between God and human beings that systematic thinking or philosophy disconnects. For example, it is God's relating to the individual soul in the command of love that answers the following question: "How should the self become a soul, when to be a soul means to escape from this self-centered isolation? How may this self step forth? Who will call it, for it is deaf? What will draw it out, for it is blind? What will it become once outside, for it is dumb? It wholly lives within itself" (Rosenzweig, *Der Stern der Erlösung* [Frankfurt am Main: Suhrkamp, 1988], 89; *Star of Redemption*, trans. by William Hallo [South Bend, Ind.: University of Notre Dame Press, 1970], 82). Note: all translations from French and German are my own.

5. Paul Ricoeur, *Penser la Bible* (Paris: Éditions Seuil, 1998), 454. *Thinking Biblically: Exegetical and Hermeneutical Studies*, trans. David Pellauer (Chicago: University of Chicago Press, 1998), 286. In this work, Ricoeur argues that modern allegorists and their literalist counterparts are both "indifferent to the conditions of reciting the canonical text anew which, in the traditions of the ancient church, enabled a Christian soul to stand in for the beloved of the Song of Songs and to sing with her the nuptial hymn. The authors of modern allegorical commentaries force themselves to take up a sort of non-place of objectivity exactly like their 'naturalist' opponents" (*Penser la Bible*, 454;

Thinking Biblically, 286). Ricoeur also points out that the charges against allegory as arbitrary, blinded by pre-supposed systems and based on questionable ecclesiastical authority, lose much of their force if one understands such allegorical interpretations as attempts to sing these songs anew by a believer removed by time and distance from the initial singers. Why are these poems handed down? Certainly we can develop theories about the origins, authorship, etc., and this is terribly important, but in the end the Song of Songs has had its impact in the retelling and singing anew of the song as a hymn to God and his mercy. See *Penser la Bible*, 458; *Thinking Biblically*, 289.

6. Though there is a strong tradition identifying the young shepherd and King Solomon, I shall maintain (as did Ricoeur) the anonymity of the two lovers in this essay.

7. It is this power, perhaps, to which Rabbi Akiba famously attests: "All the Scriptures are holy but the Song of Songs is holy of holies." This is found in Yadayim 3:5 of the *Mishna*, *Everyman's Talmud: The Major Teachings of the Rabbinic Sages*, by Abraham Cohen (New York: Schocken Books, 1949), 143.

8. *Penser la Bible*, 468; *Thinking Biblically*, 297.

9. *Penser la Bible*, 468–69; *Thinking Biblically*, 297–98.

10. Ricoeur would certainly agree with Rosenzweig that "love can never be purely human" (*Liebe kann gar nicht rein menschlich sein*). See Rosenzweig, *Der Stern*, 224; *The Star*, 201.

11. As one moves through the different roles of lover/beloved and forgiver/forgiven, the nature of love undergoes systematic changes that allow one to account for the basic conceptions of love that have dominated philosophy and theology, i.e., *agape*, *eros*, and *philia*. The fact that these modes of love can be seen as essentially related, however, argues against any rigid opposition, as was famously attempted in Anders Nygren's *Agape and Eros*, trans. Philip S. Watson (London: SPCK, 1953). See Ricoeur's critique of such a position in "Love and Justice," 320–21. Though we shall have the opportunity to see how some of these relationships might be understood, a detailed analysis is beyond the scope of this essay. Father Edward Vacek has taken up this challenge in a very important and helpful way in his book *Love, Human and Divine: The Heart of Christian Ethics* (Washington, D.C.: Georgetown University Press, 1994).

12. We should be slow to criticize even this version of eros (as selfish grasping), for as Ricoeur has noted, this more selfish and immediate desire can serve as training for other less selfish forms. See Ricoeur, "Love and Justice," 320.

13. Paul Ricoeur, *Oneself as Another* (Chicago: University of Chicago Press, 1992), 171–80; *Soi-même*, 202–11. Of course, Derrida also sees this impossible situation as the ground that also (impossibly) makes possible human action and forgiveness.

14. For a critique of such attempts to describe this distance/difference as a form of original sin, see my "Jaspers and Ricoeur on the Self and Other."

15. Sartre's early play *The Flies* captures beautifully this view of the drama of recognition between God and human beings. At the end of the play, in response to Jupiter's command that he, Orestes, recognize Jupiter's commands and the laws of his creation (his world), Orestes cries out: "Let them fall to pieces! Let the rocks condemn me and plants wilt before me. Your entire universe isn't enough to condemn me. You are the King of the Gods, Jupiter, the king of stones and stars and the king of the waves, but you are not the king of humanity" (*Huis clos suivi de Les mouches* [Paris: Éditions Gallimard, 1947], 232; *No Exit* [New York: Vintage Books, 1955], 120).

16. Paul Ricoeur, *Parcours de la reconnaissance: Trois études* (Paris: Éditions Stock, 2004). Of course, Ricoeur accepts that most of our moments of recognition arise from a

struggle begun in injustice and inequality in which a person must assert her or his personality against the violence of the other, but what he insists upon here is the primordial character of this peaceful relation—even if it is little seen in this fallen world.

17. Ricoeur here refers to the notion of *conatus* (following Spinoza), that is, the natural desire to be a subject. See *Oneself as Another*, 315; *Soi-même comme un autre*, 366. See also my "Jaspers and Ricoeur on the Self and the Other," 336–41.

18. See Ricoeur's examination of conscience in his essay on Heidegger, Lévinas, and Nabert, "Lévinas: Thinker of Testimony," in *Figuring the Sacred*, 108–13.

19. *La mémoire, l'histoire, l'oubli*, 638; *Memory, History, Forgetting*, 490.

20. Ricoeur argues forcefully in *Oneself as Another* against the notion that one's basic moral responsibility is to a principle. Ricoeur's view is that fidelity (and the related notion of attestation) cannot simply be understood as a categorical imperative that proclaims an absolute fidelity to all others. According to Ricoeur, such an empty fidelity to law or to "persons" becomes a strange sort of solipsism insofar as it wills its own abstract purity, which, because it is without concrete referent, is no true action or concrete testimony of good will. Cf. *Oneself as Another*, 264–90; *Soi-même comme un autre*, 307–37.

21. *Parcours de la reconnaissance: Trois études*, 326.

22. Both Rosenzweig and Ricoeur carefully develop the connection between the direct love of God and the reorientation to the other immediately before me. See Ricoeur, *Oneself as Another*, 169–202; *Soi-même comme un autre*, 200–36; and Rosenzweig, *Der Stern*, 229–40; *The Star*, 205–45.

23. Derrida argues that the introduction of the return-gift (*contre-don*) introduces an economy that destroys the graciousness of the gift and reduces it to a narcissistic economy or exchange. Derrida examines this subject in detail in his book *Donner le temps. 1 La fausse monnaie* (Paris: Gallilée, 1991); translated by Peggy Kamuf as *Given Time. 1. Counterfeit Money* (Chicago: University of Chicago Press, 1994). Ricoeur, too, takes note of this paradox: "Here we are presented with a paradox: how is it that the giver is obliged to give back? And if this second person (the receiver) is obliged to give back if he or she is generous, then how is it that the first gift was generous?" (Ricoeur, *Parcours*, 332).

24. Ibid., 351.

25. The two great intertwined festivals of Passover and the Eucharist both represent the story of salvation and the establishment of a community in joy. The bread and wine are served to each other in the name of salvation, that is God. It is no accident that the Gospels (Matthew and Mark) remind us that the Last Supper ended as did all Passovers with the great *Hymn* (the final Psalm of the *Hallel*). "O give thanks to the Lord for he is good; his steadfast love endures forever" (118:1).

26. Ricoeur, *Parcours*, 354.

27. Richard Kearney also links our desire for God to the dancing of David before the ark and to the "festive" when he speaks of the "play" of God. See *The God Who May Be* (Bloomington: Indiana University Press, 2001), 106–11.

5

Paul Ricoeur and the Possibility of Just Love

CHRISTOPHER WATKIN

An "ontology of totality"[1] pervades postmodern ethics, forcing a radical dichotomy of economy and excess, justice and love, framing the possibility of such an ethics—and its impossibility. Nowhere is this dichotomy more radically exposed than in Emmanuel Lévinas's *Otherwise than Being, or, Beyond Essence*,[2] in which the increasingly hyperbolic rhetoric of substitution, expiation, and the hostage disrupts, in its very excess, calculating judgment and measure. A similarly rigorous refusal of determinate commensurability is characteristic of Derridean ethics,[3] where the doubly aporetic disjunction of calculating "*justesse*" and the singular decision of "*justice*" guards against the reduction of alterity to calculability.[4] The relation of calculating justice and singular love negotiates the same problematic (non)relation of economy and excess, where justice is ranged with knowledge and totalization, and radically dislocated from uncalculating and uncalculable *agape*.

The dichotomy of love and justice is not, however, the sole preserve of deconstructive ethics, since mention could be made, for example, of Chaïm Perelman's opposition in the *New Rhetoric* between the "immediate virtue" of charity to the mediate virtue of justice,[5] or Luc Boltanski's assertion that a clash of different principles of justification fuels conflict, whereas *agape* ignores calculation and makes references to equivalence redundant.[6]

Paul Ricoeur occupies a strategic site from which to understand and critique this unbridgeable separation, writing as he does at a distance, but a sympathetic distance, from an ontology of totality and its radical disarticulation of love and justice. Sensitive to the difference between the rule of justice and the singularity of *agape*, Ricoeur's hermeneutic phenomenology does not—and here he is markedly unlike Lévinas and Derrida—consider an aporetic disjunction of love and justice to be the price to pay for maintaining an *éthicité* beyond the merely calculable.

We will consider Ricoeur's non-dichotomous thinking of love and justice through three texts. Beginning with his assessment of the Lévinasian position in *Autrement*, a reading of Lévinas's *Otherwise than Being, or Beyond Essence*,[7] we will then turn to the relation of love and justice in Ricoeur's own thought, first in the essay "Love and Justice"[8] and subsequently in the third study of *Parcours de la reconnaissance*, entitled "Mutual recognition."[9] It is a journey that will reveal how Ricoeur cautiously feels his way toward a just love, moving beyond an aporetic disjunction of justice and *agape* to inscribe the particularity of compassion at the heart of discourse.

Reading for an "Otherwise"

In the thirty-nine pages of *Autrement*, Ricoeur situates his attempt to re-think the relation of love and justice at the point of their most radical disjunction. In *Otherwise than Being*, Lévinas is at pains to disassociate the "otherwise than being" from its betrayal in all figures of the other as "being otherwise," which are systematically reabsorbed by the totalizing ontology it is his intention to disrupt. Lévinas eschews the manifestation of otherness, which merely substitutes the said for the Saying, thereby annulling it. Modeling the reduction of Saying to said on the correlation of verb and noun leads Lévinas to condemn its nominalization and ossification: to thematize is to nominalize. To forestall this collapse into nominalization, Lévinas performs a "betrayal of the betrayal" of Saying: unsaying.[10] Passionately concerned to preserve the radical nature of responsibility before the other in proximity, Lévinas rejects even the language of love, for insofar as love implies unity and agreement, it "is too easy and natural to pass for the ethical rigour of being elected to responsibility,"[11] a distinction that Lévinas seeks to preserve at all costs.

In *Otherwise than Being*, Lévinas frames the disjunction of ontology and ethics in terms of the (non)relation of, on the one hand, the escalating hyperbole of proximity to substitution, of suffering by the other to suffering for the other and, on the other hand, justice as truth and *logos*, judgment and coherence.[12] However, Lévinas also insists—and this juxtaposition is the impetus for Ricoeur's intervention—on the proximity of the Other in the call to responsibility. How, Ricoeur will ask, given both this disjunction and this proximity, might we mediate on the one hand the irreducibility of Saying to the said in the Argument of *Otherwise than Being* and, on the other hand, the discourse on proximity and substitution?

The question is critical for Ricoeur because of a danger he sees inherent in the Lévinasian argument, namely, that if an "appropriate" language for Saying is not found, the hyperbolic tropes of hostage-taking and the malice of persecuting hatred come themselves to constitute the ethical injunction as the only way to interrupt the ontological recuperation of being (A, 24). Furthermore, if there is no said appropriate to the Saying, the non-sense of the ineffable threatens both being and responsibility, ontology and ethics alike. Better, for Ricoeur, that all meaning proceed from essence, than that there be no meaning at all (A, 38). In his short study of *Otherwise than Being*, then, Ricoeur seeks to find in the Lévinasian text a reading of the relation between the ethical Saying and the ontological said otherwise than in terms of radical disjunction, setting himself the apparently Sisyphean task of "finding, for the unruly ex-ception the regime of being, the language befitting to it, its own language, the said of its Saying" (A, 2; my translation). It is the task of bringing together the economy of justice and that which exceeds and precedes it.

It is precisely the "verbal terrorism" (A, 26; my translation) of Lévinas's hyperbolic discourse of substitution and expiation that provides for Ricoeur the background to the arrival of the "third" and the discourse of justice, in terms of which he unfolds his alternative reading of *Otherwise than Being*. Whereas the singularity of Saying would seem to foreclose the possibility of comparison (A, 29), Lévinas introduces justice as "the justice that compares, assembles and conceives, the synchrony of being and peace"(A, 27).[13] The entrance of the third[14] and of justice troubles the hyperbole of responsibility, as it proclaims "Peace, peace to him that is far off, and to him that is near,"[15] refusing what Lévinas calls the "clandestinity of love."[16] In so doing, it introduces "a contradiction in the Saying." How are substitution and justice, responsibility and thought, to be related? Ricoeur takes up the Lévinasian language of a "latent birth of cognition and essence, of the said, the latent birth of a question, in responsibility,"[17] by which Lévinas does not mean to suggest that the third is chronologically posterior to the Other, born in the midst of the already established relation to the Other, for "the other and the third party, my neighbours, contemporaries of one another, put distance between me and the other and the third party" (OB, 157). The question does not totalize alterity, Ricoeur argues, but recognizes the non-recuperated distance separating alterity from the self—a distance now understood otherwise than as absolute disjunction, yet resisting the grasping gesture of co-opting alterity into the economy of the same. It is a reading that Lévinas's commitment to an ontology of totality makes him reluctant to pursue, though such a reading is announced several times in *Otherwise than Being*, and even begun under the rubric of the "third" and justice. It is a reading that it is the task of *Autrement* to develop from Lévinas's work itself, in linking the destiny of the relation between ontology and the ethics of responsibility with that of the ontological said and ethical Saying (A, 1).

Ricoeur similarly traces a middle way between absolute disjunction and recuperative appropriation in his reading of memory in Lévinas as "recognition of a temporal distance" (A, 14), a recognition he finds latent in the dedication of *Otherwise than Being:* "To the memory of those who were clos-est . . ." (*OB*, v). He uncovers in both memory and the arrival of the third the seeds of a reading of distance otherwise than as radical dislocation, a distance over which memory can range without totalizing the past in a grasping gesture of appropriation. Ricoeur is feeling his way toward the possibility of Lévinas's unexplored "otherwise said."[18] It is through the discourse of the third and justice that Saying and responsibility (an ethics without ontology) are brought together (A, 19), for "it is justice which enables the thematization of the sort of Saying that enables philosophy" (A, 28; my translation). Without reducing to the economy of justice that which exceeds it, Ricoeur shows how, on the basis of *Otherwise than Being*, they might be thought in a relation of non-totalizing distance. As Paul Simmons rightly notes, "Politics does not subsume ethics, but rather it serves ethics."[19]

Ricoeur concludes his study with four figures of what he calls Lévinas's "post-ethical quasi-ontology": the good, the infinite, "illeity" and the Name of God (A, 35–37), figures through which he rehabilitates naming otherwise (once more) than in terms of an "ontology of totality." It is the last of these four figures that Ricoeur elaborates most fully. In terms of the Name of God, and the proper name more widely, the noun is thought otherwise than as the reduction of alterity to the circle of the same, for the Name of God mediates the ethical infinite and ontological totality: an "otherwise said." This "name which does not thematize, and yet signifies" (A, 37; my translation), is a sign of the *"significance"* without which the said-less Saying would be ineffable; the question "who?" (or *"quis*-nity," as Lévinas [*OB*, 25] ventures) in contrast to "what?" or "how?" resists thematization (A, 37, quoting *OB*, 28).

Throughout *Autrement* we see Ricoeur repeatedly reading *Otherwise than Being* for hints of the possibility of relating justice and that which exceeds its calculating economy, finding latent in the Lévinasian text itself—in terms memory, the name, and the relation of Saying and the said—possibilities other than those that require the adoption of a totalizing ontology. To see how Ricoeur exploits these negotiations between love and justice in his own idiom, we now turn to his earlier essay "Love and Justice."

Love *and* Justice?

In Ricoeur's own development of the intertwining of ethics and ontology, love emerges as the lodestar of his investigation. The Lévinasian adverb *autrement* gestures aptly toward the disjunction of love and justice in Ricoeur's essay of that name, for love is not merely the other of justice, it is otherwise than justice, of another incommensurable order. Ricoeur glosses this incommen-surability in terms of two economies: justice and the economy of equivalence, and *agape* and the economy of superabundance. The question Ricoeur poses in "Love and Justice" foreshadows the concerns of *Autrement:* "If we begin by acknowledging the disproportionality [of love and justice], how can we avoid falling into . . . exaltation or emotional platitudes?" (LJ, 189). Precisely, Ricoeur will argue, by relating love and justice in terms of a "living tension."[20]

Without the ethics of love, justice would become the utilitarian *do ut des*, 'I give so that you will give' (LJ, 200). Conversely, love, the hypermoral, is for its part dependent on the structures of justice for its expression. "If the hypermoral is not in turn to be the nonmoral—not to say the immoral . . . it has to pass through the principle of morality, summed up in the golden rule and formalized by the rule of justice" (LJ, 200). Far from seeking radically to dislocate superabundant love and calculating justice, Ricoeur sees their intertwining as a condition of ethics.

Ricoeur develops this relationality in "Love and Justice" by drawing on Franz Rosenzweig's *Star of Redemption*[21] to frame love as a command, not in terms of a deontological imperative but modeled on the appeal in the Song of Solomon, "Thou, love me!": a command anterior and superior to all laws.[22] Love, then, speaks well enough, but it speaks otherwise than in the language of justice. Its pre-predicative command intervenes before *Dike's* scales begin to weigh. As he refused Lévinas's "ontology of totality," Ricoeur also resists the equation of discourse per se with reductive violence, making instead the case for an "otherwise said" that challenges the dichotomy of an impossible escape from, or collapse into, ontological language.

Ricoeur's understanding of the relation of love and justice as a "living tension"[23] is possible because both participate in the economy of the gift, not for Ricoeur an economy of gift exchange on the model of Marcel Mauss' influential study,[24] but rather a notion of the gift in terms of the tripartite division of *The Star of Redemption:* creation, revelation, and redemption. Ricoeur explores the juxtaposition of love and justice in a Rosenzweigian manner through a meditation on Luke 6:27–31, with its "strange contiguity" of the command to love one's enemies and the golden rule.[25] For Rosenzweig, creation is an originary giving of existence (LJ, 197), and the commandment to love one's enemies is an extreme form of neighborly love linked to the economy of the gift by the hyper-ethical feeling of dependence of the human creature: not "*do ut des,*" but "since it has been given you, give" (LJ, 200). The creature's relation to Torah stems from this same economy: the law is a gift, bound to the history of liberation, so "our relation both to the law and to salvation is shown to belong to this economy by being placed 'between' creation and the eschaton" (LJ, 198).

Ricoeur's association of the commandment to love one's enemies and the golden rule, of the hymn of love and the rule of justice, allows him then to move back from these theological specificities to love and justice per se, arguing that "it is legitimate for us to extend to the social practice of justice and to the principles of justice themselves the suspicion that strikes the golden rule through the logic of superabundance underlying the hyper-ethical commandment to love one's enemies" (LJ, 199). Nevertheless, the central question remains: Does the new commandment of love annul the justice of the golden rule? Do love and the logic of superabundance suspend justice and the logic of equivalence? Can love be commanded? Ricoeur returns to the troubling juxtaposition in Luke 6 with the observation that "another interpretation is possible, wherein the commandment of love does not abolish the golden rule but instead reinterprets it in terms of generosity" (LJ, 200). In this other interpretation, this interpretation "otherwise," the logic of equivalence is transformed, receiving from its confrontation with the logic of superabundance "the capacity of raising itself above its perverse interpretations." What is undermined by the "harsh words" of the logic of superabundance is "not so much . . . the logic of equivalence of the golden rule as . . . its perverse interpretation" (LJ, 200). In Ricoeur's reading, justice is understood through a hermeneutics of love.

There is no insuperable incommensurability of love and justice, if such an incommensurability is to be understood to mean that love is radically incomprehensible in the hopelessly ontologizing discourse of justice. Both Ricoeur and Lévinas have a place for hyperbolic rhetoric, but Ricoeur's is not predicated on the dichotomy of ontology and ethics that so fully determines the Lévinasian position. The extravagance of the parabolic, the hyperbole of the eschatological, and the logic of superabundance in ethics to which Ricoeur appeals are not ranged against discourse and calculation (LJ, 198). Far from it, for as Ricoeur remarks in a fleeting reference to Kierkegaard, to disorient without reorienting is to suspend the ethical (LJ, 202).

Justly Giving Love

Notwithstanding this "living tension" of love and justice in the space of discourse, Ricoeur is far from unaware of the threat, inherent in the very positing of such a space, that the discourse of "love" will become annexed as a mute legitimation of calculating justice. How can Ricoeur's economy of the gift avoid an inevitable return to utilitarian reciprocity? For a response to this question, we turn now to our final text, the third study of Parcours de la reconnaissance, and to its examination of gift exchange.

Does not giving a gift in return for a gift received reduce the gesture to a logic of equivalence, imprisoning it in an emasculating quid pro quo of calculating justice? It is surely this suspicion that prompts Derrida's posture of ingratitude in Adieu to Emmanuel Levinas,[26] and perhaps too, Stephen Webb's hasty comment that "to understand Levinas is to reject him."[27] Ricoeur, for his part, maintains a clear and crucial distinction between two different understandings of the gift: reciprocal, ceremonial gift exchange and market exchange (PR, 341), and in developing his notion of the gift in terms of the latter, he stands once more at a critical distance from the Maussian legacy and the impossible ideal of the pure, uncontaminated gift. What Ricoeur calls the "problematic of return" in gift exchange is dealt with in *Parcours* by splitting the analysis of the gift into two levels: the level of the rule of exchange and the level of the discrete gestures of individuals. The "circle of the gift," belonging as it does to the first of these two levels, is a theory for a modern description of archaic societies, but practitioners of the gift avoid the problematic of return by reorienting the question governing reciprocity from Why return? to Why give? "In place of the obligation to return, we must speak, under the sign of *agape*, of the response to a call from the generosity of the initial gift" (*PR*, 351). We must think of the second gift as the "second first gift" (*PR*, 350).

This reorientation is bolstered by a second but related shift, from a focus on the gift-object to a concentration on the relationality of giver and recipient, from the reciprocity of "return" to the mutuality of "give." From this perspective, to give a gift as a response to a gift received is not to recognize and reciprocate the gift itself but to recognize the relation of which it is a token. Reciprocity becomes mutuality (*PR*, 342).

Furthermore, *Parcours de la reconnaissance* situates the logics of equivalence and superabundance very concretely in terms of the regulated exchange of the market economy. The gift is still present in such an economy, where it is both embedded in and separate from the market laws of exchange; and there is no radical disjunction between gift and transaction, but neither is there an appropriating absorption of the gift. In *Critique and Conviction*, Ricoeur draws attention to the juxtaposition of a thriving philanthropic civil society and a market economy in the United States as a salient model of this paradoxical coexistence (we might say "living tension") of the economy of justice and the gift that cuts across it, a coexistence of "non-monetary relations to money" and "the most implacable system of profitability."[28] Though Ricoeur may find this juxtaposition "inscrutable," an important principle has been established: Gift exchange need not threaten the society of distribution and market exchange of which it is a part; just exchange and charitable excess can, while not being reduced to each other, inhabit the same social space, intertwined as they are in everyday practice (*PR*, 343).

Where Love and Justice Meet

Let us now turn to consider the ways in which this economy of the gift, this intertwining of justice and love, augments the phronetic "practical wisdom" that Ricoeur elaborates in the ninth study of *Oneself as Another*.[29] Up to a point, the gift in *Parcours de la reconnaissance* parallels the role of practical wisdom in *Oneself as Another* in mediating the deontological economy of justice and the teleological desire for the good life. There are, however, fundamental differences between the two mediations, which can be traced to the distinctions in the relation between teleology and deontology in contrast to love and justice. Practical wisdom in *Oneself as Another* is an attempt to render commensurate different "orders of greatness."[30] Each order of greatness belongs to a different "city," of which Boltanski and Thévenot name six: the inspired city, the domestic city, the city of opinion, the civic city, the merchant city, and the industrial city; the incommensurability of the different orders are summed up by Ricoeur in asking what a great industrialist would be worth in the eyes of a great conductor (*PR*, 305). The measures used in each order may be different, but measures they remain. The greatness of love, however, is precisely in that it does not measure, has no scale, does not "count the cost." Aristotelian equity, the goal of practical wisdom, is indeed a corrective to the law, but it is a justice of approximation in which the law is adjusted to the singularity of the case in a linear concern for asymptotic approximation. It is still *justesse*, as Derrida uses the term in *Force of Law*, a calculating and therefore totalizing approach. But Ricoeur's "otherwise said" exceeds justice without having to deny it in the gesture he calls "the festive gift" (*PR*, 354). Love does not stop short of justice but intensifies it in a festive mode. The festive gift is, on the gestural plane, what the hymn is on the verbal, and it also bears parallels to the demand for forgiveness: it cannot be institutionalized, but in foregrounding the limits of a justice of equivalence and opening a space of hope, all three "unleash a wave of irradiation or irrigation which, in a secret and oblique manner, contribute to the advance of history towards a state of peace" (*PR*, 354). It is neither descriptive nor normative, but optative. Perhaps we have here a mediation radical enough to constitute what Patrick Bourgeois calls, in another context, Ricoeur's "viable ethical alternative to deconstruction."[31]

The message of both "Love and Justice" and the final study of *Parcours de la reconnaissance* is that justice and love need not remain in radical disjunction if the ethical is to be preserved from an ontology of totality. Ricoeur shows, furthermore, that the resources with which to think the relation otherwise are in the Lévinasian text itself, among the paroxystic and hyperbolic discourse of *Otherwise than Being*. Ricoeur's is not simply a reading *for* just love, but also a reading *of* just love: scrupulous in its attention to Lévinas's text, always rendering a favorable, though never rose-tinted interpretation, and practicing a hermeneutics of charity. Ricoeur's reading also poses a question to the ontology of totality, interrogating the dichotomization of love and justice on which it relies. Through his elaboration of the "latent birth" of knowledge in responsibility and of the relation of the market and the gift, Ricoeur begins to articulate a common ground between what otherwise become cast as implacably incommensurable.

The wisdom of love is not to be found in an ever shriller identification of calculation with the totalizing reduction of singularity. It is not to be found in the attempt to purify ethics ever more fully from a totalizing ontology in which the persecutor issues the call to responsibility. It is to be found in a careful tracing of the intertwining of love and justice in the shared space of the economy of the gift. There is a need, as Ricoeur remarks, for "a supplementary degree of compassion and generosity in all of our codes" (LJ, 202).

NOTES

1. The term "ontology of totality" is Ricoeur's own, used to indicate the equation of being with violence in poststructuralist discourse: "For E. Levinas, the identity of the Same is bound up with an ontology of totality that my own investigation has never assumed or even come across." See Paul Ricoeur, *Oneself as Another*, trans. Kathleen Blamey (Chicago: University of Chicago Press, 1992), 335.

2. Emmanuel Lévinas, *Otherwise than Being, or, Beyond Essence*, trans. Alphonso Lingis (The Hague: Nijhoff, 1981). Hereafter: *OB*.

3. See Simon Critchley, *The Ethics of Deconstruction: Derrida and Levinas* (Edinburgh: Edinburgh University Press, 1999).

4. Jacques Derrida, "Force of Law: The 'Mystical Foundation of Authority,'" in Drucilla Cornell, Michel Rosenfeld, and David Gray Carlson, eds., *Deconstruction and the Possibility of Justice* (London: Routledge, 1992), 3–67.

5. Chaïm Perelman, *The New Rhetoric: A Treatise on Argumentation*, trans. John Wilkinson and Purcell Weaver (Notre Dame, Ind.: University of Notre Dame Press, 1971).

6. See Luc Boltanski, *L'Amour et la justice comme compétences: Trois essais de sociologie de l'action* (Paris: Éditions Métailié, 1990); Luc Boltanski and Laurent Thévenot, *De la Justification: les économies de la grandeur* (Paris: Gallimard, 1991). See also Ricoeur's discussion of Boltanski's *agapē* in: Paul Ricoeur, *Parcours de la reconnaissance* (Paris: Stock, 2004) 320–21. Hereafter: *PR*.

7. Paul Ricoeur, *Autrement. Lecture d'Autrement qu'être ou au-delà de l'essence d'Emmanuel Lévinas* (Paris: Presses Universitaires de France, 1997). Hereafter: *A*.

8. Paul Ricoeur, "Love and Justice" in *Radical Pluralism and Truth: David Tracy and the Hermeneutics of Religion*, ed. Werner G. Jeanrond and Jennifer L. Rike (New York: Crossroad, 1991), 187–202. Hereafter: *LJ*.

9. Ricoeur, *PR* 227–355. All translations of *Parcours de la reconnaissance* are my own. At the time of writing, an English translation of *Parcours* is in press.

10. Lévinas introduces "unsaying" ("dé-dire") in *Otherwise than Being* as follows: "The *otherwise than being* is stated in a saying that must also be unsaid in order to thus extract the *otherwise than being* from the said in which it already comes to signify but a *being otherwise*" (*OB* 7). Unsaying forms with saying a double movement in which language disrupts its own totalizing such that "producing more said is the proper modality of unsaying." See William Paul Simmons, "The Third: Lévinas' Theoretical Move from An-archical Ethics to the Realm of Justice and Politics," *Philosophy and Social Criticism* 25 (6): 83–104, quote on p. 89. The term is traced back to Eckhartian apophatics and developed in terms of "mystical experience" by Michel Sells in his *Mystical Languages of Unsaying* (Chicago: University of Chicago Press, 1994).

11. Stephen H. Webb, "The Rhetoric of Ethics as Excess: A Christian Theological Response to Emmanuel Lévinas," in *Modern Theology* 15 (1): 1–16, quote on p. 10.

12. Certain terminological difficulties lend added complication to the study of deconstructive ethics. Lévinas's "justice" here approximates Derrida's calculating *justesse*, Derridean "justice" to Lévinas's unthematizable proximity and substitution.

13. Quoting Lévinas, *OB*, 16.

14. The "entrance" of the third for Lévinas, famously, is not chronologically posterior to the Self-Other relation: "The third party looks at me in the eyes of the Other. . . . The face in its nakedness as a face presents to me the destitution of the poor one and the stranger . . . the whole of humanity, in the eyes that look at me." See

Emmanuel Lévinas, *Totality and Infinity: An Essay on Exteriority* (Pittsburgh: Duquesne University Press, 1969), 212–13.

15. A, 31, quoting Isaiah 57:19, here reproduced in KJV.

16. "In its frankness, it [language] refuses the clandestinity of love, where it loses its frankness and meaning and turns into laughter or cooling. The third party looks at me in the eyes of the Other—language is justice" (Lévinas, *Totality and Infinity*, 213; quoted in Simmons, "The Third," 93.)

17. *OB*, 157, quoted in A, 33. For a more detailed consideration of the place of the third and the relation between Lévinasian ethics and politics, see Simmons, "The Third," 93–96. While providing a most helpful exposition of the relation of ethics and politics in *Otherwise than Being* and other Lévinasian texts, Simmons confuses the issue in thinking in terms of an "oscillation" between ethics and politics ("The Third," 83, 84, 89, 100), whereas Lévinas speaks of their simultaneous necessity. See Emmanuel Lévinas, "Transcendence and Height," in *Emmanuel Levinas: Basic Philosophical Writings*, ed. Adriaan T. Peperzak, Simon Critchley, and Robert Bernasconi (Bloomington: Indiana University Press, 1996), 17; quoted by Simmons, "The Third," 100.

18. The title of the final section of *Otherwise than Being*, "*Autrement dit*" (*OB*, 175–85), is translated by Alphonso Lingis as "In other words." I have chosen the more literal rendering "Otherwise said" in order to preserve the resonance with Ricoeur's *autrement* motif. This section of *Otherwise than Being* comprises only one chapter, "Outside," set apart from the two sections of the main text, "The argument" (1–19) and "The exposition" (21–171).

19. Simmons, "The Third," 98.

20. The idea of "tension" will be familiar to readers of Ricoeur's earlier work, *The Rule of Metaphor: The Creation of Meaning in Language*, trans. Robert Czerny, with Kathleen McLaughlin and John Costello (London: Routledge 2003), in which he elaborates a tensional theory of metaphor, borrowing the term from Philip Wheelwright's *Metaphor and Reality* (Bloomington: Indiana University Press, 1962):

> The paradox [surrounding the metaphorical concept of truth] consists in the fact that there is no other way to do justice to the metaphorical notion of truth than to include the critical incision of the (literal) "is not" within the ontological vehemence of the (metaphorical) "is" . . . it is this tensional constitution of the verb *to be* that receives its grammatical mark in the "to be like" of metaphor elaborated into simile, at the same time as the tension between *same* and *other* is marked in the relational copula. (Ricoeur, *The Rule of Metaphor*, 302).

Tensional structures are also prominent in *Time and Narrative I*, most notably in the tension of concordance and discordance in narrative *muthos*. See Paul Ricoeur, *Time and Narrative I* (Chicago: University of Chicago Press, 1984), especially, "The Aporias of the Experience of Time: Book 11 of Augustine's *Confessions*," 5–30.

21. Franz Rosenzweig, *The Star of Redemption*, trans. from the 2nd ed. of 1930 by William W. Hallo (New York: Holt, Rinehart and Winston, 1971).

22. Ricoeur, *Oneself as Another*, 226 n. 32.

23. *LJ*, 196. It is too hasty to characterize this tension as an oscillation or dialectic, for this underestimates the disjunction of uncalculating *agape* from the economy of justice in "Love and Justice." When this important essay of Ricoeur's is overlooked, the tendency is to underestimate the disjunction in just this way. See, e.g., John Francis McKernan and Katarzyna Kosmala MacLullich, "Accounting, Love and Justice," *Accounting, Auditing & Accountability Journal*, 17:3, 327–360. It is to be hoped that the reception of *Parcours de la reconnaissance* will rectify this situation.

24. Marcel Mauss, *The Gift: The Form and Reason for Exchange in Archaic Societies* (London: Routledge Classics, 2002).

25. "But I say unto you which hear, Love your enemies, do good to them which hate you, Bless them that curse you, and pray for them which despitefully use you. And unto him that smiteth thee on the one cheek offer also the other; and him that taketh away thy cloak forbid not to take thy coat also. Give to every man that asketh of thee; and of him that taketh away thy goods ask them not again. And as ye would that men should do to you, do ye also to them likewise" (Luke 6:27–31, KJV. See LJ, 197).

26. Jacques Derrida, *Adieu to Emmanuel Lévinas*, trans. Pascale-Anne Brault and Michael Naas (Stanford, Calif.: Stanford University Press, 1999).

27. Webb, "The Rhetoric of Ethics as Excess," 10.

28. Paul Ricoeur, *Critique and Conviction: Conversations with François Azouvi and Marc de Launay*, trans. Kathleen Blamey (Cambridge: Polity Press in association with Blackwell Publishers Ltd. Oxford, 1998), 48.

29. Study nine is entitled "The Self and Practical Wisdom: Conviction." See Ricoeur, *Oneself as Another*, 240–96.

30. Ricoeur borrows the term "orders of greatness" ("*économies de la grandeur*") from Boltanski and Thévenot, *De la Justification* (see n. 6).

31. Patrick L. Bourgeois, "Ricoeur and Lévinas, Solicitude in Reciprocity and Solicitude in Existence," in *Ricoeur as Another: The Ethics of Subjectivity*, ed. Cohen and Marsh (Albany: State University of New York Press, 2002), 109–26, quote on p. 110.

6

Why There Is No Either/Or
in *Works of Love*

A Kantian Defense of Kierkegaardian (Christian) Unconditional Love

BERTHA ALVAREZ MANNINEN

Who is stronger, he who says, "If you do not love me, I will hate you," or he who says, "If you hate me, I will still continue to love you"?

—Søren Kierkegaard, *Works of Love*

According to Matthew 22:39, the second most important divine commandment is "Love your neighbor as yourself." One of Jesus' last commandments before his trial and execution was "A new commandment I give unto you, that you love one another as I have loved you" (John 13:34). The pressing question for a Christian, or indeed for *anyone* who finds these commandments morally appealing, is: How can these imperatives be applied in our everyday interactions with others; that is, how can unconditional Christian love *be practiced?* In *Works of Love*, Søren Kierkegaard's objective is to analyze the significance of this pivotal Christian commandment. In doing so, he sets up a stark contrast between unconditional love (the unconditional love of the neighbor expressed in God's commandment, or Christian *agape*) and preferential love (the limited and conditional love that human beings tend to share with specific people rather than with all human beings). Kierkegaard argues that in order to faithfully follow God's command, preferential love must yield to unconditional love; that is, we must put aside all traces of love based on preference and replace it with unconditional love for all of humankind in virtue that all are created in the divine image of God. Indeed, it is only by fulfilling God's commandment in this way that we can bridge the gap between the temporal and the eternal and have a proper relationship with God.

Given Kierkegaard's assessment of this Christian commandment,[1] it may seem at first that he is contending that it is necessary to put aside all traces of preference and personal relationships in order to obey God's edict. As Stephen J. Pope acknowledges, Christian neighbor-love, *agape*, has been interpreted by many as failing "to properly acknowledge the value of 'special relations' within the Christian moral life."[2] Stephen G. Post is very critical of such an interpretation, maintaining that many philosophers, including Kierkegaard in *Works of Love*, "depict the highest form of love as utterly heedless of self. . . . wholly devoid of self-concern. . . . [such philosophers] idealize one-way benevolence."[3] According to Post, this interpretation is deeply flawed because it ignores basic facts about the human condition: that human beings derive much meaning from personal and reciprocal relationships and that this should not be ignored when it comes to deciphering the proper way of practicing Christian *agape*. As Post writes: "Reciprocal exchanges of love merit a positive assessment because they are sources of joy in themselves. Moreover, without mutuality 'special relations' such as friendships could not develop, and moral experience would be reduced entirely to universal obligations to strangers."[4]

There are various passages in *Works of Love* that lend credence to such an interpretation of Kierkegaard. For example, he extols the love of the dead precisely because the dead can never reciprocate that love; therefore to love the dead is completely selfless.[5] Moreover, Kierkegaard maintains that "to love him who through favoritism is nearer to you than all others is self-love" (WL, 37). That is, to love someone because she is related to you in some intimate manner is really just another manifestation of self-love; that is, you love your beloved because of her relationship to *you*. As Amy Laura Hall writes:

> Even when I proclaim that I love another dearly, what I am likely cherishing is some aspect of the other that relates to my own self-centered hopes and dreams. Kierkegaard calls this preferential form of affection loving the other as the "other I" or the "other-self." . . . [W]e often do not love the other herself, but instead use her as an opportunity for our own self-defined purposes or desires.[6]

Prima facie, then, it seems as if Kierkegaard is willing to brand all instances of personal or preferential relationships as selfish, and so a violation of God's commandment to love *all* human beings as a neighbor and thus equally. Kierkegaard seems to be saying that in order to properly obey God's commandment, all such relationships should be eradicated.

If this is what Kierkegaard is demanding of us in *Works of Love* it is certainly concerning, for I would agree with Post that he is asking us to give up an integral aspect of human existence. Our personal relationships with others give life a richness and meaning that we could not do without lest we compromise the prospects for a fulfilling life. According to Kierkegaard, must we really give up so much in order to follow God's second most important commandment? After exploring Kierkegaard's arguments as to why preferential love must yield to unconditional love, I will argue, *contra* Post, that his stance does not entail an abandonment of personal relationships. That is, I will argue that Kierkegaard is not requiring us to choose between *either* personal relationships *or* unconditional love. I hope to explicate a plausible view of how this very important commandment can be followed in our lives without entailing a loss of an integral aspect of our everyday existence.

In arguing for this, I will employ the concept of overdetermination as both Richard Henson and Barbara Herman utilize it in order to defend a certain aspect of Kantian morality. A common charge against Kant is that he maintains that an action can only have moral worth if it is performed *contra* all favorable inclinations and only from duty. Both Henson and Herman maintain that what Kant really espouses is that the motive of duty ought to be the *determining* factor in acting in accordance with duty but that inclinations of, for example, sympathy or love, can still accompany, or *overdetermine*, a morally praiseworthy action. Similarly, I will argue, what Kierkegaard really maintains in *Works of Love* is that our love for each other ought to be determined by the fact that we are all created in a divine image rather than by feelings of preference. This does not entail that we can have no feelings of preference at all, but rather that those feelings must overdetermine, rather than determine, our love for the special people in our lives. Kierkegaard, then, is not espousing a rejection of personal relationships any more than Kant is rejecting the value of, for example, sympathy or empathy. Rather, Kierkegaard is emphasizing that the duty to love should be the ultimate motivation in all relationships, personal or not, and that this will prove to ensure the everlasting nature of love in all types of relationships, including the personal relationships that will be maintained.

Unconditional Love versus Preferential Love

The biblical commandment to love the neighbor as oneself "wrenches open the lock of self-love and thereby wrests it away from a man" (WL 34). This commandment requires that a person extend his own self-love to *all* people, for by "neighbor" Kierkegaard does not mean just those who live near you, but rather "all mankind, all men, *even enemies*" (WL 36; emphasis mine). We must extend our feelings of love to all human beings, from our beloved children to the alienated Iraqis across the globe, from those that add joy to our lives to those that trespass us in the gravest of ways. We must strive to love (and feed) the hungry person on our doorstep as well as the starving child in Africa. Indeed, as shocking as it may sound, we must love even the individuals responsible for the attacks on 9/11, for we are "not to make exceptions, neither in favoritism *nor in aversion*" (WL 36; emphasis mine). That is, "Whether the neighbor catches my eye or not, she is the one whom God calls me to love. The command, thus, corrects both my selfish interest in and my dismissive ignorance of each person I encounter."[7] Christian love does not play favorites; it is not "up to you" to decide who you will choose to love. You *must* love all people, whether or not they are related to you or are to your liking. For Kierkegaard, the neighbor is not restricted to family, friends, race, or even to our countrymen. In order to practice true Christian love, we must tear down the barriers of the self and refrain from making our love for others contingent on their relation to us. True unconditional Christian love "teaches love of all men, unconditionally all."[8] As Merold Westphal writes, "There is an unqualified equality about commanded love inasmuch as all, unconditionally everyone is my neighbor."[9]

Because it asks us to love one's neighbor as *oneself,* Christianity asks us to engage in proper self-love, which is not selfish love, but rather love in the sense that you can prove yourself to be the neighbor of all those that surround you. That is, proper self-love consists in being a neighbor to all of humankind:

> After having told the parable of the merciful Samaritan (Luke 10:36), Christ says to the Pharisee, "Which of these three seems to you to have been the neighbor of the man who had fallen among robbers?" and the Pharisee answers *correctly,* "The one who showed mercy on him." This means that by recognizing your duty you easily discover who your neighbor is. The Pharisee's answer is contained in Christ's question, which by its form necessitated the Pharisee's answering in this way. He towards whom I have a duty is my neighbor, *and when I fulfill my duty I show that I am a neighbor.* Christ does not speak about recognizing one's neighbor but about being a neighbor oneself, about proving oneself to be a neighbor just as the Samaritan showed it by his compassion. . . . to love yourself in the right way and to love one's neighbor correspond perfectly to one another; fundamentally they are one and the same thing.[10]

To love your neighbor as you love yourself means that you must learn to love yourself in the proper way, that is, as someone who has the ability to be a neighbor and fulfill the duty to love others. The Samaritan expressed proper self-love when helping the fallen man because he here proved himself truly to be the fallen man's neighbor. To love the neighbor and to love oneself cannot be separated from each other, since you are to view the neighbor, not as an other distinct self, but rather as you would view yourself. Therefore, the commandment forces one to transcend the world of selfish love and demands that the other is viewed with the same consideration that you would give to yourself. Moreover, since the commandment is supposed to do away with selfish love in all its forms, according to Kierkegaard, it is supposed to do away with conditional or preferential love; that is, loving the other solely because she bears a special relationship to *you,* for example as a parent, a spouse, or a child.

If one loves in this way, one is still engaging in selfish love, for *you* remain the locus of your love, since you pick and choose whom you love based on *your* feelings, *your* preferences, and what that person can contribute to *your* life. It is because God commands that we should love our neighbors as we love ourselves that he is able to help us bridge the gap between individuals, leading to an eradication of selfish love. In this sense, then, the commandment relies on selfish love transcending itself; selfish love leads to its own destruction in the face of God's commandment.

Kierkegaard (qua Johannes Climacus) makes a similar point in *Philosophical Fragments* when he argues that selfless love has its initial basis in selfish love: "Consider the analogy of erotic love [*Elskov*], even though it is an imperfect metaphor. Self-love lies at the basis of love; but at its peak its paradoxical passion wills its own downfall."[11] Selfish love seeks the love of the other, at first, purely because it desires its own happiness. However, as love progresses, it will soon realize that its happiness comes in the happiness of the other, that is, in selfless love. As such, selfish love was the starting point, but selfless love prevails, given that the happiness of the other is now what makes the self happy. As C. Stephen Evans puts it, selfless love is "the fulfillment of self-love, since it is by renouncing self-happiness that one becomes happy."[12] Paradoxically, then, proper selfish love consists in selfless love.

A similar phenomenon is described in *Works of Love*. Although selfish love must be a precondition to fulfilling God's commandment (for you must love *yourself* first if you are to love your neighbor as *yourself*), it must ultimately transcend itself into selfless love of the neighbor in adherence to God's command. Loving oneself properly consists in seeing oneself as a vehicle to help and love others in the way that God desires (which is why the good Samaritan proved himself to be the neighbor of the fallen man by his act of beneficence). Understanding this duty not only ensures that one treats all human beings as neighbors but also shows that self-love need not be grounded in the quenching of selfish desires. Quite the contrary, proper self-love consists in transcending selfish desires and realizing that you can be an instrument of love for yourself as well as for others.[13]

But loving your neighbor as you love yourself does not mean simply performing good deeds for others. Unlike Kant's interpretation of this commandment, it does not simply mean acting in a beneficent manner from a sense of duty. It seems to me that Kierkegaard's interpretation requires us to actually experience the *emotion* of love (or, as Kant calls it, "pathological love") toward all human beings in the same manner as we love ourselves. This conflicts with Stephen Pope's suggestion that loving someone with equal regard reduces to treating all human beings with equal consideration, that is, with equal impartiality and justice.[14] This is certainly part of what Kierkegaard means, but it does not capture the essence of what he means (Pope's interpretation seems much more Kantian than Kierkegaardian). Kierkegaard does interpret God's command as requiring us to have emotional attachments to all people, even strangers, in virtue of their status as my neighbor, a requirement that Pope says is really rather odd.[15] Yet evidence for this interpretation of Kierkegaard can be found when he uses the example of Jesus loving Peter even after Peter's betrayal of him in order to exemplify what proper Christian love of the neighbor consists of (WL 164–70). Jesus did not simply have "equal regard" for Peter even after the betrayal; rather, Jesus actually *loved* him. This is how we should love in order to properly obey God's command. Jesus' "love for Peter was so boundless that in loving Peter he accomplished loving the person we see" (WL 168). Jesus Christ is the exemplar of Christian *agape*. We should love as Christ loves, regardless of whether the subject of our love is our child or a stranger, whether she has betrayed us or loved us, whether she has saved our lives or killed our beloved. In Christianity, loving the other becomes a *duty*, and this requires a radical change in our conception of what love actually is. This assumes, of course, that the emotion of love, indeed that any emotion, can be commanded at all, which Kant emphatically denies. Controversial in itself, this idea is more properly the subject of another paper.

As human beings, we do sometimes tend to be kind to others, but this is not equivalent to loving the neighbor unconditionally. This is because human beings tend to reserve the emotion of love only for those we are close to; that is, human beings practice preferential love rather than the unconditional love for all humankind that Christianity demands of us. Preferential love is what Kierkegaard calls "spontaneous love," the love that is often found in friendships and erotic relationships, the type of love "found in my drives, inclinations, and feelings."[16] The main problem with this type of love is that it is dependent on these preferences and is therefore fleeting and subject to change and termination:

> Spontaneous love can be changed within itself; it can be changed into its opposite, to *hate*. Hate is love that has become its opposite, a ruined love. . . . Spontaneous love can be changed within itself; by spontaneous combustion it can become *jealousy*; from the greatest happiness it can become the greatest torment. (WL 49)

Moreover, spontaneous love has its basis in *my* desires and *my* needs, "This love is in the services of my needs and wants."[17] It is thus, according to Kierkegaard, nothing but pure self-love, for you love the other, not because of her own person, but because of how she is able to fulfill *your* desires.

In contrast, and more akin to how Jesus loved Peter—indeed, how he loved *all* of mankind—to recognize love as a duty leads to genuine love, which is love that is permanent, unchanging, and therefore can never lead to its opposite; to love from duty means that love will never turn into hate. Westphal writes: "Only when it is a duty to love, only then is love eternally secured against every change, eternally made free in blessed independence, eternally and happily secured against despair. . . . consequently, *only when it is a duty to love, only then is love eternally secured.*"[18] This is very reminiscent of Kant's argument for why an action has moral worth only if it is done from duty rather than from inclination, whether indirect or direct:

> To be beneficent where one can is a duty; and besides this, there are many persons who are so sympathetically constituted that, without further motive of vanity or self-interest, they can find inner pleasure in spreading joy around them and can rejoice in the satisfaction of others as their own work. . . . but suppose then the mind of this friend of mankind is clouded over with his own sorrow so that all sympathy with the lot of others is extinguished and suppose him to still have the power to benefit others in distress. . . . suppose that, even though no inclination moves him any longer, he nevertheless tears himself from this deadly insensibility and performs the action without any inclination at all, but solely from duty, then for the first time his action has true moral worth.[19]

Both Kant and Kierkegaard are searching for a guarantee that an agent will always do what is moral or will always love another, respectively. This means that being moral or loving another cannot be based on either inclinations or feelings of preference, respectively, *because these conditions are fleeting and subject to change.* If I were to perform an action in accordance with duty *solely* because I find myself feeling sympathetic, I would cease acting in accordance with duty if one day that feeling of sympathy were gone.[20] For example, if I decide to volunteer at a local homeless shelter *solely* because sympathy moves me to do so, I would cease volunteering if one day a "deadly insensibility" were to overcome my usually sympathetic nature. Similarly, if I were to love someone *solely* because I have a feeling of preference toward him, for example, if I love my husband just because he is *my* husband, then my feelings of love for him would be eliminated if he were one day to cease being my husband. In this sense, I love him selfishly; I love him only because of his relation to *me*. Once his relation to me is eradicated, my feelings of love towards him are eradicated as well. In other words, both Kant and Kierkegaard want to secure moral or loving behavior. Acting from inclinations or feelings of preference is simply unreliable; the security desired cannot be achieved if we act morally or love others based on vacillating emotions or upon their contingent relation to us. Just as Kant emphasizes the need to act from duty regardless of whether or not one's inclinations lean that way, Kierkegaard "counters that the Christian has a duty, *regardless of inclination*, to see the other with faithful love."[21]

From all this, I take Kierkegaard to be arguing the following: If I love someone else, not because it is my duty to love him, but solely because he is related to me in some sense (for example, as a spouse), then my love is conditional on the preferential considerations I have bestowed upon my beloved. If those preferential considerations are removed for any reason, then my love for him will either cease altogether, or worse, turn into hate. However, if I love my beloved, not in a preferential manner, but rather because I realize that it is my divinely commanded duty to love him, I love him unconditionally and throughout all changes in circumstance. For example, if I love my husband solely based on the fact that he has this special relationship to me, my love for him is not unconditional, for it would cease if his relationship to me is ever terminated. Worse yet, if we ended our relationship due to some unpleasant experience, my love for him might very well turn into hate, for according to Kierkegaard, hate is simply preferential love gone awry. However, if I love my husband, not solely on the basis that he is my husband, but because I recognize that I have an unconditional duty to love him based on God's commandment (and that this duty extends to everyone else as well), then I will continue to love him even if the personal ties are severed because these personal ties were not the determining factor of my love for him. It is only in this sense that love can come to be truly unconditional.

Preferential love is therefore neither genuine nor unconditional love. Unconditional love does not come in the form of always promising to love those whom you prefer; rather, unconditional love consists in loving all of humanity because it is your divine duty to do so. Unconditional love is not about clinging to *some* people "through thick and thin," writes Kierkegaard. "This is, by no means, loving one's neighbor" (WL 74–75). Once you recognize your duty to love due to the commandment expressed by God, therefore loving your neighbor with the same vigor and dedication that you would give to your beloved or yourself, your love will be "consciously grounded upon the eternal" (WL 46) and will therefore never be subject to change or termination. That is, in order for love to be of the kind that will never cease and never change into its opposite, we must forsake the distinctions amongst people and love them because it is our duty to do so rather than because of those distinctions, for preferential love is "always related to distinctions" (WL 79). Unconditional love, then, is the paradigm of genuine love precisely because it is not dependent on distinctions and is therefore not limited by or contingent upon them.

Unconditional love is also the way in which human beings can achieve a communion with God and be most like the divine (*imatio Dei*).[22] It is in the yielding of preferential love to unconditional love that human beings become the most like God, for God loves all human beings equally and unconditionally:

> As Christianity's glad proclamation is contained in the doctrine about man's kinship with God, so its task is man's likeness to God. But God is love, and therefore we can resemble God only in loving, just as, according to the apostle's words, we can only "be God's co-workers—in love." Insofar as you love the beloved, you are not like unto God, for in God there is no partiality, something that you have reflected on many times to your humiliation, and also at times to your rehabilitation. Insofar as you love your friend, you are not like unto God, because for God there is no distinction. But when you love your neighbor, then you are like unto God. (WL 74–75)

God's love admits of no preference. Human beings, much to our "humilia-tion," do not love like God. Whereas God loves all people equally, human beings place barriers amongst each other in the form of distinctions; we end up restricting our love to only those whom we prefer. In preferential love, I (selfishly) love a certain someone, not because he is a human being and therefore my neighbor, but because he holds a special relation *to me* and in this way he is dissimilar from all others. Again, this is not genuine love. How-ever, if we are able to yield preferential love to unconditional love, that is, if we are able to ground our love, not in selfish partiality but rather in divine duty, then we can come to love the way God loves. In such a way, then, human beings can become partners with God and thus, in some sense, divine.

An adherence to the duty of unconditional love over preferential love also guarantees that one will be surrounded by love for all eternity. If I reserve love only for those whom I prefer, then I may very well face a life without love if one day, for whatever reason, those relationships cease to be. However, if I love all people unconditionally as I love myself and as God loves us all, then I will never cease experiencing love; love will never leave me:

> Consequently, whatever your fate in erotic love and friendship, whatever your privation, whatever your loss, whatever the desolation of your life which you confide to the poet, the highest still stands: love your neighbor! As already shown, you can easily find him; him you can never lose. The beloved can treat you in such a way that he is lost to you, and you can lose a friend, but whatever the neighbor does to you, you can never lose him. . . . [i]f your love for the neighbor remains unchanged, then your neighbor also remains unchanged just by being. Death itself cannot deprive you of the neighbor either, for if it takes one, life immediately gives you another. Death can deprive you of a friend, because in loving a friend you really cling to your friend, but in loving the neighbor you cling to God. (WL 76)

Whenever I read this passage, a picture comes to mind that I hope will help to express what I understand Kierkegaard to be saying here. I know that I am guilty of preferential love. Although I try to be as good as I can to others, I do not love all people, but only those with whom I share a relationship. When I read this passage, I see myself as an old woman, sitting alone in my home, with all my loved ones either deceased or, for whatever reason, gone from my life. My life, at that point, will be without love because I restricted myself to loving only individual people rather than all people. I would now "walk alone. [I] would have no beloved to cover [my] weak side and no friend at [my] right hand" (WL 75). However, if I would have lead the type of life that God commands me to lead, a life that fulfills my duty of unconditional love, then my life would always have been full of love, for nothing, not even death, can deprive me of a neighbor. Moreover, if I restrict my love to a certain few, then I will retain a relationship with only a finite number of people, people that can sever this relationship for whatever reason at whatever time, leaving me with no one to love and no one who loves me. However, if I love unconditionally, I will be fulfilling my duty to God and as such I will be establishing a relationship to him, which is guaranteed to be eternal, and I can secure that I will always have someone to love, for I will always have a neighbor. Therefore, by loving unconditionally, by loving all people in the same way as I love myself, not only will I establish the greatest relationship possible (a relationship with God), but I will ensure that I will always have love in my life.

From all this it is possible to see why Kierkegaard advocates a yielding of preferential love to unconditional love. Unconditional love is a duty that we have in the face of God's commandment. It requires an annihilation of selfish love and a replacement of it with proper self-love (self-love that consists in extending oneself toward others as a vehicle of beneficence and love grounded on the divine duty of unconditional love, as the good Samaritan illustrates). Unconditional love unites us to God, both because it allows us to share in the type of love that God has for us, thereby giving us an opportunity to share in God's divinity, and because it establishes a relationship between us and God that can never be severed. Finally, loving the neighbor guarantees that our own lives will never be without love since it ensures that there will always be individuals present for us to share love with. Loving the neighbor, then, "has the very perfection of the eternal" (WL 76).

A Kantian Rejection of an Either/Or

It is difficult for human beings to accept this conception of love, and even Kierkegaard admits that his words will probably offend and shock us (WL 74). The reason why it is hard for us to accept unconditional love is that we take it to be part of a happy and fulfilling life that we have special relationships with certain people, and indeed it is these special relationships that give our life richness and meaning. The question now becomes: if I am to love all people the same and thus unconditionally because it is my duty to do so in the face of God's commandment, does this mean that I have to relinquish my special relationships? That is, am I failing to love in the way God commands if I do have feelings of preference for some individuals? Must the duty to love be the only possible motivation if I am to love correctly?

As mentioned above, Post certainly seems to think that this is what a Kierkegaardian interpretation of Christian *agape* requires of humans. He maintains that "Kierkegaard, for instance, viewed all friendship as a mere extension of selfishness . . . [h]ence his idealization of selflessness issues in "melancholy." The reaction against excessive self-love easily shifts to the embrace of selflessness when divine love is believed to be wholly heedless of self-concern."[23]

Post then proceeds to argue, quite successfully, I believe, that scriptural evidence supports the interpretation that God, and his physical manifestation in

Jesus Christ, does desire reciprocal love, that divine love does consist of some self-concern and thus does have selfish elements to it. Nevertheless, I think that Post's interpretation of Kierkegaard rests on a fundamental error: Kierke-gaard does not condemn friendships or personal relationships *simpliciter*, but rather he condemns certain *types* of friendships or personal relationships, the ones that depend on those preferences alone rather than on God's divine commandment. Post's criticism of Kierkegaard is rather reminiscent of an objection often brought against Kantian morality: that for Kant "an action can have no moral worth if there is supporting inclination or desire."[24] That is, Kant has also been accused of maintaining that an action is morally bankrupt if there exists in the agent inclinations that may contribute to her motivation for performing that action. If these respective interpretations of the two phi-losophers are correct, feelings of preference are, for Kierkegaard, analogous to direct inclinations for Kant in the sense that the mere presence of these condi-tions voids the proper fulfillment of duty. Yet I take this to be a faulty reading of both Kant and Kierkegaard, and in order to see how this is so I must briefly explain how apologists of Kantian morality have argued against this reading, for I will argue in favor of a similar reading of Kierkegaard.

Admittedly, I am not the only Kierkegaardian apologist who maintains that Kierkegaard's endorsement and celebration of unconditional love does not entail an abandonment of personal relationships. For example, Ronald L. Hall interprets Kierkegaard as maintaining that "Christian love supplants (*while not doing away with*) preferential love. . . . We can certainly read [Kierkegaard's] interpretation of God's command to love as not a call to rise above the human, but to embrace it as such, refusing to allow distinctions to keep us from the embrace of every human being."[25]

In his book *Love's Grateful Striving*, M. Jamie Ferreira argues that

> Kierkegaard is offering neither an attack of all self-love nor a denial of the legitimate role of preference and inclination in erotic love and friendship; rather he wants to preserve the integrity of the other, the genuine "you." . . . Although Kierkegaard is distinguishing between love based on preference and a kind of nonpreferential love, he is not recommending that relations based on the former should be eliminated or replaced by the latter. Kierke-gaard does not deny the beauty, necessity, and "delight" (WL, p. 150) of erotic love and friendship. . . . Although he distinguishes the categories of erotic love, friendship, and neighbor love, what is at issue is the contrast between preferential and nonpreferential—not an attack on the erotic as-pects of love or the congenialities of friendship.[26]

Thus, I am far from being the first person to offer such a defense of Kierkegaardian unconditional love. Yet what I want to specifically focus on, which differs from the aforementioned interpretations, is how a proper under-standing of Kant's moral philosophy can be beneficial in offering a precise elucidation of how this synchronization between unconditional Christian *agape* and preferential love is supposed to be achieved. No matter what Kierke-gaard claims to the contrary, it must be admitted that in *Works of Love* there seems to be, prima facie, "a kind of either/or about preference—preferential love can be sharply contrasted *conceptually* with nonpreferential love. Yet [Kierkegaard] claims that the goal is to preserve love for the neighbor *in* erotic love and friendship. . . . and thus that they can coincide materially."[27] That is, prima facie, Kierkegaard does seem to require an either/or choice between unconditional love and preferential love. Yet a deeper analysis of Kierkegaard, along with an understanding of Kantian morality, will aid in eradicating this apparent either/or. There is no doubt that there are Kantian undertones in *Works of Love*. Merold Westphal notes that the book has "a Kantian, deon-tological ring to it."[28] In what follows, I aim to make these undertones much more overt.

In his article "What Kant Might Have Said: Moral Worth and the Over-determination of Dutiful Action," Richard Henson maintains that attending to the concept of overdetermination can help us see that Kant was *not* arguing that no direct inclinations, for example, sympathy or empathy, can be present when acting in order for an action to have moral worth. An action has moral worth "provided that respect for duty was present and would have sufficed by itself [to produce a dutiful act], even though (as it happened) other motives were present and might themselves have sufficed."[29] That is, although support-ing inclinations could have determined the action, such an action has moral worth if it was ultimately *determined* by the motive of duty alone, and the accompanying inclinations overdetermined, rather than determined, the ac-tion. Barbara Herman also argues that the above interpretation of Kant is a faulty one: "When an action has moral worth, nonmoral motives may be present, but they may not be what moves the agent to act. . . . the motive of duty need not reflect the only interest the agent has in the action; it must, however, be the interest that determines the agent's acting as he did."[30] In her analysis of Kant's example concerning the friend of mankind who loses his sensibilities, she writes:

> Of *him* it is then said: only when the inclination to help others is not available does *his* helping action have moral worth. For of him it was true that when he acted with inclination he was not also acting from the motive of duty. This does not imply that no dutiful action can have moral worth if there is cooperating inclination. Nor does it imply that a sympathetic man could not act from the motive when his sympathy was aroused. . . . [O]ne need not be indifferent to the possible satisfactions that a dutiful action may produce. It is just that the presence of such possibilities should not be the ground of the agent's commitment to acting morally.[31]

If one accepts this interpretation, Kant is by no means arguing that a necessary condition that must be met in order for an action to have moral worth is that no direct inclinations or feelings can be present at all when the action is performed. What he arguing, rather, is that those inclinations or feelings can certainly be present in our actions *as long as these are not the determining factors for why we act according to duty*. Indeed, our action must be determined by the motive of duty in order to have any moral worth, so that if these inclinations and feelings were absent, or worse, if they went *against* what duty requires, we would still act from duty. This is a far cry, however, from arguing that the mere presence of any accompanying direct inclinations or feelings automatically empties an action of moral worth. Nothing in Kant's writings, Herman argues, "forces the reading that it is the mere *presence* of the inclination that is responsible for the denial of moral worth."[32]

It seems to me that Kierkegaard makes a very similar claim in *Works of Love*. Despite prima facie appearances, Kierkegaard is not contending that it is necessary to give up all personal feelings or relationships just because one yields preferential love to unconditional love. Instead, unconditional love should ground and permeate all types of love; it should be the ultimate motivation for the love one experiences for all people. Unconditional love for Kierkegaard is analogous to acting from duty for Kant; for both philosophers, our actions must ultimately be determined by our adherence to and respect for our duties, as expressed either by reason (Kant) or God (Kierkegaard). This does not necessarily mean that for Kierkegaard no other emotion can accompany unconditional love, just as it does not mean for Kant that no direct inclinations can accompany an action performed from duty. I can feel passion and attraction toward my husband in a way that sets him apart from other men, but it does not follow from this that my love for him is *dependent* on these feelings. What Kierkegaard is concerned with, I think, is that if I ground my love of a person on the emotions that apply only to him and his contingent relation to me, then this is what counts as preferential love and therefore not genuine love, for the instant that those emotions are taken away for whatever reason, or if ever the relation to me is severed, my love will cease to be. For Kierkegaard, it is possible to have personal relationships and still retain unconditional love *if the ultimate motivating factor for love in personal relationships is the divine duty one has to love the person* (which is the same duty that applies to all individuals, even to those for whom you have no personal feelings), rather than basing love on the preferences that one happens to have in relation to that person. That is, I only love my beloved genuinely and unconditionally if, when all my preferential feelings are stripped away, I find that I still love him.[33] I must be "able to continue finding him lovable, no matter how he has become changed" (WL 158).

Evidence for this interpretation of Kierkegaard can be found in *Works of Love* if one considers what he has to say in regard to how one ought to love a beloved:

> Go, then, and do this—take away distinctions and similarities of distinctions —so that you can love the neighbor. . . . [b]ut you are not to cease loving the

beloved because of this—far from it. If this were so, the word *neighbor* would be the greatest fraud ever discovered, if you, in order to love your neighbor, must begin by ceasing to love those for whom you have a preference. . . . It is only the preferential love that should be taken away. . . . No, love your beloved faithfully and tenderly, but let love for the neighbor be the sanctifier in your covenant of union with God. (WL 73–74)

As previously said, Christianity has not wanted to storm forth to abolish distinctions . . . but it wills that differences shall hang loosely about the individual, loosely as the cloak the king casts off in order to show who he is, loosely as the ragged costume in which a supernatural being has disguised himself. When distinctions hang loosely in this way, then there steadily shines in every individual that essential other person, that which is common to all men, the eternal likeness, the equality. (WL 96)

Notice that in these two passages what Kierkegaard wants to abolish is not *preference*, but rather *love based on preference*. This is a subtle distinction, but an important one nevertheless. This means that what ought to be eradicated is not personal relationships and preferences amongst people; rather, what ought to be eradicated is any love that is *dependent* on those preferences (analogously, for Kant, what needs to be abolished is not moral actions performed with direct inclinations, but rather moral actions that are performed on the basis of direct inclinations alone, rather than being performed primarily because of duty, with direct inclinations accompanying the action in addition).

Preferences are supposed to "hang loosely" on the individual because they should play no role in determining whether or how he is loved. Rather, all that matters when it comes to how we should love others is that we *all* resemble the eternal (for we are all made in God's image) and as such we are to love all others the same way we love ourselves because our dissimilarities are nothing more than superficial disguises. The only salient factor that ought to decide how we should love others is the "the eternal likeness" present in us all—our likeness to God.

But this does not mean that Kierkegaard refuses to acknowledge that there are dissimilarities amongst people. Kierkegaard does not condemn feelings of preference per se as long as love is not dependent on these preferences, just as Kant does not condemn feelings or direct inclinations per se as long as our acting in accordance with duty is not dependent on these feelings or inclinations. If one loves according to preferences, one would be doing a disservice to the self (by violating God's duty and not enjoying all the eternal benefits that come with unconditional love as outlined above) and to the beloved as well. Again, this is because if one loves the beloved solely based on feelings of preference, then this love would be temporary and exist only as long as those preferential feelings are present. However, if I love my beloved because it is my duty to love him, as it is my duty to love all my neighbors, then I will love him genuinely and unconditionally, even if those feelings of preference are, for whatever reason, one day abolished. This will lead to a security in genuine love that cannot be experienced in preferential love, and in this sense, "just as this command will teach every man how he ought to love himself, likewise will it also teach erotic love and friendship what genuine love is . . . in erotic love and friendship preserve love to your neighbor" (WL 73–74).

Amy Laura Hall writes: "It is rare that we walk together with our child, spouse, or parent with a lucid sense of God's immediate call."[34] Kierkegaard wants us to continue walking with these people *as* our child, spouse, or parent, that is, still as a personal beloved, but we are to step differently in our walk. We are to keep in mind "God's immediate call" and love them primarily as children of God, as a neighbor who happens to be related to me in a special way. I can still cherish that relationship without making my love contingent on that relationship, and I can desire reciprocation without making my love for them dependent on that reciprocation. Indeed, God himself expresses preferences at one time or another. For example, God expressed preference for Abel over Cain when he chose the offerings of the former but not the latter (Gen 4:4–5). It does not follow from this, however, that God loved Abel more than Cain. Post correctly argues that "Jesus, like the God of Israel, yearned for the requital of love. . . . Jesus clearly did not want his love to be rejected or unreciprocated; he did not will that the recipients of his love would reject his generosity. Indeed, he lamented over a people who 'did not recognize God's moment when it came' (Luke 19:44)."[35] Yet what Post seems to miss is that neither God's nor Jesus' love for us is contingent on this reciprocity, no matter how much it is desired. Jesus was saddened by Peter's betrayal, and he surely did not celebrate it, nor was he indifferent to it. Nevertheless, even at the hour of Peter's betrayal, Christ loved him. Indeed, he "preserved the friendship unchanged and in this very way helped Peter to become another man." (WL 168). This is how we are to love as well. I can desire reciprocation from my beloved, I can even engage in very personal and private relationships with a select group of people, but I am to love them despite their relation to me and not because of it. Preferential feelings *add* to my love, just as my direct inclinations to help others and empathize with them add to my upholding of the duty of beneficence towards my fellow human. But my preferential feelings toward my beloved do not *determine* my love; his being my neighbor in the eyes of God does that, just as I am to perform my duty, ultimately, according to Kant, because I adhere to the Categorical Imperative and not *just because* I empathize with the benefactors of my actions.

Thus, despite prima facie appearances to the contrary, there is no either/or in *Works of Love*; that is, it does not come down to a choice between *either* personal relationships *or* unconditional love. It is quite possible to maintain personal relationships and still experience unconditional love; indeed, it is unacceptable to Kierkegaard to give up the former for the latter.[36] Rather, unconditional love ought to serve as the foundation for *all* relationships, even the personal ones that are very important and indispensable. In the end, Kierkegaard puts it the most eloquently when he writes:

> Take many sheets of paper and write something different on each one—then they do not resemble each other. But then take again every single sheet; do not let yourself be confused by the differentiating inscriptions; hold each one up to the light and you see the same watermark on them all. (WL 97)

We should enjoy and acknowledge the different inscriptions that set our loved ones apart from others. But our love for them—indeed, our love for *all* human beings—should be determined, not by those inscriptions, but rather by our common watermark: our likeliness to God. In our dealings with each other, we should always remember to let "the light of the eternal [shine] through distinction" (WL 97).

NOTES

1. It ought to be noted that other philosophers have interpreted this commandment in radically different ways. For example, Kant argues in *Grounding for the Metaphysics of Morals* that the correct interpretation of this commandment is not that we are required to pathologically love all human beings equally, for we cannot be morally obligated to have certain *feelings* for other people, but rather that we treat others beneficently regardless of our inclinations: "Undoubtedly in this way also are to be understood those passages of Scripture which command us to love our neighbor and even our enemy. For love as an inclination cannot be commanded; but beneficence from duty, when no inclination impels us and even when a natural and unconquerable aversion opposes such beneficence is practical and not pathological love" (Indianapolis, Ind.: Hackett, 1981, 12). John Stuart Mill, in *Utilitarianism*, interprets the commandment as evidence that the utilitarian principle of impartiality reflects God's desires: "Utilitarianism requires [the agent] to be as strictly impartial as a disinterested and benevolent spectator. In the golden rule of Jesus of Nazareth, we read the complete spirit of the ethics of utility. . . . 'love your neighbor as yourself' constitute[s] the ideal perfection of utilitarian morality" (Indianapolis, Ind.: Hackett, 2001, 17). Kierkegaard's interpretation is certainly much more demanding than these interpretations, for he seems to construe the commandment as requiring unconditional pathological love (that is, the *emotion* of love) for all human beings equally.

2. Stephen J. Pope, "'Equal Regard' versus 'Special Relations'? Reaffirming the Inclusiveness of Agape," *Journal of Religion* 77.3 (1997): 353.

3. Stephen G. Post, "The Inadequacy of Selflessness: God's Suffering and the Theory of Love," *Journal of the American Academy of Religion* 56.2 (1988): 213–14.

4. Ibid., 214.

5. Søren Kierkegaard, *Works of Love* (New York: Harper and Row, 1962), 320. Hereafter, WL in references in the text.

6. Amy Laura Hall, *Kierkegaard and the Treachery of Love* (Cambridge: Cambridge University Press, 2002), 44 and 87.

7. Ibid., 28.

8. Ibid., 63.

9. Merold Westphal, *Transcendence and Self-Transcendence: On God and the Soul* (Bloomington: Indiana University Press, 2004), 222.

10. Ibid., 38–39; emphasis mine.

11. Johannes Climacus. [Søren Kierkegaard], *Philosophical Fragments* (Princeton, N.J.: Princeton University Press, 1985), 48.

12. C. Stephen Evans, *Kierkegaard Fragments and Postscript: The Religious Philosophy of Johannes Climacus* (Amherst, N.Y.: Humanity Books, 1998), 235.

13. This is reminiscent of Richard Swinburne's claim, in his *Providence and the Problem of Evil*, that one of the best ways to approach an instance of evil in the world (whether it be of the moral or natural kind) is to use it as an opportunity to cultivate character, to be beneficent, or, as Kierkegaard would put it, to be a neighbor: "My pain gives you the opportunity to show sympathy and help relieve it. You are fortunate to have that opportunity. I am fortunate to be able to give it to you" (New York: Oxford University Press, 1998, 167).

14. Pope, "Inadequacy of Selflessness," 371.

15. Ibid., 366.

16. Westphal, *Transcendence and Self-Transcendence*, 222.

17. Ibid.

18. Ibid., 44–45; emphasis mine.

19. Kant, *Grounding for the Metaphysics of Morals*, 11.

20. Moreover, helping another from sympathy alone does not discriminate between performing an action that is in accordance with duty and one that is against it. For example, if I am a person that is moved by the plights of others, not much would prevent me from being sympathetic to the struggling burglar trying unsuccessfully to break into my neighbor's apartment; I might even aid him in doing so, resulting in my acting against duty. That is, Kant bemoans acting from either indirect or direct inclinations, such as sympathy, not just because inclinations are, by nature, unreliable, but also because they are not necessarily directed toward performing dutiful actions. When inclinations do lead one to perform dutiful actions, it is merely "fortunately directed to what is in fact beneficial and accords with duty" (Kant, *Grounding*, 11). See Barbara Herman, "On the Value of Acting," *Philosophical Review* 90 (1981), for an excellent discussion of this aspect of Kantian morality.

21. Hall, *Kierkegaard and the Treachery of Love*, 30.

22. I take this to be a very interesting and telling aspect of Kierkegaard's theory. Often human beings are compared to God on the basis of their understanding; that is, human beings are most like God in our ability to be rational. Yet Kierkegaard does not consider rationality to be the link that unites humans and God. On the contrary, there is reason to think that Kierkegaard regards rationality as the obstacle between God and human beings. What unites God and human beings is rather, according to Kierkegaard, the ability to feel and distribute love in a nonpreferential manner. Union with God is thus more a matter of the heart than of the mind.

23. Post, "The Inadequacy of Selflessness," 216.

24. Herman, "On the Value of Acting from the Motive of Duty," 359.

25. Ronald L. Hall, *The Human Embrace: The Love of Philosophy and the Philosophy of Love: Kierkegaard, Cavell, Nussbaum* (University Park: Pennsylvania State University Press, 2000), 81; emphasis mine.

26. M. Jamie Ferreira, *Love's Grateful Striving: A Commentary on Kierkegaard's Works of Love* (New York: Oxford University Press, 2001), 44–45.

27. Ibid., 45.

28. Westphal, *Transcendence and Self-Transcendence*, 221

29. Richard Henson, "What Kant Might Have Said: Moral Worth and the Over-determination of Dutiful Action," *Philosophical Review* 88 (1979): 48.

30. Herman, "On the Value of Acting," 371–75. It should be noted that Herman is critical of Henson's interpretation that for Kant an action can have moral worth even in the face of supporting inclinations as long as respect for the moral law is sufficient for inciting one to act. While Herman agrees with Henson's use of overdetermination in order to understand Kant's moral philosophy, she argues that his interpretation is not strong enough to entail that an agent would still perform a dutiful act *contra* inclinations. That is, Henson's interpretation can account for the presence of supporting inclinations by arguing that respect for the moral law would have sufficed had those supporting inclinations been absent; but according to Herman, Henson's account leaves open the possibility that the motive of respect for duty would not have been sufficient for an agent to perform a dutiful action had the agent's inclinations actually incited him *against* duty: "On either reading of sufficient moral motive, an agent judged morally fit might not have a moral motive capable of producing a required action 'by itself' if his presently cooperating nonmoral motives were, instead, in conflict with the moral motive" (ibid., 367). Herman argues that this deficiency in Henson's interpretation of Kant is grievous because truly moral behavior, for Kant, is behavior in which a dutiful action is performed not only in the presence or absence of supporting inclinations, but even in the presence of *contrary* inclinations.

31. Ibid., 378–82.

32. Ibid, 381.

33. Kant argues in *Grounding for the Metaphysics of Morals* that, as humans, there is no way to ever really know whether one has acted from duty, or in accordance with duty but from inclinations: "When we pay attention to our experience of the way human beings act, we meet frequent and—as we ourselves admit—justified complaints that there cannot be cited a single certain example of the disposition to act from pure duty. . . . There is absolutely no possibility by means of experience to make out with complete certainty a single case in which the maxim of an action that may in other respects conform to duty has rested solely on moral grounds and on the representation of one's duty" (19). That is, given that inclinations are so intimately mixed in with our motivations, there is really no way to ever tell whether one's inclinations have served an overdetermining rather than a determining role and thus whether the motivation of duty has played its morally proper role in determining the action. As such, one can never really be sure that one as acted from duty and thus in a manner that is of moral worth. Kierkegaard's analysis may be subject to the same epistemological obstacle, for how am I to ever really know, for example, whether the love I feel for my husband is being determined by my divine duty or by my feelings of preference? I suppose the only way I *can* ever really know is by severing the relationship, therefore eradicating the distinctions between him and all others, and then checking to see if my feelings of love for him are eradicated as well. If my feelings of love are eradicated with the cessation of the spousal relationship, then I never really loved him from duty, but rather from preference. If I do continue to love him, then I love him unconditionally, both when he was my husband and now, as simply my neighbor.

34. Hall, *The Human Embrace*, 81.

35. Post, "The Inadequacy of Selflessness," 217–18.

36. A possible concern that was brought to my attention at the Wisdom of Love conference is the following. If I am to love the beloved unconditionally, the same as I

ought to love my neighbor, does not this entail that my beloved is easily *replaceable* with the neighbor, even if the neighbor were to be a complete stranger? For example, if I am to love my husband as a neighbor, and thus the same way as I am to love any other man who is also my neighbor, wouldn't this entail that my husband is easily replaceable with any other male neighbor? If so, then it seems as if Kierkegaard is requiring us to view our loved ones as replaceable, and this certainly is counterintuitive. I must admit that it took me some time to think about how I should respond to this, and I once again fall back on Kant to help me here. I believe I can argue that the reason my relationship with my husband is not replaceable with any other neighbor is because the feelings of prefer-ence that overdetermine my love for my husband make the phenomenological experi-ence of my love for him different than the love I ought to feel for all my other male (and female) neighbors. For example, take Kant's friend of mankind who decides to be charitable from duty but also has direct inclinations toward helping others that allows him to *enjoy* his charity work. Take also the man with the deadly insensibilities who still decides to be charitable from duty, although all his inclinations are against being charitable. Both men act from duty, so both actions have moral worth. Yet we cannot say that the experiences of both men are interchangeable or replaceable, since one thoroughly enjoyed his charity work, while the other perhaps moaned and groaned his way through it. While both men acted from duty, the favorable inclinations that the friend of mankind possessed that overdetermined his actions must also have contrib-uted to his experience in a positive way while he was performing the action (think of the times when we *wanted* to help someone versus a time we helped someone with very little desire to do so—certainly our experience in both of these cases was of a different phenomenological kind). Similarly, just because I love my husband and a male col-league in the same way, i.e., as a neighbor, this does not mean that my husband is replaceable with a male colleague because the feelings of preference that overdeter-mine my love for my husband will serve to make my experience of love for him phenomenologically different than the love I feel for all my other neighbors.

7

Living by Love

A Quasi-Apostolic *carte postale* on Love in Itself, If There Is Such a Thing

JOHN D. CAPUTO

If love is an unconditional gift, an expenditure made without the expectation of a return, is it not also the case that we live our lives under one economy or another, under one version or another of what St. Paul calls the "law"? Do we not have to concede that while we dream of love, in waking life we need the law for almost everything? Conversely, is it possible to be commanded to love by the law? Would it be possible to make love a matter of law? Could it be a duty to do things from love, not from duty?

I will address these age-old questions in something of an off and on dialogue with St. Paul, who has gotten a hearing among the philosophers in these postmodern times. I will do so in three voices, the first phenomenological, the second theological, and the last deconstructive. I love phenomenology, but phenomenology must beware of being too innocent and comforting. I love St. Paul's theology of love, but theology must beware of being too strong and dogmatic. That is why I finally have recourse to deconstruction, which is always affirmative, while never letting its guard down about how complicated things can be. Deconstruction is not likely to let love off the hook just because it has such a beautiful name. So, pursuing something of a certain postmodern dialogue with Paul, my project is to see if I can wring out of deconstruction a kind of apostolic letter on love, or at least a quasi-apostolic *carte postale* on love in itself, if there is such a thing.[1]

Living by Love: The Phenomenology

Shall we say that the law is sin, St. Paul asks? By no means, I answer with him, but with this more postmodern twist: because I treat love as an excess, I argue that we need the law in order to have something to exceed. We need the law the way a runner needs a hurdle to have something to surmount, the way a jumper needs a bar in order to know what has to be scaled, the way the extraordinary needs the ordinary in order to have something to stand out from. If love did not have the law, love would be lost, for what would love have to surpass? We need the law as a foil for love.

So the first model of love, the one provided by a phenomenology of love, is excess, of the eccentric, of spilling over, of Eckhartian *ebullitio:* what the law commands, love exceeds, leaps over, overrides. Love kicks in like a higher gear that leaves the law inactive, suspended, transcended, annulled. Love sweeps over the law and lifts its feet off the ground, depriving it of traction. Love obviates the need for law.

The law means obligation, while love is eager to rush in where it is not obliged to be. To respond to the law is to obey a command, to do what we are obliged to do by the other, whereas to respond to love is to answer an invitation, to respond to a solicitation, and to affirm the other without obligation. If you love me because you are obliged, well, truth to tell, I would just as soon you did not bother. The law has to do with duty, whereas love is under no duress; lovers qua lovers are not doing their duty. Doing one's marital duty sounds like it gives only a minimum of joy.[2]

The law can be formulated, compliance with the law can be measured, and one can more or less meet the demands of the law. When he was a Pharisee and a man of the law, Paul said, there was none better than he; he met every measure, and he said that "before the law" he was "blameless" (Phil 3:6). But the only formula for love is that love eludes any formula, and the only measure of love is love without measure, and love never thinks it has loved enough. In love there is no more or less, only more and more.

The law enumerates measure by measure, statute by statute, so that the perfect law would be a sprawling encyclopedia of laws, statutes, codes, and provisions covering a multitude of regions and domains, filling enough books to stock many a library. Laws are numerable—ten more or less, in several versions—but love is a single virtue that is everywhere itself yet everywhere diversified, that settles into every situation, however different.

The law is related to love the way a frozen frame or still is related to the moving picture, or the way those "instructions for assembly" that come in Sears products—with their confusing verbal directions and ambiguous drawings—are related to the sure flow of someone who knows how to put the thing together and makes it look easy. The law is like someone who has to read music, while love plays by ear. Where there is love, the law is unnecessary, redundant, even a little bit demeaning and insulting, like presenting an expert with a training manual.

The law is an economy, while love is a gift. The law is a balance of forces; it returns punishment for transgression, and it constantly seeks to maintain an overall state of equilibrium. The law has force, is enforceable, and it has well-known ways to deal with violations: civil laws have their jails and police; moral laws have their biting guilt; heavenly laws have their threat of hell. But love is weak as a lamb, as powerless as a child, as soft and tender as a kiss or a caress. Love is a gift without force, not an economy. When love is violated, it does not retaliate or wound in return or demand that its honor be restored; it suffers from the wound and continues to love in its wounded condition. The power of love is a power without power, a weak force whose strength lies, not in the force it has at its command, but in its very vulnerability. Love does not punish in an effort to restore the balance of forces; love forgives, and forgiveness is a weak force.[3]

Love is intrepid. One fears to violate a law lest one be punished, for the law always carries a threat, but love is fearless.

The law prizes obedience, right or wrong; love prizes the good, law or no law. The law is distrustful and maintains systems of surveillance that monitors right and wrong, while love believes all and trusts all, although love is not deceived.[4]

The law runs behind, whereas love runs ahead. The law is too tardy. Where the law says, "I command" or "I forbid," love says, "You are too late; that has already been done." Love anticipates what is needed, answers before it is asked, makes provisions in advance before any demands are made upon it.

Love invents, breaks new ground, imagines new ways to be, while the law codifies what has already come into being, giving statutory rights to something that love first of all invented. The law prescribes what love has first written, proscribes what love has first eschewed. Love without the law is free, but the law without love is blind, harsh, unbending.

Love is affirmation, while the law is a way to say no, for even when a law is positive, the negative threat of punishment hangs heavy over our heads. There are no truly affirmative laws, not all the way down. Every law carries a more or less overt threat. Whether it is framed negatively—thou shalt not—or positively —thou shalt!—it carries a threat. If the love we bear for our father and mother is reduced to a commandment, then that carries a threat that we will rue the day we did not do as we were commanded. Thou shalt—or else.

Dying to the Law: Strong Theology, Weak Theology

We should, then, live by love and die to the law, for the law spells death. For more help on our quasi-apostolic epistle on the undeconstructibility of love, let us turn more directly to Paul, for it is a central part of his theology that the law had the odor of death. The law kills and makes us guilty—"Where there is no law, there is no violation" (Rom 4:15)—so we should die to the law and live by love.

For Paul, we have been raised up by Christ into a new creation. To see what was wrong with the old creation, we need to go back to the first creation, to the creation narratives in Genesis. In the first narrative, the priestly author imagines Elohim to be of an expansive frame of mind, one who gives the human race, male and female equally, the whole world over which to roam and issues only positive injunctions, to cultivate the land and to multiply, both of which could be fun. But in the second (and much earlier) narrative, the Yahwist imagines two hierarchically ordered parents, set up in the lush but confined quarters of a garden, who are then instructed by the Lord to make themselves at home and enjoy everything. *Except* that tree. That, of course, is the perfect ethical storm. What *else* will they desire? That prohibition *constitutes* the tree of knowledge of good and evil as the object of desire and the object of transgression. What else is desire than the desire of what we are forbidden to have? The prohibition provoked the transgression; it practically guaranteed the transgression—and death. The Lord imagined by the Yahwist is cunning and distrustful, whereas Elohim is a serene if somewhat detached divinity, but in all, a more credible predecessor or antecedent of the God of love. Elohim loved to say that everything was good, good, even very good, yes, yes; while the Yahwist, contrary to his name (Jah-weh!), according to a famous German pun by Angelus Silesius (Johannes Scheffler), was a God of No, of prohibition, and his suspicious, prohibitionist frame of mind brought the house of creation down on his head and forced him to begin all over. From the Yahwist's twisted tale we learn that the law constitutes the desire to transgress the law; it institutes its own transgression, provokes its own overthrow, defeats its own purpose.[5]

Paul saw this point clearly. Even the example that Paul uses—coveting—is instructive (Rom 7:7–8). He does not choose murder, which is as guilty as sin all by itself, or outright stealing, which is in the same boat, but a rather more psychologically subtle phenomenon, coveting, which is something we do quietly in our heart. The law against coveting provokes coveting, provides the occasion to produce in me all kinds of covetousness, to set my mind roaming over a previously unexplored field of covetousness whose fruit I have not considered before but to which both my attention and my desire have been drawn by the very prohibition. The law sets in motion the logic, the economy, the dialectic of prohibition—a logic of death, inciting rebellion against itself.[6] To be sure, Paul abused his own insight when he did not hesitate to say that God instituted the law just in order to produce transgressions from which God could then mercifully save us by means of the grace of Christ (Rom 11:32). That makes Paul sound like the Yahwist—but a Yahwist with Christ's saving grace up his sleeve. Not so much the happy fault but the happy sting or happy setup. That is a peculiarly Pauline perversion that deserved a lot of the mean things Nietzsche said about Paul and about priests generally. Paul tried to dig out of this hole by positing a hypostatized Sin that is meant to get the law off the hook: the law didn't do it, even I didn't do it, Sin did it, which makes sin sound a little bit like over to the dark side.

Still, when Paul says that "sin, seizing an opportunity in the law" (Rom 7:7), which of itself is good and holy, wants what is against the law, we should take the point he makes seriously. Without committing ourselves to some hypostatization of Sin or some mythological combat with demons or some sweeping theological meta-narrative about the Law and Grace in the History of Salvation, the phenomenological point is sound. Once the law is proposed, it provokes a war of position and opposition: as soon as the law is posited, it rouses the forces of rebellion. The law operates inside an economy, a dialectical-oppositional scheme. Viewed from the side (the position) of the law, the law takes care to exact payment from transgressors, to punish them and bring them into line. Viewed from the side of the subject of the law (the opposition), the law arouses indignation, rebellion, resistance, spite: I am going to do it, I desire to do it, *just because* it is prohibited. To draw up a law is at the same time to draw a line in the sand and to dare someone to cross it, to institute a target for "sin." The fatal limit of the law, the reason it is death-dealing, is that it transpires on the plane of war, of order and disobedience, even if we protest that the law is on the side of the good angels and the war is with the dark side, even if we say the law is good and holy. "Wretched man that I am," to live constantly in a state of war.

Paul saw the need to overcome the law, but his weapon of choice was dogmatic-theological, that is, the grace of Christ's crucifixion and resurrection. Sometimes Paul says that the law cannot save us because we are no match for the law. We constantly fall afoul of the law and have to be saved by the redeeming and sacrificial sufferings of Jesus on the cross. But viewed more closely, as E. P. Sanders argues, that may be one of his positions but it is not his central position. Paul was not a guilt-ridden friar like Luther or a weepy, self-conscious reformed sinner like Augustine or a melancholy, solitary religious author like Kierkegaard. He was an active, robust, sharp-tongued, and irrepressible cosmopolitan with many friends (and at least as many enemies). As to righteousness under the law, if that is what you want, he said he was blameless (Phil 3:4–6); as an effective and energetic apostle of the gospel of Christ, he proudly boasted that there was none better. But Paul thought that even if we do *observe* the law, that still will not do. For the glory of the law has passed and has been replaced by a new glory. So Paul's complaint is not only or mainly about *our* defect before the law—his own observance of the law was without defect—but about the defect of the law *itself*, about the law's faded glory, even if one is impeccable about the observance of the law. For Christ's death and resurrection has initiated a new order, a new life, a new regime of grace; and with

Christ, we have died to the law. This was not an attempt to brush off good works or to show their futility, as Luther was hoping, but rather to link these good works up to a new source. Our works should indeed be good—no sleeping with your stepmother! (1 Cor 5:1)—but our good works should be the fruit of being members of Christ's body, not the fruits of the law, for we have been raised up in Christ into a new creation.[7]

There is something profoundly right about what Paul is saying, but it had one obvious limitation. It strains against the universalism and impartiality of God that Paul was pressing against Peter and James back in Jerusalem, of which Paul was one of the chief advocates in the ancient world, which is the side of Paul that Badiou has recently emphasized.[8] One God, one people; God is the God of both the Jews and the Gentiles, of the circumcised and the uncircumcised. But participating in the body of Christ is every bit as particularizing as the Jewish law, and that presents Paul with his biggest theological problem of all. If God is not partial, what about the Jews whom God has chosen and to whom God has given the law as their means of salvation? They should convert. Then what about the Jews in the ages before Jesus was born? What about the Jews who *in all good faith* have heard Paul out but simply do not agree? What about the peoples of Spain, to which Paul was never able to travel, taking "Spain" as a metonym for all those people at the end of the earth who simply have never heard of the gospel? That is a problem that I think Paul did not exactly resolve but rather simply solved with a broad stroke that brushed aside all the complications of circumcision and uncircumcision, the election of Israel and faith in Christ with which he had been wrestling. At the end of time, God is not defeated; all of Israel will be saved, everyone, everything, all creation, *ta panta* (Romans 9–11). How? That is hard to say, a mystery we cannot grasp, and we simply trust that God knows what he is doing. "O the depth of the riches and wisdom and knowledge of God! How unsearchable are his judgments and how inscrutable his ways" (Rom 11:30–36).[9]

Perhaps there is a missing "Letter to the Spaniards" in which, to the famous list in Galatians—"There is neither Jew nor Greek, there is neither slave nor free, there is no male or female"—Paul would have added what I think consistency demands, that "there are neither those who accept the gospel nor those who do not, for we are all one in love in itself, if there is such a thing, which is not deconstructible." For God is impartial. In such a fanciful letter, Paul would have forced himself to reconsider some of the things he had been saying. Hard as it may have been for Paul to swallow this, an impartial God does not harden the hearts of those who do not accept the gospel preached by Paul, who do not agree with Paul, and who prefer their own practices and do not want to be preached to, thank you very much. If God is impartial, and if God is love, then God loves everyone equally, including those whom Paul calls his enemies. Paul claimed to have had a direct communication from God himself telling him that Paul is right and the rest of the world is made up of enemies and false brethren, including Peter and James themselves, including even the very angels themselves if the latter dare to disagree with Paul. Paul's gospel was between him and God, and nothing of flesh had passed this gospel on to Paul.

That unmistakable and uncompromising militancy—persecuting Christians before his conversion, raging against those who disagree with him after his conversion—is no small part of Paul's attractiveness to neo-Marxists like Zizek and Badiou. But this is a recipe for trouble. If we turn this Pauline maxim into a universal principle, it spells war. It is an open invitation for competing apostles with quite different gospels and competing direct communications from on high and incompatible theologies to oppose him with equally uncompromising militancy. There is much to love about Paul, but this side of him is troublesome. Perhaps this is the trouble with theology as such; perhaps it is a danger only of what we might call "strong" theology, that is, one that insists in a strong way on the particulars of its own dogmatic repertoire, its own confessional apparatus, its own historical traditions. That is why I prefer to speak of a "weak theology," adapting that phrase from Derrida's idea of a "weak force" and Vattimo's concept of "weak thought."[10] The postmodern theological turn, I would argue, implies a turn to a weak theology, even as love and forgiveness are a weak force. Were I ever to write a quasi-Kierkegaardian essay entitled "What is the Difference between a Deconstructor and an Apostle?" I would start out by citing a private edition of the Sermon on the Mount that begins, "Blessed are the weak theologians, for they admit they have not seen God."

Still, I insist, there is something profoundly right about what Paul is saying. Not only had Paul identified a genuine problem, that law is a deathly economy of prohibition and transgression, but he had *also* identified the genuine way to stand clear of this war: to live by love, to elude the law's sting of death by way of love and the gift and grace, to attach our good works not to the law but to love. Paul was profoundly right to say that the answer lies in love, but his limitation from a postmodern point of view was that he had dogmatically identified access to love with those particular people who confess Christ. Love can be confessed in many ways, the particularities of the Christian confession being one among the many. (I am not trying to be condescending about Christianity in saying this, but worrying about the condescension of Christianity to others, especially to Jews.) So his dogmatic or strong theological solution to this problem would not do, but his discourse on love in 1 Corinthians 13, arguably the greatest hymn to love in Western literature, was surely right. There he said that anyone who claims to speak in the tongues of angels or to have been granted knowledge of all mysteries (a very good case in point being Paul himself!) but does not have love is a clanging cymbal. Love is patient and kind, not boastful, and it does not insist on its own way (again, exceptionally good counsel for the apostle himself!). How Paul held all these views in one head surely counts as one of these mysteries. Of course, we cannot forget that Paul was dashing off occasional letters just as the world was about to end. He was not writing a book entitled *Systematic Theology* or *Church Dogmatics* that would be analyzed half to death for two millennia and counting, that would fall into the hands of a guilt-ridden Augustinian friar or a string of popes who declared themselves infallible or the militant evangelicals of today who think that they and their Bible are inerrant and who want to take over the country, the culture, the Supreme Court, and the Constitution.

Beware of strong theology!

So let us return to the question of living by love and dying to the law, this time adopting my final voice, which—after the tempestuous voice of Paul—we may call, not unconscious of the irony, the more dulcet tones of deconstruction.

Life / Death: The Deconstruction

Let us take stock of our progress. Living by love eludes the war or economy of prohibition and transgression by ascending to another plane, above the level on which this war is conducted. On this plane, the gears of duty or obligation, of law or commandment, cannot be engaged; here the wheels of the law are lifted off the ground and lose their traction. When love is in play, the law has no work to do. Love suspends the law, rendering it unnecessary, redundant, even a little insulting—or worse still, counterproductive. Love does more graciously, more swiftly, more effortlessly, whatever the law can think to command. Live by love, die to the law.

But suppose love were commanded? Commanded love would clearly be perverse, for it would commingle the gift of love with the poison (*die Gift*) of law, producing an ill-begotten elixir called love/law, a ghastly, ghostly concoction of life/death, or gift/economy, at the very least a conundrum and a complication.

The conundrum is clear: if love is commanded, then (genuine) love would go beyond the command, while the love that is commanded would be left behind as something less than love. If love is commanded, it will be contradicted, for the very meaning of love is to transcend what we are duty bound to do and to act out of love not obligation, for love comes onstage only after duty takes its bow. If love is commanded, it will set in motion the logic of prohibition. If love is commanded, it will make hatred look desirable. If love is commanded, the flesh will war against it. If love is commanded, then love will be accompanied by the threat of retaliation—love your neighbor or else you will rue the day you did not, which is not very loving. If love is commanded, then the gift is entered into an economy. If love is commanded, it will be drawn into the fray, made a party to the very war that love is supposed to transcend. In short, if the life of love is commanded, then life is death and death puts on the airs of life.

The complication is interesting, for remember that in deconstruction nothing is simple, and nothing, however beautiful, can get off the hook. This can be seen in the deontological critique of love's attempt to exceed the law. For Kant, it is merely "beautiful" to do something from love rather than from duty, but it is non-ethical. It is not unethical, but it simply does not get recorded on an ethical register at all. For Levinas, in *Totality and Infinity*, love is "ambiguous" and has a hard time twisting free of self-love, from *jouissance*, and so its transactions do not measure up to the demands of full ethical transcendence. Furthermore, love runs the risk of drifting into something downright *un*ethical, because it is clearly *hybris*, pride, to think one could ever get out from under, or get above, the law. Estheticism and pride are two of the temptations to which love is exposed, two ways that love's yes, yes—it's way of not being puffed up, as St. Paul says—gets puffed up and goes astray. To which can be added other ways, too. We can be duped by love. Love can be a ruse, a concealed economy; love can pass itself off as self-giving just when what it has in mind all along is not a gift at all but producing debt. Love can be a way of buying favor, of demanding a return, of taking control and exerting power. So in addition to being puffed up, it can be suffocating. If truth be told, we must confess that we never really know what we desire when we desire love.

That is why, truth to tell, love *actually has been commanded*! Someone even more eminent than Paul has commanded it: "Love your neighbor as yourself: I am the Lord" (Lev 19:18).

What then?

Rather than daring to contradict anyone so eminent, we might cautiously offer a gloss on these famous words. The speaker means to say, we proffer very politely, hat in hand, that love, in itself, if there is such a thing, is the greatest *of* the commandments just in the sense that it is greater *than* any of the particular commandments, taken singly and properly so called. Love in itself, if there is such a thing, is not a *primum inter pares* but a *primum simpliciter*. It is first without there being anything second. Love is not itself a member of the set of things that it exceeds. It is not on the list of the things that it is greater than. Love does make not ten + one commandments, an eleventh and highest commandment. We are not precisely commanded to love *by the law*, but love is what *being-commanded-by-the-law* is all about. Love is not one of the things commanded by the Ten Commandments but what the Ten Commandments as a whole intend. When Jesus was asked—by a lawyer, no less—which was the greatest of the commandments in the law, he picked not one but two, the twin commands of love of God and love of neighbor, and neither one is on the list of ten. He was not saying that there are twelve rather than ten commandments, but he said that on these two are suspended all ten, and all the prophets, too (Matt 22: 37–39). If you add these two to the ten, you will still get ten, but the ten will look different. The difference will not be two more things to do, but *how* you do the ten. The two are not a quantitative two but a qualitative two, not a *what* but a *how*. The point of what you are being commanded to do when you are commanded to do the ten is to love, otherwise it is not enough. By simply doing your duty, you have not done your duty. You have to do more than you are commanded to do; otherwise, while you won't be violating the commandments, you won't be keeping them either. Without love, a commandment is less than it should be; with love, it is more than it is. Having said that much, we would then beat a hasty retreat.

For we have now admitted that things have just gotten complicated. In deconstruction, as in the Bible, as in life itself, it seems, nothing is simple. Even if love in itself (if there is such a thing) cannot be commanded, love is indeed commanded; and if commanded, then commingled with the law, positively related to or intertwined with the commandments, intermingled with the law, as their sum and substance. Paul, citing this text from Leviticus, comments that the law is "summed up" (*peplerotai*) or reaches its fulfillment (*pleroma*) in the commandment to love our neighbor as ourselves (Gal 5:14).[11] Love, we may say, is the Ten Commandments in a nutshell. Love is the alpha and omega of the commandments, their beginning and end, their résumé, their shorthand version, what is first last and always relative to the multitude of commandments. Without love, the commandments are clanging cymbals, nothing more than the hollowed out discharge of duty, mere orderliness, compliance, conformity to some code. With love, the commandments make their point and constitute so many ways to be before God. So we cannot quite say that love is not one among the commandments and this because it soars over them, for love does not exactly soar over the commandments, but it runs all through them in such a way that love animates the commandments the way the soul animates the body. The several commandments should be like so many rivers fed by the same stream of love. Or again, love is, as St. Thomas said, the form of law, while the material commands themselves are its body.[12]

But now love has sailed dangerously close to the law, and the waters of the law begin to lap over its side. Still, it is the case, a bald and inescapable reality, that like it or not, love is, in fact, *commanded.*

Love in itself, if there is such a thing, cannot be commanded.

Still love *is* commanded.

For example, what Kierkegaard writes about so powerfully under the name of "commanded love"—there is our aporia—is the love (*agape*) that does not love preferentially (*eros, philia*), that does not prefer to love, and so must be commanded to love. Commanded love is love that must be made a duty or a duty that is obliged to love; it is a duty that lets itself be touched by love or a love that has been brushed by duty. To go back to our ruling figure: we see now that the gift cannot avoid contamination by economy; that living by love cannot avoid being brushed by death. Life is life/death, *sur-vivre*, living on after a certain death. We are commanded to love even when, or rather precisely when, we prefer not to love. Love this disagreeable curmudgeon down the street, whom you do not love or prefer not to love; love that insufferable fellow you work with, whom you do not prefer to love. Love everyone, regardless, without preference, with perfect indifference to their merits—indeed, the more un-meritorious the better. For the other does not need to merit our love. Or rather, the other as other, and without regard to his or her merits, merits our love. Love not only the ones you love but also the ones you do not love, *especially* the ones you do not love. Love the unlovable. Love not only those who love you, which is a virtue honored even among thieves and crime families, but love even those who hate you, your enemies, for example, for that is what God commands, what God indeed is. The model and exemplar of that sort of love, its very incarnation, we might say, is Jesus on the cross asking God to forgive the Roman soldiers who are mercilessly carrying out this cruelest of ancient executions. That is a story of perfect and divine love, divine forgiveness—to which the rest of us unhappy things have to be commanded. But it is also the point of deconstruction: when you love what it is possible and obvious that you should love, that love is greeted with a yawn; love is really love, glows white hot with love, when you love what it is impossible to love.

So the relationship between love and the law is neither a simple contrariety (love versus the law, life versus death, the gift versus economy) nor a simple supersession (love beyond the law, life without death). It is rather a complicated interlacing or interweaving, an almost eerie intermingling or overlapping of life and death, whose only adequate model, in my view, is provided by deconstruction.

The law, the commandments, the numerable list of ten or more, ten or less, in whatever flavor—Catholic, Protestant, or Jewish—are deconstructible. That means that they are historical and positive, contingent and revisable, written and so rewritable, numerable and renumerable. Paul himself saw something of the contingency of the law, albeit through a glass darkly, when he reminded the Romans that a woman is bound to a man only as long as he lives, but she is free to marry another when he dies (Rom 7:1–3). There is something time-bound and hide-bound about law. To take another example, one that Paul decidedly did not see, I would say that Paul was against homosexual love because he was a Jew, but if he had been a Greek, he would have found beautiful things to say about adult men properly loving adolescent males. Indeed, he would have raged against his enemies who dared to disagree with him, up to and including telling these false brethren to go cut the whole thing off (Gal 5:12), a remarkable remark he makes just two verses before telling the Galatians to love their neighbor as themselves! The commandments are deconstructible, but love in itself, if there is such a thing, is not deconstructible. That is the model deconstruction provides, the model of some undeconstructible something or other, a soul or a spirit, a ghost or a specter of love, if there is such a thing, somehow or another breathing over us, insinuating itself amidst us, animating or maybe even haunting the things that are.

S'il y en a—if there is such a thing—that is the weak and whispy essence of deconstruction, its weak force, its sum and insubstantial substance, or perhaps its nutshell; and it goes a considerable way toward explaining how love is the essence of the law and the prophets.

S'il y en a: that means love is a spirit that barely exists, that we do not know if love in itself, which is not deconstructible, ever exists, even as we know that every existing love is deconstructible. We can never be sure that any existing love, that what is here and now called love, is love or not. We do not know if it is a disguised form of power, or pride, or a way we have found to make ourselves look beautiful, or who knows what, and we do not know whether it will last through tomorrow. Nor can we trust any existing love to love those whom it prefers not to love. That is why we are always and already under the law, concretely, historically situated under the law, always and already prohibited from doing some things and commanded to do other things, commanded even to love, to love when we do not prefer to love, especially then.

So then, what we have been calling the plane of pure love, where we live by love and die to the law, thus turns out to be a Rousseauian dream of life without death, of the gift without economy, of presence without *différance.* Even the image of a "plane" is the wrong figure, for phenomenologically speaking, there is only one world, one plane, the plane of immanence, of life/death, and that is where the transcendence of love—like Irigaray's sensible transcendental—if there is such a thing, will perforce have to cast its tent. Couched in the terms of deconstruction, we may say that love finds itself always and already situated in one economy or the other. There is no simple outside or exterior to economy, including to the economy of the law. We cannot simply stand outside the law and breathe the air of the pure gift or of pure love. All that actually exists is found within one economy of exchange or another, one body of laws or another, while love in itself, if there is such a thing, does not quite exist and is always to come, which is why we are in love with love with a desire beyond desire. Unhappy things that we are, we cannot live without the force of law, without the economy of the law. Unhappy things that we are, we do not have the luxury to suspend the law.

What then? Shall we say that love is impossible? Yes, but not the way a simple contradiction like $(p \cdot \sim p)$ is impossible. Love is *the* impossible, the undeconstructible; while laws, which are economies of exchange, are not only possible but actual, not only actual but inevitable. The idea would be—and this is the contribution that deconstruction makes to this discussion, the closest deconstruction can come to penning an apostolic letter, a kind of quasi-apostolic *carte postale*—on the one hand, to know that love in itself is the impossible and then to love, to know all about the ruses and risks by which love may be disturbed, and then still to make the leap of love, to live by love. But the idea is also, on the other hand, to concede that there is always and already the law, some law or other, but then to give the law a chance, to constitute the most open-ended, flexible, revisable, generous, and hospitable laws, for laws are always deconstructible. For if we must always and already operate within one economy or another, one or another system of law, and the system is constantly seeking to maintain its own equilibrium, then love must learn to operate *within* the system, interrupting the system from within, opening it up and destabilizing it from within, prodding its plodding feet to make the leap, exposing its rational functioning to madness, readying it for the foolishness of the moment of love for which the system itself has no accounting, creating openings that the system did not see coming.[13]

So then shall we say the law is death? By no means. The law is a way to protect the weak against the strong. Shall we say that love in itself is a hallucination and an illusion? By no means. Do we live by love but die by the law? Or do we merely dream of love but really live by the law? What is the difference, the *différance*, the khoral spacing, between living by love and the economy of the law?

It is, as we say in deconstruction, not a matter of choosing between the two. We live in the distance between them, negotiating the interval between the gift and economy, between love and the law, between life and death, in a fluctuating and unstable space we call history and tradition, our inherited beliefs and practices, the concreteness of factical life. And if by some gift of faith or faith in the gift we say that God is love, or at least that love is divine, then we live in the distance between the rule of God and the economy of the world, between the kingdom of God and the rule of the "world," where everything has a price and nothing is done for free. But the kingdom of God is here and now, in the world, and it contradicts and unnerves the world, exposing the world to an unheard of love.

So then, let us think of love neither as simply soaring above the law nor as doggedly pitted against the law, but rather as nestled within its provisions, inserted between the numbered planks of its imperatives. Love insinuates itself within the interstices of the law as the interruption of the law. Love haunts the law the way a preternatural specter disturbs mere mortals, giving them no rest. Love aerates the law, letting it breathe. Love is a solvent that loosens the strictures of the law. Love ruptures the law, seeking to break out of the circle of exchange, giving without the expectation of return and without being commanded to give, loving even unlovable enemies, putting the last first, and even inviting perfect strangers to the banquet. That is impossible, *the* impossible, which is why we are so much in love with love.

Love *is* the impossible, to be sure, and so we know that love's eccentric moment of madness, too, will finally be reabsorbed by the ineluctable pressures of the circle. But this is said without sadness and nostalgia, for the resulting circle, having been momentarily sundered, is rendered wider and more ample, less harsh and confining. Love makes the law more generous, more porous and open-ended, as if the law had been breathed upon by a gentle and more elliptical spirit, made soft and supple—let us say more life-like—by a very holy spirit. *S'il y en a.*

John D. Caputo

NOTES

1. I am, for philosophical purposes of my own, recontextualizing Paul's account of love and the law in the setting of Derrida's distinction between the gift and an economy. As regards historical-critical matters, my reading of Paul is largely dependent on the works of E. P. Sanders, who makes the most sense to me by situating Paul—he does the same thing with Jesus—more firmly within his Jewish setting, even if and when what Sanders says about Paul is odds with what a latter Christian theology wants Paul to be saying.

2. The aporia is this: we fall short of the ethicality of ethics, of unlimited and uncalculating affirmation, says Derrida, whenever we are acting out an ethics of duty. See Derrida's interesting and lengthy footnote in *On the Name*, ed. Thomas Dutoit (Stanford, Calif.: Stanford University Press, 199), 132–37.

3. On the idea of a "weak force," see Jacques Derrida, *Rogues: Two Essays on Reason*, trans. Pascale-Anne Brault and Michael Naas (Stanford, Calif.: Stanford University Press, 2005), xiv.

4. Kierkegaard brings out this paradox brilliantly in *Works of Love*. See *Kierkegaard's Writings*, XVI, *Works of Love*, trans. and ed. Howard Hong and Edna Hong (Princeton, N.J.: Princeton University Press, 1995), 225–45.

5. I have developed this point about the difference between the two creation narratives in more detail in *The Weakness of God: A Theology of the Event* (Bloomington: Indiana University Press, 2006), 55–75. Jack Miles, *God: A Biography* (New York: Knopf, 1995), ch. 1, does a nice job of summarizing the difference between the two stories in an accessible way.

6. Slavoj Zizek has picked up on this point in several works; see *The Fragile Absolute* (New York and London: Verso, 2000), 123–30; *The Puppet and the Dwarf* (Cambridge: MIT Press, 2003), 93–121.

7. We can all be grateful to E. P. Sanders, *Paul* (Oxford: Oxford University Press, 1991), who among others shows very nicely that Paul's *central* teaching was that the death and resurrection of Jesus raised us up to a new life of freedom and grace. As Sanders points out, Paul *also* regarded this death as sacrificial, as an atoning blood sacrifice for sin, and that interpretation preceded Paul (78–79). But if the death of Jesus is taken to be prophetic, then Jesus called the world to task for its bloody ways; and the world, in turn, ever an economy, spilled his blood in return. It was ever thus with the prophets of old and the whistle-blowers of today. I do not think there is any version of God's sending Jesus into the world to suffer and die in order to balance the scales of divine justice with a blood sacrifice that is not a perverse rendering of the God of love. That is just not how love behaves. Love, and *a fortiori* the God of love, does not set out to balance the scales of law-and-transgression—and certainly not by engaging in blood economies. I think the paradigmatic gesture of the God of love in the face of transgression as it is revealed by Jesus is found in the parable of the prodigal son—where the response to transgression is forgiveness, not a demand for sacrificial atonement—or in the passion narratives, where the word from the cross is "Father, forgive them," and there is no hint that with this suffering he is the purchasing redemption for all humankind.

8. Alain Badiou, *Saint Paul: The Foundation of Universalism*, trans. Ray Brassier (Stanford, Calif.: Stanford University Press, 2003).

9. See Sanders, *Paul*, ch. 11.

116

10. Caputo, *The Weakness of God*, 1–20. See also Jeffrey Robbins, "Weak Theology," *Journal of Cultural and Religious Theory*, 5.2 (April 2004) (*www.jcrt.org*); and Ulrich Engel, O.P., "Religion and Violence: Plea for a Weak Theology *in tempore belli*," *New Blackfriars* 82 (2001): 558–60. Engel argues that in the interests of peace and tolerance, the great monotheisms must soften their strong dogmatic traditions in favor of a weaker pacific theology. See also Gianni Vattimo and John D. Caputo, *After the Death of God*, ed. Jeffrey Robbins (New York: Columbia University Press, 2007).

11. As the citation from Leviticus 19:18 shows, one can believe firmly in the supersession of the law by love without being a supersessionist. Indeed, if that is supersessionism, the Jews are the first supersessionists. I have no truck with Christian supersessionism—the most classic form that the Christian attack on the Jew has taken. The overcoming of the law by love is itself a kind of law of the law, a law of love and a love of the law, which is the essence of the law and the prophets, what the law and the prophets are all about, what the Germans would call their *Sache*, or what we mean in English when we say "sum and substance." If we meditated long and lovingly on the essence of the law, on the inner movements of *Torah*, we would not hear only "*nomos*" or "*lex*" but also teaching, doctrine, instruction, and finally love, for what the law is continually teaching is love. So as this text from Leviticus makes plain, the essence of the Torah is love, and the Jews are already the first supersessionists. When Jesus was asked the question about the greatest of the commandments (Matt 22: 37–40), he answered by citing both Deuteronomy 6:5 and Leviticus 19:18. As Sanders shows, Jesus was being as Jewish as possible. He considered the twin laws of love the essence, the sum and the substance, of Judaism. It was no part of his thinking that this was a Christian innovation on Judaism. He never heard of Christianity. There are several and alternate ways to see that love is the point of the law, that is to say, that in love we are made a new creation—Jesus is one of them, the Torah is another. That is why I advocate weak, not strong, theology.

12. The advantage of this way of thinking about love and the law is to let love give us some leverage on the particulars of the law, to keep us on the alert about becoming legalistic and keep us focused on the point of the law. The law, then, would always be deconstructible just in virtue of the fact that love in itself, which is not deconstructible, is the point of the law, its sum and substance. Otherwise the law is terror, a monster. The law must be deconstructed in order to keep our eye on the love. The danger is, as I said above, to avoid construing this as a Christian-versus-Jewish point instead of a point about the meaning of Torah well known to the rabbis.

13. Derrida seeks to stoke up the aporetic tension around a certain "quasi-transcendental illusion" of the gift, where we must learn to enter its circle rightly: on the one hand, by responding faithfully to the command to "give," knowing well all the ruses of the gift, while also recognizing, on the other hand, that the gift gets the economy going, which means to give economy a chance. See Jacques Derrida, *Given Time, I: Counterfeit Money*, trans. Peggy Kamuf (Chicago: University of Chicago Press, 1991), 30–31. By the same token, we are arguing: know what love means to say, know all its ruses, and then love, but also give the law a chance.

PART 3.
THE SACRED

8

A Love That B(l)inds

Reflections on an Agapic Agnosticism

B. KEITH PUTT

Love looks not with the eyes, but with the mind;
And therefore is wing'd Cupid painted blind:
Nor hath Love's mind of any judgement taste;
Wings and no eyes figure unheedy haste.

—*A Midsummer Night's Dream*

But love is blind, and lovers cannot see
The pretty follies that they themselves commit.

—*The Merchant of Venice*

In *Memoirs of the Blind*, Jacques Derrida references the ancient tale of Butades, a young Corinthian woman who prepares for her lover's departure by tracing the silhouette of his shadow as a mnemonic relic that will serve as a sacramental and supplemental "presence" during his extended absence. He notes that artists who illustrate this myth of *skiagraphy*, or "shadow writing," as he terms it, often represent Butades and her lover as present but "invisible" to each other.[1] Several canvasses depict Butades as looking away from her lover's face in order to sketch his phantom outline, while he turns away from her in order to present his profile. Furthermore, Derrida indicates that in some artistic representations of the myth, an unblindfolded Cupid, the God of Love, guides Butades' hand as she lovingly, albeit blindly, delineates her lover's dark outline. He infers from such works that drawing appears to be "a declaration of love destined for or suited to the invisibility of the other," thereby inaugurating "an art of blindness."[2]

Derrida may well be making a passing reference to a "sighted" Cupid, because, as Shakespeare indicates in the two epigraphs above, Cupid traditionally appears as a sightless god, indicating that love is blind, unable or unwilling to gaze upon the visible. Love, indeed, often loathes to admit the apparent, content, instead, to embrace only its own simulations or dissimulations of reality.[3] Cataracts of desire or the myopia of passion inhibits lovers from intuiting the genuine phenomenality of the beloved, so that lovers stumble ahead through the invisibility of a projected reality like impetuous Berkleyians who "see" only through the lens of their own fervent erotic idealism. Of course, such blindness provokes a certain epistemological crisis of love in that the lover may not genuinely know the beloved, or know if the beloved genuinely reciprocates that love, or even know whether he or she genuinely loves the beloved. Love's blindness, therefore, creates an intellectual vulnerability that deception or error may exploit and that necessarily preempts any Cartesian certainty. Consequently, the idealism of love rests ultimately on the efficacy of faith, sharing with it a definite predisposition toward the risk of invisibility. Ironically, that risk of invisibility serves as the primary theme of Derrida's *Memoirs of the Blind,* which itself begins with an epigraph from Diderot—"Where there will be *nothing,* read that I love you" (emphasis added)—and ends with a personal agnostic confession of faith—"I do not know; I must believe" (*Je ne sais pas, il faut croire*).[4]

Derrida's thematic concatenation of invisibility, blindness, faith, and love becomes acutely provocative when directed toward Jesus' two great commandments to love (*agape*) God and to love (*agape*) others (Matt 22:37–39). One may inquire as to whether there are intrinsic to the structures of *agape* as un/conditional love of God and neighbor the systemic attributes of the unseen and the uncertain. This is assuredly not a gratuitous question if one considers the Apostle Paul's beautiful and powerful panegyric to *agape* in 1 Corinthians 13. There he associates love with faith and hope and concludes that love predominates within that trinity of Christian graces. By connecting love to the other two spiritual gifts, he explicitly incites deliberation on the epistemological implications of love and blindness, because he conspicuously relates faith and hope to the blindness of a functional agnosticism. He insists that for Christians, seeing is not believing, since we always walk by faith and not by sight (2 Cor 5:7). Furthermore, he claims that faith comes by hearing (Rom 10:17), thereby implying that the ears, and not the eyes, are the conduits of belief. Likewise, he distances hope from vision, insisting that "hope that is seen is not hope" (Rom 8:24). Hoping against hope always entails the invisible, that which appears neither to sight nor to foresight, precisely because no eye may see proleptically what God has prepared for those who love God (2 Cor 2:9).

Of course, Paul nowhere categorically coordinates love with blindness and agnosticism; however, the immediate context of 1 Corinthians 13 suggests just such a correlation, not only with reference to the proximity of love to sightless faith and hope, but also by virtue of his antecedent admission of the believer's currently deficient knowledge. He confesses that we have only fragmented and partial comprehension (v. 9), which, stated otherwise, means that now we may only see through a dim (*ainigmati*) mirror (v. 12). At this very moment of enigmatic, nontransparent seeing, only three virtues abide—faith, hope, and love; consequently, one might extrapolate and infer that Paul would also admit that we presently love by faith and with hope and "not by sight."

Indeed, Slavoj Zizek accentuates just such a connection when he interprets Paul as establishing love on the premise that it pertains only to "incomplete beings . . . who possess incomplete knowledge." He further glosses Paul by concluding that "only an imperfect, lacking being loves: we love because we do *not* know all."[5] Such a loving agnosticism, or agnostic loving, certainly applies to our *agape* toward God. For example, the Apostle Peter reminds his Christian readers that although they have neither seen Jesus in the past nor see him in the present, they love him and rejoice in the glory of his salvation (1 Pet 1:8). What could be more illustrative of the blindness of love? If we love God, whose face no one may see and live (Exod 33:20), with all our hearts, souls, and minds and love Jesus, who is now absent from the world having returned to his Heavenly Father, then do we not love in blindness in loving the Divine Other who cannot be perceived as visible phenomena? Are we not restricted in this existence to a tenebrous love, a blinding love, a loving blindness that never escapes the translucence of enigmatic knowledge or the fragmentation of finite cognition?

The above questions figure significantly in contemporary Continental philosophy and theology, since much of Continental, or postmodern thought adopts a hermeneutic of suspicion toward modernist paradigms of self, community, knowledge, and religion. Postmodernists cast a critical eye on the putative clarity of Enlightenment rationality, wary of claims that individuals may reach the certainty of clear and distinct ideas. This is unquestionably the case among various Continental philosophical theologians and philosophers of religion, for whom the classical onto-theological categories no longer illuminate the way to God. Jean-Luc Marion serves as an exemplary guide at this point, since he has been one of the most creative and influential theorists to prosecute the ethical, theological, and epistemological implications of love and blindness. His rather heterodox revisioning of the phenomenological method and his rather orthodox theology of the revelation of divine love may shed new light on the issues of love and faith and how both relate to an inescapable agnosticism.

Using the term *agnosticism* in the context of Marion's philosophy and theology may, at first blush, appear to be a non sequitur. As evidenced later in this essay, much of the criticism directed at his thought ensues from pretensions to certainty inherent both in his third reduction to givenness and the call and also in his phenomenology (and theology) of revelation. Neither his philosophical critics nor his theological confederates would find the term in any manner applicable. Yet I contend that "agapic *agnosticism*" functions well as a cipher for Marion's complex reflections on the impossible events of love and grace. Of course, in associating Marion with agnosticism, I am using the term, not in the colloquial sense of indecision with reference to theistic belief, but according to the more literal etymological definition of the term. To classify Marion as a theological agnostic *simpliciter* would be a gross misinterpretation at best, since he never waivers in his commitment to the reality of God. Marion most definitely writes as one with an existential certitude that God exists; indeed, his personal piety (which I share, albeit from a more Protestant perspective) identifies God as the *Christian* deity, the one revealed uniquely in Jesus of Nazareth.[6] Nevertheless, his work does manifest a systemic agnosticism *secundum quid*, if one takes seriously the term's Greek linguistic genealogy. According to its etymological definition, agnosticism names an attitude that T. S. Eliot calls the "wisdom of humility," the modest affirmation that one does not (*a*) know (*gnosis*) with absolute certainty.[7] Notwithstanding the Cartesian predispositions that make Marion vulnerable to the seductions of a *pleroma* of pure and unconditional givenness, one should not reduce his philosophical theology to a form of phenomenological gnosticism, to the arrogance of possessing secret self-confirming knowledge that establishes an inviolate dogmatism. Doing so would result in something of a perversion of his testimony of the gift, of love, and of faith. A close reading of his thought would yield a latent confession of *simul fidelis et infidelis*, an acknowledgment, if often in muted tones, that one never "sees" with total transparency. The tension between belief and unbelief prohibits Marion's reflections on love from assuming panoptical grandeur but warrants the sustaining of a residual blindness.

Adapting the Augustinian stance on the knowledge of time, Marion claims that people pretend to know what love is until asked for a specific definition. Only then does one discover that it withdraws into the penumbra of the inarticulate, dwelling beyond the light of reason and outside the clarity of language.[8] He claims that such an agnosticism of love condemns it to subjectivism and to the narcissism of self-sameness, both of which deprive love of genuine alterity and the affirmation of difference. But he insists that without otherness and difference, there can be no genuine love. He notes that the phenomenological method has been conscripted at times as a possible antidote to this contamination of heterophobia, since traditional phenomenology, through the dynamic of intentionality, has focused on the transcendent object, the "thing itself" existing beyond the *cogito* as the other and the different (*PC* 73). Marion indicates, however, that this method actually depends on the notions of conditionality and reduction, since intentionality operates only within certain horizons of expectation as the activity of a cognitive subject, an autonomous, rational self, before whom everything else becomes a noetic object. The other, therefore, ceases to be truly other, as it is transmuted into the content of the individual's proprietary "lived experience" (*Erlebnis*). Whereas love results in my encountering the other *as* other, *as* a "pure alterity" (*PC* 75), intentionality only results in my loving the other *in* myself or, worse, loving "*myself* in the other," which "inevitably ends as self-love, in the phenomenological figure of self-idolatry" (*PC* 77). Furthermore, intentionality always objectifies the other as the *noema* of my *noesis*, as the intuition that fulfills my intention. Since love should never objectify the beloved, but always treat her as another subject, love cannot be interpreted under the rubric of intentionality, and consequently cannot be deciphered through the structures of traditional phenomenology (*PC* 79–80). If one assents to Zizek's paradox of love, then to posit love "as a direct goal," as the specific aim of intentionality, would be to obliterate its status as a product of grace.[9] Or, as Marion claims, to do so would be to reduce love to an "optical illusion of my consciousness" (*PC* 75).

Nonetheless, Marion's critique of a more "orthodox" phenomenological approach to love does not prevent him from remaining within the broader structures of its method and vocabulary; consequently, he seeks to develop a "radical phenomenology" of love, one predicated, not on the intuitive visibility of an intentional consciousness, but on "two definitively invisible gazes" that call consciousness into question.[10] These invisible gazes reference, first, an emptiness—a blindness that results from a deficient intuition, from the absence of discrete, observable phenomena—and second, a fullness—a blindness that emanates from an excessive intuition, the sensory overload of an extravagant manifestation.

The first gaze directs attention to the face of the beloved other as subject, not as object, as a face that also gazes back at the lover. This reciprocal gaze of the other face intrigues Marion, since it testifies to an inescapable and non-exploitable invisibility. When one sees the other's face, one actually looks into the eyes, specifically into the pupils that serve as the media for the other's gaze. In the darkness, or "black holes," of those orbs, one encounters a nothingness "in the very midst of the visible . . . nothing to see, except an invisible and untargetable (*invisable*) void."[11] The invisible gaze of the other is indeed *invisable*, that which cannot be the target of an intention, that which cannot be "aimed at" as if it were an object. Indeed, the invisible, *invisable* gaze of the other aims at *me*, summons *me* to accountability, makes *me* an object of an injunction.[12] One might express it in a more Levinasian form as the gaze that obligates me, binds (*ligare*) me toward (*ob*) the other so that I might surrender myself to the other, speak the "ocular" phrase of commitment: *me voici*—"here I am," "*see* me here."[13] Marion identifies this reciprocal gaze of the other as an iconic gaze and differentiates it from the idolatrous gaze of self-sameness. He claims that the icon never reflects the gaze of the subject back onto itself, as does the idol, but looks upon the subject as the object of an obligating gaze. In other words, he maintains that "in the icon, the gaze of man is lost in the invisible gaze that visibly envisages him" (*GWB* 20). As a result, this binding love of obligation is a blinding love that looks into the face of the beloved without seeing her with total lucidity.[14]

The second invisible gaze of love avoids reductive objectification by overwhelming intentionality through the bedazzling givenness of a "blinding intuition," what Marion terms a "saturated phenomenon" (PC 65ff.). Borrowing Kant's notion of an "aesthetic idea," he reverses Husserl's contention that an intuition can fail to fulfill the surplus meaning of an intention and insists that through an "excess of *donation*," the superfluity of intentional givenness, a phenomenon can manifest itself in such a way as to saturate conceptuality, thereby rendering it blind by an "excess of light."[15] Marion labels such a saturating phenomenological event an "impossible experience," impossible on the grounds that it transcends every condition of possibility dictated by the horizonal forestructures of conscious intentionality and the noetic capacity of a constituting ego.[16] Of course, Marion contends that the invisibility and *invisabilité* of a saturated phenomenon does not constrain visibility per se, but visibility as "regardability." He argues that the blindness evoked by the saturated phenomenon does depend upon a "seeing," in that one must be able to recognize the glory of the intuition; however, one certainly cannot "look" at the phenomenon, that is, regard it, or intuit it, as the aim, or target, of an intentionality.[17] To do so would pervert the saturated phenomenon by constraining it within the "limits of a concept" and under the dominating "initiative of the gaze" of a constituting "I" (BG 214). Instead, the saturated phenomenon gives its phenomenality as an "auto-manifestation," creating the conditions for its reception in its givenness itself (BG 219). Consequently, the saturated phenomenon "gives nothing to see," but this blindness simultaneously reveals a vision of extravagance that, although visible, cannot be sustained (BG 203).

The iconic gaze *sous rature*, under erasure, and *sous sature*, under saturation—that double blindness of the invisible gaze and the incandescent profusion of bedazzlement—both come to expression in the face of the other, in the inexhaustible and impossible experience of the other as other.[18] As my gaze crosses with the counter-gaze of the other, the other "comes to meet me only while remaining invisible . . . strictly speaking, there is nothing to see" (BG 243). Of course, I may see the face as a simple object, something of a *Vorhandensein* without bedazzlement; however, I cannot see the face as the face of the other qua other. The face as the revelation of the singularity and alterity of the other manifests a "phenomenon of inaccessible meaning," a phenomenon that reminds me that I can never know the other completely, that it "would take an eternity to envisage" the other. Interestingly enough, the asymptotic nature of the iconic gaze places Marion in close proximity to Derrida's concept of undecidability, in that the icon "definitively exceeds the scope of expectation, terrifying the desire, [and] annulling the anticipation."[19] In other words, the iconic gaze prohibits any manipulation by or imprisonment in the closed structures of horizons of expectation. Consequently, the face of the beloved exposes the reality that I can never see the other with total transparency; it enables me to see that I cannot see, but must accept, the blindness of an "infinite hermeneutic" of the other, that is, recognize that I must continually "interpret [the other] in loving [the other]."[20] In other words, I must make decisions as to the identity of the other, constantly interpreting whom I love when I love the other and accepting no termination to the process of discovery inherent in love. Yet this infinite hermeneutic requires faith, a trusting that the future holds further disclosures of meaning, that I can learn more about the person even after her death.[21] An infinite hermeneutic of love, therefore, necessarily entails a particular agnosticism, an intellectual invisibility, or blindness, that, with reference to loving the other, would logically lead Marion to affirm: "*Je ne sais pas, il faut croire.*" Or perhaps one should state it: "*Je ne sais pas, il faut aimer*"—"I do not know; I must love."

The conjunction between love and faith figures significantly into the theological application of Marion's radical phenomenology of *agape*. The religious prominence of the issue stems from his privileging what David Tracy calls the "ruling metaphor" of Christianity, "God is love" (1 John 4:8, 16), as the source of the "most theological name" for God (GWB xvi). If God bears the name *agape*, then God reveals Godself as pure gift, as a "givingness" that exceeds every human attempt to domesticate it within the cognitive claustrophobia of any idolatrous conceptuality. God's donation of unconditioned and unconditional love shatters every horizon of expectation and refuses to be objectified by the intentional regard of a constituting ego. In other words, God manifests Godself iconically in an invisible gaze *sous rature* and *sous sature*; consequently, this gaze induces a blindness of love as *kenosis* (emptiness), as the gaze that cannot be gazed upon, and as *plerosis* (fullness), as the gaze that cannot be sustained (GWB 46–47). The blindness in loving God depends not only on the absence of any intuition of the divine, on the "failure of the visible" vis-à-vis God's "face," but also on the bedazzling brilliance of certain theophanies of *agape*, those revelations of divine love that irradiate the shadows, which often eclipse human existence, through the impossible experiences of saturated phenomena. Indeed, for Marion, such saturated phenomena of *agape* may actually manifest that "the ultimate icon is . . . revealed as a 'living icon of charity.'" (CV 85). Zizek might well interpret such saturated phenomena of *agape* as expressions of the "excess of life," of the "too-muchness of life" beyond good and evil, or in Pauline terms, outside the "morbid cycle of law and sin."[22] Zizek interprets these phenomena as intimations of the mercy of love—"the excess of mercy without proportion."[23] Marion claims that one can "see" such phenomena of excess "only by blinking," by squinting at the "surfeit of intuition [that] leads to the paradox that an invisible gaze visibly envisages me and loves me."[24]

Marion admits his Christian prejudice and proclaims the centrality of Christ as the most conspicuous appearance in the flesh of the saturated phenomenon of *agape*; however, he also concedes that Jesus' embodiment of the divine love "surpasses all knowledge, with a hyperbole that defines it and, indissolubly, prohibits access to it" (GWB 108). He writes of the "paradox of the face," with reference to Christ, by which the invisible glory of the divine achieves a certain phenomenality through the visibility of Jesus' embodied humanity. Such a paradox dazzles and shocks the gaze, actually wounding it through "its very excess of visibility" (CV 1–2).[25] Yet this saturated visibility does not preempt a residual invisibility, since he claims that "Christ Jesus offers not only a visible image of the Father who remains invisible but even a (visible) face of the invisible itself (the Father), a visible image of the invisible as *invisible*" (CV 58). Consequently, the saturated phenomenon of the Christ event maintains the reality of the distance between God and humanity, since the face of Christ may only be "seen" through a vision that "is exhausted in sustaining with a blinking gaze the darkness that makes up bedazzlement." In other words, "the Christ paradigmatically receives the paradox of distance and renders it absolutely (in)visible."[26] Thereby, Jesus functions as the icon of the Father, who remains invisible in the visible face of the Christ, and brings divine distance into proximity through the event of the cross (ID 176).

With something of a Kierkegaardian humility, Marion admits that although Christ's face reveals the "face" of God, when one looks into Jesus' eyes, one cannot see the gaze that looks back (CV 17).[27] Of course, the contemporary believer cannot even look into Jesus' eyes, which remain hidden until the eschatological disclosure at his second advent. Nevertheless, Marion considers Christ's crucifixion to be the premier event that communicates both the *kenosis* and the *plerosis* of divine love. Jesus' selfless gift of self, *usque ad mortem*, reveals a "love without reserve, universal and hence all-powerful." This fullness of love, however, occurs in the midst of darkness, a darkness that not only enshrouds Jesus' agony from the crowd but also shrouds God from Jesus' sight: "My God, My God, why have you forsaken me?" (Mark 15:34). Marion asserts that Jesus dies without any absolute assurance that God will resurrect him. He is blind to any absolute future, unable to see with intellectual certitude that God will be faithful to the promise of Easter morning. Consequently, the "logic of love" does not lead to necessary truth and Cartesian certainty; it does not grant enlightening assurances; instead, it abandons Jesus to the risk of agnosticism, to the sightlessness of faith and hope (GWB 193). Consequently, even the saturated phenomenon of divine *agape* that inspires the incarnate Christ fails to avoid completely the shadows of doubt.

Marion concludes from his radical phenomenology of divine love that God "can be reached only so long as one receives him by love"; that is, one only "knows" God through a love that surrenders in obligation to the holiness of God, a love that, although blind, trusts in the invisible God of grace and promise (PC 61). This iconic divine invisibility signifies for Marion that the distinction between love and faith is the "smallest of abysses," an abyss so small perhaps that no functional distinction may be made between them (*PC* 65). The Apostle Paul reports that faith is nothing without love (1 Cor 13:2), but likewise, love is nothing without faith. Since *agape* never escapes the double blind of the invisible gaze and the saturation of an immoderate grace, it double binds us to God and to each other on the basis of systemic uncertainty. Whereas the conceptual idolatry of epistemological confidence may promise absolute knowledge, the iconic gaze of divine *agape* stares into and out of the blinding abyss of agnosticism and risk.

The question may well remain, however, whether Marion's radical phenomenology of love genuinely appreciates the abyssal character of faithful agnosticism, primarily because of its gloss on the second form of blindness, the saturated phenomenon. He does indeed insist that in the impossible experiences of bedazzlement, the visible reveals itself through the invisible and offers a type of phenomenality that, although overwhelming *noesis* with excessive *noema*, nonetheless does "give" something to be seen, something that can be known, albeit through an impoverished intentionality. Likewise, he prosecutes the saturated phenomenon as a pure and unconditional intuition, one that automanifests the required structures of receptivity without depending on any prior existential horizons or categories of expectation.[28] The automanifestation of the saturated phenomenon establishes the self-confirming dynamic of its phenomenality, which, in turn, suggests a 20/20 clarity of (in)sight and a transparent certainty in the reception of the experience. In other words, it appears that an agapic "gnosticism" emanates from the revelatory effulgence of Marion's saturated phenomenon and establishes something of an eidetic reduction, not a reduction to an intentional idea of the epistemological subject, but to the form of the phenomenon itself, resulting in a clear and distinct essence, which grants Cartesian certainty. Marion's third reduction, therefore, solicits the question of whether or not he advocates a phenomenological essentialism.

Some variant of the above question echoes as a constant refrain within the responses of several of Marion's critics. For example, Mark Dooley catalogs Marion's theory of the saturated phenomenon as one more failed attempt to construct an essentialist ontology of irreducible phenomena that, in turn, produces a "form of intuitive realism."[29] Such an account of a theory-less reality independent of any cultural-linguistic milieu and/or personal consciousness putatively supplies a *fundamentum inconcussum* of pure phenomenality; however, Dooley argues that such an epistemological foundationalism no longer finds purchase in a post-Kierkegaardian, postmodern world.[30] Dominique Janicaud concurs with Dooley and protests against what he considers Marion's apostasy from traditional Husserlian phenomenology when he discounts the phenomenological character of Marion's claim that one can detach "an unconditional principle-givenness-from the limits of every horizon."[31] Such a detachment results in "an autosufficiency (pure givenness 'gives *itself*'!) that restores *metaphysica specialis*—and its favorite trick, auto-foundation."[32] Consequently, Janicaud inquires as to whether Marion's third reduction and his idea of saturated phenomena do not reprise the idea of "a metaphysics of love" under a different alias.[33]

Christina Gschwandtner joins Janicaud in finding problematic Marion's preoccupation with identifying phenomena that are "given in pure and total appearance." She is particularly concerned with the effects of Marion's phenomenology of the unconditional on the nature of prayer. She contends that his theology of prayer parallels "his desire to formulate a radical phenomenology that presses experience to its purest form," which ideally converts phenomenology into a "pure, radical, and undetermined" first philosophy."[34] She considers this intent to result in a phenomenology of certainty, which she then finds troubling for a theology of prayer that seeks to escape the narcissistic. Joseph O'Leary applies something of the same dissension to Marion's theory of gift and its influence on a theology of grace. He fears that Marion's reduction to pure givenness produces an essentialism that undermines the reciprocal nature of grace as the foundation for relationship. In agreement with Gschwandtner, O'Leary considers that a residual Cartesian subjectivity haunts Marion's best efforts to escape the transcendental "I" and undermines his sincere intention to correlate giving and love. In the third reduction, gift functions "as a simple, universal ontological law," a function that, as a theology of grace, "seems to override the contributions of interpretation and faith."[35]

Finally, John Caputo inquires as to whether Marion's radical phenomenology is radical enough, given that it appears to allow for a theology of glory in which the eyes of faith may sporadically peek out from under their blindfold and catch a glimpse of a discrete and identifiable theophany.[36] Of course, Caputo certainly appreciates how Marion develops his phenomenology and does find pleasing much of what he sees when looking from Marion's perspective.[37] For example, he too accepts "love" as a central name for God, even going to the extreme of saying that the love of God, in both senses of that genitive, is the "Archimedean point" from which to define religion.[38] Furthermore, he joins Marion in speaking the idiom of "the impossible." He has no problem in accepting the saturated phenomenon as an "impossible experience," especially when that phenomenon is a theological "manifestation" of the love of God. On the other hand, Caputo would convert the word order and claim that loving God is not just an "impossible experience," but is an "experience of the impossible," a "passion for the impossible," even a movement "*by* the impossible."[39] Indeed, he considers the "passion for the impossible" to be synonymous with love—the love of the other as other, as wholly other, whether that other is God or some other person.[40] Caputo would also use this nomenclature to express Marion's contention that love is the *invisable*, that which cannot be the object of an aim or the source of an intentionality. He considers "the impossible" to be an expression of undecidability and unprogrammability,[41] to be both beyond the clairvoyance of any horizon of expectation and also a transcendent alterity that cannot be reduced to the self-sameness of an ego's gaze.[42] Loving God as a "passion for the impossible," then, requires the blindness and agnosticism of faith, what Caputo calls its *non voir* and *non savoir*—its not seeing and not knowing.[43]

Notwithstanding the areas of consonance, Caputo contends that Marion does not remain faithful to the *non* but eventually replaces it with the *avec*, for Marion concludes that the saturated phenomenon of divine *agape* does give a type of *hyperousiological* insight into the "God without Being." In other words, Caputo fears that Marion replaces faith with a functional dogmatism, which may not correct our spiritual vision to a 20/20 insight but does allow for an experience of God *avec voir* and *avec savoir*. As he "poetically" states it, "Marion will not go gladly into that dark night of non-appearance."[44] Claiming that God manifests Godself iconically in and as love, as the effulgence of pure givenness, and that we encounter this God in love, knowing God only through the surrender and trust that love evokes, does not extricate one from the confinement of conceptuality or the contextualization of a horizonal condition.[45] As Rama-Kandra tells Neo in *The Matrix Revolutions*, "love" is a *word*, and consequently, love is still a semiotic mediation vulnerable to the limitation, fragmentation, and uncertainty inherent in human knowledge. Caputo is simply pointing out linguistically that we "see" through a mirror darkly, even when we look at God through the eyes of love.

The preceding criticisms of Marion's third reduction to givenness and vocation are not without merit, and they are certainly not without foundation. Marion does, indeed, propose a pure and unconditional saturated intuition that gives itself *ohne warum*, without any preceding horizons or intentional structures and that results in a form of the visible "without reserve or retreat." The gift breaks into "broad daylight" with an "intuitive saturation" that "phenomenalizes itself of itself insofar as it shows itself as it gives itself," thereby becoming the "figure of all phenomenality."[46] There seems little room here for an agapic agnosticism or any sort of blindness. Yet when one considers the complexities of Marion's phenomenology, one discovers that it is not completely devoid of the uncertain and the agnostic. In other words, along with his prescription of the possibility of a bedazzling revelation, one that saturates intuition, that gives without why, and that illuminates a transparency of (in)-sight, one may also discern his affirmation of unknowability, of that which cannot be named, and of the systemic blindness that affects us as we see through the dark mirrors of faith and love.

One may confirm such a discernment by examining several ideas that function within the nuances of Marion's thought as arguments for agnosticism. First, Marion never relinquishes throughout the development of his thought the significance of distance, specifically as it relates to the relationship between God and humanity. In his early work *Idol and Distance*, he establishes what he terms the "advent of withdrawal," which he connects with the paternal imagery that Scripture uses for God. God as Father both proceeds toward humanity through the excess of revelation and also recedes from humanity as the unthinkable one (*ID* 138–40). The revelation of the divine name to Moses in Exodus 3:14 illustrates this "advent of withdrawal," in that Yahweh reveals the divine covenant name as nameless, as a name that is no name. Instead of a name with semantic content, God reveals a name that serves as a sign of the divine presence as beyond human thought and domination.[47] It is "the donation of the Name, whose unthinkability silently and overabundantly graces us at a complete distance."[48] Robyn Horner correctly traces the tenacity of this concept from *Idol and Distance*, through *God Without Being*, where it lies behind Marion's conceit to write the name of God *sous rature*, and up to the third reduction in *Reduction and Givenness*, where it informs the horizon of the call that constitutes subjectivity.[49] She demonstrates that Marion never compromises his belief that no phenomenology or theology can ever overcome the epistemic distance between God and humanity and, therefore, can ever speak of God with absolute certainty or clarity. Actually, Marion contends that it is this distance that lies behind the Apostle Paul's admonition that knowledge leads to arrogance, while love edifies (*ID* 145). Edifying love is not an issue of knowing as much as of being known; therefore, in love one embraces the unthinkable as a gift that "requires distance (as unthinkable), in order that participation be fortified in, and reinforce, the mystery of alterity" (*ID* 156). In summary, Marion's agapic agnosticism remains consistently Pauline, since he agrees with the apostle that one should seek "'to know the [*agape*] of the Christ which surpasses all knowledge' (Ephesians 3:19): charity goes further than knowledge" (*ID* 248).

The distance revealed as unrevealedness in the theophany to Moses also addresses the second argument for agapic agnosticism. Marion reprises this revelatory event in *Being Given* and interprets the nameless naming as an example of "the radical anonymity of what calls" (*BG* 297). When Moses responds to the vocation sounding forth from the burning bush, he does not know to whom he responds. Furthermore, even after God identifies Godself as Yahweh, the "I am who I am," Moses is not given full knowledge of the source of the summons. Marion contends that this uncertainty is not an ad hoc experience on Moses' part, but it actually characterizes the essence of the third reduction to the call that establishes every identity. The constituting call that establishes the "I" in the accusative of response perpetually comes as a surprise, as what disrupts and interrupts every horizon of expectation and transcends every intentional consciousness. That is to say, the source of the call remains anonymous as inherently unknowable.[50] Is the call from Being, from God, or, perhaps, from one's own projected conscience? Who knows? It cannot be known. The call just comes from somewhere and from someone, or something, who remains nameless as the source of the surprising summons, and I simply must respond to that anonymous call. Or, to state it otherwise, there is—*il y a, es gibt, cela donne* (it gives)—the call. Yet to translate the vocative reduction into the language of gift just accentuates the anonymity of the call. One may not—indeed, need not—know the identity of the giver in order to receive a gift. Actually, bracketing the personality of the giver results in establishing the gift *as such*, as beyond the restraints of the economic: "The giver acts perfectly because he disappears perfectly" (*BG* 94–97). This disappearance from sight becomes acutely significant when the issue of gift connects with the issue of love, because Marion insists that the only way "to recognize the giver without cognizing him" would be through the risk of love (*BG* 101). Consequently, Marion once again establishes grounds for an agapic agnosticism within the broader structures of his third reduction. Who calls? Who gives? *Je ne sais pas, il faut répondre-il faut recevoir.*

The third argument for agnosticism emerges out of Marion's elaborations on the intricacies of the saturated phenomenon. In a seminar held in 2003 at the Mater Dei Institute in Dublin, John O'Donohue asked Marion to respond to Meister Eckhart's "subversive" confession "God becomes and God unbecomes" as an expression of inescapable apophaticism. In his answer, Marion states categorically that no contradiction obtains between that statement and his notion of the saturated phenomenon because the excessive nature of such a phenomenon "may be felt and expressed as a disappointment." He insists that an "experience of disappointment means that I have an experience which I cannot understand, because I have no concept for it. . . . I am in the situation of making the encounter without having the possibility to understand it." He then actually concludes this explanation with a statement that sounds quite Derridean: "The saturated phenomenon doesn't mean that we are never in the experience of 'being in the desert' "[51] Interestingly enough, "desert" joins "aporia," "*khôra,*" and "*différance*" as a significant sign in Derrida's semantics of undecidability.[52] But as discussed above in relation to Marion's idea of the icon, undecidability signals the humility of finite knowledge, the wisdom that one can never have absolute certainty in this existence; consequently, one always decides out of undecidability, takes a risk in making choices, proceeds into a future that exists proleptically in the shadows of the inexact. In other words, with his "desert" imagery, Marion seems to be saying that the saturated phenomenon, in its very revelatory prodigality, exposes the individual to an experience of the *non savoir* implicit in undecidability.

Of course, for Derrida, undecidability serves as a quasi-transcendental grounding for the non-closure of hermeneutics, that is, as the *différance* that defers establishing a final and precise meaning.[53] Since Marion appears to acknowledge undecidability in his agnosticism of disappointment, the question remains as to whether he would also assent to an open process of interpretation vis-à-vis the saturated phenomenon. Richard Kearney broaches this very issue with him during an interview by suggesting that his notion that the saturated phenomenon occurs as transcendent to every horizon and beyond every intentionality of a knowing subject seems to quarantine such phenomena away from any hermeneutical contamination.[54] In other words, the saturated phenomenon seems to be a pure event that escapes the conflict of interpretations and justifies an absolutely precise meaning. In response, Marion insists that the excessive character of the saturated phenomenon, what he terms its "surplus of intuition," does not separate the phenomenon from hermeneutics but in reality demands an open-ended process of interpretation. He argues that "hermeneutics is generated when we witness an excess of information rather than its lack" and concludes that "hermeneutical investigation never completes its mission."[55] He relates this openness to the idea of revelation, contending that while one may claim that everything has been fully revealed, "we don't know, we can't know, how far it reaches."[56]

The inherent *non savoir* of revelation might well be illustrated by two Johannine references Marion makes regarding the complete knowledge of the divine. First, he relates the narrator's pronouncement in John 1:18 that "no one has seen God at any time" to Yahweh's prohibition in Exodus 33:23 that "My face cannot be seen." Marion states that the invisibility of God results not only from finitude's inability to bear the glory of the Infinite but also from the Infinite's inherent non-conceptualization. For him, it is not enough simply to assert that God remains God whether one knows the divine essence or not; he avows more decisively that God "remains God only on condition that this ignorance be established and admitted definitively." One must avoid the "idolatry of the concept" by which one deceives oneself into believing that God may be held within a determinate gaze. Marion believes that "the Revelation of God consists first of all in cleaning the slate of this illusion and its blasphemy."[57] Second, he also accepts the narrator's conclusion in John 21:15 that the world could not hold the books necessary to recount all of the acts of Jesus. As a saturated phenomenon of revelation, Jesus demands "a never definite plurality of horizons," which prohibits the world from ever fully comprehending the meaning of his message (*BG* 239). Implicit in these Johannine illustrations, therefore, may well be the answer to Marion's own rhetorical question: "If the *phenomenon* of revelation could be seen without lack, indeterminacy, or bedazzlement, would it be manifest more perfectly as phenomenon of *revelation* or, on the contrary, would it be disqualified?" (*BG* 244).

The above arguments for agnosticism bear directly on the topic of this essay, since Marion identifies the "experience of the Other, in love" to be "the experience of the saturated phenomenon par excellence."[58] All of the complementary concepts applicable to the saturated phenomenon—revelation, event, icon, gift, and vocation—coalesce in the theme of love. But as stated earlier in this essay, love, for Marion, cannot escape correspondence to faith. To be in love is to be confronted by the "silence of a gaze" that can be seen by no one but the lover. But when the beloved is God, that gaze initiates with the blindness of bedazzlement, especially the radiance of divine holiness (*BG* 204). Loving

God, therefore, accentuates the risk of surrendering one's gaze in love to the gaze of the other, a surrendering that Marion declares "requires faith" (PC 100–101). But if he remains consistent with his Pauline provenance, Marion must recognize that faith retains a certain blindness, which means, in turn, that love maintains an agapic agnosticism.

"What do I love when I love my God?" Caputo proclaims that the theology of undecidability comes to expression in this Augustinian/Derridean question. For him, it synopsizes the open question of faith, the constant inquest that we make as we make our way through the flux of existence. Caputo likes the words "God," "love," "justice," and other labels that serve as "the least bad" means for denominating what we love when we love our God, for naming our passion for the impossible, and perhaps even for naming God's love for us.[59] But who knows what exemplifies what? Do we love God, or justice, or gift, or love itself? But is this theology of undecidable love so far removed from Marion's theology of the saturated phenomenon? I think not. As argued above, Marion's theology of the gift also factors into experience a persistent *non savoir* whenever we attempt to comprehend and communicate what we interpret as encounters with the saturated phenomena of divine grace and love. Granted, Marion's agnosticism generates out of the *sous sature*, the *plerosis* of an excessive experience of revelation, whereas Caputo's finds root more in the desert, the *sous rature* of *kenosis*. Yet functionally, both agree that answering the question of what we love when we love God depends on a hermeneutical wager and not on absolute certainty.

Like postmodern "Timothys," both Marion and Caputo remain faithful to the Apostle Paul and his optics of belief: we walk—and love—by faith and not by sight. Who knows when one might stare into the depths of existence and for once, then, see something—perhaps something beyond, something more, something blurred?[60] Faith is a *hermeneusis*, a way of construing experience, an agnostic affirmation that, as we gaze into the abyss, we might "see" loving divine eyes gazing back. On the other hand, they may be only reflections or projections of our own eyes, mere hallucinations and optical illusions of hopeful souls. Who can say with any finality? Certainly, believing that one can see nothing is not equivalent to believing that there is nothing to see. So love consorts with invisibility and blindness, with faith and hope, with interpretation and agnosticism. Perhaps Caputo and Marion would both agree that in the end loving God is a *caritas quaerens intellectum*:

> What do I love when I love my God?
> *Je ne sais pas, il faut croire.*
> *Je ne vois pas, il faut aimer.*
> (I do not see; I must love.)

NOTES

1. Jacques Derrida, *Memoirs of the Blind: The Self-Portrait and Other Ruins,* trans. Pascale-Anne Brault and Michael Naas (Chicago: University of Chicago Press, 1993), 51.

2. Ibid., 49, 51.

3. Jean Baudrillard distinguishes between dissimulation and simulation as follows: "To dissimulate is to pretend not to have what one has. To simulate is to feign to have what one doesn't have. One implies a presence, the other an absence" (*Simulacra and Simulation*, trans. Sheila Faria Glaser [Ann Arbor: University of Michigan Press, 1994], 3).

4. Derrida, *Memoirs of the Blind*, 1, 129.

5. Slavoj Zizek, *The Puppet and the Dwarf: The Perverse Core of Christianity* (Cambridge: MIT Press, 2003), 115; *The Fragile Absolute: Or, Why Is the Christian Legacy Worth Fighting For?* (London: Verso, 2000), 147.

6. Jean-Luc Marion, *God Without Being: Hors-Texte*, trans. Thomas A. Carlson (Chicago: University of Chicago Press, 1991), xix. Hereafter in text as *GWB*.

7.   The only wisdom we can hope to acquire
       Is the wisdom of humility: humility is endless

The Four Quartets, "East Coker," lines 97–98.

8. Jean-Luc Marion, *Prolegomena to Charity*, trans. Stephen E. Lewis (New York: Fordham University Press, 2003), 71. Hereafter in text as *PC*.

9. Zizek, *The Puppet and the Dwarf*, 19.

10. Jean-Luc Marion, *Being Given: Toward a Phenomenology of Givenness*, trans. Jeffrey L. Kosky (Stanford: Stanford University Press, 2002), 203 (hereafter, *BG*); *PC* 85.

11. *BG* 232; *PC* 81. Marion's position here is quite similar to Derrida's investigation into the correlation between touch and sight in his encounter with Jean-Luc Nancy. When Derrida asks poetically what happens when eyes touch, he identifies the ocular touch with the intersecting look that hesitates "infinitely between the two Orients, between the visible eye (which it is therefore possible to touch) and the seeing eye (which is finally, essentially, absolutely untouchable)" (*On Touching—Jean-Luc Nancy*, trans. Christine Irizarry [Stanford, Calif.: Stanford University Press, 2005], 281). He further broaches the issue of the invisible gaze by asking, "When eyes meet-intensely, infinitely, up to the point of the abyss, plunging Narcissus into the chasm . . . is it day or is it night?" (306).

12. Jean-Luc Marion, *In Excess: Studies of Saturated Phenomena*, trans. Robyn Horner and Vincent Berraud (New York: Fordham University Press, 2002), 118.

13. Jean-Luc Marion, "The Final Appeal of the Subject," in *The Religious*, ed. John D. Caputo (Oxford: Blackwell, 2002), 137.

14. Kierkegaard introduces an interesting gloss on the relationship between love and blindness, specifically with reference to who the other of obligation truly is. For him, the obligation to love, to speak the *me voici*, comes not only from the other person but also ultimately from the Wholly Other as a divine commandment to love the neighbor (*Works of Love* [Princeton: Princeton University Press, 1995], 24–43). The "neighbor" signifies an equality of persons before God; that is, the commandment centers, not on the preferential loving of only the beloved or the friend, but on loving everyone equally on the basis of the individual's loving God first (60). Of course, Kierkegaard affirms that this commandment includes intrinsically what Jesus com-

mands extrinsically in the Sermon on the Mount, "Love your enemies," since the enemy is the neighbor from the perspective of the universal equality before God. He admits that loving an enemy seems impossible for human beings, since "enemies are hardly able to endure the *sight* of one another" (emphasis added). He suggests, therefore, that the individual *shut her eyes* so that the enemy will then look like the neighbor! As a result, "one sees the neighbor only with closed eyes, or by looking away from the dissimilarities" (68). So God obligates the individual to love in blindness, to close her eyes "to weakness and frailty and imperfection" in the other (163).

M. Jamie Ferreira addresses the apparent reduction to abstraction that Kierkegaard's blind love for the other might evoke. She indicates that one could infer from Kierkegaard's position that the other should not be recognized in her/his individuality and concreteness, that Jesus' commandments to love the neighbor and the enemy actually diminish both by interchanging each with every other other so as to deny the uniqueness of person (*Love's Grateful Striving: A Commentary on Kierkegaard's* Works of Love [New York: Oxford University Press, 2001], 54). She rejects such a misreading and insists that the blindness of equality that Kierkegaard prescribes seeks only to emphasize the universality and unconditionality of the commandments (56, 112–13).

Not surprisingly, Marion also regards love of enemy to be a particularly compelling instance of the gratuitous nature of love as gift. He acknowledges no better way to give love without expectation of return, without intention or aim to receive any compensation, than to give love to one who will not reciprocate it ("Sketch of a Phenomenological Concept of Gift," in *Postmodern Philosophy and Christian Thought*, ed. Merold Westphal [Bloomington: Indiana University Press, 1999], 138).

15. Jean-Luc Marion, "The Saturated Phenomenon," in *Phenomenology and the "Theological Turn": The French Debate*, trans. Bernard G. Prusak, Jeffrey L. Kosky, and Thomas A. Carlson (New York: Fordham University Press, 2000), 197.

16. Ibid., 184.

17. Ibid., 198, 209–10; *BG* 213.

18. Writing *sous rature*, under erasure, is a semiotic conceit that Marion borrows from Heidegger, who writes the word "Being" *kreuzeweise durchstreichung* (Beng). Marion applies it to the sign "God" (Gd) in order to avoid conceptual idolatry, that is, in order to signify that God cannot be manipulated by, or confined within, cognitive schemas. He claims that writing God in such a manner denotes that "the unthinkable enters into the field of our thought only by rendering itself unthinkable there by excess, that is, by criticizing our thought. To cross out Gd, in fact, indicates and recalls that Gd crosses out our thought because he saturates it" (*God Without Being*, 46). Obviously, therefore, Marion writes Gd *sous rature* as an expression of the saturated phenomenon of divine revelation; consequently, writing *sous rature* is another way of writing *sous sature*.

19. Jean-Luc Marion, *The Crossing of the Visible*, trans. James K. A. Smith (Stanford: Stanford University Press, 2004), 33. Hereafter in text as *CV*.

20. Marion, *In Excess*, 126–27.

21. Marion, *PC* 101; *In Excess*, 124.

22. Zizek, *The Puppet and the Dwarf*, 97–98.

23. Ibid., 110.

24. Marion, "The Saturated Phenomenon," 215.

25. See also *In Excess*, 113–19.

26. Jean-Luc Marion, *Idol and Distance: Five Studies*, trans. Thomas A. Carlson (New York: Fordham University Press, 2001), 157. Hereafter in text as *ID*.

27. Søren Kierkegaard, *Fear and Trembling/Repetition*, eds. Howard V. Hong and Edna H. Hong (Princeton: Princeton University Press, 1983), 66.

28. Jean-Luc Marion, "The Reason of the Gift," in *Givenness and God: Questions of Jean-Luc Marion*, eds. Ian Leask and Eoin Cassidy (New York: Fordham University Press, 2005), 134; *Reduction and Givenness: Investigations of Husserl, Heidegger, and Phenomenology*, trans. Thomas A. Carlson (Evanston: Northwestern University Press, 1998), 197–98; 204–205; *Being Given*, 197.

29. Mark Dooley, "Marion's Ambition of Transcendence," in *Givenness and God: Questions of Jean-Luc Marion*, ed. Ian Leask and Eoin Cassidy (New York: Fordham University Press, 2005), 190–92.

30. Ibid., 193.

31. Dominique Janicaud, *Phenomenology "Wide Open": After the French Debate*, trans. Charles N. Cabral (New York: Fordham University Press, 2005), 11.

32. Dominique Janicaud, *The Theological Turn in French Phenomenology*, in *Phenomenology and the "Theological Turn": The French Debate* (New York: Fordham University Press, 2000), 65.

33. Janicaud, *Phenomenology "Wide Open,"* 11. Along with this critique of a phenomenology *sans* horizons, Janicaud also casts suspicion on several other aspects of Marion's thought. First, he considers Marion's distinction between Revelation and revelation to be an untenable artifice (8). Second, he mistrusts Marion's semantics with reference to "givenness" (*donation*), the "*es gibt*" (*cela donné*), and "saturated." The first term may not be an adequate translation of Husserlian *Gegebenheit*; the second term conceptualizes as "it gives" what for Heidegger is a non-conceptual linguistic conceit; and the third term, which means "to sate," or "to fulfill," fails to translate the Cartesian notion of the Infinite, which means "that which surpasses" leaving in its trace a dissatisfaction (36–41).

34. Christina M. Gschwandtner, "Praise—Pure and Personal? Jean-Luc Marion's Phenomenologies of Prayer," in *The Phenomenology of Prayer*, ed. Bruce Ellis Benson and Norman Wirzba (New York: Fordham University Press, 2005), 176–77. Ironically, Gschwandtner criticizes Marion's third reduction to certainty because it disallows a kataphatic naming of God. Although an iconic experience of God through the liturgy might be pure and certain, no language can express that experience; consequently, prayer predicates nothing *of* God but only directing the individual's egocentric attention *to* God (168–69). Although Gschwandtner does take Marion to task for proscribing a communal context for prayer, she does appreciate that he preempts the egocentric with reference to love, which she says he connects to "a kind of loss of consciousness that gives itself to another in reciprocal vulnerability" (179). Indeed, she agrees with the basic thesis of this essay that Marion's theology of love never escapes invisibility.

35. Joseph S. O'Leary, "The Gift: Trojan Horse in the Citadel of Phenomenology?" in *Givenness and God*, 135–36, 141, 148.

36. John D. Caputo, "Apostles of the Impossible," in *God, the Gift, and Postmodernism*, ed. John D. Caputo and Michael J. Scanlon (Bloomington: Indiana University Press, 1999), 209. Caputo takes seriously the Lutheran polarity between a "theology of glory" and a "theology of the cross," personally identifying with the latter. The former results in a triumphalism of rationality and human cognition in that it holds to the possibility of a clear and distinct understanding of God by an analogy of Being or a transparency of experience. Conversely, the theology of the cross results in a knowledge of God "*per contraria*," through the "backward" routes of foolishness, weakness, and a certain "kingdom of God" madness. As Caputo states it, knowledge through the cross is

"something that is neither visible to the senses nor understandable to reason but that is accessible only to faith." Consequently, a genuine Christian theologian "relies not on reason but faith and . . . proceeds not from the visible manifestations of God's glory but from the scenes of ignominy and distress that beset the human condition under which God has paradoxically revealed himself precisely by concealing himself from human wisdom" ("Toward a Postmodern Theology of the Cross," in *Postmodern Philosophy and Christian Thought*, 212–13).

37. B. Keith Putt, "What Do I Love When I Love My God? An Interview with John D. Caputo," in *Religion With/Out Religion: The Prayers and Tears of John D. Caputo*, ed. James H. Olthuis (New York: Routledge, 2002), 162–63, 176–77.

38. John D. Caputo, *On Religion* (New York: Routledge, 2001), 5.

39. John D. Caputo, *Deconstruction in a Nutshell: A Conversation with Jacques Derrida* (New York: Fordham University Press, 1997), 145; *The Prayers and Tears of Jacques Derrida: Religion Without Religion* (Bloomington: Indiana University Press, 1997), 332; *More Radical Hermeneutics: On Not Knowing Who We Are* (Bloomington: Indiana University Press, 2000), 263.

40. Caputo, *Prayers and Tears*, 49.

41. One should not confuse undecidability with indecisiveness, since the former does not mean the *inability* to make a decision but the *necessity* in having to make one (*Deconstruction in a Nutshell*, 137). Undecidability means "that our lives are marked by a radical, structural inability to settle archi-questions, even as it insists on keeping them alive, which is what the name of God means for Derrida" (*More Radical Hermeneutics*, 262).

42. Caputo illustrates this point with the Markan narrative of the widow's irrational and immoderate gift of her entire "fortune" to the temple coffers, an appropriate example, given that he identifies the "pure gift" as such as "how *the* impossible happens" (*Prayers and Tears*, 160). The widow's gift shatters "the horizon of expectation" as something "unplannable and unforeseeable" (ibid., 176). It also reveals a dispossession of self-love, a sacrifice of her own well-being for the sake of the "other." He claims that she gives *ohne warum*, without why, without calculating any reciprocal economy of self benefit. Her gift is a gift, not an investment, the madness of an "expenditure without reserve" (ibid., 203). He concludes that this story of a non-conditional and non-reductive giving reminds him of one of his favorite Augustinian apothegms: "*delige, et quod vis fac*"—"love and do what you will" (ibid., 177).

43. Caputo considers Derrida's "faith without religion" to be a performative, not a constative. It seeks not so much to describe the truth of faith according to a dogmatic or systematic structure as to prescribe faith as *facere veritatem*, a doing of the truth. Consequently, faith does not focus on religious visions or revelations; instead, it is "*sans vision, sans verité, sans révelation*" (*Deconstruction in a Nutshell*, 166). Or, as he restates it in *More Radical Hermeneutics*, Derrida's faith is in the "name of what throws everything into bottomless questionability, and beyond questioning, the name of what we desire and love without question, *sans voir, sans avoir, sans savoir*" (263). Cf. also Caputo, *Prayers and Tears*, 332.

44. Caputo, "Apostles of the Impossible," 210.

45. John D. Caputo, "How to Avoid Speaking of God: The Violence of Natural Theology," in *The Prospects for Natural Theology*, ed. Eugene Long (Washington, D.C.: Catholic University of American Press, 1992), 135–36.

46. Marion, "The Reason of the Gift," 116, 129–31.

47. On the basis of the distance revealed in the nameless naming of God, Marion

advocates a theological linguistics of "de-nomination." Our attempts to name God must always de-nominate God by "saying (affirming negatively) and undoing this saying of the name" ("In the Name: How to Avoid Speaking of 'Negative Theology,'" in *God, the Gift, and Postmodernism*, ed. John D. Caputo and Michael J. Scanlon [Bloomington: Indiana University Press, 1999], 27). Ultimately, this de-nomination leads theology to privilege the *lex orandi* that governs hymnic language, accentuating the more performative language of prayer and praise over the constative language of predication; consequently, naming gives way to "aiming," as "in the direction of . . . , of relating to . . . , of comporting oneself towards" (30).

48. Ibid., 143.

49. Robyn Horner, *Rethinking God As Gift: Marion, Derrida, and the Limits of Phenomenology* (New York: Fordham University Press, 2001), 107–108. Cf. also her *Jean-Luc Marion: A Theo-logical Introduction* (Aldershot: Ashgate, 2005), 51–60.

50. Marion, *Reduction and Givenness*, 201–202.

51. Jean-Luc Marion and Richard Kearney, "Giving More," in *Givenness and God*, 246–47.

52. Cf. Jacques Derrida, *On the Name*, ed. Thomas Dutoit, trans. David Wood, John P. Leavey, and Ian McLeod (Stanford, Calif.: Stanford University Press, 1995), 53; *The Specters of Marx: The State of the Debt, the Work of Mourning, & the New International*, trans. Peggy Kamuf (New York: Routledge, 1994), 90; *Writing and Difference*, trans. Alan Bass (Chicago: University of Chicago Press, 1978), 82.

53. Cf. Jacques Derrida, *Positions*, trans. Alan Bass (Chicago: University of Chicago Press, 1981), 8.

54. Jean-Luc Marion, "The Hermeneutics of Revelation," in *Debates in Continental Philosophy: Conversations with Contemporary Thinkers*, ed. Richard Kearney (New York: Fordham University Press, 2004), 15.

55. Ibid., 16.

56. Ibid., 21.

57. Marion, "In the Name," 34.

58. Marion and Kearney, "Giving More," 252–53.

59. Caputo insists on the "endless substitutability and translatability" of the name "God" (*Prayers and Tears*, 52). In other words, "God" is a sign among many signs that may name what we love when we love God, or that may reference the object of our passing for the impossible. He contends that we only traffic in the "least bad names we have, names for the conditioned, empirical counterparts of something unforeseeable, unconditional, and nameless" (*The Weakness of God*, 294). See also *On Religion*, 26, and *Deconstruction in a Nutshell*, 173.

60. Others taunt me with having knelt at well-curbs
    Always wrong to the light, so never seeing
    Deeper down in the well than where the water
    Gives me back in a shining surface picture
    Me myself in the summer heaven, godlike
    Looking out of a wreath of fern and cloud puffs.
    Once, when trying with chin against a well-curb,
    I discerned, as I thought, beyond the picture,
    Through the picture, a something white, uncertain,
    Something more of the depths—and then I lost it.

Water came to rebuke the too clear water.
One drop fell from a fern, and lo, a ripple
Shook whatever it was lay there at bottom,
Blurred it, blotted it out. What was that whiteness?
Truth? A pebble of quartz? For once, then, something.

Robert Frost, "For Once, Then, Something"

9

Absence Makes the Heart Grow Fonder

BRIAN TREANOR

For one being to love another: that is perhaps the most difficult of all our tasks, the ultimate, the last test and proof, the work for which all other work is but preparation.

—Rainer Maria Rilke, *Letters to a Young Poet*

Postmodern philosophy has a curiously schizophrenic relationship with love, and nowhere is this more the case than in postmodern thought at the intersection of philosophy and theology. On the one hand, postmodern thinkers return to the theme of love again and again. For example, Emmanuel Levinas asserts, "From the start, the encounter with the Other is my responsibility for him. That is the responsibility for my neighbor, which is, no doubt, the harsh name for what we call love of one's neighbor."[1] Likewise, deconstruction has turned out to be a philosophy of love, for Derrida "loves the impossible."[2] In fact, deconstruction "never proceeds without love."[3] However, on the other hand, postmodernity exhibits a surprising suspicion of love. Levinas concludes the passage just cited by stating, in seeming frustration, "I don't very much like the word love."[4] And, despite his many direct and indirect references to love, Derrida claims at one point, with similar frustration, "I have nothing to say about love."[5]

The conflicted relationship with love that characterizes postmodernity in general and deconstruction more specifically is the result of postmodern assumptions about the otherness of the other. Deconstruction serves as useful focal point for our inquiry insofar as it represents the culmination of a certain philosophy of otherness. If Levinas instituted the emphasis on the absolute otherness of the other in Continental thought, Derrida carried it to its logical conclusion. The movement from Levinas's "other with an alterity constitutive of the very content of the other" to the Derridian claim that *tout autre est tout autre* ("every other is wholly other"), is not surprising.[6] Indeed, this development seems inevitable if the otherness of the other is absolute. However, the characterization of otherness in absolute, all-or-nothing terms places deconstruction—especially the religious reading of deconstruction—in an awkward position. Deconstruction is all about love; but paradoxically, deconstruction does not love.

"You must therefore be perfect . . ."

In the United States, it is not uncommon to think of love in terms that are overtly, if unreflectively, Christian. I have been to weddings where Paul's Letter to the Corinthians—"Love is always patient and kind; love is never jealous or conceited" (1 Corinthians 13:4)—was part of a ceremony uniting agnostic or even avowedly atheist couples. However, few Americans, secular or Christian, seriously consider the full implication of subscribing to a Christian view of love. Love, especially as articulated in Judeo-Christian terms, is an incredibly demanding standard, which calls us to a difficult, perhaps impossible, task.

> One of the scribes came up and heard them disputing with one another, and seeing that he answered them well, asked him, "Which commandment is the first of all?" Jesus answered, "The first is, 'Hear, O Israel: The Lord our God, the Lord is one; and you shall love the Lord your God with all your heart, and with all your soul, and with all your mind, and with all your strength.' The second is this, 'You shall love your neighbor as yourself.' There is no other commandment greater than these." (Mark 12:28–32)[7]

This bifurcated first commandment calls us to love God and other people; and the hyperbole that marks an affinity between deconstruction and Christian theology is already evident in these two injunctions. The command to love one's neighbor as one loves oneself is, as we all know, difficult to say the least; but this command is complicated by its pairing with another imperative directing us to love God, not our neighbor or ourselves, with *all* our heart, soul, mind, and strength.[8]

Although loving God and loving our neighbors are challenging, one might argue that these loves are nevertheless relatively natural. However, the demands of love are not satisfied with these "easy" loves. Christ's Sermon on the Mount ratchets up the demand of love to a fever pitch where love of one's neighbor becomes love of one's enemies and persecutors. "You have heard that it was said, 'You shall love your neighbor and hate your enemy.' But I say to you, Love your enemies and pray for those who persecute you" (Matt 5:43–47). To love those who hate, persecute, torture, or kill us requires an almost unimaginable degree of charity. In response to this demand, Derrida points out that the Sermon on the Mount hinges on the notion of "a love without reserve."[9] Love our enemies? Without reserve? Is this possible?

The commands to love God with all one's focus, to love one's neighbor as one loves oneself, and to love one's enemies are progressively more difficult, more demanding, and certainly border on impossibility. However, the prophetic hyperbole that characterizes the Sermon on the Mount ends with an aporetic demand that puts to rest any hope that we might satisfy the demands of love: "You must therefore be perfect, just as your heavenly Father is perfect" (Matt 5:48). "*Perfect*"? Well then, we might as well throw in the towel. Perfection is not possible; indeed, it seems to run contrary to an enormous tradition that emphasizes coming to terms with human imperfection. The Christian view of love, far from the easy congeniality and pleasantries of Sunday school caricatures, requires an almost incomprehensible level of charity and sacrifice. Indeed, we are called to a love in a manner in which we are incapable of loving—such love is impossible.[10]

"O my love, there is no love."

However, if Christian love is, strictly speaking, impossible, it should offer us one of the best examples of the sort of "pure," hyperbolic, and aporetic relationship with which postmodernity is fascinated. Nevertheless, deconstruction remains suspicious of love. Why? At the heart of deconstruction is the desire for difference or otherness, which, following Levinas, it construes in terms of absolute alterity.[11] "Deconstruction . . . is the thought, if it is a thought, of an absolute heterogeneity that unsettles all the assurances of the same within which we comfortably ensconce ourselves."[12] The relationship to absolute otherness is, again following Levinas, construed in terms of desire. Deconstruction is a "passion" for the impossible (*tout autre*), for something new, something other than what is present and accounted for. Derrida tells us that he never loved anything but the impossible.[13] However, desire for absolute heterogeneity comes with a substantial challenge: the *tout autre* is by definition always *a-venir*, never present, hoped for but unforeseen, which is why otherness is characterized as "impossible."[14] For deconstruction, "love . . . is [the] infinite renunciation which somehow *surrenders to the impossible* [*se rend à l'impossible*]."[15] However, the object of such love never arrives; toward the loved other, we can say nothing but "*Oui, viens!*"

The upshot of this radical openness is that deconstruction loves the other, "no matter whom."[16] Because deconstructive love is directed toward the *tout autre*, toward "I know not what," it resolutely refuses to fix in any way the object of its desire. To love the other is to surrender to otherness, to be open to all others without question and without reservation. All others are accepted with the same generous, hospitable love. And here we have the remarkable parallel between deconstruction and Christianity: to love means to *love without regard,* to love one's neighbors as one loves oneself, to love the "widow, orphan, and stranger," one's enemies, one's persecutors, and the wicked, as well as one's neighbors.

In fact, the history of Christianity—which includes excommunications, wars, persecutions, and inquisitions—has led some to point out that deconstruction is in some sense *more* thoroughly loving than many determinate religions. At the very least it seems likely that deconstruction's passion for the *tout autre* guards against the perversions of love that have characterized much of Christianity's history. Its relentless focus on the other as *tout autre* keeps love "safe from Hegelian and from Christian blackmail," which all too frequently tend to love as a "common (*com*) defense (*munis*) against the other."[17] That is, to love one's neighbor at the expense of the stranger, who is repulsed, excluded, exiled, stripped, or killed.[18]

However, a Christian account cannot easily come to terms with an absolute vision of otherness. For Christianity, otherness is never really absolute. After all, God, the other par excellence, "emptied himself, taking the form of a slave, becoming as human beings are; and being in every way like a human being . . ." (Phil 2:7). As Kierkegaard—who is generally thought of as an ally of the religious reading of deconstruction—notes, there can be no communication with absolute otherness. Communication requires a measure of equality, which in this case is brought about by the willingness of God to become human. "It is indeed less terrifying to fall upon one's face while the mountains tremble at the god's voice than to sit with him as his equal, and yet the god's concern is precisely to sit this way."[19] God, of course, does not need us, so such a debasement could only take place through God's love. "Only in love is the different made equal, and only in equality or unity is there understanding."[20] If even God is not absolutely other, then otherness is always relative. However, from the perspective of deconstruction, this relative view of otherness leads, predictably, to a desire for communion and an emphasis on similarity rather than difference. The Christian account (as well as other accounts based on a relative notion of otherness) leans sharply toward "the side of the same," while deconstructive love leans sharply toward "the side of the other."[21] Christianity, no doubt influenced by Neoplatonism, is far too willing to think of love in terms of proximity, intimacy, contact, and union.[22]

"Don't *love* me; *respect* me"

Thus, deconstruction remains understandably suspicious of love in the Christian tradition, precisely because of the many ways in which Christians have failed to love over the past 2000 years. Love is dangerous, and is fully capable of leading to both domination (loving one's idea of the other rather than the other herself) and exclusion (preference for the loved other at the expense of other others). In order to avoid these degradations, deconstruction demands a rigorous attention to the otherness of the other—*tout autre est tout autre*—which has a dramatic effect on how deconstruction thinks of love. On this view, love is not about understanding or intimacy, but about maintaining distance and difference.

> Love . . . *surrenders to the impossible* [*se rend à l'impossible*]. To surrender to the other, and this is the impossible, would amount to giving oneself over in going toward the other, to coming toward the other but without crossing the threshold, and to respecting, to loving even the invisibility that keeps the other inaccessible.[23]

Love is about difference, distance, and respect—terms normally associated with justice rather than love—as opposed to understanding or intimacy; it is unwilling to trespass on the otherness of the other in the name of a comfortable fusion of horizons or a romantic ideal.

Efforts to close the distance that separates the self from the other in the name of love are characterized as fundamentally violent; and so, for philosophers of absolute otherness, the archetypal intersubjective relationship is justice, which respects distance, not love, which desires to traverse it. Or, put another way, such philosophers construe love in terms of preserving the otherness of the other, which is in many ways remarkably similar to the disinterestedness associated with justice. Love *is* responsibility (Levinas) or love *is* justice (Derrida). This preference for justice is quite clear in the work of Levinas: "*Socialité première: le rapport personnel est dans la rigueur de la justice qui me juge et non pas dans l'amour qui m'excuse.*"[24] Likewise, one of Derrida's most direct treatments of love (as *philia*) is a book about politics (i.e., justice). For deconstruction, love is a gesture of sorts toward "I know not what," an unconditional openness or welcoming. However, because the *tout autre* is always *a-venir*, in our relationships with actual other persons love has *already* been compromised or betrayed.[25] All we can do is remind ourselves of the hyperbolic and always-already betrayed demand of "pure" love in order to minimize the violence (thematization) and exclusion (of other others) inherent in all actual intersubjective relationships. While we hope for love, the best we can expect is justice.

(Some) Absence Makes the Heart Grow Fonder

Clearly, these two accounts of love rest, ultimately, on two different understandings of otherness itself: absolute and relative. The upshot of the relative view of otherness that characterizes Christianity, as well as certain hermeneutic philosophies, is that it leads to relationships in which there is some hope for "better" understanding of the other. However, it must be acknowledged that a relative view of otherness is also open to all sorts of perversions and abuses. An absolute, all-or-nothing view of otherness would avoid some of these problems, because the other qua other is always beyond the grasp of the same and so cannot be limited or restricted. However, while philosophies of love based on a relative understanding of otherness are shot through with assumptions that may lead to domination and exclusion, the deconstructive account of love is not without significant problems of its own.

Deconstruction "loves the impossible," and this does constitute a passion of sorts. However, because the *tout autre* is always *a-venir*, deconstruction's love is something like holding a place at the table for an unknown guest whose arrival is *infinitely* deferred.[26] If the guest ever arrives, she is no longer wholly other and thus no longer the object of deconstruction's love. I love otherness when the other is not present, when she is unknown; however, as soon as the other is present, she is no longer *tout autre* and thus, strictly speaking, no longer the object of my love. Deconstruction loves the other "no matter whom" but only when "no matter whom." As Dostoevsky points out, it can be the case that "the more I love mankind in general, the less I love people in particular."[27] Or, in the case of deconstruction, to love others generally—or better yet love otherness itself—while failing to love any particular other. But surely this is problematic.

> Those who say, "I love God" [the *tout autre* if there is one], and hate their brothers or sisters are liars; for those who do not love a brother or sister whom they have seen, cannot love God whom they have not seen. The commandment we have from him is this: those who love God must love their brothers and sisters also. (1 John 4:20–21)

The Judeo-Christian retort to deconstruction's love of otherness is that one cannot love otherness without loving actual others in the specificity and particularity of their *haecceitas*. We cannot love the *tout autre* without loving particular others. Deconstruction loves everyone (no matter whom) but paradoxically loves no one. Or again, it desires to love all others, but fails to love any particular other. Although it has been argued that deconstruction is concerned precisely with the *haecceitas* of the other—the "proper name" of the "singular event," the "*effanineffables*"—rather than universals or generalities, this point is made in the context of justice, not love.[28] Deconstruction uses "love" either as synonym for justice or as a name for the passion for *the* impossible, which is always *a-venir*, not for the *haeccitas* of the concrete other here before me. In either case, deconstructive love is at pains to accentuate the distance and difference of the other, viewing any intimacy in terms of violence of one sort or another. "O my love, there is no love."[29]

In another way, we might say that deconstruction loves *love* but does not love others. However, being "in love with love" is subject to numerous pitfalls, as Augustine chronicles in his *Confessions*. It is not enough to passionately desire something, which can often lead to very unloving relationships. We must passionately desire in the right way. People in love with love love the novelty of love, the newness and freshness of something unfamiliar. However, this is problematic in terms of fidelity. One in love with love may find it difficult, perhaps impossible, to undertake the hard work of fidelity, rushing from one position—religious, political, ethical, or romantic—to another with alarming ease and frequency. The positive spin on such behavior is that it remains "open to everything." However, another view might note that because such people remain committed to nothing other than the willingness to remain open to new perspectives, they run the risk of changing perspectives haphazardly. And those who do shift perspectives with such fluidity and frequency never really understand anything about any of the perspectives they inhabit—their experience never penetrates the surface toward any deeper understanding. It should go without saying that remaining flexible and open are an essential virtues that stem from an admirable desire not to close off discourse, but such flexibility must have limits. Remaining open is virtuous, but being open to anything is not the same thing. Real love endures beyond the heady upheaval of infatuation or the exigence, feeble or urgent, for something new (i.e., other). Surely there is an Aristotelian mean to be found here.

Deconstruction's willingness to forego an account of loving particular others out of a desire to avoid the debased forms into which such love is capable of falling is not unlike an epistemological proclivity noted by William James. While James agrees that truth (in this case understanding of an other that would in some way mitigate the claim that *tout autre est tout autre*) is a moving target subject to reevaluation and revision, he also makes an important distinction between two epistemological impulses: avoiding error and seeking truth.

> There are two ways of looking at our duty in the matter of opinion,—ways entirely different, and yet ways about whose difference the theory of knowledge seems hitherto to have shown very little concern. *We must have the truth*; and *we must avoid error*.—these are our first and great commandments as would-be knowers; but they are not two ways of stating an identical commandment, they are two separable laws. Although it may indeed happen that when we believe the truth A, we escape as an incidental consequence from believing the falsehood B, it hardly ever happens that by merely disbelieving B we necessarily believe A.[30]

The trouble with fueling one's deconstructive or pragmatic skepticism with the impulse to avoid error rather than the impulse to seek truth is simply that it will not get you anywhere. Skepticism is useful, even essential; however, elevated to the level of first commandment it tends to be something of a nonstarter. Seeking only to avoid error, we will never find truth, and seeking only to avoid debased forms of love, we will never love.

So it seems that relative accounts of otherness run the risk of domination and exclusion, and absolute accounts of otherness, while avoiding these dangers, fall short in terms of applicability. The problem here lies in two unacceptable accounts of otherness. The solution lies in a rehabilitated notion of relative otherness, one that takes seriously the critique and the valid concerns of philosophies of absolute otherness, but that does so without lapsing into the ultimately unnecessary hyperbole of absolute otherness. At this point, we can offer only the briefest indication of how such an account might proceed.[31]

First, otherness cannot be simply relative. We must acknowledge and affirm the irreducible alterity of every other. Emmanuel Levinas, Jacques Derrida, John D. Caputo, and other postmodern philosophers have made this point well. To rehearse their critiques of relative alterity in the tradition is neither possible nor necessary in this context. Suffice it to say that without real alterity there is no other, and without otherness there is no love.

Second, however, otherness cannot be absolute. Any other with whom we have, or could have, a relationship—any other we might love—cannot be absolutely other. If there is such a thing as an other that is wholly, absolutely other, we would not know about it either directly or indirectly. Absolute otherness cannot surprise us, or jolt us out of economic existence, or call us into question, or question the naïve spontaneity of freedom, or found freedom, or found discourse, or any other such thing because otherness qua absolute otherness cannot be encountered, experienced, or revealed. Absolute otherness, being absolutely incommensurable with the world in which we perceive and think, would not register on our radar screens, so to speak, not even as a "trace." Being absolutely unaware of such an absolute other, we would not love it (as God) or fear it (as in the nocturnal menace of the *il y a*). We would not be called into question by its vulnerability or challenged by the "undecidability" of it. Moreover, we would not write philosophy books, even under erasure, or hold philosophical conferences about it, even to speak negatively or to unsay what we have said. *Absolute* otherness can communicate nothing, not even its own alterity. Beyond the God of apophatic theology, beyond the impossible of Derrida's deconstruction, otherness that is wholly, absolutely other is something that would go absolutely unnoticed, unmentioned, and unthought.[32]

Even when we desire "otherness," even when we cannot name that for which we hope and resign ourselves to hoping for "we know not what," our desire is not for absolute otherness. Imagine the person beset with nonspecific, existential angst, or with a sort of global malaise or ennui. Or indeed, imagine a person filled with a passion for God, or justice, or any of the other examples of the impossible to which philosophies of absolute otherness resort. Such a person may well desire something unexpected or novel to come and shake things up. However, this is not a desire for absolute otherness, for the person in question desires a change in *her* situation, that is, a change within the world she inhabits.[33] And a change in the world one inhabits is not an encounter with absolute otherness but with relative otherness, that is, with aspects of alterity imbedded in, or interwoven with, aspects of similitude.

In order to offer an alternative in the entrenched debate between absolute

and relative otherness, we must distinguish between relative otherness as traditionally construed and relative otherness construed in hermeneutic-chiastic
terms. Relative otherness need not imply that the otherness of the other is
relative to me in the sense that it is determined by me or must conform to a
system I have created. Otherness is precisely that which does not conform to
my system. The point is rather that the otherness of the other is not complete
or absolute; therefore, it might be helpful to think of relative otherness in terms
of non-absolute otherness. Rejecting an all-or-nothing account of otherness,
the hermeneutic-chiastic position maintains that, while there may be some
aspects of the other that are foreign and even absolutely obscure to the self,
these aspects exist alongside others that are in some measure familiar.

It may help to differentiate between "otherness" and "alterity" when con-
trasting each with "similitude." Similitude is that aspect of things, and others,
that is in some way familiar or understandable. On the most basic level, this
means that any other that I encounter appears or manifests itself in some
determinate way. Alterity is that aspect of things, and others, that is unfamiliar,
alien, or obscure. There are always aspects of any other to which I have no
clear or direct access. Indeed, there may be aspects to which I have no access at
all. Otherness, then, is the chiastic relationship of alterity and similitude.
Thus, qua alterity, the other is that which can reveal or bring about something
new and unforeseen; however, qua similitude, the other is also susceptible to
some measure, imperfect though it may be, of understanding. No other is
wholly, absolutely other because any other with which or with whom we are in
relationship is both other-qua-alterity and other-qua-similitude. Neither alterity nor similitude actually exists independently. No other whom we experience or to whom we relate is either completely foreign or perfectly intelligible.
Alterity and similitude are always encountered together as aspects of otherness,
the otherness in ourselves or the otherness of the other.[34]

Advocates will argue that deconstruction rejects the notion of "pure" or
"perfect" love (or giving, or hospitality, etc.) in the name of affirming actual,
imperfect loves (or gifts, or acts of hospitality). However, if this is the case, it
does so in an exceedingly awkward manner. While it is true that the initial
point is often that the "pure" relationship is impossible, the language is such
that the skepticism and critique inevitably bleed into even the impure, imperfect manifestations of the relationship in question. Moreover, if the deconstructive point was merely to deny that the pure relationship to the other is
possible, it is not clear why the language of absolute otherness is necessary for
this task. A hermeneutic-chiastic account of otherness agrees that perfection
(as perfect love, or perfect understanding of the other) is impossible, but does
so without resorting to excessively hyperbolic language that argues or implies
that anything short of perfection is equally flawed. Not all actual loves are
equally imperfect. Or, stated positively, some loves are better than others.
Likewise, some gifts are more selfless than others, some examples of hospitality

are more genuine than others, some instances of forgiveness are more sincere than others, and some examples of understanding an other are better than others—and, in each case, only a relative account of otherness will allow us to make this judgment.

So the hermeneutic-chiastic account of otherness can be circumscribed by two claims. First, every other is truly other; that is, every other is marked by an irreducible alterity. Second, this element of alterity notwithstanding, no other is wholly other. We love both that we have come to understand someone or something better—in both the veridical and ethical senses—and that there is an inexhaustible measure of alterity which we do not understand. An other who is absolutely other is an other with whom no relationship is possible, and a relationship with an other who is not genuinely other is nothing more than a relationship with an idea of the other. Absence makes the heart grow fonder, but complete absence leaves us with nothing of which we are fond (other than the absence itself). What is called for is a hermeneutic-chiastic account of otherness that views every other as a crossing of alterity and similitude. Every other is genuinely other, but no other—no other we relate to or love—is wholly other.

NOTES

1. Emmanuel Levinas, *Entre Nous: Thinking of the Other*, trans. Michael B. Smith and Barbara Harshav (New York: Columbia University Press, 1998), 103.

2. "Circumfession," in Geoffrey Bennington and Jacques Derrida, *Jacques Derrida*, trans. Geoffrey Bennington (Chicago: University of Chicago Press, 1993), 3. John D. Caputo's *The Prayers and Tears of Jacques Derrida: Religion without Religion* (Bloomington: Indiana University Press, 1997) offers the clearest and most persuasive reading of deconstruction as religious and loving.

3. Jacques Derrida, "The Almost Nothing of the Unrepresentable," in *Points . . . Interviews, 1974–1994*, ed. Elisabeth Weber, trans. Peggy Kaumf (Stanford, Calif.: Stanford University Press, 1995), 83.

4. Levinas, *Entre Nous*, 103.

5. *Derrida* (Jane Doe Films, 2002). See note 25 below regarding this and other references to this film.

6. Emmanuel Levinas, *Totality and Infinity: An Essay on Exteriority*, trans. Alphonso Lingis (Pittsburgh: Duquesne University Press, 1969), 39; and Jacques Derrida, *Sauf le nom*, in *On the Name*, trans. David Wood, John P. Leavy Jr., and Ian McLeod (Stanford, Calif.: Stanford University Press, 1995), 74.

7. A similar tension is found in the Jewish tradition, where we find "You shall love the Lord your God with all your heart, and with all your soul, and will all your might" (Deut 6:5), as well as the wonderful story of Rabbi Hillel who, when challenged by someone who promised to convert if he could be taught the entire Torah while the Rabbi stood on one leg, lifted his leg and said "What is hateful to you, do not do to your friend. This is the entire Torah; the rest is interpretation, which you must go and learn" (Babylonian Talmud, *Shabbat*, 31A). Paul's letters to the Galatians and Corinthians echo this sentiment: "My brothers, you were called, as you know, to liberty; but be

careful, or this liberty will provide an opening for self-indulgence. Serve one another, rather, in works of love, since the whole of the Law is summarized in a single command: Love your neighbor as yourself" (Gal 5: 13–14). Also, in the course of enumerating the spiritual gifts, Paul writes: "So faith, hope, love abide, these three; but the greatest of these is love" (1 Cor 13:13).

8. See my *"Plus de Secret:* The Paradox of Prayer," in *The Phenomenology of Prayer,* ed. Bruce Ellis Benson and Norman Wirzba (New York: Fordham University Press, 2005).

9. Jacques Derrida, *The Gift of Death,* trans. David Wills (Chicago: University of Chicago Press, 1995), 97.

10. Of course, one might argue that human imperfection can be perfected through God's grace, as in the case of Augustine's conversion in the garden. See Augustine, *Confessions,* trans. Henry Chadwick (Oxford: Oxford University Press, 1991), 149–54.

11. Deconstruction follows Levinas but surpasses him as well. Although postmodern philosophy tends to think of otherness in absolute, all-or-nothing terms, deconstruction has further hyperbolized Levinas's position, as we noted above. Thus, while both Levinas and Derrida think of otherness in absolute terms, from the Derridian perspective Levinas fails to follow through his insight regarding the *absolute* otherness of the other. See, for example, Caputo, *Prayers and Tears,* 20–26.

12. Caputo, *Prayers and Tears,* 5.

13. Derrida, "Circumfession," 3.

14. *The* impossible is not impossible *simpliciter,* "the non-sense of something absolutely absolute" (Caputo, *Prayers and Tears,* 23); however, the *tout autre,* as *the* impossible, is infinitely deferred and never arrives. This has significant import for a philosophy of love based on an absolute conception of otherness.

15. Derrida, *Sauf le nom,* 74

16. Ibid.

17. Caputo, *Prayers and Tears,* 248.

18. See Levinas, *Totality and Infinity,* 82.

19. Søren Kierkegaard, *Philosophical Fragments,* trans. Howard V. Hong and Edna H. Hong (Princeton, N.J.: Princeton University Press, 1985), 35.

20. Ibid., 25.

21. The image of "leaning toward" the side of the same or the other is actually employed by Derrida in the context of discussing Cicero (and deconstruction) on the topic of friendship. See Jacques Derrida, *The Politics of Friendship,* trans. George Collins (London: Verso, 1997), 4. Nevertheless, the use of the image here, in the context of distinguishing (the historical manifestations of) Christian love from deconstruction love is certainly in the spirit of Derrida's work.

22. For example, marriage is thought of, at least in part, as the union of two people who subsequently become one (Gen 2:24 and 1 Cor 6:16); community is thought in terms of a collectivity: "You are the body of Christ and individually member of it" (1 Cor 12:27); and, finally, the relationship with God is thought of in terms of a final union with the Creator (in Plotinus and other Neoplatonists). Love is a relationship that collapses distance and brings people together.

23. Derrida, *Sauf le nom,* 74.

24. "This is the primary sociality: the personal relation is in the rigor of justice that judges me and not in love that excuses me." See Emmanuel Levinas, *Totalité et Infini* (The Hague: Martinus Nijhoff, 1961), 340. This preference for justice is the result of Levinas's all-or-nothing view of otherness, a view that profoundly influences Derrida.

25. Perhaps this accounts for the frustration with love exhibited by both Levinas and Derrida that we noted at the outset. Levinas, for example, tells us that he does not like the word "love," which he characterizes in terms reminiscent of adolescent infatuation (*Entre Nous*, 103). He also writes: "Language as the presence of the face does not invite complicity with the preferred being, the self-sufficient 'I-Thou' forgetful of the universe; in its frankness it refuses the clandestinity of love, where it loses its frankness and turns into laughter and cooing" (*Totality and Infinity*, 213). Likewise, Derrida claims at one point that his "head is empty" with respect to the question of love and insists that the properly philosophical question is not the question of love but the question of being.

This highly provocative insight into Derrida's view of love can be seen in Kirby Dick and Amy Ziering Kofman's bio-documentary film, *Derrida* (Jane Doe Films, 2002). When Ziering-Kofman asks Derrida what he thinks of "*l'amour*," Derrida thinks at first that he has been asked about "*la mort*," a misunderstanding only partially attributable to Ziering-Kofman's French. Given the extent to which love characterizes deconstruction's desire for the *tout autre*, one would think that Derrida would have a great deal to say on the subject, that he would have significant resources at his disposal for an extended discussion, even extemporaneously, on the subject. However, when Amy Ziering-Kofman puts this question to him, Derrida is frustrated, even flustered, and insists, "I have nothing to say about love." Now, on many levels, it would be unfair to hold Derrida accountable for his response in this interview. After all, he notes several times in the film—both in its final version and in deleted footage—that the final product will not be Jacques Derrida, but a construct, a statement by Ziering-Kofman. Moreover, Derrida's frustration in that moment was as much with the clumsiness of Ziering-Kofman's question as with the topic itself. He characterizes her question as "very American," which is itself the topic of another interview left on the cutting room floor. It is, Derrida insists, unfair and typical of the utilitarian and abusive traits that characterize many Americans, to think that one may approach him, press a button, and receive a "ready-made" discourse on, for example, Being (or love). He insists, "I have nothing ready-made." Likewise, he admits, "I don't particularly like improvising" (Derrida, *Points*, 197). If ready-made statements and improvisation are both less than ideal, Derrida's preference is obviously for the "favorable conditions" (ibid.) of a carefully constructed position; indicating, perhaps, a preference for written philosophy over spoken discourse—although Derrida himself dismisses this dichotomy (ibid., 198). Fair enough. Derrida did not have an editorial hand in the film—although he did give the final cut his approval prior to the premiere—and the manner in which the question was put to him may well have been unexpected. Nevertheless, his treatment of love in this interview is well worth examining. What Derrida does say, both in this segment and in other scenes of the film, about love and philosophy is quite surprising, and we remain surprised that a philosopher so committed to love would be at such a loss when asked to speak, even extemporaneously, on the subject.

26. "Deconstuction *is* the preparation for the *tout autre*" (Caputo, *Prayers and Tears*, 21).

27. Fyodor Dostoevsky, *The Brothers Karamazov*, trans. Richard Pevear and Larissa Volokhonsky (New York: Vintage Classics, 1990), 57

28. See John D. Caputo, *Against Ethics: Contributions to a Poetics of Obligation with Constant Reference to Deconstruction* (Bloomington: Indiana University Press, 1993), ch. 4 passim. Of course, any talk of *haecceitas* would appear to violate the claim *tout autre est tout autre*. Even when deconstruction operates as a "preferential option"

for the different and the disenfranchised, it must choose which other it will advocate for, to which silent minority it will lend its voice. However, in choosing one disenfranchised other, we fail to choose other disenfranchised others, and unless we are to admit that our choice is simply random and without meaning, we must be comparing the disenfranchised others in order to speak for one other before the other others—and if we choose to represent one other for a reason, the otherness of the others cannot be absolute.

29. A play on a statement attributed to Aristotle by Montaigne ("O my friend, there is no friend."), which Derrida uses as a tapestry for his meditations on friendship in *The Politics of Friendship*.

30. William James, *The Will to Believe* (New York: Dover, 1956), 18.

31. I discuss the valid epistemological and ethical concerns of philosophies of absolute otherness, as well as the way in which a properly developed philosophy of relative otherness can answer these concerns, in my "Constellations: Gabriel Marcel's Philosophy of Relative Otherness," in *American Catholic Philosophical Quarterly* 29:2 (2005), as well as in *Aspects of Alterity: Levinas, Marcel, and the Contemporary Debate* (New York: Fordham University Press, 2006).

32. Ironically, Derrida makes a similar point: "The other cannot be what it is, infinitely other, except in finitude and mortality (mine *and* its)." See Jacques Derrida, "Violence and Metaphysics," in *Writing and Difference*, trans. Alan Bass (Chicago: University of Chicago Press, 1978), 114–15.

33. Moreover, one's desire is rarely, if ever, for any change whatsoever. Some changes can be much, much worse than the status quo. The desire for something new (i.e., other) is, even when the desire appears contentless, a desire for something good, something better. This is why Derrida and Caputo construe the messianic *a-venir* in terms of justice rather than injustice.

34. Thus, Ricoeur maintains that selfhood and otherness "cannot [be] thought of without [each] other . . . instead one passes into the other." See Paul Ricoeur, *Oneself as Another*, trans. Kathleen Blamey (Chicago: University of Chicago Press, 1992), 3. Richard Kearney's goal is to "make the foreign more familiar and the familiar more foreign," as he puts it in *Strangers, Gods and Monsters* (London: Routledge, 2003), 11.

10

Creatio Ex Amore

JAMES H. OLTHUIS

—poetic prologue—

And God stepped out on space,
And She looked around and said,
"I'm lonely—
I'll make me a world."
As far as the eye of God could see
Darkness covered everything,
Blacker than a hundred midnights
Down in a cypress swamp.

Then God smiled,
And the light broke,
And the darkness rolled up one side,
And the light stood shining on the other,
And God said, "That's good!"
. . .
Then God walked around,
And God looked around
On all that She had made.
She looked at Her sun.
She looked at Her moon.
And She looked at Her little stars;
She looked on Her world
With all its living things,
And God said, "I'm lonely still."

Then God sat down
On the side of a hill where She could think;
By a deep, wide river She sat down;
With Her head in Her hands,
God thought and thought,
Till She thought, "I'll make me a human!"

> Up from the bed of the river
> God scooped the clay;
> And by the bank of the river
> She kneeled Her down;
> And there the great God Almighty,
> Who lit the sun and fixed it in the sky,
> Who flung the stars to the most far corner of the night,
> Who rounded the earth in the middle of Her hand—
> This Great God,
> Like a mother bending over her baby,
>   Kneeled down in the dust
>   Toiling over a lump of clay
>   Till She shaped it in Her own image;
>   Then into it She blew the breath of life,
>   And human became a living soul.

James Weldon Johnson[1]

If God is love, and God is all in all, then without love, there is nothing, which means, as James Weldon Johnson's evocative 1927 poem "The Creation" poetically presages, that the world was not created *ex nihilo*, but *ex amore*. That is the central theme of this essay: we would do well to replace the doctrine of *creatio ex nihilo* with its emphasis on God's omnipotent power, with *creatio ex amore* and its accent on God's generating and regenerating love.

Although the focus of this essay is theological and philosophical, the exegetical and hermeneutical considerations of such a reconceptualization are, I suggest, so striking that I cannot resist at the outset presenting one example: Genesis 3: 9. "And the Lord God called out to Adam, and said unto him, Where art thou?" (KJV).

Traditionally, this text has generally been read—I first heard it in catechism classes more than fifty years ago—as an angry God taking humans to task. Beginning *ex amore*, another reading suggests itself. Looking forward, as was God's wont, to walking with Adam and Eve in the garden in the cool of the day, God is disappointed when they are nowhere to be found, and calls out: "Where are you guys? I'm missing you."

When God locates Adam and Eve, they point fingers, assign blame, implicate the animal world, in effect accusing God the creator of all, after which follows the curse as God's declaration of humankind's future in sin. Such a reading—with its focus on intimacy, communion, and loneliness—does, I suggest, more justice to the actual words of Genesis. In the text, God does not play the heavy hand, accusingly pointing the finger, "What have you guys done now?" Rather, distressed at being stood up, God cries out, "Where are you?"

wild spaces, wild times

Everything that happens, happens in time and space. When we begin *ex amore*, time and space are not neutral, empty receptacles, but God's primings —occasions and places for giving and receiving love. There is no meaningless time, only time to be full-filled in love (or impaired by hate). There is no vacuous space, only space as the abodes of love (or the haunts of evil). Created beings are called to live side by side, dwelling in enduring relations with each other.

Indeed, as I have become fond of saying, the spaces and times of creation are the wild spaces and times of love.[2] Wild, because they are uncharted and unpredictable—to venture into them is to take the beautiful risk. Spaces can turn out to be healing meadows, or they may become killing fields. Time can make for fulfilling or distressed connections. Although space can be traversed and time filled, there is no guarantee of enduring connections or healing moments.

Moreover, in regard to both space and time, if we attempt to tame the space and determine the time in order to guarantee the outcome, we may have control, manipulation, aggression, co-option, domination, subjection, bullying, intimidation—but never meeting nor intimacy, never fulfillment. In the spaces and times that we are given, we are called to negotiate ways together of hope and healing.

Trading on the many African and Asiatic rituals in which the metaphor of the world as dance has symbolized these negotiations,[3] we are called to dance together in the wild spaces and times of love. Choreography is always required, with the risk of wrong moves, black-and-blue shins, not to mention hurtful tumbles, bruised egos, abused bodies, and betrayed hearts. The dance metaphor nicely links space and time in rhythmic movement. In rhythm, "space is measured in terms of time, and time in terms of space."[4]

Moreover, one of the most compelling images of the Trinity in the patristic church is that of the "sacred dance-play between three persons" known as the *perichoresis*, which literally means "dance (*choros*) around (*peri*)."[5] The celebrated Shaker song, "The Lord of the Dance" trades on these images, with the Son as the Lord of the dance inviting all of humanity to join, as Lucian stated it, in the "great dance of creation and rebirth."[6] Thirteenth-century Beguine Mechtild of Magdeburg talks of God as "playmate":

> I, God, am your playmate!
> I will lead the child in you in wonderful ways
> for I have chosen you.
> Beloved child, come swiftly to Me
> For I am truly in you.[7]

A timed/spaced creation is God's adventure in love, the original blessing[8] in which God both loves creation into being and desires to be loved by creation. It was God's let-there-be's of love that brought forth time and space for the great dance of creation. Eleventh-century mystic Hildegard of Bingen exclaims:

> For it was love which was the source of this creation in the beginning when God said: "Let it be!" And it was. As though in the blinking of an eye, the whole creation was formed through love.[9]

There it is: *ex amore*. Everything in creation speaks and bespeaks love, which means that it is not only *ex amore*, out of love, but also *cum amore*, with love, and *ad amorem*, to love.

Spacing and timing are the between-ings of love, which can be become meetings-in-the-interval, passages of visitations of love, with-ings[10] of the Spirit. Time and space are holy containers, wombs primed for love, spaces for the formation of love.

Simone Weil declared that "time is the waiting of God, who begs for our love." Upon reading this description, Emmanuel Levinas substituted "who commands our love" for "who begs for our love."[11] Time—and I include space—are the waitings of God, and at the same time, they are also the yearnings of God, gifting us for love, calling us to redeem the time.

Since the gifting God, in the beginning, *ex amore*, made the world, we, image-bearers of God, both receive and find our being *ex amore*. The question is not Shakespeare's: To be or not to be. Rather, the make-or-break question— God's question, one could say—is: To love or not to love. And in the degree that we love, we are, and in the degree we fail to love, we are not. Instead of "I think, therefore, I am"—Descartes' classic starting point—it is "I was loved, therefore, I am." Indeed, we are Love's agents in the world—in the double sense of being both agents *of* love and *for* love. To be a lover is to be caught up in the intrigue of love even as we are an active agent of that love.

Waging love, rather than waging war, is no easy matter in our world that knows so much violence and brokenness. Too often the reality is one in which we turn the spaces and times of love into killing fields and instants of terror. In a world in which compassion is in exile, the practice of compassion—redeeming time and space—is a working and a waiting in faith, living in hope and by grace, a beautiful risk, a ministry of encouragement.

We are, says the Apostle Peter, in these between times, to adopt a double strategy, waiting for, and at the same time, hastening the coming of the "kindom" of God (2 Peter 3:12). Kindom, with its connotations of partnership, family, friendship, and kindred spirits, seems more becoming to me than the more political, militaristic image of the kingdom. Waiting and hastening at the same time is not easy. With one eye fixed on Christ's coming and one eye fixed on our task in this world, we are, so to speak, cross-eyed—even if starry-eyed—

witnesses. Our focus is never 20/20. We, "lovers in a dangerous time," sorely need to hold on to each other in the fellowship of faith and communion of the spirit as, in the words of Bruce Cockburn, we "kick at the darkness till it bleeds daylight."[12]

Love as Strange Attractor

In *The Beautiful Risk* I have further elucidated what it means anthropologically that love is who we are, rather than something we do. In this essay I want to deepen this understanding by exploring some cosmological implications of beginning *ex amore*. If God creates *ex amore*, then creation not only lives out of love, but love is the cosmic energy of creation, one could say the oxygen, the glue, and the fire of the universe. Love is the being and becoming of created reality. Love is the oxygen of the universe without which we cannot live even though we cannot see it. At the same time, when it is not there we know it, we gasp for breath, slowly dying.

Love is the glue of the universe, the staying power that acts to hold it together in all its contingency and randomness. One of the most striking features of contemporary chaos theory is the attention it pays to the reality that in and through the open-ended, chaotic systems of nature is an emergent force that lures and evokes new patterns of novelty and surprise. This force has been designated the strange attractor. Love, I want to suggest, is not just a random effect; rather, love is the strange attractor luring creation into new life, and God is the divine attractor.[13] Indeed, in a recent book Richard Middleton makes a similar claim that "not only does Genesis 1 depict a fractal universe, but it depicts a creator less like a Newtonian lawgiver and more like a strange attractor."[14]

Love is the fire, the driving force of the universe. Creation, fired by the love of God, will always tend toward the fullness of love, as the lover searches for the beloved. The spirit of love, the Divine Eros, lures creation and its creatures to participate in the creative process itself toward ever new and widening spirals of love. The cosmos in this way, speaking the language of Whitehead, has a divine aim. Creation is not only *ex amore*, but *cum amore* and *ad amorem*.

Love measures us, not we, love. Without love's grace, imagination and vision are finally very limited, for the graceless mind proves in the end to be boring, caught in its own repetitive reverberations—shades of Levinas—in which the regime of the same conquers. Without love, we measure the other on the basis of our own insights and interests, and in so doing, there is a failure of hospitality, a hardening of arteries, a closing off, a becoming unavailable, a violation of the other. With love, there is a suffering-with—a standing-with the other, giving and forgiving.

Love is the echo before the anonymous, menacing, rumbling, of "the impersonal *there is*[15] (*il y a*), the recurrence that interrupts and breaks open any congealed or clotted identity. The law of friendship is, as Derrida demonstrates, that "one must always go before the other," that one must always die before the other.[16] When love (as well as justice) is undeconstructible, the law of friendship receives another face: Yes, one must go before the other, but meanwhile, one may go *with* the other. Friendship, life as a whole, is a risk, and there will be wounds and death, but life is a beautiful risk to run because it holds within it the graced possibilities of connection, not being alone, being touched by love. At the same time it is true, I suspect, that a mark of true friendship in distinction from acquaintance relations is the frightening realization between friends that one will die before the other.

All these considerations point in one direction: the logic of creation, in its height and depth, in its human and non-human dimensions is the logic of love. If this is the case, there is an impressive case to be made for replacing our doctrine of *creatio ex nihilo* with *creatio ex amore. Creatio ex nihilo* emphasizes the difference, the externality, between God and creation, God the infinite transcendent creator, who brings forth the finite creaturely universe as something separate from God.

In other words, too often the difference between God and the world is radically misunderstood as the difference between two discrete entities that extrinsically relate. In this view God is a kind of master craftsperson, divine architect, mastermind who designs and creates, connecting the parts, and who thereafter, because of sin and evil, reconnects and repairs. Often this is coupled with an interventionist view of divine action in which God—who is immutable, unmoved, and unaffected by anything—from time to time miraculously intervenes.[17]

Viewing the God-creation relationship as external in this way does not do adequate justice to the biblical testimony that God is love, tending to bracket, if not abrogate, the uniquely personal and mutually participatory relationship between God and creation. As love, God cannot be related to the world in extrinsic fashion such as in deism or dualisms of any sort.

Moreover, as Catherine Keller summarizes in her provocative *The Face of the Deep*, "although the *creatio ex nihilo* has reigned largely uncontested in the language of the church since the third century ACE" (FD 4), more and more biblical scholars are recognizing that the Bible does not support it. Thus, Jon Levenson claims that the "overture to the Bible, Genesis 1:1–2:3, cannot be invoked in support of the developed Jewish, Christian, and Muslim doctrine of *creatio ex nihilo*."[18] In fact, it needs to be noted that the Bible does not talk about a creation from nothing, but "knows only a formation of something new from something-*else*, something yet unthinged, unformed, some sort of marine chaos" (FD 25).

However, the alternative to *creatio ex nihilo* need not leave us with a Plotinian emanation in which the creation is an efflux of the divine selfsame— one of the alternatives that *creatio ex nihilo* was constructed to avoid. Instead of a pure dualism (God and nothing), we need a "third possibility" as Karl Barth also recognized.[19]

My "third space of beginning" (*FD* 12) is *creatio ex amore*, which shifts the focus from an understanding of God who creates by omnipotent power over and periodic divine intervention in creation, to a God whose unconditional love gives birth to creation and intimately and enduringly suffers-with creation, redeeming and renewing it.

Along these lines, creation is not the demonstration of God's almighty power, but the communication of God's unfailing, unconditional love. "Creation," exclaims Jürgen Moltmann, "is not a demonstration of his boundless power, it is the communication of his love, which knows neither premises nor preconditions: *creatio ex amore Dei*. In Dante's words,

> From the Creator's love came forth in glory the world . . ."[20]

In contrast to the *creatio ex nihilo* doctrine that emerged in the third century, as Gerhard May has documented, "to express and safeguard the omnipotence and freedom of God acting in history,"[21] *creatio ex amore* would emphasize "the risk-taking, power-sharing character of God" (*LI* 287), passionately involved with the creation. In creating, God took the supreme risk of love, letting the other be.

The Let-there-be's of Genesis One

The concept of an omnipotent God in splendid supremacy masterfully ordering creation does not fit the picture of creation in Genesis 1. The let-there-be's of Genesis are, Richard Middleton reminds us, not "imperatives at all, but Hebrew jussives (which have no exact counterpart in English)"; but, even as they may range "from the very strong (almost a command) to the very soft (almost a wish)," they always possess a "voluntary element" (*LI* 265). "God said, 'Let the *earth put forth* vegetation, plants yielding seed etc. . . . .' And it was so. The *earth brought forth* vegetation; plants yielding seed of every kind." Indeed, "the earth is *agent* of *Elohim's* creation. . . . The same again with the sea. . . . *Creation takes place as invitation and cooperation*" (*FD* 195).

William P. Brown concludes that the creative process described in Genesis "does not thereby imply a God who simply imposes order on unruly matter or creates everything *ex nihilo*," but the let-there-be's can be "read as invitations to enter into the grand creative sweep of God's designs." Indeed, "God chooses and implements noncoercive ways of creating, thereby allowing the elements to share positively in cosmogony."[22] This fits very well with Catherine Keller's suggestion that in Genesis 1 we have the impetus for a "theology of creation, in which the chaos is neither nothing nor evil; in which to create is not *to master the formless, but to solicit its virtual forms*. Such solicitation, when expressed as divine speech, may sound less like command than a seduction" (*FD* 115). Keller talks of a *creatio cooperationis* (*FD* 117). She asks: "Does not the vibratory proximity of *ruach* upon the waters suggest that intimate co-generativity?" (*FD* 121).

Richard Middleton goes even farther, surmising that the text of Genesis "depicts God's founding exercise of creative power in such a way that we might appropriately describe it as an act of generosity, even of love" (*LI* 278).

In the advent(ure) of creating, God put Godself at risk. God gave Godself over to the adventure and risk of time and space, inviting, hoping, wooing all the family of God's creatures to participate in the creative process itself. God as love yearns for and desires another, not out of lack or need, but out of the profusion or abundance of love as self-giving and out-going. God's life as love spills over into what is other than God, birthing creation, empowering and inviting creation into a covenant partnership. Rather than being a supreme display of power, creation is a revelation of the power of love in which the Godhead becomes vulnerable, risking rebuff, refusal, and hurt. In place of power as demonstration of mastery and total control (power-over), we have the power of love as opening to the other, gifting to and calling for partnership (power-with).

Thus, in our turn away from God in the Fall, God was deeply wounded, as our previous reference to Genesis 3 reminds us, and still suffers yearning/waiting for us to pass love on rather than hoard it. Yet the risk and vulnerability of Divine Love is at the same time its very power. Love is unstoppable; it never stops coming—reaching a particularly marvelous climax in the coming of Jesus, love incarnate. And even when we killed Christ on the cross, love was born anew in his resurrection.

God's heart of love can be wounded, it can be violated and betrayed, but it cannot be destroyed. God's love keeps on coming back. That, in fact, is the meaning of the crucifixion and Easter. God redemptively suffers with the world and its creatures to the point of death, so that all things might be made new in the power of the resurrection. Love, if there is such a thing, is indeconstructible.

No matter what—even death, as Christ proved on the cross—Love can never be defeated because it keeps on coming back in resurrection power, suffering with us now and in the future until the end. Love is stronger than death—period.

—interlude—

Without the Word of God no creature has meaning.
God's Word is in all creation, visible and invisible.
The Word is living, being, spirit, all verdant greening,
all creativity.
This Word manifests in every creature,
Now this is how the spirit is in the flesh—the Word is
indivisible from God.

Hildegard of Bingen[23]

Omnipotence as Unfailing Love

Thinking of creation *ex amore* opens, I want to suggest, new and promising ways for approaching some of the most baffling and controversial issues having to do with God's relation to creation. First is the question of omnipotence that we have just broached. Instead of speaking of God's omnipotence in terms of sheer power over any and everything—which always raises a host of haunting questions: How can an omnipotent, good God allow evil and suffering? Why does not such an all-powerful God intervene? and If God could, but does not, how are we to distinguish God from an arbitrary and sadistic despot?—we can say that God's omnipotence is the unfailing, boundless power of love, a vulnerability that can never, despite sin and evil, be defeated. Love cannot not come back. That is who God is, that is who God will be, that is who God always has been, life.

In the face of evil, with a traditional view of God's omnipotence, it is usually said with orthodoxy that God freely restricts his/her power. That, however, leaves unanswered the cluster of questions that we have just mentioned. More recently, realizing the need for a different approach, John Caputo, pointing to the *tohu wa bohu* of Genesis 1:2 argues that "God's power only extends so far, that is, up to the point of the formless void which is of itself, not from God. So God can only do so much."[24] Richard Kearney is even more blunt: "God can't stop evil. . . . God has no power over what God is not—namely, evil. . . . God is *not* omnipotent when it comes to evil. God is utterly powerless. And that's terribly important."[25]

Although I fully share Caputo's and Kearney's dissatisfaction with God's self-limitation of his/her power, it strikes me that they are still working too much with power as power-over. If, instead, we understand the power of love as power-with, another possibility suggests itself.

God's love is omnipotent in respect to evil because love outlasts evil. The power of love de-stings the sting of death, not by redeeming evil, but by redeeming from evil. Evil is/will be defeated by love because, despite everything that evil conjures up, God's infinite love does not/cannot/will not stop coming.

Inordinate Intrigue: *ebullitio*

Secondly, traditionally, it has often been asked: Did God create out of necessity or out of freedom? However, to say that it was necessary to the Godhead that God create not only brings with it the suspicion that God lacked something, but it leaves little room for joy and spontaneity on God's part: God had to do it—which seems cold, impersonal, and disheartening. On the other hand, to say that God was free to create or not to create brings with it, besides a certain arbitrariness in God, the idea that creation is external to God—a kind of wonderful afterthought, an amusement for a lonely deity—that God didn't have to create—which also seems disconcerting.

In contrast, when we conceive of God as a Trinity of Love—ebullient, exuberant, passionate, bubbling or boiling over, gushing forth creatively— God's relation to creation can be framed in ways that avoid or go beyond the confines of the necessity/freedom binary. Creation begins, not as the Big Bang, but as the Bursting out of God's love. Considering the hotness of God's love, it's ebullience—*ebullitio*, boiling over, said Meister Eckhart[26]—creation was bound to be as an outbursting of love. If God is love, creation will be God's self-giving love going out to the other for the sake of the other. In that way, creation is not the result of an external act of God, which God could or could not have made, but proceeds quite naturally from the heart of God's love. On the other hand, for love to be love, it needs to be spontaneous, unconditional, and gratuitous rather than necessitated, forced, or programmed.

In understanding God as love, to be God is to be creator. This means that God's acting as creator is not something that is added to the divine essence. That is, "to be in relation to creation as the Creator, is not a relation added on to the divine essence, ancillary to God's being. To be God is to be the Creator of the world."[27] Creation's "reason," then, is hidden in the inscrutable mystery of God as self-originating and self-giving love. "While the world is the gracious result of divine freedom, God's freedom means *necessarily* being who and what God is. From this standpoint the world is not created *ex nihilo*, but *ex amore, ex condilectione*, that is, out of divine love."[28]

In *creatio ex amore*, we have a creation that, although not a necessary emanation from God with its pantheistic overtones, is nevertheless in all its difference from God, internally, intrinsically, and intimately—as opposed to deistically, distantly, externally—connected/covenanted with God. In this way, creation is not a self-same emanation of the Godhead, but a creation of a different sort out of God's love. However, if the difference between God and creation is from the Godhead, there is just as much reason to posit that this establishes the most intimate intrinsic connection precisely in the differentiation. *Ex amore* emphasizes the connection-in-difference between God and creation.

Theologically, such a connection-in-difference points in the direction of panentheism (God-in-all and all-in-God) as an alternative to either deism or pantheism. At this point, I am resistant to describing my position as panentheism because of fears that it will be seen as yet another metaphysical construction that seeks to capture or bracket the holy mystery. At the same time, a mystical *"apophatic panentheism,"* of the kind that Catherine Keller is suggesting, that "retains what all theism desires: a 'Thou' different enough and intimate enough to love and be loved" (*FD* 219) is attractive. Particularly, this would be the case when the fundamental distinction between creation and Creator is heightened in intensifying the relationality, and when the "in" of panentheism would begin "to designate creation as incarnation" (*FD* 219).

Levinas, at this point, afraid of any totalizing ontology, talks of the "intrigue of infinity," the "inordinate intrigue"[29] of God. Inordinate intrigue are words that seem particularly apt for the holy mystery of the omnipotence of

Divine Love in *creatio ex amore*. In this understanding, if God is love, God could not be God without a bestowal of the Godself in love.

To-Be Is To-Be-Related

Another crucial advantage of talking of God as love means that we can give up our focus on God as Being, as *causa sui*, which historically (whatever the details) has developed into ontologies of maintenance, control, domination: power-over. In the world of being-as-power, suffering has no legitimate place. Pain and suffering are diminutions of being. Is this perhaps a telling reason why the philosophical idea of the impassibility of God has often, even to the present, prevailed over the biblical teaching of the suffering love of God?

Beginning *ex amore* gives legitimate place to suffering, not as a diminution of being, a suffering-from, but as suffering-with, a becoming-with, withings that comfort and heal, enriching and transforming. Love as excess seeps into life's cracks and fissures as suffering with. In the words of Leonard Cohen, "There is a crack in everything, that's how the light gets in."[30] We have the promise that the wounds of creation, suffering, and death will be taken up in the wounds of Christ—not erased, but transformed. We are heirs of Christ, says Romans 8:17, provided we suffer with him. Love turns us to the other, not as foe, not as a diminution of being, but as enrichment, hospitality, and celebration.

When the Love of God is the Spirit of Life, creaturely life is life-with-God. For God so loved that creation came forth. Creation as the first incarnation of love. *Ex amore*. For God so loved the world that God gave us the Son. The Word becoming flesh in Jesus Christ for our redemption as the second incarnation. *Cum amore*. For God so loved the world that God sent us the Spirit. The Spirit of Love aflame in the hearts of God's people as a third incarnation. Such incarnations of love both in suffering-with and celebrating-with each other and the whole family of God's creatures help fill up what is lacking in the sufferings of Christ (see Col 1:27). From before the foundations of the world God destined us in love, says Ephesians, to be God's sons and daughters. *Cum amore*. For God so loved the world that in the end God will be all in all, the fourth incarnation, we could say. *Ad amorem*.

When love is the being of being, we allow space for the deep mystery of God's dance of love with the creation. We make space, then, for the Yes of Love most ancient to sound forth from before the very beginning, resounding as the norm for all of life, including the disciplines of philosophy and theology, even as it invites that we end our endeavors in doxology, in praise and thanksgiving. Emphasizing that God created because God is relational and made a creation that is at heart relational also fits well, as we noted earlier, with contemporary physics that tells us that relationality is the prime feature of the universe in which we live.

What I am saying amounts to a suggestion: What if we were to set aside our focus on God as Being, and talk of God as love, beyond both the categories of being and non-being? Without love, nothing. Love calls into existence everything and anything that is. To-be is to-be-related. Creation is then conceived, not as *ex nihilo*, but as *ex amore*. As the creative Love that exceeds all systems, physical and metaphysical, and yet evokes such systems, God may be said to be beyond creation, the excessive. As the Love revealed and incarnated in the world, God is not-beyond. Then we can perhaps begin to move beyond our squabbles about whether talking of both the being of creation and of God is to be interpreted univocally, equivocally, or analogically.

Indeed, I am left wondering about the usefulness of any kind of infinite/finite, transcendence/immanence, archetypal/ectypal, being/non-being scheme for envisioning the creator/creation relationship. In such binaries, there is not only the pull to prefer one term as superior to the other, but even more sinister, each term gets defined in terms of the other so that an emphasis on one is taken at the expense and cost of the other. The difficulties of such binary schemes are astronomically amplified when applied to the God/creation relation because even when God is identified as infinite or transcendent or Being (in contrast to the finite, non-transcendent, non-being), God, who as creator is not a creature, is placed within a human conceptualization. Regardless of how God's infinity is explained, whether as so-called bad or good infinity, God is subjected and understood in terms of what needs to be more fully recognized as human (non)understandings. In the process, it is not only God who suffers, but the excellence of humankind, as a good creation, is eclipsed: in contrast to the infinite, the "being" of the finite is always limited, inferior, contingent.

Developing a radical ontology of love as a with-paradigm (rather than an oppositional paradigm of comparison) would, I suggest, provide new openings. "With" speaks of difference-and-connection, non-oppositional difference, without definition of one in terms of the other and without valorization of one above the other.

At the same time, I want to acknowledge that suggesting that we would be better off with love than being doesn't mean that the problem of conceptualization is solved. Being a philosopher indeed entails precisely that I need to translate the intuitions of my faith into philosophical concepts. The secret that is no secret but is revealed—God's love—can only be thought through and worked out by philosophers and theologians in terms of concepts. *Ex amore*, even as a faith response, involves conceptualization. So when I suggest that "love" is the preferable term, as other than being and different than being, when love and loving become the conditions for being and becoming, love functions as an ontological category, the condition of possibility for being itself. Love is other than being and yet the condition of being. Love, in this way, becomes, one may say, the being of being. All I can say, following Derrida, is that at these limits, speaking of the conditions from within the conditioned makes for a certain conceptual incoherence.

My argument, however, is that whereas a metaphysics of being or substance is designed to understand the world in terms interior or intrinsic to individual entities, inside-out, with relationality always an accidental property, a radical ontology of love begins as it were outside-in, from inter-relationality as the warp and woof of creation. Instead of talking in terms of being with its connotations of substance, confinement, definition, boundaries, totality, and independence, talk of love emphasizes relationality, inter-relationality, inter-subjectivity, openness, excess, infinity.

When "being" is taken as the central concept—whether of God or of creation—love, as the dynamic source and end of being, can too easily be eclipsed or lost. It is as if being is possible without love, with love becoming the ethical imperative that we attend to once we exist as beings. In contrast, *ex amore*, we only are, we only exist, insofar as we love. *Ex amore*, God only exists, is, insofar as God loves.

God as Love is not the "being" above in the splendid isolation of *epekeina tes ousias*, but the gracious, passion-filled *inter-esse*, the being-with. God, as the *Logos* by whom all things were created, as the *Logos* Incarnate, Emmanuel (God-with-us), is the Logos of Love, the *Meta-Logos*. *Logos* as *Meta-Logos* offers a more fruitful image for moving us beyond divine aseity, with its immutable, impassible God, to a God who, as Scripture reveals, sojourns and journeys with us, lamenting, mourning, redeeming, loving.[31]

The medieval mystic Angelus Silesius said: *Gott spricht nur immer Ja* (God only always says Yes). That is the yes of love, the yes of being human. Humans, with ears to hear, eyes to see, and hands to touch, are called in all they do to individually and communally say, Yes, Yes, to each other as they dance—and, when appropriate grieve, resist, and say No—in the wild spaces and times of love.

Life—all of creation—is God-with-us: Love. "God is love, and those who abide in love abide in God and God abides in them" (1 John 4:16). We, as human creatures, participate with God in the ongoing adventure of creation until Love is all in all. God lives as the mystery of love. Which means that life in all its mystery is *ex amore, cum amore, ad amorem*.

—*poetic epilogue*—

The God Who Only Knows Four Words
    Every
    Child
Has known God,
Not the God of names,
Not the God of don'ts,
Not the God who ever does
    Anything weird,
But the God who only knows four words
And keeps repeating them, saying:

"Come dance with Me."
   Come
   Dance.

The Ambience of Love
We all
Sit in His Orchestra
Some play their
   Fiddles,
Some wield their
   Clubs.
Tonight is worthy of music.
Let's get loose
With
Compassion,
Let's drown in the delicious
   Ambience of
   Love.

Sufi Master Hafiz[32]

NOTES

1. James Weldon Johnson, in *God's Trombones* (New York: Viking Press, 1927). In this rendition, in reference to God, "she" replaces "he," and in reference to human beings, "human" replaces "man."

2. See James H. Olthuis, *The Beautiful Risk* (Grand Rapids: Zondervan, 2001), 48.

3. Jürgen Moltmann, *God in Creation*, trans. M. Kohl (London: SCM Press, 1985), 304.

4. Ibid., 306.

5. Richard Kearney, *The God Who May Be* (Bloomington: Indiana University Press), 109.

6. Ibid.

7. Sue Woodruff, *Meditations with Mechtild of Magdeburg* (Santa Fe, N.M.: Bear & Co., 1982), 47.

8. Matthew Fox, *Original Blessing* (Santa Fe, N.M.: Bear & Co., 1983).

9. *Hildegard of Bingen's Book of Divine Works* ed. Matthew Fox (Santa Fe, N.M.: Bear & Co. 1987), 308.

10. On with-ing, see Olthius, *Beautiful Risk*, 48.

11. See G. Fuchs, H. Henrix, eds., *Zeitgewinn. Messianisches Denken nach Franz Rosenzweig* (Frankfurt, 1987), 163–83.

12. Bruce Cockburn, "Lovers in a Dangerous Time," 1984 Sony/Columbia, from the album *Stealing Fire.*

13. When preparing this essay for publication, I was pleasantly surprised that Catherine Keller has raised the same possibility: "Might we every now and then imagine Elohim as the strange attractor of the creation?" (*Face of the Deep* [London: Routledge, 2003], 198). Hereafter in text as *FD.*

14. J. Richard Middleton, *The Liberating Image* (Grand Rapids: Brazos Press, 2005), 286. Hereafter in text as *LI*. "Whereas the world rhetorically depicted in Genesis

1 is certainly ordered, patterned, and purposive . . . , this world is not mechanistically determined, as if it were governed by ineluctable, ironclad Newtonian laws. . . . The God who is artisan and maker, reflected rhetorically in the complex literary artistry of the text, does not overdetermine the order of the cosmos. . . . [T]he process of creation [is] God sharing power with creatures, inviting them to participate (as they are able) in the creative process itself," 285–87.

15. Emmanuel Levinas, *Totality and Infinity*, trans. A. Lingus (Pittsburgh: Duquesne University Press, 1969), 190.

16. Jacques Derrida, *The Work of Mourning*, ed. P. Brault and M. Naas (Chicago: Chicago University Press, 2001), 1.

17. Thus, physicist-theologian Arthur Peacocke judges that our understanding of God as creator has been "too much dominated by a stress on the externality of God's creative acts. . . . We should work the analogy of God creating the world within herself. God creates a world that is in principle other than himself, but creates it within herself" ("Theology and Science Today," in *Cosmos as Creation*, ed. T. Peters (Nashville: Abingdon, 1989), 36.

18. Jon Levenson, *Creation and the Persistence of Evil: The Jewish Drama of Divine Omnipotence* (Princeton, N.J.: Princeton University Press, 1988), 24 or 121.

19. Karl Barth, *Church Dogmatics* III/1, ed. Bromiley and Torrance (Edinburgh: T & T Clark, 1960), 104. However, Barth's third possibility is to demonize the chaos: "Nothingness is not nothing . . . it 'is' nothingness" with its "own being, albeit malignant and perverse" (III/3, 349). See Keller's chapter on Barth in *FD* 84–99.

20. Jürgen Moltmann, *God in Creation*, trans. M. Kohl (London: SCM Press, 1985), 76.

21. Gerhard May, *Creatio Ex Nihilo: The Doctrine of "Creation out of Nothing" in Early Christian Thought*, trans. A. Worall (Edinburgh: T & T Clark, 1994), 180.

22. William P. Brown, "Divine Act and the Art of Persuasion in Genesis One," in *History and Interpretation: Essays in Honour of John H. Hayes*, ed. M. P. Graham, William Brown, and Jeffrey Kuan (Sheffield: JSOT Press, 1993), 28, 32.

23. Gabriel Uhlein, *Meditations with Hildegard of Bingen* (Santa Fe, N.M.: Bear & Co., 1982), 49.

24. John D. Caputo, "Olthuis's Risk: A Heretical Tribute," in *The Hermeneutics of Charity*, ed. James K. Smith and Henry I. Venema (Grand Rapids: Brazos Press, 2004), 46.

25. Richard Kearney, "Philosophizing the Gift," in *The Hermeneutics of Charity*, ed. James K. Smith and Henry I. Venema (Grand Rapids: Brazos Press, 2004), 59.

26. Meister Eckhart, as cited in "Introduction" to *Meister Eckhart The Essential Sermons, Commentaries, Treatises, and Defense* trans. and intro. E. Colledge and B. McGinn (Mahwah, N.J.: Paulist Press, 1981), 38–41. "The differences between *bullitio* and *ebullitio*, between the emanations of the divine Persons and the creation of the universe, were frequently highlighted by the Meister, but their inner connection was never in question," 39.

27. Catherine Mowry LaCugna, *God for Us* (San Francisco: HarperSanFrancisco, 1991), 355.

28. Ibid.

29. Emmanuel Levinas, "God and Philosophy," in *Basic Philosophical Writings*, ed. A. Peperzak, S. Critchley, and R. Bernasconi (Bloomington: Indiana University Press, 1996), 135, 146.

30. Leonard Cohen, "Anthem," 1992 Sony Music Entertainment, from the album *The Future*.

31. S. Goiten has interestingly proposed a morphological correlation between God as love and Exodic naming of Yahweh. Comparing the Hebrew Tetragrammaton *YHWH* with certain Arabic roots, he suggests that the "I am that I am" of Exodus 3:14 may be translated as "I shall passionately love whom I love" ("*YHWH* the Passionate: The Monotheistic Meaning and Origin of the Name *YHWH*," *Vetus Testamentum* 6 [January 1956]:2).

32. Hafiz, *The Gift* trans. Daniel Ladinsky (New York: Penguin Compass, 1999), 270, 186.

11
Militant Love

Zizek and the Christian Legacy

TYLER ROBERTS

What can one make of episodes like this, unforeseen, unplanned, out of character? Are they just holes, holes in the heart, into which one steps and falls and then goes on falling?

—J. M. Coetzee, *Elizabeth Costello*

Acts and Passages

When scholars invoke the "turn to religion" in Continental philosophy, they generally are referring to a trajectory of phenomenological thought rooted in Heidegger and developed most prominently by Levinas, Marion, and Derrida. But today the question of religion is arising in new ways in other Continental thinkers, notably in the Marxist and Lacanian work of Alain Badiou and Slavoj Zizek. We should proceed carefully before calling this another "turn to religion." For one thing, both Badiou and Zizek position themselves in staunch opposition to phenomenological postsecularism and its ethics of the other. In contrast to the messianism of this ethics, Badiou's and Zizek's commitment to Marxist politics leads them to focus on radical change in the present and on the importance of community and universalism. For his part, Badiou argues that he really has no interest in "religion" per se, but rather appeals to St. Paul and offers significant readings of Pauline love, hope, and faith in order to extract their "secular" meaning for a world in which, he thinks, the "fables" of religion can no longer exert a serious claim. Zizek's case, however, is perhaps more complex. Zizek agrees with Badiou that the particular form of universalism first articulated by Paul can ground a contemporary anti-liberal and anti-capitalist politics. But his interest in Paul extends to Christianity more generally and to the complex relationship between Judaism, Christianity, and Marxist materialism. Most importantly, it extends to the claim that Christian love—*agape*—is the key to radical politics. It is this "turn to *agape*" that I want to explore here.

Badiou and Zizek theorize radical change in terms of a revolutionary break from established social and historical structures of meaning and value: Badiou calls the break the "Event"; Zizek calls it the "Act." For Zizek, though, there is much more than a difference in terminology here. Badiou, he argues, fails to theorize adequately the "passage" from the revolutionary break of Act/Event to new meaning and commitment, a passage Zizek attempts to theorize through the psychoanalytic category of "sublimation." Basically, sublimation, for psychoanalytic theory, is "the process by which the energy of the drives is taken up and directed toward 'higher,' more creative aims."[1] Sublimation, in other words, is the process by which meaning and subjectivity is created from the meaningless, machine-like movement of the drives. What is it about Zizek's understanding of sublimation that he thinks distinguishes him from Badiou? And what is the role of love in this "passage" from the Act? These questions are my focus here.

Zizek's thinking on this has gone through at least two phases. In *The Ticklish Subject*, Zizek argues that where Badiou focuses on the reconstruction of the symbolic order in fidelity to the Event—Badiou calls this reconstruction a "truth-procedure"—Zizek follows Lacan by stressing the "symbolic death" of the break itself.[2] This has important consequences for their views of subjectivity, according to Zizek. Badiou claims that we only really become "subjects" when, in fidelity to the Event, we participate in the creation of new meaning. Zizek, by contrast, argues that the Lacanian position he embraces views the subject *as* the (negative) Act, the break itself. Here, then, it appears that it is Badiou, not Zizek, who is focused on the passage to new meaning. However, in a more recent engagement with Badiou, Zizek has addressed this issue, in large part, it seems, in response to a reading of Lacan's negativity offered by Bruno Bosteels. Bosteels contends that by stressing the negativity of the break, Lacan is forced to denounce as "illusory" every effort to forge a passage beyond it with the creation of a new order.[3] Any sublimation, then, any new meaning emerging from the break, will be grounded in a false consciousness that represses or distorts the fundamental negative reality. But Zizek counters Bosteels by claiming that Lacanian "sublimation" is the movement from the "shattering encounter of the Real," in the Act, to "the ensuing arduous work of transforming this explosion of negativity into a new order" (PS 177). But this sounds a lot like Badiou as Zizek described him in *The Ticklish Subject*, so Zizek is forced to nuance his criticism of Badiou. He does this by claiming that in Badiou the work of transformation toward a new order effaces—that is, "masks" or "gentrifies"—the negativity of the subject.[4] One gathers from this engagement that for Zizek an adequate account of the passage of sublimation must (1) have as its condition the "Act" of radical negativity that "momentarily suspends the Order of Being," and (2) involve the creation and attachment to a new symbolic order in which this negativity "continues to resonate" (TS 162–63). Somehow, even as we create and commit ourselves to new meaning and value, we must retain a sense of the abyss of negativity that underlies it all.

Love is central to Zizek's efforts to theorize this form of sublimation, which is a major reason why, in a series of recent books, he has argued that even radical militant materialists must learn to affirm what he calls "the Christian legacy."[5] Here too, his differences with Badiou are illuminating. Badiou insists that we can identify four distinct kinds of truth-procedure, that is, four fundamental modalities of the reconstruction of symbolic order following the Event: these are art, politics, science, and love. However, Zizek argues that Badiou is unable to consistently confine love to a discrete truth-procedure—the erotic love between two people. In fact, Zizek argues, love functions for Badiou as an "excessive" truth-procedure or as the "formal principle or matrix" for truth-procedures in general (PS 170–1).[6] Zizek argues that love is such a matrix, that it is at the heart of all sublimation, all efforts to create new meaning and reshape human collectivities. This is Zizek's primary concern in writing about love and Christianity: the possibility of a radical politics as passionate attachment to, that is, love for, a "cause." Theorizing this love, Zizek claims not only to counter Badiou by opening a non-ideological passage to new meaning, but also to expose the shortcomings of the postsecularist messianism found in Derrida and driven by a deconstructive "undecidability" that precludes all radical commitment.[7]

My purpose here is to examine the link Zizek wants to forge between Christian *agape* and sublimation. I will argue that to do so it is necessary to specify the difference between the two forms of sublimation I have already identified: an "ideological" sublimation in which the negativity of the "Act" is masked, and the passage to a new symbolic order in which this Act "resonates." Zizek has taken significant steps to articulate this distinction, and these have allowed him to usefully push the Continental turn to religion in some provocative and potentially illuminating directions. Yet he is inconsistent in applying this distinction to his political theory, and I will argue that this inconsistency prevents Zizek from clearly articulating the relationship between passionate love for other individuals and political or collective love for community.

Breaking from Desire

"The fact that we cannot ever 'fully know' reality is not a sign of the limitation of our knowledge, but the sign that reality itself is 'incomplete,' open, an actualization of the underlying virtual process of becoming" (TR ix).[8] With this, Zizek summarizes his basic ontological, epistemological, and psychoanalytic positions, which all revolve around his appropriation of the Lacanian

"Real." What does Zizek mean by the "Real"? From the perspective of ontology and epistemology, the Real is the "Void" or the "incompleteness" of reality that is exposed in the break of the Act. The "Void" underlies or, more precisely, exists as a "gap" between the various symbolic orders human beings construct. But where Kant posited an external, unknowable noumenal reality behind or beneath all the phenomena produced by human interaction with the world, Zizek reads Hegel to argue that there is no ontologically complete reality behind or beneath human symbolic orders, only the "inconsistency/gap between" these orders (*PD* 66).[9] This gap is the Real. The break exposes the Real and thus the contingency of any particular symbolic order. In the psychodynamic register, the Real is "excess," "jouissance," and even "subject." For Zizek, each of these terms points to the same modality of psychosexual energy that both "sticks out" from and supports the symbolic order as a material "remainder." Eric Santner has described this aspect of the Real in terms of a "constitutive too-muchness that characterizes the psyche."[10] This excess is produced as the developing self is called out—is "interpellated"—to assume a socially prescribed identity, to take one's place as part of a particular symbolic order. In and through our relations with others, we contract an identity and attach ourselves to this world of meaning. But we encounter others not just on the level of shared meaning but as bearers of an unconscious, that is, of erotic energy operating on the boundaries of physiology and culture. These are "enigmatic signifiers," fleeting transmissions that we seek to decode and process, captured by the idea that the other wants something specific from us, something that will legitimate us in their eyes, if only we could figure out what it is. But we inevitably fail to figure it out, because there is no specific articulate desire being transmitted, just unconscious erotic force. The trauma of this failure produces knots of psychic energy that constitute the excess of the Real as a psychoanalytic category, the uncanny excitement of pleasure/pain, the insistent, driven mindlessness or "excessive intensity" that Lacan identified as jouissance (*ES* 29) and that Zizek identifies *as* the subject (*PD* 94). As such, the subject cannot be integrated into the symbolic order; it stands out from this order as "part with no part" or a "constitutive" excess (*TS* 158).

Ordinarily, our psychic economy is shaped by an attachment to a particular symbolic order and the repression of the Real. Here the desire for and pursuit of particular objects allows us to hide from ourselves the Void of our subjectivity. Zizek follows Lacan in distinguishing such objects of desire from the actual cause of desire (*FA* 21; *TS* 291). What is the "cause" of desire? For many psychoanalytic theorists, this "cause" is the immediate bliss of mother/infant relationship that is then prohibited by the castrating Law of the Father. On this model, desire is conceived to have a definite end—the mother—that must be endlessly deferred in favor of socially acceptable substitutes. Zizek though, following Jean Laplanche, offers a more radical view by theorizing that the social order is not a substitute for, but is in fact an *escape from*, the mother—or, more precisely, from the traumatic, overwhelming nature of the mother's, and thus ultimately from the subject's own, enigmatic jouissance.[11] From this perspective, desire and law go hand in hand, because both protect the subject from the Real of jouissance (B 76–77). In this view, one submits one's psychic life to the law of the social order and its prescribed "objects" of desire because it promises an "answer" to the disturbing question posed by the other's jouissance: "What does she want from me?" But, again, there is no real answer to this question, and this realization is what must be repressed: there is no true end or goal of desire.

What does this mean for sublimation? Zizek wants to think a sublimation in which the Void resonates. But if desire represses this Void, Zizek's sublimation must break from the repressive "economy of desire" without destroying the possibility of a new symbolic order; that is, it must be a sublimation that works through an alternate psychic economy, through "love" rather than "desire." Whereas the latter cuts us off from "the primordial encounter of the Unconscious" (TS 284), in love, as Zizek understands it, object and cause of desire coincide. That is, in love one person becomes passionately attached to another, not because they possess a particular, desired, quality, or because they meet some particular need, or because they offer one legitimation, but rather one affirms the other precisely in his or her enigmatic *jouissance*, or, as Zizek puts it, "on behalf of the very unnameable X in him/her" (TA 255).

Love beyond the Law

This distinction between sublimation of desire and sublimation of love is at the heart of Zizek's recent writing on religion, for he employs it to interpret the difference between Judaism and Christianity. Both traditions, he argues, are organized around an encounter with the Real, which means that both make possible a radical break from the social order. But they do so in very different ways. Judaism, claims Zizek, is embedded in the economy of desire, with its paradoxical symbiosis of desire and law. Christianity, by contrast, breaks from desire to love, that is, to a "jouissance outside the Law." For Zizek (as in Badiou), Paul provided the first conceptual account of this shift when he saw that the law itself produces not only a sense of obligation to the law but also the desire to transgress it. This creates a vicious cycle in which law "generates and solicits" sin, which in turn provokes guilt and so binds us ever more tightly to the law (PD 113). Under the regime of desire, then, our capture by the Law is sustained not only by our fantasy of legitimation, but also by our libidinal attachment to fantasies of transgression, to the Law's "obscene underside."[12] As Freud showed in *Moses and Monotheism*, Judaism remains attached to such transgression, repressing the primordial murder of Moses so that it continues to haunt the tradition as an undead specter, a haunting at the basis of Judaism's passionate attachment to the Law.

With Paul and Christianity, however, the violent underside of the Law is revealed in the crucifixion of Christ, which repeats the murder of Moses. And this revelation makes the break from the law possible. Of course—and this is crucial for Zizek—for Paul this does not mean that you no longer obey the Law, but that you should "obey the laws as if you are not obeying them." That is, "unplugging" from the law—to use the term Zizek borrows from Santner (ES 27)—involves not a definitive escape from the law or the symbolic order, but rather a change in our libidinal attachment to them, a suspension, as Zizek puts it, of "the obscene libidinal investment in the Law" (PD 113).

Another way to look at this is to recall Zizek's claim that the subject *is* in excess of the symbolic order. Eric Santner helpfully elaborates this point by distinguishing between two forms of "interpellation": first, the social and psychological processes by which we are called to a particular *identity* and thus become an identifiable part of a larger social whole; and, second, a revelatory experience of divine love that singles us out as a "part which is no part (of a whole)," that is, singles us out in the excess of our jouissance. As Zizek puts it, this involves "an uncanny 'interpellation' beyond ideological interpellation" (PD 113), or, elsewhere, a form of "grace." God's love, in other words, affirms us as "subject," as that which stands out from, cannot be encompassed by or accounted for in the terms of the symbolic order or law. This love, argues both Zizek and Santner, has the effect of releasing us from our compulsive attachment to the symbolic without denying the ways in which, as a person with this or that particular identity, we remain a part of that order. In and through this release, one rejects the fantasies of completion that sustain the economy of desire and that construct others as holding the keys to this completion. In turn, this means that one no longer "desires" others but "loves" them, which allows one to encounter and affirm them in the opacity of their jouissance.[13] Such love, claims Zizek, is what is meant by the biblical command to "love thy neighbor" (FA 111).

These two forms of interpellation provide the grounds for what I am calling the sublimation of desire (interpellation to identity) and the sublimation of love (interpellation to singularity). We can see Zizek working with this distinction in at least two important contexts. The first is his treatment of the passage from Judaism's transcendent God to Christianity's incarnate God. In Judaism, sublimation involves the elevation of finite objects to the status of God as "Real Thing of Beyond" whose name cannot be spoken (FA 104). In Christianity, by contrast, the distance between God and human is closed, meaning that Christ "is not sublime in the sense of 'an object elevated to the dignity of a Thing.' He is not a stand-in for the impossible Thing—God; he is, rather 'the Thing itself,' or, more accurately, 'the Thing itself' is nothing but the rupture/gap which makes Christ not fully human" (PD 80). In Jesus' cry of anguish on the cross—"Why have you forsaken me?"—the Jewish distance between God and human becomes a distance *internal* to God, understood as the gap of the Real. In Christ, in other words, a certain identification of God and human is achieved, not in a collapse of the divine into the human, but in the recognition that the divine is the inhuman excess of the Real. Here the divine is encountered in exposure to the jouissance of the other.

We also see the distinction between two forms of sublimation in Zizek's distinction between "idealization" (sublimation of desire) and "sublimation" (sublimation of love). In "idealization," the other becomes the projected object of my fantasy, that which will provide the "answer" to my desire. By contrast, "sublimation," as "true love," is love for the other "the way he or she is" and is made possible through the "traversal of fantasy" (FA 128). Here, Zizek's designation of the other as he or she is, means he or she as "subject," as excess, or what Zizek also calls the "unnameable X." Desire seeks to repress this "X," while love embraces it. But what is crucial for Zizek's sublimation is that this embrace takes place only in and through engagement with the other in their symbolic identity, in their full, concrete being in the world. That is, in "true love," the other as unnamable X, the other in his or her singularity or jouissance, becomes visible *in and through* their ordinary, everyday life. This is Zizek's "fragile absolute" (B 41), the convergence of the divine and the human manifested in Christ and visible in the neighbor through love. Access to this dimension is made possible by the grace of love in which something happens to turn the other, in all their ordinary reality, into the "Thing I unconditionally love."

It is here, then, that we see the Void of negativity, the Real, resonating in the midst of the symbolic. Where desire seeks to possess its object in the quest for self-legitimation and thus idealizes the object and so fails to see the other for what he or she really is, love, Zizek claims, finds satisfaction in a directedness to the other that is always both constantly approaching and missing it, as a planet in orbit around a sun. The sublimation of love, Zizek says, "eternalizes" drive: where desire always misses the object because what it takes as objects are never "really it," drive "finds satisfaction in circulating around the object and repeatedly missing it" (B 78). This means, more precisely, that the sublimation of love finds satisfaction in the irreducible mystery—that "nothing" at the heart of and resonating in one's everyday engagement with the other. Finding enjoyment in this engagement, we no longer are compelled to possess and distort the other; rather, in love, we are captured precisely by the other's idiosyncratic expression of jouissance.

"Who Is Really Alive Today?"

To this point, I have focused on sublimation as manifested in one's love for another person. But as I have noted, the real impulse behind Zizek's attention to sublimation and the "Christian legacy" is political: he is trying to give an account of political commitment to a "cause." Sublimation in the richest sense, he thinks, is the arduous work of forming "authentic" political collectivities, grounded in passionate belief that results from the uncanny interpellation of love. The Christian community provides Zizek with the model and the theoretical underpinnings for this form of commitment. After the death of Christ, he writes, "there is no place for the God of the Beyond: all that remains is the Holy Spirit, the community of believers onto which the unfathomable aura [sublimity] of Christ passes once it is deprived of its bodily incarnation" (B 91). In this sense, the "fragile absolute" is visible, not simply in the individual in front of me, but also in the community itself for which one struggles and sacrifices.

Yet, like many Hegelians, Zizek argues that the specifically *Christian* form of such community needs to be *aufgehoben* into something new: "The ultimate heroic gesture that awaits Christianity [is that] in order to save its treasure, it has to sacrifice itself—like Christ, who had to die so that Christianity could emerge" (PD 171). For Zizek, the "cause" of contemporary politics is carried by "authentic psychoanalytical and revolutionary political collectives" (FA 160). What does Zizek mean by "authentic" and "revolutionary"? More precisely, what kind of cause can capture us in the interpellation of love? We get some clues in the following:

> Who is really alive today? What if we are "really alive" only if and when we engage ourselves with an excessive intensity which puts us beyond "mere life"? What if, when we focus on mere survival, even if it is qualified as "having a good time," what we ultimately lose is life itself? What if the Palestinian suicide bomber on the point of blowing himself (and others) up is, in an emphatic sense, "more alive" than the American soldier engaged in a war in front of a computer screen hundreds of miles away from the enemy. . . . Or, in terms of the psychoanalytic clinic, what if a hysteric is truly alive in her permanent, excessive, provoking questioning of her existence, while an obsessional is the very model of choosing a "life in death"? . . . It is a properly Nietzschean paradox that the greatest loser in [the obsessional's] apparent assertion of Life against all transcendent Causes is actual life itself. What makes life "worth living" is the very excess of life: the awareness that there is something for which we are ready to risk our life (we may call this excess "freedom," "honor," "dignity," "autonomy," etc.)." (PD 94–5)

Here a cause is something "excessive," for which one is willing to risk one's life. But as we have seen, Zizek's conception of "excess" is much more specific and uncanny than is suggested the idea of "something for which we are ready to risk our life." This excess, for Zizek, does not include many of things we ordinarily think of as the object of self-sacrifice. Thus, in another context, distinguishing between masculine and feminine forms of subjectivity, Zizek writes: "While men sacrifice themselves for a Thing (country, freedom, honor), only women are able to sacrifice themselves for nothing" (B 78). In this context, he clearly privileges the feminine form of sacrifice as "the Christian gesture par excellence" (B 79). In the sublimation of love, then, one does not love the other or a particular cause for the sake of the positive characteristics of the other or the cause, but "for nothing." What does this mean? Theologically, for Zizek, it means that one's passionate belief is directed not to a symbolically glorified, publicly visible cause like kin or country, but to the "nothing" of the "fragile absolute," of the excess or jouissance that shines through the surface of the other or the community. Politically, it means that commitment is structured by a "subtractive universality," a concept central to Zizek, Santner, and Badiou. Santner's distinction between "global" and "universal" perspectives on otherness and plurality is helpful for understanding this idea of "subtraction."[14] Global consciousness distinguishes between people and groups on the basis of those positive characteristic by which each person is part of a larger "natural" community: nationality, ethnicity, race, and so forth. Universal consciousness, by contrast, focuses on the singularity or alterity in each one of us, on the subject as excess. What binds together the "authentic" collectivity and makes it "universal" is not any particular positive characteristic shared by all—any "identity"— but rather the "excess" that is "immanent to any construction of identity" (ES 5): we all share the fact that we are always more (perhaps it would better to say less) than our identities. In this sense, the universal cuts across and disrupts all constructed social orders; it is "subtracted" from them. It is shaped only through the constant and never-completed work of unplugging from our organic communities and so disrupting our identities, as in the psychoanalytic work of traversing our fantasies and so recognizing the Void at the heart of our own subjectivity. This, for Zizek, is the "arduous work of love."

For Zizek, this is not an abstract universality, but rather one that "shines through" *marginalized* social groups, that is, groups "in excess" of the social whole.

> Politics proper thus always involves a kind of short-circuit between the Universal and the Particular, the paradox of a "singular Universal," of a singular which appears as the stand-in for the Universal, destabilizing the 'natural' functional order of relations in the social body. . . . [T]his identification of the non-part with the Whole, of the part of society with no properly defined place within it (or that resists its allocated subordinated place within it) with the Universal, is the elementary gesture of politicization." (TA 166)[15]

The absolute shines through marginalized groups, not because of any positive characteristic they happen to possess, but because they make manifest the process of exclusion that helps support the structural coherence of the Whole —even as it also disrupts it. For Zizek, anyone can be called to this marginalized position and participate in the work of sublimation that forms the political collectivity:

> From a truly radical Marxist perspective, although there is a link between "working class" as a social group and "proletariat" as the position of the

militant fighting for universal Truth, this link is not a determining causal connection, and the two levels must be strictly distinguished: to be a "proletarian" involves assuming a certain subjective stance . . . which in principle, can be adopted by *any* individual—to put it in religious terms, any individual can be "touched by Grace" and interpellated as a proletarian subject. (*TS* 226–27)

The Politics of Sublimation and the Problem of Violence

At a time when terms such as "truth" and "universality" are usually disqualified from the start in religious or political engagements, Zizek's vision of belief and politics is refreshing and important. Particularly promising, I think, is Zizek's effort to distinguish between the sublimation of desire, which we might simply call "ideology" and connect to Santner's "global consciousness," and the sublimation of love considered in terms of a "subtractive universality." I have taken some steps here to analyze this idea and so to elaborate this promise, but I will conclude by arguing that Zizek has to this point failed to rigorously apply this distinction to his efforts to think love and politics together. This becomes especially clear in the prominent—and, I will argue, problematic—role that Zizek assigns to violence in his vision of passionate attachment to a cause.

Christian love, as Zizek understands it, is a violent love. With the names of Lenin and Che Guevara resonating in the background, Zizek describes "Christian, intolerant, violent Love" as "a passion to introduce a Difference, a gap in the order of being, to privilege and elevate some object at the expense of others." Such violence, he goes on to say, is already evident in "the love choice as such, which tears its object out of its context, elevating it to the Thing" (*PD* 32–33).[16] There are two key issues here. First, there is the traversal of fantasy that entails the violence of "unplugging," of rupturing old relationships and sacrificing aspects of self, family, and community that one holds dear. There is, I think, something right in describing this, and so Christian love generally, as "violent." Take, for instance, Martin Luther King's "nonviolent resistance." Some will argue that this example in fact shows that Christian love and politics can be nonviolent. But the fact is that King's resistance incited violence and in some ways depended on it for success. To say this is by no means to belittle or criticize his work. Nor is it to ignore the fact that segregation and racial oppression in the United States in King's day was already inherently violent or to deny a crucial difference between using what we might call "active" violence to resist oppression and, as King did, refusing such means. But King's resistance did "introduce Difference"—and it relentlessly insisted on it in a way that not only demanded the "violence" of change but provoked the violence of blood. To the extent that the violence Zizek invokes is of this type, I think he is right that when it comes to politics, or at least when it comes to any form of resistance to the status quo, love and violence are closely connected.[17]

But we also need to consider a second issue regarding this "passion to introduce a Difference." Here, I think, Zizek's claims about the violence of Christian love are misguided and seem to contradict the view of sublimation I have been elaborating. As noted above, for Zizek this passion takes the form of a love that "tears its object out of its context, elevating it to the Thing." But this is precisely the (standard Lacanian) definition of sublimation that I have been arguing Zizek rejects: it is the sublimation of desire that, through fantasy, mistakes a particular object for the Real and so confuses the object of desire for the cause of desire.[18] As I have indicated, when Zizek contrasts "the Real Thing of the Beyond" as the transcendent, sublime God of Judaism with the "rupture/gap which makes Christ not fully human," he articulates a different form of sublimation, one that does not elevate a particular object to the status of "Thing." Thus, while Zizek offers the theoretical resources for this new conception of sublimation, his discussions of violence, even in his latest works, depend on the earlier, Lacanian view of sublimation.

This inconsistency creates the theoretical space for a problematic valorization of violence, which has its roots in Zizek's dissatisfaction with a politics of resistance and his efforts to defend a politics of the new order. Such a politics, he claims, was Lenin's achievement, which is the point behind his contrast between the Leninist who is "fully aware of what it actually means to take power and to exert it" and the liberal leftist who "wants true democracy for the people, but without the secret police to fight the counter-revolution" (B 4). And Zizek sees Paul as Lenin's predecessor in this: "Was not Paul, like Lenin, the great 'institutionalizer.' And, as such, reviled by the partisans of 'original' Marxism-Christianity? Does not the Pauline temporality 'already, but not yet' also designate Lenin's situation . . . ? Revolution is already behind us, the old regime is out, freedom is here—but the hard work still lies ahead" (PD 9). For Zizek, the left should not be satisfied with simply resisting the current hegemony of global capitalism, but, out of passionate love for the cause, should put aside liberal qualms about secret police and do the hard and sometimes violent work of creating and protecting the new order.

But here, I think, Zizek fails to work hard enough. Returning to his embrace of Christ, the "Thing" as gap, it is necessary to keep in mind that when we are grasped in a relation of love to the "fragile absolute," we are continually "missing" the object of our love. Thus, with respect to the individual, the work of love is in large part the work of traversing fantasy in a way that enables us renounce the desire for possession and to love the other as he or she is—as an imperfect being, through whom the absolute shines. This is, as Zizek puts it, to forsake "the promise of Eternity itself for an imperfect individual" (PD 13). Politically, this means that it is necessary to carefully articulate the political work of de-sublimation, that is, to discipline our passionate commitment to the cause by the traversal of fantasy. One way of doing this, if Jesus is to be an example, is to focus not only on his "hatred" (leaving one's family to follow him, coming with a sword, etc.), as Zizek tends to do, but also on his compassion, his more "positive" acts of love. It would also mean thinking more carefully about the model of the Christian community, something Zizek hints at but does not develop explicitly. Thus, the ambiguity in his work with respect to sublimation finds a parallel in his treatment of the collectivity. On the one hand, as I have just indicated, he sees Lenin and Paul as great institutional-izers. But on the other hand, in what I see as a more promising move, he affirms the "return to Lenin" in terms of "a collective organization [that] does not yet fix itself into an Institution (the established Church, the IPA, the Stalinist Party-State)" (B 4). There is an important difference here, one that Zizek has not developed, between an institutionalized order invested in pro-tecting itself and a "collective" that, although not necessarily "nonviolent," has less invested in the "new order" and so is less willing to resort to violence to protect its own power, or perhaps more open to nonviolent ways of expressing and exerting its power.

In the end, though, even if one agrees that Zizek needs to address more clearly what we might describe as a politics *between* resistance and order, I think one also should agree that the problem he is grappling with here is a crucial one: global capitalism's threat to the "fundamental matrix of sublima-tion." Is it possible to believe or commit today? This, to be only a little simplis-tic, is the real question behind Zizek's criticisms of deconstruction and "post-secular ethics." Though many of the critical comments he directs at Derrida, Levinas, and postsecular thought strike me as more of the bluster to which Zizek is prone and as obscuring the fact that he is closer to a postsecular ethics of the other than he admits, his focus on sublimation and belief identifies a site for significant comparison and debate.

"Derrida reduces Otherness to the 'to-come' of pure potentiality, thor-oughly deontologizing it, bracketing its positive content, so that all that re-mains is the specter of a promise" (PD 140). On Zizek's reading, deconstruc-tion is a form of symbolic death without the resurrection of a new sublimation. Thus, Derridean themes such as "messianism to come" and "undecidability" are symptoms of the contemporary threat to commitment. By contrast, Zizek's "fragile absolute" and his work on sublimation are precisely attempts to avoid the politics of such "bracketing" to think about a form of sublimation that can commit to "positive content." Zizek's, then, is a "messianism" in which the Messiah has arrived already and opened up a new space for us. It is now our duty to act, to "help God" by "drawing the consequences of the Act" (PD 136–37). Yet perhaps something like the work of deconstruction is precisely the kind of work of de-sublimation that Zizek has left out of his account. If so, then thinking carefully and non-polemically about the distance that separates these two "turns to religion" might help to resolve some of the questions about politics and violence I have raised here.

NOTES

1. This is the definition offered by Jonathan Lear, *Love and its Place in Nature* (New York: Farrar, Straus, and Giroux, 1990), 179.

2. Slavoj Zizek, *The Ticklish Subject* (London: Verso, 1999), 159. Hereafter in text as *TS*.

3. Slavoj Zizek, "From Purification to Subtraction: Badiou and the Real," in *Think Again*, ed. P. Hallward (New York: Continuum, 2004), 171. Hereafter in text as *PS*.

4. Badiou's sublimation thus remains captive to ideology, for Zizek, who defines ideology as the "mitigation of the Real," a definition derived from his reading of the late Lacanian concept of the "sinthome" (Zizek, *The Fragile Absolute* [London: Verso, 2000], 116–17; hereafter *FA*). For the early Lacan, the goal of psychoanalysis was to bring the analyzand to terms with the "symbolic," the linguistic and social order of the "big Other." The symptom, on this view, signaled the subject's alienation from this order, his/her refusal to accede to the demands of the "big other." Later, Lacan argues that the symbolic order should be understood as "sinthome," *itself* a symptom of the repression or "mitigating" of the Real that masks the fundamental incompleteness of reality and subject.

5. In addition to *The Fragile Absolute*, I include here *On Belief* (London: Routledge, 2001; hereafter in text as *B*) and *The Puppet and the Dwarf* (Cambridge: MIT Press, 2003; hereafter in text as *PD*).

6. The place of love in Badiou is a difficult one, in large part precisely because, as Zizek sees it, there seems to be a disjunction between the relatively circumscribed role he assigns what is basically erotic love as one of four truth-procedures and the seemingly more foundational role he assigns to love elsewhere. For an example of the latter, see the chapter on love in *Saint Paul* (Stanford, Calif.: Sanford University Press, 2003), 86–92.

7. This latter problem is the context in which, in the opening chapters of *The Fragile Absolute*, Zizek rejects politically correct tolerance in favor of the "proper political hatred" necessary for committed political struggle (*FA* 11). Zizek believes that the kind of commitment in which political love and political hatred are closely intertwined has become more and more difficult, not simply because of the imperative to "tolerance" but also because "the very fundamental matrix of sublimation . . . seems to be increasingly under threat" (*FA* 26). In short, he claims, we are losing the ability to "believe" (*PD* 7; *B* 14–5, 109).

8. Slavoj Zizek, "The Descent of Transcendence into Immanence, or, Deleuze as a Hegelian," in *Transcendence*, ed. R. Schwarz (New York: Routledge, 2004), 244.

9. Politically, the key term here, which Zizek borrows from Laclau and Mouffe, is "antagonism," which refers to historically and socially constructed conflict between perceptions of reality that gives any given symbolic order its particular ("distorting" or, we might say, fictional) shape yet cannot itself be articulated from within this order (*PD* 75).

10. Eric Santner, *On the Psychotheology of Everyday Life* (Chicago: University of Chicago Press, 2001), 8. Hereafter in text as *ES*. In what follows, I rely frequently on Santner's insights and formulations to help clarify Zizek's thinking. This is possible because in many fundamental respects, the two thinkers are very closely aligned. Nonetheless, it is important to emphasize that on the issue of the relation of Judaism to Christianity, and on the possibilities of a Jewish ethics of the other, there are important differences between them. Basically, where Zizek argues for the importance of the

sublation of Judaism into Christianity, Santner, following Rosenzweig, has a more positive reading of the theological and ethical promise of Judaism. Given the proximity of their thought in so many crucial respects, it would be fascinating to explore this difference in more detail.

11. Slavoj Zizek, *Did Someone Say Totalitarianism?* (London: Verso, 2001), 56–8.

12. This underside has been theorized by Carl Schmitt in terms of the "logic of exception," which points to the founding transgression (or in Benjamin's terms "divine violence") by which the law is instituted in the first place. This idea is exerting renewed force today not only in Zizek but in Agamben and Derrida among others

13. Zizek puts it this way in *The Abyss of Freedom* (Ann Arbor: University of Michigan Press, 1997), 25: "When do I effectively encounter the Other 'beyond the wall of language,' in the real of his or her being? Not when I am able to describe her, not even when I learn her values, dreams, and so on, but only when I encounter the Other in her moment of jouissance."

14. It is important here to distinguish Santner's and Zizek's "subtractive" universality from the universality that is suspended in Kierkegaard's suspension of the ethical.

15. Zizek's work here owes much to the political theory of Jacques Ranciere. See Ranciere, *Disagreement: Politics and Philosophy*, trans. Julie Rose (Minneapolis: University of Minnesota Press, 1999).

16. "[I]n true love, I 'hate the beloved out of love': I 'hate' the dimension of his inscription into the socio-symbolic structure on behalf of my very love for him as a unique person. . . . In this 'uncoupling,' the neighbor is thus reduced to a singular member of the community of believers . . . reduced to the singular point of subjectivity" (FA 126–27).

17. I make no claims here to have provided anything like a satisfactory argument that Christian love and social action necessarily involves violence. Obviously, such an argument would need to be constructed with far more breadth and far more detail than I offer here. It is to suggest, though, that I am suspicious that any such argument could succeed and that the issues involved are more complex than many imagine.

18. See also FA 20, 49, 158.

12

Love as a Declaration of War?

On the Absolute Character of Love in
Jean-Luc Marion's Phenomenology of Eros

CHRISTINA M. GSCHWANDTNER

The lover "declares his love, as one declares war." So insists Jean-Luc Marion repeatedly in his investigation into the nature of the erotic phenomenon.[1] War, of course, is here "only" a metaphor illustrating the absolute commitment of the lover. Yet the fact that this analogy is used several times throughout the book seems to indicate that it is a bit more than merely an insignificant example. Rather, it points to a problematic aspect of Marion's treatment of eros, namely the extreme—if not almost militant—character of this love. And the careful reader finds the connotations of absoluteness exacerbated by another sub-theme, stated even less obviously: the parallel between this phenomenological analysis of eros and Marion's (earlier) theological analysis of charity. Combined, they lead to a troubling conclusion. The lover, on Marion's account, will turn out to be like a God declaring war. In the following, I will (ab)use four of Marion's comparisons of love to war in order to highlight the absolute character of his treatment and show how in each case the divine emerges surreptitiously. Before analyzing these comparisons more carefully, however, let me briefly provide some context for Marion's exploration of love.

In *Le phénomène érotique*, Marion outlines what he calls an "erotic reduction" in six meditations. Such an erotic reduction sets metaphysical constrictions aside and reconfigures the notions of time and space. It is also able to overcome the metaphysical dichotomies of subject and object, on the one hand by articulating a self after the subject that is not autonomous and self-sufficient, and on the other hand by approaching a truly individuated other. Marion begins with the claim that we are today no longer concerned with

Cartesian certainty. Instead, questions of meaning and affirmation touch us much more profoundly. We particularly desire the assurance that somebody loves us. He shows that we are unable to provide such assurance ourselves by outlining the failure of self-love that ultimately leads to hatred of both self and others. He therefore suggests that love must start, not with my own desire to assure myself that I am loved by someone else, but rather with my decision to love another. He articulates love first of all as a meeting of the flesh (instead of bodies) where I phenomenalize the flesh of the other while the other phenomenalizes my flesh: we both give each other the experience of our own flesh. Marion speaks of this as a mutual, yet not reciprocal, relationship. He then goes on to show how this love incarnate in the flesh must always come to a halt (e.g., after the rapture of orgasm) and therefore seeks to express itself in a third that would bear witness to the fidelity and reality of that love. The child can do so only temporarily and unsuccessfully. Marion therefore concludes by articulating a language of love that would express the whole range of its experience, even as it always admits its inability to express this impossible event. Outlining and describing these various moves, Marion also provides analyses of seduction, betrayal, hatred, jealousy, fidelity, friendship, and many other aspects of love.

War is not an explicit aspect of this treatment. Marion does not consciously compare love and war. There is no separate section on the relationship between or similarity of love and war. Yet he uses war as an analogy for love several times and in different contexts. It is this apparently innocent metaphor and especially its repeated occurrence that makes us aware of something disquieting emerging in Marion's treatment of love. I will consider four of these comparisons, each emphasizing a different aspect of Marion's account of love: first, the lover who declares love; second, the beloved to whom love is declared; third, the language of this declaration of love; finally, the quality of this love and especially its univocal character.

The One Who Declares

The first comparison is the one mentioned in the opening sentence. It appears when Marion begins to insist on the lack of reciprocity in the loving relationship that must escape all danger of metaphysical reason and economy. Marion compares love and war as both being beyond reason in their escape from calculation and commerce: "As a war finally breaks out without reason, by deflagration and transgression of all better reasons, the lover makes love break out. He declares his love, as one declares war—without reason. That is to say, at times even without taking the time and the trouble to make such a declaration" (*PE* 129; *EP* 79). We engage in both love and war with passion and abandon, without cool consideration, without hesitation, without rational boundaries. What Marion emphasizes in this context (as is, of course, also very evident in the comparison itself) is the importance of the lover's initiative. Marion had originally begun his treatment with the desire of the subject to find meaning in life. In order to escape the attack of "vanity," I wish to be assured that I am loveable (and that somebody does actually love me). It is in consequence of my failure to love myself sufficiently or to find another who will love me satisfactorily, that Marion suggests we must abandon all search for self-fulfillment, assurance of being loved, and even reciprocity (*PE* 114ff.; *EP* 68ff.). Instead of requiring to be loved by the other, I must take the initiative in loving; I must first become lover before I can find myself beloved. Marion insists that this separates love from "being" and overcomes metaphysical constrictions.[2] He compares the love that I give freely, even if it is not returned, to the gift that escapes any commerce or need for reciprocity. In loving with abandon, even if that love is rejected by the other, I find meaning and assure my identity and dignity as lover (*PE* 122; *EP* 76).

To some extent, this emphasis on making the first step in love seems to connote selflessness, vulnerability, and generosity, which are obviously all aspects that Marion desires to stress. Yet even these apparently positive connotations seem problematic if they indicate an exclusive emphasis on the lover. And the insistence on the primacy of the lover becomes even stronger in a following section, where Marion argues that the mere decision to love is already sufficient to mark me as lover.[3] Marion highlights the significance of this decision to love first: Even if I do not love well or perfectly and cannot measure the quality of my love, I must make a decision to love as first lover. This decision is fully accomplished even if my love never elicits any response (*PE* 146). Since I could never accomplish love perfectly anyway, I need not wait for a complete performance of love. The decision alone is sufficient. My phenomenality decides itself only in my decision for the other. I can and must at least decide to love, "love to love" [*aimer aimer (amare amare)*] (*PE* 148). Although I can never love fully, it suffices to love "love" in order for me to appear as lover. I must act *as if* I love. The initiative of love lies fully with the lover, who depends only on him- or herself. I fall in love only on my own account, not by chance or by accident or by the other's initiative. Throughout these passages, Marion repeatedly emphasizes the lover's sole initiative on which everything depends here (PE 146–52).[4] Yet a lover who can become lover solely by his or her decision, by a solitary choice, and needs no interaction with another in love seems extremely problematic.[5] Surely, loving *love* is decidedly not equivalent to (nor the first step toward) loving *another*. And while Marion is certainly right to refuse a requirement of reciprocity in the loving relationship and to describe love primarily as a freely offered gift, neither of these aspects ought to lead to an elimination of the role of the other in this relationship to the point where the sole focus is on the choice of the lover.

Marion insists on the absolute importance of this initiative of the lover because, so he suggests, it individuates the self for the first time fully:

> I do not become myself only because I think, doubt or imagine (because others can think my thoughts, which besides often do not concern me but the objects of my intentionalities); or because I will, desire or hope (because I never know if I intervene in first person or only as the mask which hides—and supports—the pulsations, the passions and the needs which play in me without me). But I become definitely myself each time and as long as, as lover, I can love first. (*PE* 125)

I become individuated in my acts as a lover and in my choice to love because neither depends on other objects or on a reciprocal relationship. I gain assurance, not of another's love, but of my own ability or decision to love. This assurance allows me to overcome my self-hatred and counters the "attack of vanity." By thus assuming what is "most proper to me," I am able to become truly myself and am no longer dependent on anything else to affirm my existence or my worthiness.[6]

This first love that has to be prior to any response, that is freely given as gift (and that apparently speaks more of me than of the other) already seems to carry religious overtones. And in fact, biblical imagery pervades the treatment. It is a love thoroughly kenotic in character, patterned on the infinite divine love for finite humanity. Marion explicates what he calls "remarkable postures of love" by taking up the Pauline definitions of love from 1 Corinthians 13: The lover supports all and prepares everything for the beloved (*PE* 138; *EP* 85). The lover believes all and endures all with a kind of "sovereign power" that requires no response (*PE* 139; *EP* 86). The lover loves without sight and thus hopes all (*PE* 140; *EP* 87). This love is not only self-emptying but also overpowering in its intensity. It abandons itself in complete commitment and profound vulnerability. Yet it is the lover who makes the first move, who decides to love, and who prepares all conditions for intimacy to become possible. One wonders if any beloved would still be able to resist such powerful advances. Maybe this is an appropriate description of the incarnation, but is it also a good paradigm for all human love? Marion insists, of course, that my initiative as lover does not merely serve to individuate me but also the beloved. Yet even the distinction itself between "lover" and "beloved" appears to suggest the superiority of one and the dependence of the other.[7] It is always the "lover" who phenomenalizes the "beloved" and allows him or her to appear. The next comparison serves to highlight this even more clearly.

To Whom One Declares

This second (briefer) example appears only a few pages after the first in the context of Marion's analysis of Don Juan as an example of the advance of the lover (*PE* 133ff.; *EP* 82ff.). Marion claims that "those to whom he declares love, as those on whom he declares war (often these are the same) appear in their increasingly extreme singularity" (*PE* 134; *EP* 82). The seducer especially exemplifies love in his or her abandonment and total commitment to the cause that is akin to that of the soldier. Both are passionately devoted to the "object" of their pursuit that is thus highlighted in its singularity and specificity. Again, the initiative of the lover (as the one who makes the declaration of love/war) and his or her complete dedication to the movement of eros is emphasized. Yet what Marion also highlights in this case is that the lover actually allows the phenomenon of the other to appear for the first time in the way in which a declaration of war singularizes the enemy.

Not only does my initiative as lover allow me to find myself, but also it becomes the condition for the individuation of the other. In the erotic reduction, the beloved appears for the first time as an individuated person and not merely as an object of my consciousness. Marion argues that the lover allows the other to emerge and makes him or her visible through the erotic reduction: "The other phenomenalizes himself in the exact measure in which the lover loves him and, Orpheus of phenomenality, tears him away from obscurity, makes him remount from the ground of the unseen" (*PE* 130; *EP* 80). Making something "remount from the ground of the unseen" is an expression Marion has used repeatedly in order to depict the work of an artist (especially in painting).[8] Creativity means to make visible as a phenomenon what was before unseen.[9] Yet even if the work of art is not an object (as Marion of course wants to insist also about the beloved) but a saturated phenomenon—a bedazzling and incomprehensible experience—it still seems extremely problematic to imply that the lover "creates" the phenomenon of the beloved in a manner similar to the painter's creation of a work.

And Marion continues to emphasize this parallel. Only the lover sees truly and allows the other to emerge: "The lover, and he alone, sees something else, a thing that nobody except him sees—precisely no longer a thing, but, for the first time, this other, unique, individualized, furthermore cut off from economy, disengaged from objectness, unveiled by the initiative of love, surging up as a phenomenon so far unseen" (*PE* 131; *EP* 80). The lover is the condition of possibility for the phenomenon of the beloved who appears on the horizon of the lover's consciousness. This seems to go beyond vulnerability and generosity to give the lover both power and control over the beloved, despite all of Marion's affirmations of the contrary. Even if the beloved saturates or even explodes the screen of consciousness, the lover must first provide the screen and horizon that is being transgressed. If the lover allows the beloved to emerge, allows the beloved to become visible, and is like the painter who permits the invisible phenomenon to emerge, then this primacy includes at least a measure of mastery.[10]

And has not much of this insistence on the initiative of the lover likened him or her to God? In *Prolegomena to Charity*, Marion compares the lover's initiative more explicitly to a divine initiative, while also using the imagery of creativity: "It is up to me to set the stage for the other, not as an object that I hold under contract and whose play I thus direct, but as the uncontrollable, the unforeseeable, and the foreign stranger who will affect me, provoke me, and—possibly—love me. *Love of the other repeats creation through the same withdrawal wherein God opens,* to what is not, the right to be, and even the right to refuse Him" (*PC* 167; emphasis mine). The imagery of painting therefore becomes loaded with a weightier creation, the divine one. Although Marion does not make the same connection explicit here, he does affirm later that God is the first and primary lover, the one who precedes us and by whom we are always loved prior to our own loving another (*PE* 341; *EP* 222).

The employment of the figure of Don Juan in this context seems particularly unfortunate. Although Marion censures Don Juan's obsession with seduction, he praises him for his advances. He explains that the problem in this context is not that Juan advances in his desire to seduce, but rather that he breaks off too quickly and thus continually and obsessively repeats the movement with a new person. In true love, the lover would need to maintain the initiative more faithfully and more persistently toward the same person: "Don Juan does not love too much—on the contrary, he loves too little, too briefly, without enough impetus; he loses his advance. Don Juan loves too little, not because he desires too much, but rather because he does not desire enough, nor long enough, nor strongly enough" (*PE* 137; *EP* 85). Yet is there not something deeply problematic about seduction apart from its lack of fidelity and its need for repetition? Surely "advance" can here become very quickly much too demanding and violent? The space to resist or reject this advance of the seducer seems to recede from view, especially as Marion calls for an even more persistent pursuit, ideally one that lasts to eternity.[11] And not only does Marion resort to biblical imagery and theological language here, but he also calls for such language in the discourse of the lovers, as will be seen in the context of a further comparison of love to war.

How One Declares

In this third passage, Marion points to the repetition of the imagery himself: "Once again, the lovers declare their love to each other as one declares war: claiming to love equals a provocation without return" (*PE* 230; *EP* 147). As in the previous occurrences, Marion wishes to stress the absolute and total commitment implied in one's declaration of love that is like one's total involvement in a war; yet he is particularly concerned with the *language* of love in this context. Like the declaration of war, the declaration of love is performative, not descriptive. In declaring my love (as in declaring war) I do not describe a state of affairs or investigate an object, but I engage in an activity to which I commit myself completely. Erotic language is performative or pragmatic in two ways. On the one hand, it does not really "say" anything, because it makes no statements of fact or description and often does not even make sense. It is therefore neither descriptive nor logical speech. On the other hand, it makes possible the actual "performing" of the activity: it excites the flesh and enables its reception; it invites the coming of the other; it commits the lover by an oath of fidelity. Like the declaration of war, it announces an incoming event and makes this activity possible, instead of describing an abstract statement of truth.

Again, what Marion says about the language of love parallels what he has said earlier in his more theological work about the language of prayer and praise. He has usually employed the threefold Dionysian distinction of an affirmative (or kataphatic), a negative (or apophatic) and a third way, a hyperbolic way of praise, which is not prescriptive or descriptive but purely performative.[12] In the liturgical acts of prayer and praise, the person praying approaches God and allows him- or herself to be envisaged by the divine, to become open to the crossing of gazes that happens within this act of prayer.[13] The performative (or pragmatic) language of prayer therefore accomplishes a relationship similar to that between lover and beloved. Prayer neither describes nor denies description, but it performs an activity. Like the performative language of love, praise and prayer are not logical, at times not even coherent. And, like love, prayer opens me to the coming of another, commits me to a certain kind of life. This similarity would not be troubling if it were a mere parallel: prayer is one example of performative language; the declaration of love is another. Yet Marion actually insists in his analysis of eros that the language of mystical theology is absolutely essential for an appropriate expression of erotic love and as the culmination of such talk.[14] The excess that is represented by the excitement of the flesh overflows in a discourse that for Marion is always that of mystical theology. The language of love *must* express itself in a mystical and quasi-divine discourse. Marion even explicitly likens the three vocabularies for love that he has outlined (obscene, infantile, mystical) to the three ways of Dionysius (*PE* 233; *EP* 149). Erotic language must not only employ the vocabulary of mystical theology, but any terminology it does employ finds its place in a relationship of discourse patterned on theological affirmations about God. Of course, erotic imagery and language have indeed been employed in mysticism, and theological language has been used to describe sexuality. Yet to insist that erotic language must *of necessity* be theological and that chastity is the "erotic virtue par excellence" (*PE* 283; *EP* 183) seems a bit extreme.

Within *Le phénomène érotique* Marion only mentions this "necessary" connection of erotic language to mystical theology briefly. He explores the parallel between the two in much more detail in a recent article where he analyzes the nature of erotic statements in greater detail.[15] He contends that "I love you!" does not "say something about something" [a locutionary act that is signifying or predicative] or even "performs what it says' [an illocutionary or performative act], but that it "does what it says to someone." He identifies this as a "perlocutionary" act, namely, one that intends to have an effect on the interlocutor without necessarily accomplishing its intent.[16] These effects might include provocation, intrigue, compulsion, or seduction and are concerned more with the person to whom one speaks than with either the utterance or the speaker. After identifying erotic language as such a perlocutionary act, Marion goes on to analyze what he sees as its "three paths," which correspond again to the three paths of mystical theology.[17] He spells out an affirmative, apophatic, and hyperbolic path in erotic dialogue. Although "I love you!" cannot be verified (is not locutionary or illocutionary), it does *affirm* the effect that it intends to produce, namely to individualize the other and to open the space for a response. This affirmation leads to *negation* in that the speaker must listen to the effect the speech act has produced, knowing that no clear response is possible at this moment. There is always a temporal delay in an answer fraught with ambiguity. The affirmation of love thus must ceaselessly be repeated in a final *hyperbolic* movement: "I keep saying and repeating 'I love you!' precisely because, on the one hand, I cannot guarantee it, and, on the other hand, I cannot give up trying. Short of answering the question, 'Do you love me?' I repeat the perlocutionary act that instigates it, 'I love you!' It is neither a question of kataphasis, nor of apophasis, but rather of a temporalizing language strategy, a repetition that affirms nothing, negates nothing, but that keeps alive a dialogic situation."[18]

Marion concludes his article by linking this erotic discourse explicitly to mystical theology and by insisting on their univocality.[19] He denies the suggestion that the two discourses are merely parallel but wants to establish a deeper connection between them. Both types of language "mobilize three types of names" for the beloved (or God) and do so in a parallel fashion. He employs the story of Christ's three-fold question to Peter whether he loves him to show that its three stages exemplify the paths of mystical theology and of erotic discourse. Consequently, "between God and man everything remains ambiguous except, precisely, love."[20] Already the theological nature of this phenomenological exercise has become very apparent. This is made even more explicit in the final reference I will examine.[21]

Why One Declares

This final instance occurs when Marion is speaking of the need for a third to witness to love, while simultaneously pointing out the insufficiency of the child to do so. The fact that the child will grow and no longer witness to the couple's love, he sees as further consolidating the impossibility of reciprocity between lovers. He emphasizes this by saying: "The lover enters into the advance as one enters into war or into religion—by burning one's bridges and without hope (and the least desire) to return to the equilibrium of exchange" (*PE* 315; *EP* 204). This comparison is again intended to stress the complete and total character of love and the abandon with which one engages in it, that allows no reflection or reversal. Yet in this case, religion is included in the comparison, making explicit (maybe involuntarily) what has become clear in the preceding: the univocity between divine and human love.

Indeed, Marion insists repeatedly on the need for a univocal description of love. He outlines how important it is that anything having to do with love, including the moves of seduction and betrayal, can be described with the same paradigm. Purely carnal desire, friendship, affection between parents and children, erotic intimacy, religious or mystical union with God—all must display a similar pattern. After comparing the most extreme cases (of desire for money or drugs with love for a human being or God), Marion concludes that there can be no equivocity in love: either erotic reduction is practiced fully and in the same fashion, or there is no love involved in the desire at all (*PE* 335; *EP* 217).[22] For Marion, all types of love function in the same manner, even erotic love and friendship. Friendship does not formally differ from erotic love except in "the tonality of its figures" (*PE* 336; *EP* 218). As we have seen, the recent article similarly insists on the univocality of the languages for divine and human love.[23]

Yet why must all these instances of love be the same? Why are they necessarily mere modulations of the same thing? It appears inadequate, for example, to describe the affection of a young girl for her grandmother as a mere immature stage of a later development of deeper erotic sentiments and sexual urges. Nor does it seem appropriate to describe friendship, as Marion does, as erotic love minus orgasm. The fact that there is no "object" involved or that neither is concerned with possession or economy is not enough to indicate the phenomenological similarity of the various figures.[24] Yet to show the univocal character of love is one of Marion's explicit goals from the very beginning of the treatment. Even in the introduction, he claims that to distinguish between different kinds or modes of love is to compromise its unique character (*PE* 14–15; *EP* 4–5). One ought not to oppose eros and charity, or even eros and *agape*, to each other. A true concept of love, for Marion, must of necessity be a univocal one. The apparently strict distinction between his earlier theological reflections on charity and his present phenomenological treatment of eros, then, is far from clear. The insistence on love's univocal character and the rejection of any distinctions between eros and charity/*agape* make evident that Marion does seek to appropriate his theological insights for his phenomenological treatment, or at the very least that he wants to guide the phenomenological consideration back to theological reflection.[25]

This becomes explicit in the final paragraphs of the book, where Marion examines the traditional distinction between human eros and divine *agape* and rejects it, since true human love does not possess (and thus is like *agape*), and since God's desire is as strong as any human eros (and thus qualifies as erotic). He concludes that God loves in the same way that we do and performs the erotic reduction in a parallel fashion: "God practices the logic of the erotic reduction as we do, with us, according to the same rite and following the same rhythm as we do, to the point where we can even ask ourselves whether we do not learn it from him and from none other. God loves in the same way we do" (*PE* 341; *EP* 222). All love, then, ultimately functions in an identical fashion for Marion. The various aspects of eros that he has outlined apply to all human beings and to God in the same way. Erotic intimacy is an indication of divine *agape*. And God's love provides the blueprint for any truly loving human relationship. We must learn to love divinely.

This is, of course, also something Marion has argued in his earlier theological work. In an article on the ascension, Marion depicts the relationship between the disciples and Christ as the paradigm for a self that is related in total abandonment and love to God.[26] The disciples take on the role and persona of Christ. Christ was the first to measure the divine distance successfully and to do so as a human being. To assume the role of Christ is to be able to engage in the play of distance with right measure and to recognize that it is a game of charity that is played only with the measure of love. The disciples (then and now) must live out this new vision of charity by playing the role of Christ in mutual love, as if it were a performance in a theater that they must continually reinvent (as a *commedia dell'arte*): "Distance allows the disciples to become not servants but friends, not spectators but actors of the redemptive and revelatory action of Christ. They themselves occupy the place, the role, and the charge of Christ" (*PC* 145). To instantiate love truly is to become like Christ, maybe even to become divine.[27]

Finally, not only do all loves proceed in a parallel manner, but also for Marion all erotic love ultimately appears to dissolve into divine *agape*.[28] One loves authentically only when one loves like God in an abundant self-giving kenosis. Marion certainly never claims explicitly that all true love is divine. Yet he constantly courts this danger by his insistence on the univocality of these experiences and of the discourses employed to describe them. As we have already seen, the initiative of the lover is analogous to the divine initiative. The arising of the other parallels a kind of creation. The language to describe this encounter is that of mystical theology. So Marion concludes his entire treatment of the erotic phenomenon by making explicit what has been implicit all along, namely, that divine love is the origin and culmination of all human loves:

> When God loves (and in fact he never ceases to love), he simply loves infinitely better than we do. He loves to perfection, without fault, without error, from beginning to end. He loves as the first and the last. He loves like no one else. In the end, I discover not only that an other loved me before I love him, thus that this other played the lover long before me, but especially that this first lover, from always, is named God. . . . God precedes and transcends us, but in that first and foremost because he loves us infinitely better than we love ourselves and we love him. God surpasses us as the best lover. (*PE* 341–42; *EP* 222)

God is the only true lover. All human love is authentic only as it approaches the character and direction of this divine love. All humans must consider themselves loved by God before they are truly capable of love. Ultimately, their love becomes a mere repetition of the divine one. God enables, sustains, and perfects all human love. While this might be a convincing *theological* account of love, it seems deeply problematic as a *philosophical* analysis of eros.[29] Despite all of Marion's groundbreaking work on the erotic phenomenon and at times beautiful descriptions of its various aspects, this love just seems a bit too overwhelming. A love initiated by an absolutely committed lover who prepares all conditions for the beloved and declares this love in a divine fiat—such love really does seem to strike the bedazzled beloved like a "declaration of war."

NOTES

1. Jean-Luc Marion, *Le phénomène érotique: Six méditations* (Paris: Grasset, 2003), 129; henceforth cited as *PE*. I also provide references to the English translation: *The Erotic Phenomenon*, trans. Stephen E. Lewis (Chicago: University of Chicago Press, 2007), cited as *EP*. In some form or another Marion has been occupied with the topic of love throughout most of his work. His most recent work on the erotic phenomenon merely crowns a much older concern that was previewed in *The Idol and Distance* (New York: Fordham, 2001; cited as *ID*) and prepared in *Prolegomena to Charity* (New York: Fordham, 2002; cited as *PC*). At the same time, this is a very intimate work: Marion suggests in the introduction that he speaks primarily from his personal experience (*PE* 22; *EP* 10). Not having shared this experience or spent a comparable amount of time on this topic, I do not presume to criticize Marion's work on eros and charity in its entirety. And in fact his book (and his work overall) includes many trenchant analyses, brilliant insights, and beautiful reflections. Yet the comparison of love with war seems to highlight a problematic aspect of Marion's work on this topic that I wish to explore in this paper. I focus on Marion's explication of love in this particular book, which is his most recent and definitive work on the topic; however, I supply references to earlier works when appropriate.

2. This claim has been contested by several of his readers, but I am unable to examine it here.

3. *PE* 143ff.; *EP* 89ff. Even a bit earlier he emphasizes that "the lover loves to love for the love of love" [*L'amant aime aimer pour l'amour de l'amour*] (*PE* 140; *EP* 87).

4. Consider the following example: "In fact, falling in love depends solely on me" (*PE* 150; *EP* 94).

5. Of course, Marion would respond that we are still in the beginning of the treatment, that we have not yet spoken of the intimacy of the flesh or even of the necessary appearance of the third in the figure of the child. Yet the fact that love must necessarily begin with my initiative and that I can become lover solely by my own choice and without interaction with the other still appears somewhat alarming.

6. It is not entirely clear to me why this avoids the return of any notions of self-sufficiency or autonomy.

7. It is particularly troubling here that he exclusively uses the male pronoun for the lover and often switches to the feminine pronoun when speaking of the beloved, in

particular when describing the need to "enter into" the beloved. In one passage he seems to realize this himself: "*Il voit avec les yeux de l'amour, c'est-à-dire en s'aveuglant (la grande est majestueuse, la petite délicieuse, l'hystérique passionnée, la garce excitante, la sotte spontanée, la raisonneuse brilliante, etc.—et on peut le transposer au masculin)*" (*PE* 130–31); "He sees with the eyes of love, which is to say by blinding himself (the large woman is majestic, the petite, delightful; the hysterical, passionate; the bitch, arousing; the silly, spontaneous; the argumentative, brilliant, etc.—and one can easily transpose these so that they apply to men, too)" (*EP* 80). It is not entirely clear to me that one could really so easily "transpose this into the masculine." See Stephen Lewis's comment on this in the English translation (*EP* 24).

8. See especially the first two sections (which analyze painting) of Jean-Luc Marion, *The Crossing of the Visible*, trans. James K. A. Smith (Stanford, Calif.: Stanford University Press, 2004; cited as *CV*) and chapter 3 of Jean-Luc Marion, *In Excess: Studies of Saturated Phenomena*, trans. Robyn Horner and Vincent Berraud (New York: Fordham University Press, 2002), in which he explicates the painting as a saturated phenomenon of "quality," namely, by giving more than we can bear.

9. Marion does employ painting imagery and terminology in this section by speaking of the "field of vision," of "vanishing lines," and of the "empty frame" (*PE* 137; *EP* 84).

10. In *Prolegomena to Charity*, Marion describes this even more bluntly: "Only charity (or however one would like to call it, if one is afraid to acknowledge its name) opens the space where the gaze of the other can shine forth. The other appears only if I gratuitously give him the space in which to appear. . . . I must take from myself, in order to open the space where the other may appear" (*PC* 166).

11. In a later passage, he suggests that the future of the erotic experience coincides with the hope of Christian eschatology (*PE* 325; *EP* 210). We must always love as if the first time were the last: "The lovers accomplish their oath in the adieu [*adieu*]—in the passage to God [*à Dieu*], who they convoke as their final witness, their first witness, the one who does not leave and never lies. Therefore, for the first time, they tell each other 'adieu' [*adieu*]: next year in Jerusalem—the next time for God [*à Dieu*]. To think of God [*à Dieu*] can be accomplished, erotically, in this 'adieu' [*adieu*]" (*PE* 326; *EP* 212).

12. See especially the final chapter of *In Excess*, but also passages in *Idol and Distance* and Jean-Luc Marion, *God without Being*, trans. Thomas A. Carlson (Chicago: University of Chicago Press, 1991).

13. Marion analyzes the activity of prayer most explicitly in *The Crossing of the Visible*. His analyses of art or painting in general (*CV* 1–45), of the contemporary status of the image in our media-centered world (*CV* 46–65), and finally of the significance of the religious icon (*CV* 66–87) center around a rethinking of the subject as a kenotic self that is radically envisaged by another (namely, God) and receives true identity as a person only from the one who holds it in this divine gaze. The icon initiates a liturgical exchange in which "the gaze sees him who, praying, raises his gaze toward the icon" (*CV* 20). Distance must always be preserved here, for the "crossing of gazes" is a kind of participation in a dance, not a simple amalgamation or direct identification. This is a paradox of self-giving where I abandon myself to the gaze who envisions me. The emphasis on abandonment and self-sacrifice is here connected with a recovery of personhood and self-identity. In contrast to contemporary culture, where I lose all identity because I am constituted only by the gazes that evaluate me as an image on a screen, where I become an idol, fully seen and fully determined by the tyranny of the other's gaze, and where all invisibility is eliminated, the icon makes possible a recovery of self through vulnerability and devotion to God. The icon thus invites veneration,

welcomes the crossing of gazes instead of aiming at control or possession. The self is dispossessed, dislocated, and unsettled in prayer as it is in the erotic experience. Kenosis does not mean losing one's face before the other but exposing oneself to the other's gaze in a fashion parallel to the vulnerable exposure of my flesh in the intimacy of love. Only such prayerful exposure ultimately makes a communion of love (which preserves distance) possible. Hence, even in this analysis of prayer, Marion identifies the encounter as a movement of love or charity. Prayer or praise is the performative language that accomplishes the loving relationship.

14. "It [the erotic word] must therefore *inevitably* employ the words of mystical theology" (*PE* 233; *EP* 149; emphasis mine). "Come," the word of the eschatological future of erotic reduction, he points out, is also the final word of Revelation. The erotic word *must* employ "this language of the spiritual union between God and humans" (*PE* 233; *EP* 149).

15. Jean-Luc Marion, "The Unspoken: Apophasis and the Discourse of Love," *Proceedings of the American Catholic Philosophical Association* 76 (2002): 39–56. The quotations in the next sentence are taken from the headings of several sections of the article.

16. "The Unspoken," 47–49.

17. He summarizes as follows: "It has now become possible to describe the perlocutionary act that I accomplish when I say 'I love you!' or at least to trace a sketch. It is thus an act, in which not only the fact *that* I speak is more important than *what* I say, but in which, the fact *that* it is spoken has an effect on the person *to whom* I said it. This characteristic, which goes beyond the field of language (*langue*) and its use (*langage*) to give preponderance to individual speech (*parole*), establishes a structure that is essentially pragmatic, and in this case dialogic. This act speaks in as much as it calls out. This call elicits a response and, eventually, a response to the response, without there necessarily being an end in sight. Thus erotic discourse unfolds according to a call, a response, and a counter-call that can also be seen as following three paths" (ibid., 49; emphases his).

18. Ibid., 51–52.

19. This is the concluding section of the paper. Ibid., 52–54.

20. Ibid., 54.

21. Another reference, which occurs in the fifth meditation, is much less explicit, and I will not be able to explore it in this context. Marion is here dealing with the issues of betrayal and veracity. In this particular section, he describes two false moves: either I advance fully but am abandoned by the other and thus fall into a void (my love is not returned), or I deceive the other by pretending to offer myself fully but holding something back. This second move is compared to capitulation in a siege: "I do not want to show [lit. "declare"] my face openly, as one declares a town open because one has renounced defending it and has surrendered it to the supposed good will of the victor" (*PE* 262; *EP* 169). It is not entirely clear from the French whether the "openness" of the abandoned town is here compared to the false or the right openness of love, and this reference would not be particularly problematic if it were not part of a larger pattern.

22. This implies for him that desire for objects (including rape, which turns the victim into an object) is excluded from the erotic reduction and thus is not love (*PE* 335; *EP* 217–18).

23. Marion does point out that he is more concerned with raising the question of univocality than with firmly establishing it. But he expresses strongly his desire that "in this sense, mystical theology would no longer constitute a marginal and insignificant

exception in language theory, but would, on the contrary, indicate a much more central and vast domain, where, among other things, pragmatics, perlocutions, and what they render utterable unfold. It is no longer a question of a discourse about beings and objects, about the world and its states of affairs, but rather the speech shared by those who discourse on these things when they no longer discourse on them but speak to one another . . . we could then interrogate the dimensions of this encounter between erotic discourse and mystical theology" ("The Unspoken," 52).

24. This is especially true in that Husserl himself never saw univocity as a result of reduction but rather emphasized how reduction makes possible a multiplicity of noetic figures.

25. The article on the parallel between erotic language and mystical theology, in fact, begins with a consideration of "negative theology," although it then goes on to spend the bulk of the article on analyzing erotic language, returning only at the end to more theological considerations. Both the theological framing of the analysis of eros and the abstract introducing the article, which only concerns mystical theology and says nothing about love at all, indicate the theological concern that guides this exploration of eros.

26. "The Gift of a Presence," in *PC* 124–52.

27. See especially Marion's repeated references to the need for *theosis* (deification) in his theological work, e.g., *ID* 160.

28. Not only does all love seem to become a mere version of divine *agape*, but it also seems a bit blasphemous (especially considering Marion's prior work on apophaticism) to claim that God loves in the same way that we do, that God's love is univocal to ours. Why would love escape the danger of idolatry that Marion has highlighted so consistently throughout his work? Others have, of course, made this criticism already in the wake of the publication of *God without Being*. See, for example, Kenneth Smith's review of *God without Being*: "The God of Love," *Thomist* 57:3 (1993): 495–508; and Géry Provoust's review of *Questions cartésiennes II*: "La tension irrésolue: Les *Questions cartésiennes, II* de Jean-Luc Marion," *Revue Thomiste* 98:1 (1998): 95–102.

29. While I find Marion's account much more convincing as a theological reflection, I would surmise that the association of love with war would be equally problematic on a theological reading.

PART 4.

RETHINKING HUMANITY

13

Liberating Love's Capabilities

On the Wisdom of Love

PAMELA SUE ANDERSON

There are plenty of good reasons to reflect upon the wisdom of love rather than the love of wisdom. My argument is that such wisdom derives from "liberated love" rather than "bonded love"—a distinction that, however contentious, I employ from the outset of this chapter. It is also my view that the practical wisdom of contemporary women and men finds itself at a moment when our critical reflections should be compelled to reject the bonded love that is associated both literally with violence and symbolically with death. To support this, it is imperative to reject the symbolism of a self-destructive bonding to an unenlightened other and begin to recognize the nature of liberated lovers. Looking closely at symbols and myth is a highly abstract exercise; nevertheless, this is substantially supported by cutting-edge work on "the philosophical imaginary"[1]—the decisive significance of which will guide these reflections on love.

To begin our critical reflection, consider two claims:

> Liberated love is superior to bonded love: Wise lovers are not only more joyous, but more effective and beneficent than unenlightened lovers.[2]

> By refusing to accompany her father in his blindness; by saving herself and her child instead of obeying her husband, by opening her eyes and seeing with whom she is living, Psyche has walked out of the Oedipus plot.[3]

The first quotation above, concerning liberated love, assumes that love can and should be freed from a certain sort of bondage. This is a huge and contentious assumption. Can, and if so, should, love be liberated? It might be thought that by its very nature love binds those who love to others—so that love is always in some sense bonded. For the sake of my argument, let us suppose that love *can* be liberated and see if my readers can be persuaded. The initial question is, From who or what precisely—and to what degree—is love freed? At the very least, love can be freed from total passivity.

The second quotation above suggests an answer in the interpretation of mythical imagery: the blindness of a familial relation, as portrayed in this case by the plot of the Oedipus myth, renders these bonds of love less effective by preventing the daughter from seeing reality. To put it simply, we will see that the young girl, Psyche (taken from the Cupid and Venus story), has the capability to reject the plot in which the man literally or symbolically marries his mother and the woman simply accepts the patriarchal authority. The first quotation implies that wisdom liberates and creates "enlightened lovers." But from where does the wisdom of love arise?[4]

This chapter sets out to argue that the wisdom of love comes from liberating love's capabilities, especially from the bondage of patriarchal myths, and that these liberated capabilities are expressed in the retelling of the stories about the gendered relations between human beings themselves and between human and divine. In the telling and retelling of love stories, we shall seek to imagine how the wisdom that remains latent in the mythical configurations of these relations both enlightens and is enlightened by love's capabilities.

Myths by Which We Live: Dark and Difficult Symbolism for Wisdom

I propose that instead of focusing on everyday stories of love and family life, which normally goes on without any philosophical reflection, we seek love's deeper wisdom in philosophical stories. The stories that remain decisive for the wisdom of love contain significant symbolic and mythical elements, especially narratives that in their telling bring together human and divine characters. If we add gender to the mix of the crucial attributes of these characters, then we can, perhaps, come close to the necessary ingredients for configuring and reconfiguring the hierarchal relations that have been crucial to "the myths we live by."[5]

The contemporary British philosopher Mary Midgley defends the existence of myth as "symbolic stories which play a crucial role in our imaginative and intellectual life by expressing the patterns that underlie our thought."[6] She maintains that anyone who denies that myth underlies their thinking simply has not become aware of "the general background within which all detailed thought develops."[7] Midgley even employs myth and its symbolism to make sense of the significance of philosophy in her own personal life. She introduces her memoirs, *The Owl of Minerva*, with two non-human figures from ancient mythology: the female deity, Minerva (Athene is the equivalent in ancient Greek myth), and her owl, representing wisdom.[8] The figure of Minerva is also famously employed by G. W. F. Hegel in the nineteenth century to describe the moment in the history of philosophy when an era would seem to be at an end. We can glimpse the nature of wisdom assumed in Hegel's own words:

> [O]n the subject of *issuing instructions* on how the world ought to be: philosophy, at any rate, always comes too late to perform this function. . . . it is only when actuality has reached maturity that the ideal appears opposite the real and reconstructs this real world, which it has grasped in its substance, in the shape of an intellectual realm. When philosophy paints its grey in grey, a shape of life has grown old, and it cannot be rejuvenated, but only recognized, by the grey in grey of philosophy; the owl of Minerva begins its flight only with the onset of dusk.[9]

So, like Hegel, Midgley points to the wisdom recognized at dusk, at a moment of difficult transition, of loss or death. Her choice of this imagery toward the end of her own life, as well as in the wake of the philosophical life that she shared with her husband, who is deceased,[10] tells us something about her view of wisdom: it emerges in difficult or darkening times. Minerva's owl symbolizes the wisdom of being capable of seeing in the dark at the end of a day or of an era. The owl sees in the dark. Yet I would like to stress that the darkening at dusk is not permanent; nor is the imagery of dusk alone adequate for a fair picture of Mary Midgley.

Each night is followed by a new dawn. The break of day, the rising of the sun, the beginning of a new day, and similar images constitute imagery for thinking after the long night of late-twentieth-century postmodernism. Speaking metaphorically, this is the night when the light of reason is eclipsed by uncertainty and obscurity. Moreover, the symbolism of light remains most appropriate to a philosophical imaginary that recognizes a lasting debt to ethically significant aspects of seventeenth- and eighteenth-century Enlightenment philosophy in Europe at least. And yet Midgley still employs imagery from ancient Greek mythology and modern German philosophy to capture the nature of wisdom in the context of the dark difficulties of death: "Going out in the dark brings danger of death. But, if you have to go out, then it is surely a good thing to have with you a creature that can penetrate the darkness."[11] In this, she is pragmatic: when things get tough we have to turn to the wisdom in philosophy; thus, the wise philosopher is a necessity. And what subject is more difficult to grasp or darker in its depths, especially in its loss, than excessive love!

At this point I will mention a contentious reading of Midgley's discovery of wisdom in certain philosophical difficulties. This wisdom expressed symbolically as the danger brought about by death could be explained by psycholinguists as the mode of the philosopher who remains in melancholia.[12] To treat this as one possible explanation, consider Julia Kristeva's psycholinguistic description of the woman who has successfully shifted her attachments away from the security of maternal love:

> Shifting the symbolic *at the same time* as [shifting] to a sexual object of a sex other than that of the primary maternal object represents a gigantic elaboration in which a woman cathexes a psychic potential greater than what is demanded of the male sex. When this process is favourably carried out, it is evidenced by the precocious awakening of girls, their intellectual performances often more brilliant during the school years, and their continuing female maturity. Nevertheless, it has its price in the constant tendency to extol the problematic mourning for the lost object . . . not so fully lost.[13]

Melancholia that follows after the loss of love can generate great psychic potential for intellectual performance. But to use Kristeva's imagery, "black sun" also haunts the wisdom of a melancholic woman. I will return to explore critically the decisive problems with a Kristevan conception of love's wisdom. Alternatively, the feminist philosopher of religion Grace M. Jantzen might well have argued that Midgley remains caught up in the masculinist symbolic of death, which displaces both beauty and natality; Jantzen advocates natality as life-affirming.[14]

A less contentious reading than either of these two psychoanalytic positions would simply recognize how the myths of patriarchy have configured Western relations between men, women, and the divine. Under patriarchy, love's capabilities are configured in ways that variously empower love's characters; patriarchal myths have given authority on matters of ethical wisdom to fathers and sons over mothers and daughters as well as to men generally over other women and young girls. Think of the ways in which the myth of Oedipus determined twentieth-century accounts of familial and other love relations. Think of the unforgettable myth of Eve's eating the forbidden fruit of the tree of knowledge of good and evil. In the patriarchal telling of these myths, love is portrayed as both liberating and constraining gendered relations. Ultimately, the patriarchal "resolution" of these constraints on gendered relations eclipses the ethical wisdom of women.[15]

The contemporary French philosopher Michèle Le Doeuff demonstrates, with a creative discovery of liberating myths, how to unearth the obstacle in relations between women and everything or everyone else. The difficulty is the identification of the obstacle: "that barely perceptible reality which does not speak its name."[16] In this chapter I am arguing that we should seek to create or recreate myths that can liberate those eclipsed capabilities that have been hidden by oppressive or dark forms of love. This means liberating our gendered forms of love according to the specificities of the lives of actual women and men who are each distinguished by the complexity of many factors, including age, race, class, ethnicity, religious and sexual orientation. *Agape* (charity), *philia* (friendship), *eros* (desire), and other affections contain the capabilities[17] that are integral to, yet often enslaved by, human love.[18]

In his last writings on memory, forgiveness, and love, the French philosopher Paul Ricoeur describes how human capabilities have been wounded by painful affection.[19] His mythical descriptions of the enslavement of the triad freedom-goodness-love assumes the loss of human capabilities.[20] In various ways across the course of his writings, Ricoeur contends that the symbolic and mythical language of slavery expresses this loss as an enslaved freedom. "The captive free will" is enslaved to evil. Nevertheless, we can and should recover freedom's more primordial (original) ground of goodness.[21]

In one sense, our myths about love are timeless. But in another sense, the myths that structure our love stories are about time and the variable relations of human subjects to eternity and divinity. In my writings on feminist philosophy of religion, I have been repeatedly struck by how much philosophy has unwittingly or wittingly relied on myths to support its norms.[22]

Midgley presents a highly relevant account of imagery concerning wisdom. But I contend that the imagery of Minerva's owl is only part of the picture of wisdom. A network of symbolic relations certainly constitutes the structure of myths portraying wisdom. This network gives significance to stories and to a whole range of interrelated imagery. In addition, a myth is cultivated by composing narratives that make sense of the lived experiences of individuals; this composition brings together the rational, attentive, and conative[23] capabilities of individual women and men. I employ "capability" in line with the later writings of Ricoeur to describe human subjects in terms of their potentiality, especially the powers that enable us to relate and to love as moral beings.[24] Ricoeur's final portrait of the capable human being is deliberately neo-Aristotelian and post-Kantian, but perhaps not post-Hegelian.[25] His self-description is revealing, but it also fits nicely with the picture developing here.

A Myth for Wise Lovers: Joyful and Hopeful Symbolism for a New Enlightenment

Le Doeuff has uncovered a symbolic figure and myth that differ significantly from Minerva and her owl, from Psyche and Cupid, or from Eve and Adam. In her recent, as-yet-unpublished Weidenfeld Lectures, University of Oxford, Le Doeuff demonstrates the ethical significance of a highly distinctive myth for twenty-first-century men and women:[26] essentially, to gain ethical wisdom we should take care not to force a girl to grow up to be a goddess of maternal love with sacrificial and tragic relations to men, other women, other gods and goddesses.[27] A novel story told by Le Doeuff lends itself to a recreation of a timely contemporary myth about a young girl, Dawn, whose vulnerability needs to be protected in order for her heart,[28] which is reason, to enlighten us. Dawn provokes qualities of tenderness, attentiveness, and wise generosity in those who love her.

Le Doeuff herself discovers the main elements of this story from her reading of Maria Zambrano.[29] Educated in philosophy, Zambrano wrote fiction and nonfiction in Spanish and contributed to a conception of poetic reasoning in which the symbolic has a philosophically significant role. Le Doeuff picks up crucial elements from what becomes *"la philosophie imaginaire"* of Zambrano to challenge traditional stereotypes about young girls, reason, mature women, motherhood, and divinity. In telling Dawn's story, Le Doeuff appropriates Zambrano's poetic reasoning about a girl whose heart is reason, in order to create an ethical figure of hope for women and men in philosophy. The heart becomes a symbol for a fresh understanding of a human soul and human love. If we extrapolate a bit more, this mythical language about a young girl's heart begins to personify liberated love, not the bonded love of a female deity, whether a goddess of wisdom or of motherhood. Le Doeuff asserts that Dawn should not be forced to become divine.

My own contention is that Le Doeuff's retelling of Dawn's story offers us a new Enlightenment narrative. Of course, other narratives could be created or similarly reconfigured to avoid the pernicious dangers in apotheosis, but for this context consider a retelling of the story about Dawn. Each dawn begins anew, offering us hope for each woman and each man to be attentive and tender to one another; to learn to love a young girl involves practicing tenderness, not unthinking force. A revised ethics is implicit in this Enlightenment story whereby a young girl holds out a promise for practical wisdom, while women and men create ethical dispositions (e.g. tenderness) in being drawn to the vulnerability of Dawn. Le Doeuff insists that European Enlightenment philosophy was unethical when it came to women and the potential of a woman's ethical wisdom. Yet Le Doeuff's new myth, unlike Midgley's memoir, does not take its starting point from the symbolism of dusk. Instead, the starting point of this alternative myth is dawn, which comes after "the dark." Whether this imagery refers to the era of medieval or of postmodern darkness, Dawn brings light to certain unfathomable difficulties, especially to the sexual violence and living death which have enslaved women.

Le Doeuff is not preoccupied with any postmodern imaginary or any assumed death of Enlightenment philosophy, which can arguably be read as melancholia. In sharp contrast to either a medieval or a postmodern imaginary, Le Doeuff's story is about a new Dawn who/which has the capacity to enlighten, to teach us unwittingly how to protect a heart that symbolizes an unenslaved reason. This Enlightenment narrative does not oppose reason to love, or mind to body. Instead, reason, like a pre-adolescent heart, can, if it is cultivated, enlighten love in others too. Thus, the mutually produced wisdom of love comes with Dawn, at the break of day, and not exclusively with Minerva at dusk.

Elsewhere I have pointed out that Le Doeuff draws productively on the imagery in women's writings to make sense of a movement for women's recognition.[30] She focuses on the imagery of dark and light in the movement of waves as they break, seemingly between sea and sky. Even if unaware of her impact, Le Doeuff shifts an imaginary relationship from dusk and darkness to the dark and light oscillations on the sea at dawn. This shift away from a struggle between light and dark to both light and dark, struggling to represent more is read in the imagery with which Virginia Woolf begins her twentieth-century novel *The Waves:* "The sun had not yet risen. The sea was indistinguishable from the sky, except that the sea was slightly creased as if a cloth had wrinkles in it. Gradually as the sky whitened a dark line lay on the horizon dividing the sea from the sky."[31] In this way, Le Doeuff's enlightened preference reveals hope even when the political climate is dark or darkening. Consider her references to joy and hope in the light that continues to dawn across the horizon of the sea every morning:

> The waves of hope rise and fall: "The grey cloth becomes barred with thick strokes moving, one after another, beneath the surface, following each other, pursuing each other, perpetually. As they neared the shore each bar rose, heaped itself, broke and swept a thin veil of white water across the sand. The wave paused, and then drew out again, sighing." These opening sentences from Virginia Woolf's *The Waves* might well contain the poetics of our collective historical experience. Successive waves of women have joyfully fought, convinced that once we had at last gained the right to, for example, a job, education, citizen's rights, or a sexuality freed from the chains of reproduction, something fundamental would have changed in the general female condition. A thin veil of white water across the sand: those gains have hardly even yet been gained and the radical transformation that we expected along with civil equality or birth control has not come. Besides, like harbour pools governed by a complex system of locks and sluices, particular social spaces open to us and then close off again.[32]

Le Doeuff confirms that each woman's joyful expression of her own wisdom is shaped around the collective history of an ethical movement for reciprocal equality, or recognition.[33] This history includes the ebb and flow of the imagery and political ideas of each woman. Here feminism is implicit as a politics constantly moved forward by both successes and failures of women individually and collectively. The movement creates the shifts in the philosophical imaginary:[34] this is essentially the symbolic and narrative patterns of thought that often unwittingly shape philosophical texts. For Le Doeuff, Woolf becomes a paradigmatic figure of and for a woman's writing speaking profoundly to her readers, even in this new century, about how patriarchy has disinherited women.[35] This lack of inheritance means that women have mainly been separated from their own ideas, which have been given away or cast off without any rightful recognition of their ownership by or origin in a specific female thinker.

The imagery of the waves is a case in point. To illustrate how the failure of inheritance might be reversed, Le Doeuff picks up and exploits the metaphorical and mystical language making up Woolf's novel in order to express the rise and fall of hope in a woman's collective inheritance. This exploitation means that Le Doeuff's imagery points beyond the intended significance in *The Waves*. But she also disagrees with Woolf's writings on women when Woolf fails to recognize ideas that have been generated by women from past centuries.[36] So "waves of feminism" present themselves on a political scene as historical movements of individual women: they are like the recurring lines rising and falling on the sea waters each dawn. Thus the imagery of waves gives expression to the complex patterns and shifts in the relations of *each* woman to one another and to all of those others whom they love. Love relates them individually and collectively to the larger reality of patriarchy.

The crucial point is that Le Doeuff would find any exclusive reflection on the grey on grey, whether taken from Woolf or Hegel, as missing the significant light shed on the crest of waves. The symbolism and myth of this ethical wisdom emerge like the light shining from the lives of each woman who is part of a vibrant, if hidden, collective historical experience. The task is to claim each woman's wisdom as part of our philosophical inheritance; that is, an inheritance of the ideas of past women whose writings were quickly cast off.[37] My present argument takes support from Le Doeuff to contend that *the wisdom of love* can be found in both the imagery of protecting a young girl's heart and the larger picture of our collective inheritance. So the philosophical imaginary would no longer picture a woman exclusively in the shadow of a man: not just Geoff Midgley with Mary, or Hegel with the owl of Minerva, but Mary Midgley with the wise men and women who have learned to liberate love's capabilities. Perhaps they have learned about love from a reason freely expressed and a heart tenderly received.

"Not a goddess, she!" is Le Doeuff's crucial cry. If Dawn grows up *without* having *imposed* those humanly impossible patriarchal gender roles that enshrine a goddess in bonded love and stereotypical beauty—and yes, ethereal beauty can also be sexist—*then* her reason will enable non-oppressive love and thus goodness to shine upon humanity and its relations. This myth implies that a woman's oppression begins in adolescence, at which point the myths of patriarchy enslave the relations of men and women. Yet liberation can be achieved when the young girl develops an adolescent heart that is treated tenderly, but this must be prior to her (maternal) sacrifice to the god(s).

Alongside the so-called French feminists[38]—Hélène Cixous, Luce Irigaray, and Julia Kristeva—Le Doeuff looks unique, and not only because, unlike the others, she was born in France. Le Doeuff exhibits no psycholinguistic interest in sexual difference and desire. In contrast, Kristeva and Irigaray tackle patriarchy's myths in order to rethink female desire, sexually specific pleasure, and the oppressive forms of paternal or fraternal love. A crucial psychoanalytic aim is to liberate women's pleasure and maternal relations, including mother-daughter relations, as necessary for the psychological and sexual health of women and men. Le Doeuff rejects the essentialism that is assumed in discussions of a distinctively female sexual pleasure. Instead, Le Doeuff focuses on certain philosophical virtues, including joy, hope, and charity, as well as the rational and conative capabilities that are the ground of goodness for knowledge (*la science*) and wisdom (*la sagesse*). Admittedly, all of these virtues and capabilities will still appear obscure without concrete examples and detailed definitions. Le Doeuff gives us only the abstract—yet imaginative in the sense of creative—framework as the structure from which we can begin a transformation of debilitating bonds.

Without moralizing in a wholly negative sense or denying the crucial role of the body in love, I am arguing that for the philosopher, with Le Doeuff as a prime example, the wisdom of love is another matter from the expression of a sexually and bodily specific desire for pleasure associated with the idealized maternal bond. Wisdom is a capability, that is, an ability or potential that can be cultivated into a disposition by love that is free. Before some more elaboration of the specific capabilities of love, I offer exposition of the psycholinguistic readings of patriarchy's bonded love. My contention is that love fails to be unbonded as long as it is exclusively focused on melancholia, on the one hand, and on female sexual pleasure on the other.

A Psycholinguistic Reading of Myth:
Bonded Love and Sexually Specific Pleasure

From the beginning of a psycholinguistic reading of love, we find stories. These love stories vary precisely because of their origin in myth. Put simply, each myth has an invariable core, which includes central figures, their human or divine attributes, and their basic relations and significant actions. At the same time, the variability of myth's plot and its resolution gives the possibility for creating various stories that can be partial or whole reconfigurations of the significance of the myth's narrative.

If we look critically at the ancient Greek figure of Psyche, a psychoanalytic configuration of her story stresses the significance in the birth of her daughter, who symbolizes Pleasure. Psyche is the youngest and most beautiful of three daughters, who is so beautiful that she becomes the envy of all women. This beauty leads her to be called the new Venus. Yet even when worshipped by all, she is loved by no one. Moreover, at the same time as Psyche is made into an envied beauty, Venus herself, who is the real goddess of love, sends for her son, Cupid, and beseeches him in the name of the maternal bond to punish the defiant young beauty. Inevitably, as the story unrolls, Cupid falls in love with Psyche. The patriarchal configuration of the story of the male god Cupid gives a distinctively tragic end to Psyche: she is made to become a wife, a mother, a goddess of sacrificial love and ethereal beauty—essentially, Venus. Nevertheless, the ending and upshot of the myth of Psyche and Cupid become a matter of dispute for contemporary feminists.

In one reading of love, Western discourses contain stories that, like the human and divine relations of Psyche and Cupid, portray a recurring struggle between human (temporality) and divine (eternity) for possession of the female soul. Genesis tells the story about Eve, who falls from the paradise created for humans by God. Eve's fatal choice to eat the forbidden fruit ensures that the incompatibilities between divine perfection (in eternity) and human sin (in time) will endure for men and women. Love of divine wisdom is, then, the focus for human subjects who worship divine perfection; some would urge loving God's wisdom after having lost their own innocence at a particular point in time. This raises a crucial question concerning love in the myths of divine-human relations and female-male capabilities. Does the god's love, whether pagan or not, save humans from the consequences of sin by changing them into divine beings? Or is the idea of apotheosis a matter of human arrogance, not divine love?

Against a certain amount of opposition from other feminists and masculinists in philosophy, I would contend that Psyche's bondage is her apotheosis, that is, being made divine in her marriage to Cupid. Symbolically speaking, women under patriarchy are ironically kept from the recognition of love's wisdom by the bonded love of wisdom. That is, *liberating love's capabilities* would free gendered subjects from *the bondage of patriarchal myths*. The symbolism of salvation in bondage renders the bondage of women in love a symbolism of death.[39]

A woman becomes symbolically bonded to death when oppressive and/or self-destructive relations to a male god's love support her idealization and apotheosis.[40] To undo this, a woman's liberation comes from remaining human, precisely, because this would liberate the capabilities—including attentiveness, tenderness, patience, and hope—for the wisdom of love. Thus Le Doeuff's cry, "Not a goddess, she!" also becomes my rallying call against those who insist that women's liberation from patriarchy lies in becoming divine.[41]

The American psychotherapist and gender theorist Carol Gilligan claims that "the myth of Psyche and Cupid was written at a time when the hegemony of male gods was becoming unsettled, a time in this respect, very much like our own."[42] But what precisely, then, is the significance of the human-divine battle for the female's soul? For one thing, Cupid's divinity derives from his father, while Psyche's humanity derives from the human mother who gives her birth. For another thing, a renewed focus on the outcome of Psyche's story as a myth of the female (mortal) soul and the male (immortal) love could initiate a revolutionary change in the love story of Western patriarchy. Yet would Gilligan agree with Le Doeuff's caution against apotheosis? To compare critically Psyche's way out of the Oedipus plot to Dawn's escape from the deification plot would require a critical study of Gilligan's ending to the love story.

Instead of assessing Gilligan on Psyche, let us stay with Kristeva's psycholinguistics on love. For psycholinguists, language is the condition for the meaning and values of sex/gender[43] relations, as well as the condition for wisdom. The psycholinguistic progression in Kristeva's "Christianized history" establishes no particular Christian exegetical or doctrinal truth. Instead, it articulates both the gender and the psychosexual dynamics in the ethical development of "Westernized" patriarchy. For my purposes, Kristeva's plausible account of the West's intellectual-social history of myths on love establishes a critical, even if ultimately problematic, psychosexual background for recognizing and liberating love's capabilities. Her liberating intention is comparable to Gilligan's intended retelling of the story about Psyche and Cupid; each is aimed at a transformation of patriarchy in the birth of maternal pleasure.

Kristeva begins with the philosophical discourses of Plato, which contain myths concerning love: first, his *Phaedrus*, and second, his *Symposium*. In the former dialogue, Plato symbolizes Eros as "essentially the desire for what man lacks,"[44] displaying the "libidinal economy" of Eros.[45] Kristeva points out that in the *Phaedrus* Psyche and Eros are interdependent. The dynamic they share is "phallic appetition": "the imagery-laden description . . . an erection of . . . feathers, of warming, swelling, or ebullition . . . compels recognition of its sexual, penial nakedness." This erotic ascent of a masculine soul to the wisdom of love is compared to the flight of a bird: "Through Eros . . . through philosophy, the fallen soul, having lost some feathers in the fray, will be feathered again and climb toward celestial or even supercelestial heights that still activate its mobility . . . its love."[46]

Second, in the *Symposium* love as Eros is again symbolized as a lack. Kristeva claims that "with love as with desire, the object is [in Plato's words] 'that which he has not already; and which is future and not present, and which he has not, and is not, and of which he is in want.' "[47] But the "mania" of Eros in this dialogue is less about possessing oneself (as in the *Phaedrus*) than becoming one. Consider the two myths presented in the *Symposium*. The first myth is spoken by Aristophanes, who tells a story about the desire of the Androgynes, whose original union of male and female made them unisexual. This is different from bisexual. The union exists only until a failed challenge to the gods results in division into two sexes. Kristeva names this act of dividing "sexualization": Eros becomes the sexual desire of each sex for union with its other half; only an ideal union could reconstitute the Androgynes. The second myth is spoken by Diotima, who tells about the birth of Eros from Penia (poverty) and the male god Poros (resource; read as plenty), who together configure procreation. In this story Eros is the "go-between," going between mortal and immortal, poverty and plenty, while desiring what is lacking: beauty, goodness, truth, and, ultimately, wisdom. Eros is always seeking the wisdom of love.

The crucial element in this reading of Plato is the erotic. A contrast could be drawn between Plato's portrait of a beautiful boy, Eros, as "a glowing, soothing, ebullient vision"[48] and the imagery of the young girl, Dawn, whose heart is reason. Yet we will continue with Kristeva's history, for next Plotinus internalizes the Platonic ascent of Eros. Plotinus' discourse takes the violence of mania into the inner space of "an alter-ego, an idealized Ego, sustained by a new myth, that of Narcissus."[49] Essentially, the mythical figure of Narcissus represents a fixed love of one's own self-image.

The myth of Narcissus tells a story of a young man who falls in love with his own reflection. The gods punish him with paralysis for ignoring a fair maiden, Echo, so that he can only ever see his own face in a pool of water. In psychoanalytic terms, "primary narcissism" is a developmental stage in the formation of an individual's identity, normally when an infant is entirely focused on itself. The problem is that debates continue between Freudians and post-Freudians, Anglo-American and French psychotherapists, whether narcissism remains in the adult as inherently pathological. The feminist and philosophical value of this debate is recognizing that a fixation on a single gendered image remains an obstacle to change and to recognition of an independent reality. As long as narcissism persists, the lack of recognition of the self as distinct from an independent reality undermines honest love relations to others.[50] According to Kristeva's *Tales of Love*, when narcissism is found symbolized within the social history of Christian discourses, it reflects back on the individual history of psychosexual development. To confront the narcissistic obstacle to self-giving love, Christian myth requires, at least at an imaginary level, the death of the mother and a violent struggle with the figure of transference love, who Kristeva identifies as "the father of an individual pre-history."[51]

Kristeva sees the possibility of self-recognition when the narcissist generates an awareness of the unfathomable, formidable Other: "This mini-revolution has bequeathed us a new conception of love—a love centered in the self although drawn toward the ideal Other. This is a love that magnifies the individual as a reflection of the unapproachable Other whom I love and who causes me to be."[52] At this point, the self just begins to shape her or his self-reflection in relation to the unapproachable Other. Contrast this to the earlier account from Hegel concerning the point at which "the grey in grey," or "actuality," reaches its "maturity" when "the ideal appears opposite the real."[53] The ethical imperative is for mutual recognition between self and other, ideal and real; an inevitable and relentless narcissism would be an obstacle to Hegel's vision.

Nevertheless, after the mini-revolution where the lover recognizes the Other as an ideal love and cause of being, Kristeva's psycholinguistic history moves to the so-called Westernized scriptures, in particular, to the Song of Songs in the Old Testament.[54] From these scriptures, Judaism is read as revolutionary in prescribing heterosexual love on the basis of the family, reproduction, and the chosen people who understand the word of the Father (God). To this Kristeva draws a contrast: "Eastern eroticism" appears as "pleasure of [the body's] organs, swell[ing] to infinite proportions in the bursting of its pleasure, quietly dependent upon the nourishing mother."[55] She concludes that love "for the other sex, came to us for the first time through King Solomon and the Shulamite—a precocious yet fragile triumph of heterosexuality, tinged with impossibility."[56]

Taking a closer look at the Christian Gospels, Kristeva recognizes a distinctive emergence of Christianized discourses on *agape*. Instead of Eros and its so-called mania, *agape* names a love "always already ensured by a Father who loves us before we are to love him."[57] Although Kristeva claims that "the prudence of family fervour and the tension emanating from a non-representable, impossible biblical love, as fervid as it is distant, in the manner of the Song of Songs" is added to the New Testament texts, the Greek erotic remains, as "disguised in the dramas of a passion of the flesh."[58]

After this, Kristeva indicates the changes in the discourses on love that are anticipated in the twelfth century but ultimately brought about by St. Thomas Aquinas (1227–74). Aquinas makes self-love "the linchpin of salvation-love,"[59] connecting self-love with love of the good—being itself.[60] Kristeva identifies some "perverse"[61] prescriptions of maternal love, prior to this Thomistic account of love, in a certain number of the Franciscans, the Jesuits, and followers of Bernard of Clairvaux (1091–1153). For the latter, love is always a lack, but also an affliction with physical suffering and violence. Aquinas shifts the focus from any question of the irrationality of such carnal desire to the rationality of knowing and loving. Yet the perversions of Christian love as a physical affliction have been easily repeated historically. This happens whenever the discourses on love shift away from the self-love that is grounded in the good of the prior love of the Father to "a violent, consuming, impetuous love" for the maternal union. The urgent need for a transformation of the latter carnal love generates "the *holy violence*" of a love seeking "the ideal";[62] that is, the mother-child union, like the Virgin with Child imagery, becomes "the pedestal for what is most dear to love—what is most reassuring, fulfilling and sheltering when confronting the abyss of death."[63]

Clearly, the decisive problem is the inevitability of the destructive violence that is generated in relation to a maternal ideal, or what I would identify as a bonded love. The choice, which is arguably no choice, appears between violence in the consuming passion for returning to the ideal love of a mother-child union or violence in sacrificing the maternal body for a paternal-fraternal love grounded on self-love. Ultimately, the conclusion to Kristeva's psycho-linguistic search for sexually specific pleasure demonstrates the inevitability of both the symbolic sacrificial death of the mother (matricide) and the consequent melancholia of the wise woman, or man, for the foundation of Christian forms of patriarchy.[64]

This conclusion implies that the West's most enduring myths of love derive from the material making up the Christianized discourses on narcissistic, paternal, and maternal forms of love. In this way the gendering of Christian myth informs the portrayal of love in Western literature. At least in her *Tales of Love*, Kristeva maintains that whatever literary classic we name, whether Shakespeare or Goethe, we can draw out their Greek, Hebrew, or Christian mythological backgrounds. Kristeva demonstrates the many and problematic ways in which the ancient myths of patriarchal forms of love live within us through the history of our literature and art.

Love's Capability in the Search for Wisdom

Similar to Kristeva and other French psycholinguists, Gilligan unearths the sexually specific pleasure of women as mothers in the wisdom of lovemaking. With her use of the Psyche myth in psychotherapy and in gender studies, Gilligan assumes a new path to enlightenment, away from the tragic stories of love, in "the birth of pleasure."[65] However, in this context, I maintain that Psyche's "wisdom" in *jouissance* should not be what concerns us most as philosophers. Instead, another path in contemporary French philosophy directs us to a different "course of recognition," which remains more consistent with Le Doeuff's new Enlightenment story. This path draws on Le Doeuff but also on those philosophers informed by the liberated love of Spinoza.[66]

To recall Le Doeuff's story, if the heart of the adolescent Dawn remains free to reason and to grow, both loving freely and being tenderly loved, then it will generate a mutual response of attentiveness to her as much as to others. In this autonomous process, each of us learns to cultivate our attentive, rational, and conative capabilities. Dawn symbolizes for us love's capabilities to see reality, to know the world, and to strive to love humanity. In brief, these human capabilities would enable the wisdom of love, especially in an ethical sense. Both men and women would have to seek the ground of goodness if we are to recover love's capabilities from humanity's self-inflicted incapability.[67]

Add this picture of human capabilities to the women in the two myths of patriarchy. First, in the Genesis story of Adam and Eve, the woman's desire to eat from the tree of knowledge of good and evil is portrayed as an act of disobedience of God's commandment, the consequence of which is a fall from God's grace, resulting in human sin and suffering. But why not rewrite the fate of Eve and so Adam in recognition of wisdom as a capability (of love)?[68] Le Doeuff's retelling of the Genesis myth liberates Eve and her descendants in recognizing that the sin of this "first" woman is not disobedience but laziness. Eve wanted the easy way to ethical wisdom, eating the fruit of moral knowledge. But wisdom avoids the sin by liberating Eve's reason with the hope and joy of her own capabilities; that is, the woman is no longer "the second sex" in the sense of being devalued or oppressed by the patriarchal symbolism of love's bondage. Instead, she uses her attentive reason to see, feel, think, and love wisely.

Second, the ancient myth of Psyche and Cupid has similar dangers in its patriarchal telling. Although, as we have seen, recent feminists have attempted to rewrite the ending of the story in order to liberate Psyche from the gods and goddesses, the patriarchal version has Cupid's love for his goddess mother, Venus, transforming Psyche's beauty into the second Venus: the son falling in love with a mother-like goddess, with Psyche becoming divine. One feminist retelling of this myth has Psyche's liberation in apotheosis and birthing: the new Venus is liberated by the birth of Pleasure, that is, by her daughter. But in the context of this chapter, serious reasons have emerged for us to question the psycholinguistic goal of maternal *jouissance*.[69] Even if the mother is not transformed into a deity, there remains the problem of projection, whereby love is fixed on impossible gendered ideals, whether Virgin mother or Savior father.

What affinity does a woman's *jouissance* have to the philosophical sense of joy that has been described as an intellectual love of God?[70] The myth of Psyche is still a tragedy of patriarchy: as long as the young woman becomes divine and enshrines all of the imposed gender qualities of patriarchy, her story is not compatible with the new Enlightenment myth of Dawn. Making the object of love an idealization is not much different from the divinization of woman; both are equally obstacles to acquiring the wisdom of love.

Furthermore, Ricoeur and Le Doeuff inform the following two major points on the wisdom of love. First of all, human subjects can each take hold of "the human condition" in love. Here are Le Doeuff's enthusiastic words:

> Being born into knowledge is nothing other than reaching out with two hands to grasp the human condition . . . a condition one can love . . . and that, incorrigible meliorist that I am, I believe one can also make more lovable.[71]

Is there nothing to stop each of us from grasping human affections, passions, and reasons? What precisely is the condition that we can love and that can make our world more lovable for women and men? For answers, we have been seeking to see the reality of our lives, of self- and other-love, of the divine-human relations, and of our search for the wisdom of love.

Second, we can turn to our human capability for self-reflection, including philosophical conceptions of oneself and another. These conceptions are revealing on love.[72] Ricoeur's "Epilogue: Difficult Forgiveness" is a brilliant example of the potential in self-reflection, in this case, on the heights and depths of love in relation to forgiveness and (in)justice. We are confronted with philosophical questions concerning the role of the self and the role of the other in love, especially when we must risk forgiveness in the face of injustice for the sake of love. For instance, a critical difficulty for love as *agape* has to do with the rightful form of self-love. How do those women or men who lack self-esteem comprehend or realize self-giving love? The problem of self-destructive love relations can undermine the wisdom of love, especially that of *caritas* or *agape*. It becomes absolutely necessary to recover love's rightful capabilities.

This recovery of ethical wisdom has been portrayed by the story of Dawn: it is unethical to force a woman into the role of maternal goddess or into the idealization of a fixed gender identity insofar as this forceful imposition has violent consequences for self-other relations; it also undermines human capabilities such as loving attention to another and to oneself as another.

To address the difficult balance between gaining and losing a proper sense of self, I will refer all too briefly to the ethically significant notion of "de-creation," which derives from French philosopher Simone Weil. In a recently published essay I have discussed de-creation in terms of (un)selfing in love as a necessary ground for the self's arresting attention to the reality of the other.[73] Weil's de-creation involves a critique of rationalists' self-conceptions insofar as they remain at one of two extremes: an egoism that eclipses the other, and altruism that is self-deceptive in relation to another. Weil's critique of these extreme conceptions of selfhood is both ethically and spiritually significant for liberating human capabilities. I submit that Weil anticipates crucial contemporary retrievals of Spinoza's account of the self's persistence in being; Spinoza has become attractive to those philosophers (often women) who find a rationalist dualism of mind/body and a privileging of mind over body highly problematic.[74] Kristeva herself names Spinoza "the great philosopher of bliss" because, crucially, he "equates 'self-love' with love of God,' even love of God himself."[75]

In Amelie Rorty's provocative reading of Spinoza's philosophical account of (self)-love, she recovers the idea of a liberated lover. Returning to my opening quotation, I add two sentences for context to dissociate liberation from an overly Platonic ideal:

> Spinoza thinks that liberated love is superior to bonded love: Wise lovers are not only more joyous, but more effective and beneficent than unenlightened lovers. How do the wise act on behalf of those they love?[76]

Spinoza's wise lovers also desire to unite with what they love, but this is a consequence rather than the essence of love. The wise are known by the nature of their actions on behalf of those they love. But it is not enough to say that love's essence is the wisdom that renders us enlightened—and liberated—lovers. We must understand both the capabilities and the complexities of this wisdom in action.

Complexities in the Gendering of Love's Wisdom

It should follow from the previous sections of this chapter that gendered stories remain implicit in our conceptions of the three forms of love already mentioned: *agape, philia,* and *eros.* This means gender and the gendered relations in Western myths have shaped love as a self-giving (*agape*) that should also be a self-making, along with both love as friendship (*philia*) and love as sexual desire (*eros*). But I have not said much directly about what these forms have to do with capabilities.

These forms of love are a matter of feeling, but each of these also involves an "attention to X," that is, to a loved object or another self. This attention to X constitutes a conscious capacity that can be cultivated cognitively along with the receptive and conative elements of the original disposition; this generates a certain know-how, or practical *capability* to love.[77] So the forms are linked with actions, dispositions, and passions because we possess the capabilities that serve as the rational, conative, and attentive potentialities of love. The best way for me to illustrate this fact has been with stories about the wisdom of love.

Although significant, the forms of love are difficult to distinguish in reality because of the actual messiness of love. (This is one reason for the necessity of abstract and mythical examples in this chapter.) We cannot always separate out the erotic, philial, or agapic dimensions of actual practices. This is simply a fact—but it also creates a problem. The difficulties arise from the ambiguities in our living and loving that render self-deception and relentless egoism[78] constant threats to the wisdom of love. It is not that every sexual desire (*eros*) or that the predisposition to love is hopelessly egocentric and so unethical. Remember that Spinoza's positive account of rightful self-love constitutes an intellectual love of God. Yet there remains a constant danger of love's illusions: for love to project its own self onto another, projecting one's own desires onto the desires and/or needs of another. We have illustrated this danger in the various configurations of our mythical women, men, and gods/goddesses.

To return to address the contested problem of self-projection in love, eclipsing the differences between the lover and the beloved, let us consider a final definition of love. If love is essentially a feeling, with a complex capability —that is, the potentiality of love's rational, conative, and attentive elements— that can be cultivated, then the aim of this cultivation would be a settled disposition in reasoning about, striving for, and attending to a loved object or the beloved. How does one render the capabilities of this disposition a source of wisdom for wise lovers? We have mentioned that certain feminist philosophers of religion argue that women need to become divine.[79] However, this argument runs into difficulties—some of which have been suggested in my resistance to an Irigarayan imperative. The imperative to become divine undermines the very idea of love's human capabilities, balancing a difficult self-giving and an incomplete self-making.

Recall the difficult nature of forgiveness in the face of injustice. This difficulty generates a paradox for self-giving and self-making love. Nevertheless, for love to be achieved and sustained, a positive role should be given to a degree of (un)selfing.[80] A critical balance between selfing and unselfing is meant to avoid debilitating contradiction without enslaving. Any imagery or myths concerning divine women or men has to be modified for humans so that actual women and men are able to confront the critical role of the self in the context of the socially and materially specific lives of each human lover.

Confronting the complexity that surrounds the rightful role of (un)selfing is a necessary condition for the cultivation of the wisdom of love; complexity is consistent with the situated nature of a subject's love. In support of this confrontation, Midgley offers some incisive comments about "the lure of simplicity" that characterized philosophy in the twentieth century.[81] She sees the danger in modelling philosophy too strictly on a principle of simplicity that derives from a modern conception of science. Love is complex, but this does not render it completely unknowable or inappropriate as a subject of wisdom for contemporary philosophy. In Midgley's words,

> [The] clash is sharpened today by the notion we now hold of ourselves as thoroughly scientific beings, individuals too clear-headed and well-organized to use blurred or ambivalent concepts. The concepts that we need to use for everyday life are, however, often in some ways blurred or ambivalent because life itself is too complex for simple descriptions. For instance, notions such as love, care, trust and consent are incredibly complicated. The concept of a friend is not a simple one, and people who insist on oversimplifying it cannot keep their friends, nor indeed be friends themselves, because they do not properly understand what a friend is.[82]

Love, like friendship (as one significant form of love), involves ambivalence and thus complexity. There is nothing unphilosophical about this: mutuality is not straightforward for a self who is in process. In fact, it is quite the reverse. It follows that our wisdom will not always be able to bring the theoretical to apply perfectly to the practical, or the concept to the experience or practice; that is, it will not apply at all until we are willing to deal with the complex as much as (and sometimes more than) the simple. We should not allow science to render out-of-date the wisdom of love; the lure of scientific simplicity may cover over complexity, but genuine wisdom would seek to avoid the very dichotomy of simple versus complex. Reductive forms of simplicity are not the same as perfect simplicity achieved by the wise art of love's complexity.

In addition to Le Doeuff and Ricoeur, Kristeva and Gilligan, Midgley and Weil each provide us with philosophical tools for seriously and self-consciously learning to grasp the capabilities of love in a careful and arresting attention to the real in our lived experiences.[83] A close contemporary of Midgley since their early years in Oxford, Iris Murdoch identifies the force behind this careful attention to the reality of another: love joins subjects to goodness. This implies a search for goodness, but such goodness is very close to what we have sought as the ethical wisdom of love. In contrast to any neutralized (value-free or impartial) self, Murdoch advocates a lover who aspires toward perfection in goodness—but we have also learned that this perfection is not achievable by either a man or a woman alone. Instead, we might say that wise lovers would aspire to wisdom in knowing her or his own limitations, even while aspiring to move beyond these limits in recognizing love's liberated capabilities. This would be the outcome of one's attention to the real as refined by a search for wisdom. In Murdoch's own words,

> Love is . . . *capable* of infinite degradation and is the source of our greatest
> errors; but when [love] is even partially refined it is the energy and passion
> of the soul in its search for Good, the force that joins us to Good and joins us
> to the world through Good. Love's existence is the unmistakable sign that
> we are spiritual creatures, attracted by excellence and made for the Good. It
> is a reflection of the warmth and light of the sun.[84]

Here we return to the image of the enlightened lover. But does this imagery reflect a problematic Platonism, restricting the wisdom of love to the ethereal?

For Murdoch, *eros* motivates an arresting attention to see what is real in nature, in beauty, in ethics, and especially in love of the other as well as the self. Murdoch's terms also recall the myth of Psyche and Cupid in bringing together the soul of the lover and the energy of the erotic. The latter appears crucial as the psychic and spiritual energy motivating a movement toward a unity that integrates the various forms of love. Murdoch calls this a movement toward the real non-representable union of love in pleasure or extreme delight. It would follow that the latter includes *jouissance*. But would the intellectual love of wisdom mitigate the narcissistic dangers of eros by joining lovers to the world through God?[85] At the same time that *eros* seeks its fulfilment in an idealized union with the beloved, Murdoch brings in benevolence, in the sense of a mutual concern for the well-being of the beloved, that is, a friend, as a necessary form of love's wisdom. Yet the relationship itself—in this case, friendship—would be a consequence of love, not to be confused with the wisdom of love itself.

In fact, I have followed Murdoch in turning to Weil's de-creation in love to address the dangers of narcissism in terms of un-selfing.[86] This mitigates the idealizations of a Christian form of Platonic love with mutual benevolence. Never should either blindly sacrificial love, as in extreme altruism, or patriarchal pride, as in unacknowledged egoism, be confused with the wisdom of love. Thus, in the light of Murdoch and everything else we have learned about love's capabilities, the reductively Christianized (i.e., overly simple) stereotypes of a woman's sacrificial love and a man's assertive eros will no longer do.

The argument of this chapter supports the rejection of the simplistically fixed gender roles and gendered relations as well as the reductive norms that patriarchal myths of love have ordained, apparently by divine fiat. Essentially, a bonded love that has been symbolized by patriarchy only enslaves our capabilities in love. So what are the myths by which we should live today? Myths that would create narratives about enlightenment, appropriately balanced at times by dark uncertainty, by symbolism to do with human and divine attributes, as well as by imagery of enlightened lovers, that is, wise lovers attentive to one another, all play parts in the chapter's reflections on liberating love's capabilities.

But there remains a distance to go before we can be confident and clear about the complexities in contemporary discourses on love that are no longer self-destructively bonded and before we can feel certain about the exact capabilities to be found today in the wisdom of love. Indeed, one cannot give an exhaustive definition of love or an exhaustive framework for the wisdom of love; however, our first steps toward such definition acknowledge that love is a highly complex matter and that a framework for liberating human capabilities should go hand in hand with new and renewed myths as fruitful guides on a path to the wisdom of love.

NOTES

1. Michèle Le Doeuff, *Recherches sur l'imaginaire philosophique* (Paris: Payot, 1980); English: *The Philosophical Imaginary*, trans. Colin Gordon (London: Athlone Press, 1989; Berkeley, Calif.: Stanford University Press, 1990); republished (London: Continuum, 2002). Cf. Max Deutscher, ed., *Michèle Le Doeuff: Operative Philosophy and Imaginary Practice* (New York: Humanity Books, 2000); see also notes 22, 33, and 34 below. For a recent statement on the urgent need for a feminist imaginary, see Penelope Deutscher, "When Feminism Is 'High' and Ignorance Is 'Low:' Harriet Taylor Mill on the Progress of the Species," *Hypatia* 21:3 (Summer 2006): 147.

2. Amelie Rorty, "Spinoza on the Pathos of Idolatrous Love and the Hilarity of True Love," in *Feminism and the History of Philosophy*, ed. Genevieve Lloyd (New York: Oxford University Press, 2002), 222; cf. Spinoza, *Ethics*, trans. and ed. G. H. R. Parkinson (Oxford: Oxford University Press, 2000), 314–16. For reference to a Western problematic of love as "bonding," see Birgitte Huitfeldt Midttun, "Crossing the Borders: An Interview with Julia Kristeva," *Hypatia* 21:4 (Fall 2006): 168–69.

3. Carol Gilligan, *The Birth of Pleasure: A New Map of Love* (London: Chatto & Windus, 2002), 40.

4. For the claim that philosophy is "the wisdom of love in the service of love," Emmanuel Levinas, *Otherwise than Being*, trans. A. Lingis (The Hague: Nijhoff, 1981), 162. For a gloss on Levinas: "the Said said in the service of the Saying, the 'justified Said,' in which wisdom has learnt from love, or in which politics is not uninformed by ethics," see Stella Sanford, *The Metaphysics of Love: Gender and Transcendence in Levinas* (London: Athlone Press, 2000), 91.

5. Mary Midgley, *The Myths We Live By* (London: Routledge, 2004), xi, 1, 2, 5.

6. Mary Midgley, *The Ethical Primate: Humans, Freedom and Morality* (London: Routledge, 1994), 109: Midgley asserts that "Myths are not lies, nor need they be taken as literally true" and gives a highly useful philosophical definition of myth; this basic, relatively uncontentious treatment renders mythical symbolism a necessary addition to scientific facts. For her initial use of the term, see Mary Midgley, *Wickedness: A Philosophical Essay* (London: Routledge & Kegan Paul, 1984), 10–12 and 162. For the more technical use of myth, see Midgley, *Ethical Primate*, 109, 117–18; the latter is repeated and elaborated ten years later in *Myths We Live By*, xi, 1, 2, 5. See note 22 for additional references to discussions of 'myth'.

7. Midgley, *Ethical Primate*, 117, and, more generally, 109–20. To read more from this:

> The way in which myths work is often very obscure to us. But, besides their value-implications—which are often very subtle—they also function as summaries of certain selected sets of facts.

. . . When we attend to the range of facts that any particular myth sums up, we are always strongly led to draw the moral that belongs to that myth. But that range of facts is always highly selective. It is limited by the imaginative vision that lies behind that particular story. This vision can, of course, generate actual lies, which is what makes it plausible to think of the myth itself as a lie. Thus, myths about the inferiority of women, or of particular ethnic groups, have supported themselves by false factual beliefs about these people. (117–18)

8. Mary Midgley, *The Owl of Minerva: A Memoir* (London: Routledge, 2005), x–xii.

9. G. W. F. Hegel, *Elements of the Philosophy of Right*, ed. Allen W. Wood and trans. H. B. Nisbet (Cambridge: Cambridge University Press, 1991), 23.

10. If one wanted to make this argument, a premise would need to be defended; that is, Mary's memoirs testify to Geoff Midgley's wisdom, which lives in the various forms of her love and her practices of philosophy. But it is unfair to push the argument this far. The reverse is more likely to be true: Mary is the source of inspiration for Geoff's wisdom.

11. Midgley, *Owl of Minerva*, xi.

12. Cecilia Sjoholm, *Kristeva and the Political* (London: Routledge, 2006), 50, 54–58; cf. Julia Kristeva, *Black Sun: Depression and Melancholy*, trans. Leon Roudiez (New York: Columbia University Press, 1989), 27–30.

13. Kristeva, *Black Sun*, 30; also see note 51.

14. Grace M. Jantzen died May 2, 2006. So this present claim extrapolates from the project on which she was working—a first volume of which is published: *Foundations of Violence: Death and the Displacement of Beauty*, vol. 1 (London: Routledge, 2004), 11–20. For other references to Jantzen, see notes 41 and 64.

15. For the examples and implications of this eclipse, see Michèle Le Doeuff, *Hipparchia's Choice: Women, Philosophy, Etc.*, trans. Trista Selous (Oxford: Blackwell, 1991; rev. trans., New York: Columbia University Press, 2006), 28. Cf. Michèle Le Doeuff, *The Sex of Knowing*, trans. Kathryn Hamer and Lorraine Code (New York and London: Routledge, 2003), esp. Part 1, "Cast-offs."

16. Le Doeuff, *Hipparchia's Choice*, 28; cf. Le Doeuff, *The Philosophical Imaginary*, 100–128.

17. Paul Ricoeur, "Ethics and Human Capability: A Response," in *Paul Ricoeur and Contemporary Moral Thought*, ed. John Wall, William Schweiker, and David Hall (New York and London: Routledge, 2002), 280, 282, and 284.

18. I will return to these forms of love in the section "Complexities in the Gendering of Love's Wisdom," 216–20 (below).

19. Paul Ricoeur, *Memory, History, Forgetting*, trans. Kathleen Blamey (Chicago: University of Chicago Press, 2004), 460.

20. Ibid., 459–66.

21. Ricoeur, "Ethics and Human Capability," 284. On the captive free will, see Paul Ricoeur, *The Symbolism of Evil*, trans. Emerson Buchanan (New York and London: Harper & Row, 1967), 152. On original innocence, see Paul Ricoeur, *Fallible Man*, trans. Charles A. Kelbley (Chicago: Henry Regnery, 1965); rev. trans. by Kelbley with a new Introduction by Walter J. Lowe (New York: Fordham University Press, 1986), 9–15, 144–45; and *Symbolism of Evil*, 156–57.

22. Pamela Sue Anderson, *A Feminist Philosophy of Religion: The Rationality and Myths of Religious Belief* (Oxford: Blackwell, 1998), esp. 4, 21–22, 113–14, 138–43, and 245–47; "Myth and Feminist Philosophy," in *Thinking Through Myths: Philosophi-*

cal Perspectives, ed. Kevin Schilbrack (New York and London: Routledge, 2002), 101–22. Midgley's understanding of symbolism and myth in the wisdom of our living, learning, and knowing bears similarities to an earlier argument presented on the philosophical imaginary; see Le Doeuff, *The Philosophical Imaginary*, 1–20; cf. Midgley, *Myths We Live By*, esp. 1–5, 88–93, 97–101.

23. The adjective "conative" recalls Baruch Spinoza's conception of *conatus* as the human persistence in being, or striving to be; see notes 70, 74 and 76 below.

24. Ricoeur, "Ethics and Human Capability," 282–83.

25. Paul Ricoeur, *The Course of Recognition*, trans. David Pellauer (Cambridge, Mass.: Harvard University Press, 2005), 91, and more generally, chap. 2.

26. Michèle Le Doeuff, "The Spirit of Secularism: On Fables, Gender and Ethics," Weidenfeld Professorial Lectures, University of Oxford, Trinity Term 2006.

27. Le Doeuff, "Spirit of Secularism," Lecture 4: "Not a goddess, she!"

28. This reference to "the heart" has a crucial significance as different from either mind or body, male or female, encompassing aspects of both sides. It is not exactly the soul either, yet it is clearly significant for the distinctive identity of the young girl prior to her adolescence, at which time her self-identity becomes challenged by her changing body, her sexuality, her female beauty, her sexually specific pleasure—a joy that will be more than sexual. We might compare this intellectual joy with Spinoza's intellectual love of God (see notes 70 and 74 below). In this light, the heart is a fundamental and encompassing term for what needs to be protected in the young girl as she grows up, generating the wisdom of love. Le Doeuff leaves us to wonder whether the heart of a young boy is more easily protected from the illusions and oppression of imposed social-sexual stereotypes. For a crucial backdrop to Le Doeuff's thinking on "*le coeur*," see Maria Zambrano, *Les Clairières Du Bois*, translated from Spanish by Marie Laffranque (Paris: Éditions de L' Éclat, 1989), 65–80; and note 29 below.

29. Maria Zambrano was born in 1904 Andalousia, attended the University of Madrid, where she studied philosophy, and died in 1991. Zambrano wrote numerous books in Spanish—one of which inspired Le Doeuff with a story about Dawn, who, unlike the goddess "Dawn" of classical literature, remains human. For the challenge of "*la philosophie imaginaire*" in Zambrano to the traditional gender stereotypes of divine women, see Mary Zambrano, *De L'Aurore*, translated from Spanish by Marie Laffranque (Paris: Éditions de L' Éclat, 1989).

30. See Pamela Sue Anderson, "Feminism and Patriarchy," in *The Oxford Handbook to English Literature and Theology*, ed. Andrew Hass, David Jasper, and Elizabeth Jay (Oxford: Oxford University Press, 2007), 810–28.

31. Virgina Woolf, *The Waves*, ed. Gillian Beer (Oxford: Oxford World's Classics, Oxford University Press, 1992), 3. For example, Woolf moves from the light-dark imagery of waves rising and falling to the figure of a rider on a proud horse who faces a dark enemy advancing against her or him (247–48).

32. Le Doeuff, *Hipparchia's Choice*, 242–43; cf. Woolf, *The Waves*, 3. For a contextualization of French feminism in terms of waves, see Lisa Walsh, "Introduction: The Swell of the Third Wave," in *Contemporary French Feminism*, ed. Kelly Oliver and Lisa Walsh, Oxford Readings in Feminism series (Oxford: Oxford University Press, 2004), 1–11.

33. For more on recognition, or reciprocal equality, see Le Doeuff, *Hipparchia's Choice*, 278–79; and Pamela Sue Anderson, "Life, Death and (Inter)subjectivity: Realism and Recognition in Continental Feminism," *International Journal of Philosophy of Religion*, Special edition: Issues in Continental Philosophy of Religion 60: 41–59 (2006); DOI 10.1007/s11153-006-0013-6.

34. For a gloss on this conception, see Le Doeuff, *The Philosophical Imaginary*, esp. 3–10 and 20.

35. Hamer and Code translate Le Doeuff's French term *déshérences* as "cast-offs," see Le Doeuff, *Sex of Knowing*, 18. Instead, to emphasize the lack of inheritance in this context, the albeit awkward "dis-inherited women" is my translation.

36. For example, Le Doeuff points out that Woolf fails to recognize any renaissance or medieval woman writer, so Le Doeuff singles out a counterexample: Christine De Pizan, a fourteenth-century woman writer who did much to demonstrate the crucial significance of the imaginary for the successful living and thinking of women; see Le Doeuff, *Sex of Knowing*, ix–x, 119, and 135–38; Christine De Pizan, *The Book of the City of Ladies*, trans. Rosalind Brown-Grant (London: Penguin Books, 1999).

37. See note 35.

38. The prominent late-twentieth-century "French" feminists included Hélène Cixous, Luce Irigaray, and Julia Kristeva—none of whom are French by birth. For background on the label "French feminists" and for their contribution to topics in religion, see "Introduction: French Feminisms and Religion," in Morny Joy, Kathleen O'Grady and Jill L. Poxon, eds., *French Feminists on Religion: A Reader* (New York and London: Routledge, 2002), 1–12. Recall that Kristeva recognizes forms of love as bonding; see Midttun, "Crossing the Borders," 168.

39. I will return to the problematic role of the self in this picture in the section "The Complexities of Love's Wisdom." I think that the gendering of Christian (self)-love often creates a debilitating tension between extreme altruism (sacrificial love of the mother) and relentless egoism (the male arrogance that supports matricide).

40. Anderson, "Life, Death and (Inter)subjectivity."

41. See Luce Irigaray, "Divine Women," in *Sexes and Genealogies*, trans. Gillian C. Gill (Ithaca, N.Y.: Cornell University Press, 1993), 55–72; Grace M. Jantzen, *Becoming Divine: Toward A Feminist Philosophy of Religion* (Manchester: Manchester University Press, 1998). For criticism of the Irigarayan imperative "become divine [women]," see Pamela Sue Anderson, "Divinity, Incarnation and Intersubjectivity," *Philosophy Compass* ⅓ (2006): 335–56; DOI 10.1111/j.1747-9991.2006.00025.x.

42. Gilligan, *Birth of Pleasure*, 20

43. For an early discussion of the sex/gender distinction, see Anderson, *A Feminist Philosophy of Religion*, 5–8, 44, 102 and 113–14.

44. Julia Kristeva, "Manic Eros, Sublime Eros: On Male Sexuality," in *Tales of Love*, trans. Leon S. Roudiez (New York: Columbia University Press, 1987), 62; and for further discussion of Plato's *Phaedrus* by Kristeva, 63–69.

45. Ibid., 72. For a relevant philosophical account of Sigmund Freud's conception of libido and libinal energies, see Jonathan Lear, *Love and Its Place in Nature: A Philosophical Interpretation of Freudian Psychoanalysis* (New York: Farrar, Straus and Giroux, 1990; reprinted New Haven/London: Yale University Press, 1998), 140–41 and 148–55.

46. Kristeva, "Manic Eros, Sublime Eros," 63 and 64. To add Kristeva's critical comment: "In its transparent sexual connotation, one can only share the hesitancy of the Fathers of the Church in granting a soul to . . . women" (64).

47. Kristeva, "Manic Eros, Sublime Eros," 63, see also 69–76; and Plato, *Symposium*, trans. Alexander Nehamas and Paul Woodruff (Indianapolis, Ind.: Hackett, 1989), 43:200e. For a highly provocative account of a woman whose wisdom of love is spoken by a man, see Luce Irigaray, "Socrerer's Love: A Reading of Plato, *Symposium*, 'Diotima's Speech,'" in *An Ethics of Sexual Difference*, trans. Carolyn Burke and Gillian C. Gill (London: Athlone Press, 1993), 20–33.

48. Kristeva, "Manic Eros, Sublime Eros," 59, 62–82.

49. Ibid., 59; also see Kristeva, "Freud and Love: Treatment and Its Discontents," and "Narcissus: The New Insanity," in *Tales of Love*, 21–45, and 105–109, 115–21, respectively. For a classical account of Narcissus, see Ovid, *Metamorphoses* (Harmondsworth, Middlesex: Penguin Books, 1955), 84–86.

50. For a philosophical interpretation of this recognition process, see Lear, *Love and Its Place in Nature*, 134–42 (on narcissism), and 198–204 (on the necessity of individuation and the violence of the individuating act). Also, for Kristeva's account of Narcissus' perverse entry into Christian discourses on love, see "Our Faith: The Seeming," in *Tales of Love*, 122–23.

51. For the problem and possibility of an alternative to the idealized mother, see Kristeva, "Stabat Mater," in *Tales of Love*, 234–63: "This motherhood is the *fantasy* that . . . involves less an idealized archaic mother than the idealization of the *relationship* that binds us to her, one that cannot be localized—an idealization of primary narcissism" (234). On "the father of individual pre-history," see Kristeva, "Freud and Love," 33; and "Don Juan, Or Loving To Be Able To," 202, in *Tales of Love*; and *Black Sun*, 23–24. Kristeva stresses the need for two facets of this fatherhood (of the psychoanalytic "imaginary") to enable a blending of the abstract and the affective in language; a successful transition of the infant to language will retain a connection with the prelinguistic realm of affection, i.e., the maternal; so this imaginary father unites the maternal and paternal functions in identity formation.

52. Kristeva, "Manic Eros, Sublime Eros," 59.

53. See note 9 above; cf. Hegel, *Elements of the Philosophy of Right*, 21.

54. Kristeva, "A Holy Madness: She and He," in *Tales of Love*, 83–100.

55. Kristeva, "Manic Eros, Sublime Eros," 60

56. Ibid.; and "A Holy Madness," 88–94, 99–100.

57. Kristeva, "Manic Eros, Sublime Eros," 60; and see note 51 above.

58. Ibid.; also see Kristeva, "God is Love," and "Ego Affectus Est. Bernard of Clairvaux: Affect, Desire, Love," in *Tales of Love*, 139–50 and 151–69, respectively.

59. Kristeva, "Manic Eros, Sublime Eros," 60. Also compare Kristeva, "Our Faith," and "Ratio Diligendi, or the Triumph of One's Own. Thomas Aquinas: Natural Love and the Love of Self," in *Tales of Love*, 122–23 and 172–78.

60. Kristeva, "Ratio Diligendi," 170–87.

61. For her post-Freudian conception of perversion in this context, see Kristeva, "In Praise of Love," in *Tales of Love*, 9–12; see also "Manic Eros, Sublime Eros," "Narcissus," and "Stabat Mater," 60, 115–17, and 260, respectively. For the twelfth- and thirteenth-century accounts of love, distinguishing the violent (irrational) and the rational, see Kristeva, "Ego Affectus Est." 154, 161–66; see also "Ratio Diligendi," 176–77.

62. Kristeva, "Ego Affectus Est," 166. In this chapter Kristeva also discusses the role of apotheosis in the writings of these twelfth- and thirteenth-century philosophical theologians (160, 163, and 166).

63. Kristeva, "Manic Eros, Sublime Eros," 60; cf. "Stabat Mater," 235.

64. For additional references to Kristeva and my earlier discussions of matricide and melancholy, see Anderson, *A Feminist Philosophy of Religion*, 109–14 and 122. On motherhood and primary narcissism, see Kristeva, "Stabat Mater," 243–63. Cf. Grace M. Jantzen, "Death, Then, How Could I Yield to It? Kristeva's Mortal Visions," in *Religion in French Feminist Thought*, ed. Morny Joy, Kathleen O'Grady, and Judith L. Poxon (New York/London: Routledge, 2003), 117–30.

65. Gilligan, *Birth of Pleasure*, 208: "Once we un-focus our eyes and let go an

accustomed way of seeing [then] we recognize that a path has been laid out in our midst. A path, not the path. If we mark the places where pleasure is buried and the seeds of tragedy are planted, then when we arrive at these places, we can take an alternative route." I have reconfigured the myth of Psyche and Cupid to give an account of the birth of pleasure in the beauty of love; see Anderson, "Beauty," in *Encyclopedia of Religion*, 2nd ed., ed. Lindsay Jones (Farmington Hills, Mich.: Thomson Gale, 2005), 2:810–14.

66. For Le Doeuff's philosophical attempt to unsex "the sex" of knowing, see Le Doeuff, *Sex of Knowing*; and for philosophical imaginings after Spinoza, see Rorty, "Spinoza on the Pathos of Idolatrous Love"; and note 74 below. See also Ricoeur, *The Course of Recognition*, esp. chap. 2.

67. Ricoeur, "Ethics and Human Capability," 284.

68. Le Doeuff, *Sex of Knowing*, 28–34; and Pamela Sue Anderson, "An Epistemo-logical-Ethical Approach to Philosophy of Religion: Learning to Listen," in *Feminist Philosophy of Religion: Critical Readings*, ed. Pamela Sue Anderson and Beverley Clack (London: Routledge, 2004), 90–92 and 100.

69. *Jouissance* often appears in English theoretical texts on French feminism untranslated; the French word *jouir* refers to sexual pleasure that is both physical and symbolic, but it can also refer to enjoyment as a legal or social possession, privilege, or right. For its significant link with the maternal in an early account of *jouissance*, see Julia Kristeva, *The Revolution in Poetic Language*, trans. Leon Roudiez (New York: Columbia University Press, 1984), 75–85, 178–81, and 244.

70. This philosophical sense of joy is given content from the seventeenth-century philosopher Baruch Spinoza, who conceives self-love to be roughly equivalent to what might be called "the intellectual love of God"; see notes 74 and 76 below.

71. Le Doeuff, *Sex of Knowing*, 68.

72. Paul Ricoeur, *Oneself as Another*, trans. Kathleen Blamey (Chicago: University of Chicago Press, 1992), 240–96; and Ricoeur, "Epilogue: Difficult Forgiveness," *Memory, History, Forgetting*, 457–506.

73. See Pamela Sue Anderson, "Un-Selfing in Love: A Contradiction in Terms," in *Faith and Enlightenment? The Critique of the Enlightenment Revisited*, ed. Lieven Boeve, Joeri Schrijvers, Wessel Stoker, and Hendrik M. Vroom, Currents of Encounter series 30 (Amsterdam and New York: Rodopi, 2006), 243–67, esp. 245 n. 8, 246, 249, 254, 257–58, and 261–62. See references to Murdoch in notes 78, 84, and 86 below.

74. Susan James, "The Power of Spinoza: Feminist Contentions. Susan James Talks to Genevieve Lloyd and Moira Gaten," *Women's Philosophy Review* (1998): 6–28; Genevieve Lloyd, *Spinoza and the Ethics* (London: Routledge, 1996); and Lloyd, "What a union!" *Philosophers Magazine* 1 (2005): 45–48. Judith Butler connects her own keen interest in Spinoza's account of the desire for life (i.e., Spinoza's *conatus* as persistence in being) to Hegel's later account of the desire for recognition; see "Can the 'Other' of Philosophy Speak," in *Undoing Gender* (New York: Routledge, 2004), 198, 235–37.

Ricoeur refers in numerous places to Spinoza's *conatus* alongside Jean Nabert's conception of "the desire and effort to be"; see, e.g., Paul Ricoeur, "The Demythization of Accusation," in *The Conflict of Interpretations*, ed. Don Ihde (Evanston, Ill.: Northwestern University Press, 1974), 340–42; and Ricoeur, *The Course of Recognition*, 92–93 and 114. Compare this to Kristeva's account of Spinoza on love in *"Ratio Diligendi,"* 186–87.

75. Kristeva, *Ego Affectus Est*, 168; and *"Ratio Diligendi,"* 186–87.

76. Rorty, "Spinoza on the Pathos of Idolatrous Love," 222. On love in Spinoza, see Lloyd, *Spinoza and the Ethics*, 76–77, 110–14, and 137–38. See also note 2 above and Spinoza, *Ethics*, 305–16.

77. For "care-knowing" as an example of such know-how, see Anderson, "An Epistemological-Ethical Approach to Philosophy of Religion," 88, 92–94.

78. Iris Murdoch, "On 'God' and 'Good,'" *The Sovereignty of Good* (London: Routledge & Kegan Paul, 1970), 47–54.

79. Jantzen, *Becoming Divine*.

80. See Anderson, "Unselfing in Love," 246–48.

81. Midgley, *Myths We Live By*, 5–6, 128–29, 137, and 142–45.

82. Ibid., 137.

83. I have derived this idea of an arresting attention from Simone Weil, *Gravity and Grace*, Routledge Classics (London: Routledge, 2002), 96–97, 116–21.

84. Murdoch, *Sovereignty of Good*, 103; emphasis mine.

85. Murdoch herself replaces "God" with "the Good"; note 78 above.

86. For critical discussion of Murdoch, see Anderson, "Unselfing in Love," 246–48, 253–54, and 260–62.

14

The Genesis of Love

An Irigarayan Reading

RUTHANNE S. PIERSON CRÁPO

. . . male and female He created them. . . .
—Genesis 1:27b

In the Beginning Was Space for Two

Luce Irigaray has rightly understood the creation of a good world, where in the beginning is *space* and where God, as time itself, lavishes, or exteriorizes, Godself in the world. Inhabitants live in this space, both male and female, but in the genealogy of philosophy, male becomes time and female becomes the space of inhabited places. A fall occurs. Female is subsumed into the radical interiority of the subject itself, and the male subject, the master of time, becomes what Irigaray dubs "the axis of the world's ordering."[1] Instead of the goodness of two sexes and the revelation possible in the other sex, "a revelation in and of itself," declares Irigaray, "the race of men claims a monopoly on truth and the exclusive right to legislate everything: philosophy, law, politics, religion, science."[2] To borrow the conceptual framing of Al Wolters, this is no structural fall—it is an ethical fall.[3] It is an ethical deviancy where the self equals *one* not *two*,[4] a sameness, and a split in sameness that ignores the *other*.[5] Phallocentrism displaces and replaces sexual difference, treating the two sexes as if they are two variations of the one sex.[6] There is no longer two, but one sex, one master discourse, and only one desire—the masculine. Where is the feminine? Where is her desire, her language, her sex, her God? Irigaray realizes that the call for redemption can no longer be found in an ethic where one sex turns to itself for consciousness raising, where one sex understands the symbolic mysteries of the unconscious and interprets them for the other sex.

Which will we choose: to separate or to align? If we choose the latter, space and time must be rediscovered, perhaps "time must *redeploy* space."[7] We must reconsider the immanent and the transcendent in a way that we have never traversed: through the female sex. A place is needed where the kingdom of God occurs in the *here and now*—a place where the angel and the carnal touch.[8] Irigaray begins this quest in a third world order that she sees, not as the order of the Old Testament (the age of the Father), or as the order of the New Testament (the age of the Son), but as the order of a Third Testament (the age of the Spirit and the bride), where she observes a "coupling."[9] No longer is the masculine secure in his absolute knowledge of one subject, of one gender. The very notion of divinity is now a God of "flesh and sex." Irigaray queries,

> Would a couple god have more to say, and more dialectically yet? No man or woman would achieve absolute knowledge within or according to his or her gender. Each would be constituted in time through a constant articulation between the genders, a dialectic between two figures or incarnations of the living that are represented in sexual difference, and there alone.[10]

A genesis of love between the sexes springs forth "from the smallest to the greatest, from the most intimate to the most political. A world that must be created or re-created so that man and woman may once again or at last live together, meet, and sometimes inhabit the same place."[11]

It must be acknowledged first that sexual difference has been marred by a world of patriarchal subjugation and male misogyny. Sameness has caused language to be always centered on the phallus; the refuse rejected by the phallogocentric language is what is left to woman.[12] She has no created language of her own. While this is certainly Irigaray's fundamental critique, her philosophy advances to another level—a utopian vision of what could be if sexual difference were realized. Irigaray's philosophy has been called utopian, in the sense that she must try to "imagine the unimaginable—namely where we're going before we're there."[13] Utopia is not above us or ahead of us—it is here amongst us. This is not a static perfection, but a process. As Margaret Whitford astutely observes, "The possible articulation of material and symbolic is not worked out by Irigaray *except at the junction of the two in language and in the bodies of women.*"[14] Like social feminists, Irigaray wants change to happen to real women and for it to affect their day-to-day realities, but utopia is now between us. Utopia will never be found within an individual. The reign of the one is over. It can only be found between us, amongst us. I now have an intersubjective need for another, and an other of the other. The interval, or that real space between us, becomes the position where two subjects meet: woman to woman, woman to man, man to woman, woman to God, God to woman, woman to creation, creation to woman. I seek to track these two moments of both critique and visionary hope within her work that creates the possibility for intersubjectivity between men and women, uncovering a normative guide for a genesis of love.

In order to understand sexual difference, we must think of the intersection of various planes: the reuniting of the masculine and the feminine, the horizontal and vertical, the terrestrial and heavenly. We must think there is a possibility for the vertical and the horizontal to come together, a "sensible transcendental," a "divine enstacy."[15] This will take all the power (puissance) of the gods, and a rethinking of love and its wisdom.

This essay will seek to understand the discourse surrounding the Genesis account and re-read the creation/fall story as a story of sexual difference. It will rely on an Irigarayan reading, while attempting to uncover the creation of the female genesis narrative, invoking a place for two origins and two genealogies that is in reality the genesis of many. I engage Irigaray to critique notions of philosophy that have construed woman as an indispensable construction for the masculine subject,[16] yielding a fragmented self for both sexes. I suggest that in order for both sexes to be subjects in their own right, they each need a genesis of sexual difference that creates the conditions of possibility for love. For Irigaray, a masculine sex has been thoroughly instantiated and dominant in our culture to the point of covering or subsuming female subjectivity; what is missing is a birth and development of a female genealogy.[17] This essay will conclude by problematizing the challenges and impossible possibility of love for being two in our world.

The Death of Mother/Daughter

Under patriarchy, the mother has no possibilities of expression; she is an exile, as is her daughter, from her own origin and her development as a woman. Instead, the daughter is offered to take her mother's place in the reproductive cycle, symbolically "murdering" her in madness similar to Electra. Irigaray depicts the ancestry of woman as thus:

> The need for the daughter to turn away from the mother, the need for hatred between them, without sublimation of female identity being an issue, so that daughter can enter into the realm of desire and law of the father. This is unacceptable.[18]

I agree with Irigaray, but how can a proper space of identification be formed between mother and daughter that does not enter the dialectical symmetry of the phallic order, or the competitiveness of the female economy that vies for status within a phallic logic? Irigaray's quest for restoration will have to be multidirectional, a search for history/herstory that has been rendered invisible, leaving the safety of the maternal, a haven that has historically brought rejuvenation and restoration to the identity shared by mother and daughter. No more can a fear of abandonment or slavery to the pretense of security overpower the independence and assertion for power of women by seeking protection in an object of love that is also her identity. Irigaray calls for a restoration of relationship between mother and daughter with a purview to the articulation of their identities as women. She wants the debt of the mother to be legitimated, freeing the mother to her own desire and her own sexual identity and thus allowing her daughter a place other than an undifferentiated sexual economy—a fusion, in Elizabeth Grosz's words, that is neither residue nor loss.[19] A positive place is now established, woman to woman: "We are luminous. Neither one nor two. . . . An odd sort of two. And yet not one. Especially not one. Let's leave *one* to them: their oneness, with its prerogatives, its domination, its solipsism: like the sun's."[20]

Left with lack, deficiencies, negatives, Irigaray creates a beauty out of the ashes of sameness—difference.[21] Never completed, but embracing ourselves whole, one no longer has to be the real and the other the copy. We can now be safe in our own skin.

The Origin of the Unacknowledged Mother in the Biblical Account

The unacknowledged mother has been forgotten even longer than perhaps Irigaray suspects.[22] Her eclipsing goes back to creation itself. Biblical scholar Victor P. Hamilton brings to light some of the darkness historically shrouding the Genesis account of our first mother, Eve. Hamilton notes as remarkable the large section of the creation story given over to a separate and distinct account of the creation of woman. According to Hamilton, "Such a separate narration of woman's creation is without parallel in ancient Near Eastern literature."[23] Hamilton makes several observations. First, both male and female are created in the image of God; neither one is the "Master Signifier." The command to rule and steward creation is directed at both male and female. Second, Hamilton notes their similar origins—the raw material of rib and dirt—"Neither is actively involved in the creation of the other."[24] But what I find particularly interesting is the description of woman as a "helper fit" for Adam. Hamilton clarifies the importance of this statement: "Interestingly, the writer has described Eve with a word which preponderantly is applied to God elsewhere in the Old Testament. The 'helper' par excellence is God. The helper who is invoked for assistance normally is stronger than the one who stands in need."[25] Fourth, on seeing Eve for the first time, Adam exclaims, "This at last is bone of my bones and flesh of my flesh" (v. 23a). Hamilton notes that similar words are employed in Genesis 29:14, Judges 9:2, and 2 Samuel 5:1 and 19:12–13, where a case could be made for the phrase *your bone and your flesh* as an affirmation not simply of kinship but of loyalty. That is, circumstances will not dictate or determine or undermine this relationship. Hamilton's fifth observation is that Genesis clearly sets subordination of the woman to man, not in the context of creation, but in the context of the Fall (see Gen 3:16).

While Hamilton's arguments carry a certain residue of a binary opposition, he has, I believe, uncovered vital understandings of our origin. There was no

Master Signifier in creation, only in our fall. Eve's origin is separate from Adam; her singular appearance carries a dissymmetry to Adam's creation account. Her genealogy is separate from Adam's but rooted in the same image of a complex YHWH whose image must bear the origin of the female as well as the male if she is created in his/her image. She has her own story of creation, fall, redemption, and consummation, which cannot be subsumed into a neutered or neutral story of beginnings.[26] Yet together they can have a loyalty to one another; the lack between the two can be overcome when they are *with* one another, not as One + One, but as Female and Male—a space/time modality created separately for each of them. Irigaray's cries of absence find an audience in the biblical story that records mother's presence, her being, her space and time in history that cannot be denied. Her sexual identity is different. She no longer has to fear abandonment by the Law/Father, or desire what he possesses. She has her own story, her own God, her own origin, her own desire; she is a dissymmetrical conundrum of delight to both God and man.

Too Much, Too Little: Respecting the Space for Difference

The fall of our ethical relationship can be understood in James Olthuis's concept of too much, too little.[27] When we give too much space between male and female, there is estrangement, distance, a cold disdain. We began our fall, in an Irigarayan sense, when we started with too much, too much of the One sex, one discourse, one signifier, one desire, one language. The male's refusal to recognize the other (not as the negative of himself) has been complemented by woman's own acceptance of her lack of subjectivity.[28] She has mirrored the male's perception of the image: the denial of herself.[29]

But now the converse is possible. Theorists like Irigaray make us aware of the duping of philosophy, science, and history. We must re-historicize our genealogies, our stories, our myths, and our divinities. We need space of our own, air to breathe of our own, time to become. But what will we do with our space, our time, our air? Some may attempt to protect female autonomy by resisting passionate involvement with men because their sexuality is bound up with the fantasy of submission to an ideal male figure, and this undermines their sense of a separate self.[30] We cannot say yes in the double bind of not wanting to mimic the phallocratic order of the masculine;[31] the yes must come from another source, something deeper, richer, more original—the "yes" more ancient. When man constructs his own architecture of safety, when woman goes amazoning with her own sex, each slips into their solipsism from the other sex, and there is too little. How can we not slip into the threat of too much (absorption) or the loss of too little (isolation)? We need the wisdom of love if this is to be possible.

To Be Two and Together

Love, according to Hegel, was something in which a woman could not partici-pate because love is a labor of the universal, a universal delimited by man.[32] Men are the assumed citizen and family representative of public life.[33] For a couple within this system, argues Irigaray, the ultimate aim of love is the accumulation of family capital—both being enslaved to the State, to religion, to the accumulation of property.[34]

In contrast to this model of coupling, Irigaray offers a process, a dynamic potential for growth; only through the acknowledgement of difference can the possibility for true togetherness actually flourish. Currently, what we find are attempts to integrate the other into our country, our culture, our house; but she laments that we still lack a culture of relation with the other.[35] For there to be exchange, Irigaray insists, "it is essential that the other touch us, particularly through words."[36] What we have known in touching through words has been fusion, a speaking that has distanced each of us from ourselves, destroying that in which we have been touched. The words that claim to lead the transcen-dental cannot be deprived of their sensibility:

> Touching must remain sensuous, join the near, without dissolving it in the surroundings. Touching must reach it and, as a result, close it again, with-drawn. Enfolded in a proper, which does not make it imperceptible to the other but reveals it to the other, while preparing a proximity between us.[37]

We need an interval, a medium—the elements of earth/nature itself, Being par excellence—the matter of the transcendental.[38] Our proximity, our space-time continuum, must not be calling the other equal, thereby calculating the value of the subject. The feminine subject, instead, has interest in the relationship between two, in communication between people.[39] If our culture has been a culture of monosubjectivity, as Irigaray postulates, then aiming at a culture of at least two subjects must be a constant gesture. Yet the discourse of exchange has been thoroughly saturated in a masculine discursive logic.

Is there no escape from the effects of phallogocentrism? Has Irigaray developed an imminent critique that is only descriptive and not prescriptive? I suggest that her prescription is a nondiscursive philosophy that cannot be merely theorized but must be lived and fleshed out through an intersubjective participation that aims at opening and retaining fluid space between at least two subjectivities. In many ways, her philosophy is an attempt to create bridges between language and the body—bodies that are sexually differentiated. Her philosophy moves beyond the discursive. It is a saying other than words, to sing together, sharing breath, a sharing of desire, of love. She develops a notion that words (or *logos*) are formed through and conducted by air, and air or breathing becomes a crucial symbol for a conduit that resists the mechanization or containment by the masculine economy.[40] Air or breath represents that which cannot be enslaved, enveloped, or controlled; it must be shared. There are thus far at least two implications in Irigaray's theory of intersubjectivity that I want to articulate.

First, Irigaray's conception of breath powerfully connects to Genesis and has ethical repercussions. Breath, the breath of God, and the Age of the Spirit encircle the Genesis myth. Irigaray observes that God sending his breath into matter, into earth, created humans. When sin occurs, both man and woman are redeemed through the generation of a woman; the breath of the Spirit inhabits both Mary and Jesus. In the third age, after the age of the world's redemption, Irigaray theorizes that humanity must itself become divine breath. She postulates, "The accomplishment of humanity, its perfect realization, requires the cultivation of one's breath as divine presence, in ourselves, and between us."[41] We must learn to breathe on our own and then breathe together for subjectivity to become redemptive intersubjectivity.[42]

Second, according to Irigaray, the saying belongs to two: the two can grow, flourish, and dance when there is a desire to not possess or fuse with the other.[43] By recognizing sexual difference, we do not stifle the origin, continuing the death of the unheralded mother. Rather, desire renders the I-me together with the I-you, not in a possession, submersion, or nausea; they are not ambiguity or "the feminine body and the feminine." It is an encounter belonging to a faithful sexed nature, the recognition of another whom I do not possess; it is a quest for new words, an alliance that does not reduce the other to an item of property.[44] Irigaray celebrates the careful dance of two subjects in the dance of intersubjectivity:

> In my desire for you, in the love that I share with you, my body is animated by the desire to be with you or to you, with me or to me, and it also longs for the existence of a between-us. . . . I seek an alliance between who you are and who I am, in myself and in yourself. I seek a complex marriage between my interiority and that of a *you* which cannot be replaced by me, which is always outside of me, but thanks to which my interiority exists.[45]

In her conception of love, Irigaray places a "to" between "I" and "you" to resist subjugation or reduction of the other: the "to" maintains intra-transitivity between persons, between interpersonal questions, speech, or gift.[46] Therefore, I speak to you, I ask of you, I give to you, I love to you. No master commands his slave, no doctor prescribes his remedy, no teacher inscribes truth; rather, I ask you, I am attentive to you, I ask to stay with you. The "to" prevents domination and barriers against alienation:

> *I love to you* thus means: I do not take you for a direct object, nor for an indirect object by revolving around you. It is, rather, around myself that I have to revolve in order to maintain the *to you* thanks to the return to me. . . . The "to" is the guarantor of two intentionalities: mine and yours.[47]

In conclusion, Irigaray offers us several areas for reflection in order to be two together:

1. To be two together means acknowledging the death of mother. We must acknowledge the debt we owe to our origin, allowing the mother her own desire, not being an object of desire or sharing the Father's desire. Intersubjectivity begins with acknowledging the baggage of our own sense of lack.

2. To be two together means neither domination nor alienation. To be two means we are not the same; the other does not signify the Master Signifier. There are two economies, dissymmetrical in their genealogies, but they are not doomed to never touch.

3. To be two together means language must not house the same. The poetic, the song, the breath we use to speak must listen and speak to *parler femme*, that which breaks out of the binary opposition of metaphysics and allows for multiplicities and an imaginary of female voice, agency, and empowerment.

4. To be two together means to respect the interval between and fill that space with love, a love that is possessed by neither, a gift, impossible, but at the same time possible. A love to another, without expectation or return, from me to you, from you to me. We seek to retain the intra-transitivity of love, where one is not the subject and the other the object.

5. To be two together means we do not work toward a teleological end, but embrace the process, the utopia of struggling in the hard work of earth, relationships; we labor together in love.

Clearly, to be two means much more than what I have highlighted. But Irigaray's process is a journey, not a destination, and it is never final. It has only just begun.

NOTES

1. Luce Irigaray, *An Ethics of Sexual Difference*, trans. Carolyn Burke and Gillian C. Gill (Ithaca, N.Y.: Cornell University Press, 1985), 7.

2. Luce Irigaray, *Sexes and Genealogies*, trans. Gillian C. Gill (New York: Columbia University Press, 1993), 114.

3. I refer to reformational philosopher Al Wolters, who argues that "structure denotes the 'essence' of a creaturely thing, the kind of creature it is by virtue of God's creational law. *Direction*, by contrast, refers to a sinful deviation from that structural ordinance and renewed conformity to it in Christ." See Wolters, *Creation Regained: Biblical Basis for a Reformational Worldview* (Grand Rapids, Mich.: Eerdmans, 1985), 73.

4. I do not believe Irigaray is talking about a literal two; instead, she is trying to raise our awareness of the primacy of One, and the fact that the history of subjectivity has been One + One + One. I agree with Gail M. Schwab that Irigaray is really interested more in what is "left over," that which lies between the integers. See Schwab,

"Mother's Body, Father's Tongue: Mediation and the Symbolic Order," in *Engaging with Irigaray: Feminist Philosophy and European Thought*, ed. Carolyn Burke, Naomi Schor, and Margaret Whitford (New York: Columbia, 1994), 363 n. 1.

5. Irigaray, *Sexes and Genealogies*, 115.

6. Differences are reduced to similarity, they are commensurable, with one inferior notion: the female becomes the "castrated" sex. For further discussion, see Luce Irigaray, "Another 'Cause'—Castration," in *Speculum of the Other Woman*, trans. Gillian C. Gill (Ithaca, N.Y.: Cornell University Press, 1985), 46–54.

7. Irigaray, *Ethics of Sexual Difference*, 18.

8. Ibid., 17.

9. Margaret Whitford acknowledges Gillian Rose's observation of Third Testament found in Deleuze, *Différence et Repetition* (Paris: Presses Universitaires de France, 1969). She turns to Rose's notation that Joachim of Fiore, c. 1132–1202 divided history into three periods: the Age of the Father (Old Testament), the Age of the Son (New Testament and 42 subsequent generations), and the Age of the Spirit, in which all humanity would be converted. Irigaray adapts this scenario to include the woman. Whitford, *Luce Irigaray: Philosophy in the Feminine* (London and New York: Routledge, 1991), 30 n. 13.

10. Irigaray, *Sexes and Genealogies*, 110.

11. Irigaray, *Ethics of Sexual Difference*, 17.

12. I am referencing Irigaray's critique of Jacques Lacan's theory of the phallus as the veiled master signifier by which all discursive symbols are positioned and woman becomes the signified. See Lacan, "The Signification of the Phallus," and "Guiding Remarks for a Convention on Female Sexuality," in *Écrits*, trans. Bruce Fink (New York: W.W. Norton, 2006, 2002) 685–584, 610–20.

13. I am quoting from Whitford's commentary in *Daring to Dream: Utopian Stories by United States Women: 1836–1919*, ed. Carol Farley Kessler (London: Pandora, 1984) 7.

14. Whitford, *Philosophy in the Feminine*, 21.

15. I borrow this term from James Olthuis, "Divine Enstacy: Luce Irigaray's 'Sensible Transcendental'" (working paper, Chair of Philosophical Theology, Institute for Christian Studies, Toronto, 2001).

16. According to Irigaray, the Freudian and Lacanian accounts of subjectivity postulate that female subjectivity is a myth, since it exists only in its relation to the male symbolic. According to this logic, a little girl is merely an inferior little boy, and a woman is a woman as a result of a certain lack of characteristics. The overwhelming power of the phallic economy can only position female subjectivity as an object in relation to male subjectivity, creating a strange and harmful dependence on the female to be an object to reflect or mirror male subjectivity. See Luce Irigaray, *Speculum of the Other Woman*, trans. Gillian C. Gill (Ithaca, N.Y.: Cornell University Press, 1985), esp. 25–33, 119–122, 168–179.

17. While I believe Irigaray has communicated a stunning absence of authentic female subjectivity, I concede that she in many ways leaves male subjectivities as an ultimately negative force. In an interview, she surmises, "Research of this kind [sexual difference] aims at offering women a morphologic that is appropriate to their bodies. It also aims at inviting the male subject to undertake his own self-redefinition as a body, with a view to exchanges between sexed/gendered subjects" (in *Shifting Scenes: Interviews on Women, Writing and Politics in Post-68 France*, ed. Alice A. Jardine and Anne

M. Menke, trans. Margaret Whitford (New York: Columbia University Press, 1991), 103). I read her as suggesting that her work is leaving space for intersubjective relations between two sexes to revolutionize the ethical and ontological nature of the male subject. I assume she senses that she cannot adequately address male subjectivity since she is a woman, but would it not follow then, that philosophy has rightly ignored female subjectivity because its canon is written overwhelmingly by men? Can each sex only write about its own sex? I sense that she would not want to make such a definitive conclusion, and that as such, her work ought to offer a utopian possibility for a normative understanding of ethical male subjectivities, apart from the negative description she has critiqued.

18. Luce Irigaray, *Thinking the Difference: For a Peaceful Revolution*, trans. Karin Montin (London and New York: Routledge, 1994), 109.

19. Grosz, *Jacques Lacan: A Feminist Introduction* (New York: Routledge, 1990), 183.

20. Luce Irigaray, *This Sex Which Is Not One*, trans. Carolyn Porter (Ithaca, N.Y.: Cornell University Press, 1985), 207.

21. To be clear, Irigaray is not postulating a sexual difference that follows traditional notions of gender, where woman becomes inferior, opposite, or complementary to men. For Irigaray, female subjectivity is primordially different, and this upsets previous renderings of history and philosophy and has implications for intersubjectivity. Many have misread Irigaray's account of sexual difference as "essentializing" woman's nature, that is to say, the belief that woman has an essence that can be specified by one or a number of inborn attributes that transcend culture and time. As Margaret Whitford has already established, the debate regarding essentialism has actually put into question the binary pair of essentialism/anti-essentialism, allowing one to interpret essentialism "as a position rather than as an ontology and Irigaray to be interpreted as a strategist" (*Engaging with Irigaray*, 16); see also Tina Chanter's helpful essay, 'Tracking Essentialism With the Help of A Sex/Gender Map," in *Ethics of Eros: Irigaray's Rewriting of the Philosophers* (New York and London: Routledge, 1995), 21–46; and Naomi Schor, "This Essentialism Which Is Not One: Coming to Grips with Irigaray," in *Engaging Irigaray*, 57–78.

22. The creation story is often told only from the Genesis account. The book of Proverbs also records images of the creation and pre-creation, specifically noting the presence of another character in the creation story—*Sophia*, or Lady Wisdom. In Proverbs 8:27–33 she declares, "When he prepared the heavens, I *was* there; when he set a compass upon the face of the depth: When he established the clouds above: when he strengthened the fountain of the deep: when he gave to the sea his decree, that the waters should not pass his commandment: when he appointed the foundations of the earth: Then I was by him, *as* one brought up *with him:* and I was daily *his* delight, rejoicing always before him; Rejoicing in the habitable part of his earth; and my delights *were* with the sons of men" (KJV). Clearly, her presence there was originary and pre-originary, bringing another sex to a traditionally masculinized account.

23. Hamilton, *Handbook of the Pentateuch: Genesis, Exodus, Leviticus, Numbers, Deuteronomy* (Grand Rapids, Mich.: Baker Book House, 1982), 28.

24. Ibid.

25. Ibid., 28–29.

26. Irigaray theorizes that the story of original "sin" for woman is almost contrary to the sin of man: "she has to care about turning back to herself, respecting the *I* and the *you* as *I-she* and *you-she/her*, being faithful to feminine values, in talking and acting in

daily life. . . . Woman has to praise the grace of being born a woman without being envious of a masculine being or existence" (in *Key Writings*, ed. Luce Irigaray [London and New York: Continuum, 2004], 146).

27. Olthuis, "Divine Enstacy."

28. See Jessica Benjamin, *The Bonds of Love: Psychoanalysis, Feminism, and the Problem of Domination* (New York: Pantheon Books, 1988), 85–132.

29. Irigaray cites another "too much," the women's egalitarian movement that bought into the master signifier, and sought to be One + One + One. She argues that they mimicked the phallic order and wanted to be "equal to them," which is not equality at all, but a sacrifice of our mothers and daughters on the alter of economic gain without concern of our own particularities, sexes, genealogies. See especially her controversial interview in Margaret Whitford's *The Irigaray Reader* (Cambridge: Blackwell, 1991), 30–33.

30. For further discussion, see Benjamin, *Bonds of Love*, 185–218.

31. This is a critical juncture where Irigaray is deeply at odds with egalitarian feminists such as Simone de Beauvoir. According to Irigaray, egalitarian feminists have centered their concerns largely on having the same rights, access, and wages as men. While she clearly sees these as important realizations, she is concerned with the *aim* of such logic—that is, to reduce woman to a masculine identity, reinstating a second genocide of female identity. She suggests that feminists became so bound up in identifying with the resources of patriarchal privilege that they began to identify with the norms, values, goals, and methods devised and validated by men. While her project does have political aims, she believes these aims must originate through the sexual identification of each sex, not just the masculine sex. In Irigaray's words, "And the matter is not of reaching the highest position in a patriarchal or phallocratic tradition but of bringing about her own values in a human world" (*Key Writings*, ix).

32. Irigaray, *I Love to You*, 22.

33. For a fuller examination of Hegel's understanding of family and the sexual division of roles within family life, see his section on the family and the ethical order in G. W. F. Hegel *Elements of the Philosophy of Right*, ed. Allen W. Wood, trans. H. B. Nisbet (Cambridge: Cambridge University Press, 1991), 199–219; G. W. F. Hegel, *Phenomenology of Spirit*, trans. A. V. Miller (Oxford: Oxford University Press, 1977), 266–294.

34. Irigaray, *I Love to You*, 23.

35. See especially her most recent work, *The Way of Love*, trans. Heidi Bostic and Stephen Pluháček (London and New York: Continuum, 2002), ix.

36. Ibid., 18.

37. Ibid.

38. Ibid., 19.

39. Ibid., 24.

40. Irigaray's philosophy systematizes and addresses each of Empedocles' classical elements of fire, earth, water, and air. In her book *The Forgetting of Air in Martin Heidegger*, trans. Mary Beth Mader (Austin: University of Texas Press, 1999), she devotes a substantial amount of work to the question of Being and its connection to the earth, namely, the way philosophers constitute metaphysics to privilege solid planes, ignoring the fluid modalities of fire, water, and air. For Irigaray, air or breath becomes a nondiscursive way to articulate the connection between language and bodies: "Breathing can create bridges between different peoples or cultures, respecting their diversities. It is particularly of use in our time in order for women and men to enter into relation in

spite of their different subjectivities and cultures" (*Key Writings*, 146). For other essays on air or breath as a symbol for intersubjectivity, see "The Air of Those Who Love Each Other," and "Words to Nourish the Breathe of Life" in *Why Different? A Culture of Two Subjects: Interviews with Luce Irigaray*, ed. Luce Irigaray and Sylvère Lotringer, trans. Camille Collins (New York: Semiotext(e), 2000), 129–41.

41. Irigaray, *Key Writings*, 169.

42. For Irigaray, cultivating a sense of self is the primary moment that determines the outcomes of our intersubjectivity. Breathing becomes a metaphor for the connection between the exterior cosmos and the interior of the self. According to Irigaray, "the difficulty for a woman is to remain both in the fluidity and in herself, in her interiority. Also here, a possible way for uniting these two necessities lies in the cultivation of breathing, in a culture of breath. . . . It grants the woman autonomy as well as interiority, two indissociable dimensions of subjectivity" (*Key Writings*, 170).

43. An acknowledged difficulty in Irigaray's work is her insistence to use coupling or pair bonding as the primordial medium through which intersubjectivity is experienced and normalized. Critics also view her theory of intersubjectivity to be "heterosexualist" in its formation, with little space for alternative sexualities. It should also be noted that she can be read as privileging sexual difference over and against other forms of difference; and given the complexity of individuals' subjectivities, sexual difference is always in play with other differences such as race, ethnicity, religion, age, orientation, and the like. But as Alison Stone argues, it would be over-hasty to dismiss her cogent and complex account of a philosophy of nature, where sexual difference clearly exists and has vast political, social, and cultural ramifications. For a more developed account of the merits and deficiencies in Irigaray's philosophy of nature, see Alison Stone, "The Sex of Nature: A Reinterpretation of Irigaray's Metaphysics and Political Thought," *Hypatia* 18 (2003): 60–84; and *Luce Irigaray and the Philosophy of Sexual Difference* (New York: Cambridge University Press, 2006), esp. 87–121.

44. Irigaray, *I Love to You*, 11.

45. Luce Irigaray, *To Be Two*, trans. Monique M. Rhodes and Marco F. Cocito-Monoc (London and New York: Routledge, 2001), 28.

46. Irigaray, *I Love to You*, 109.

47. Ibid., 110.

15

You'd Better Find
Somebody to Love

Toward a Kierkegaardian Bioethic

AMY LAURA HALL

How could one speak properly about love if you were forgotten, you God of love, source of all love in heaven and on earth: you who spared nothing but in love gave everything; you who are love, so that one who loves is what he is only by being in you!

—Kierkegaard, *Works of Love*, 3–4

One aims at her with the ethical category, shuts the eyes, thinks of the absolute in the ethical requirements, thinks of man, opens the eyes, fastens one's gaze upon this demure miss who is being constructed in one's imagination to see if she meets the requirement; one becomes embarrassed and says to oneself: Ah, this surely is a jest.

—Kierkegaard, "In Vino Veritas," 48

Is this indeed love, to want to find it outside oneself? I thought that this is love, to bring love along with oneself. But the one who brings love along with himself as he searches for an object for his love (otherwise it is a lie that he is searching for an object—for his love) will easily, and the more easily the greater the love in him, find the object and find it to be such that it is lovable.

—Kierkegaard, *Works of Love*, 157

Enough!

Does an orphan in the woods have a voice if there is no one to hear her cry? What if another forest-dweller perceives her as his next meal? Is this propositional orphan a "she" in any meaningful sense, calling in any relevant way for care or attention from those who would neglect, manipulate, or devour her? The biotech revolution evokes again this question—a question that is much older than the Human Genome Project or the debate over embryonic stem cell research. How does one detect the features attending a life worth living, a life worth saving, or a life worth protection? Working within the field of "bioethics," I am deluged by colleagues and students with stories that beg for a definitive, compelling, clear-cut account of *the person* to whom we are responsible. My electronic inbox sags with HEADLINES from the frontier of morality:

1. "Sacrifice Self and Avoid Being Nuisance"—Baroness Warnock, a leading British bioethicist, defended voluntary euthanasia to the *Sunday Times* in 2004. "In other contexts, sacrificing oneself for one's family would be considered good. I don't see what is so horrible about the motive of not wanting to be an increasing nuisance."[1]

2. "No More Stupid People"—James Watson argues that parents should have routine genetic veto over the make-up of their child, insisting, for example, "Most mothers wouldn't want to have dwarfs."[2] Watson has also gone on record promoting the elimination of "stupid" people and the genetic enhancement of female beauty.[3]

3. "Only Quality Children"—According to reports in the United States, Canada, and the United Kingdom, around 9 out of 10 fetuses detected for Down Syndrome through prenatal testing are terminated. The rates of termination after prenatal detection of conditions involving genital ambiguity, club foot, and cleft palate are also growing, according to physician reporting in the United States.[4] Bob Edwards, world-renowned embryologist and IVF pioneer, declared in 1999, "Soon it will be a sin for parents to have a child that carries the heavy burden of genetic disease. We are entering a world where we have to consider the quality of our children."[5]

4. "Bad Genes"—Regarding concerns about reports that the foster children of Texas were being treated disproportionately with psychiatric drugs, Dr. Joseph Burkett, Tarrant County medical director, representing the Texas Society of Psychiatric Physicians suggested, "A lot of these kids come from bad gene pools."[6]

5. "Humanlike Animals"—Researchers at the Mayo Clinic have created pigs with human blood flowing through their bodies, and scientists at Stanford University are experimenting on mice with human brains. *National Geographic News* reports: "The more humanlike the animal, the better research model it makes for testing drugs or possibly growing 'spare parts,' such as livers, to transplant into humans."[7] Such "humanized" animals could have countless uses.

A More Primal Truth?

The relatively new field of bioethics runs on the motor of boundary-breaking science. As university scientists craft pig-people and "humanzees," as pregnancy.com offers women the opportunity to terminate for sex selection "before they show," some moral philosophers and theologians seek to call a halt by digging into the definitive markers of humanness. Inasmuch as it is part of the task of human life to love one's neighbor, it is important to be able to discern whether this or that entity *is* a neighbor. Is the embryo a person? Will the bionically enhanced cyborg still be human? There is a sense among some bioethicists that it is important to discern the more primal truths about human existence, in part by way of determining the basic characteristics attending to human life as such. The medical industrial complex is producing novel ways to detect, eliminate, use, and ostensibly enhance human life, and it seems a time ripe for finding and protecting *the human.* There is a sense, in other words (using Darby Slick's words, to be exact) that moral philosophers must excavate our increasingly technologized existence in order to find somebody to love. In this essay I propose to enlist Søren Kierkegaard for the purposes of just such an excavation and to make explicit his potential as a source for bioethical reflection.

There are now various voices shouting *Enough!* in the United States. Drawing on different strands within Western philosophy and theology, American scholars who agree on little else find themselves eager to cooperate to delineate the boundaries of truly human life. McKibben's eco-interrogation of medical technology, *Enough: Staying Human in an Engineered Age,* has become a key text for lefties suspicious about unfettered biotech. Warning in particular about human germline genetic intervention, McKibben suggests that post-genetic enhancement generations may be, in an important sense, *no longer human;* grandchildren will no longer be the same sort of creatures as their grandparents. In the face of this disconnect with our primordial genetic heritage, it is time to say *Enough,* for, McKibben concludes, "We're [already] capable of the further transformations necessary to redeem the world."[8] Here McKibben evokes what he deems to be the common moral sense of the importance of basic struggle toward a human goal. To oversimplify a complex (and compelling) argument, McKibben suggests that to engineer our children on the genetic level is, potentially, to save them from those very limitations and difficulties that make us human. Genetic enhancement threatens to pull humanity out of those essentials that are simply *given* in our nature and in the surrounding natural world. Humanity, as it currently is, is enough—enough, even, to "redeem the world."

Francis Fukuyama draws similar conclusions in his current work on bioethics. Drawing from his previous Hegelian interpretation of democracy as a kingdom of ends, Fukuyama now hopes to shore up the basic contours of given human existence against erosion through biotechnology. He seeks to recover and protect the blurring margin of natural and unnatural, a margin that delineates the line between inhumane and humane democracy. Here Fukuyama is involved in natural moral philosophy, shorn of its potentially divisive history in religious tradition. Using literature, philosophy, and trenchant cultural analysis, Fukuyama wishes to evoke in his readers the realization that something is gravely awry and getting worse. In his book *Our Posthuman Future: Consequences of the Biotechnology Revolution*, Fukuyama opens the first chapter with a quote from Martin Heidegger's *The Question Concerning Technology*:

> The threat to man does not come in the first instance from the potentially lethal machines and apparatus of technology. The actual threat has always afflicted man in his essence. The rule of enframing (Gestell) threatens man with the possibility that it could be denied him to enter into a more original revealing and hence to experience the call of a more primal truth.[9]

The sense that there is, underneath the accretions of culture, the "call of a more primal truth" propels both Fukuyama's and McKibben's resistance to *Our Posthuman Future*. The source of that truth, according to Fukuyama, may be found within a basic foundational layer running beneath the specific traditions of Western religion.[10] Of vital importance in discerning "legitimate and illegitimate uses" of biotechnology, according to Fukuyama, is a basic agreement on "the centrality of human nature to our understanding of right and wrong."[11]

In teaching undergraduates, this task becomes immediately applicable. I have found myself thinking: "Surely, buried under the technological accretions of the new generation's cyborg existence there is some sense of what it means to be purely, naturally *human*." I have also found myself relying on the reality of a discernible division between past and future. Again, I tell myself as I prepare pedagogically to tackle cloning, chimeras, or prenatal testing, "Even those within the Ipod/Tivo generation surely must perceive the truth of a boundary between, on the one hand, a truly human, more natural *prior* and, on the other hand, a biotechnologized *future* that is becoming post-human." At my most desperate, I find myself taking up the persona of Dana Carvey's Church Chat Lady, mixed with his rendition of the Grumpy Old Man. "Why, when I was a kid, we didn't *need* pre-implantation genetic testing or somatic cell nuclear transfer, and if we had, we would have recognized them as tools of *Satan*."

The quest for a verifiable humanness and some boundary between before and after biotechnologized existence is appealing, but this form of argument depends on a pre-biotechnological strand of human nature on which to pull in order to elicit a moral response to the problems of a biotechnological future. Some of the most eloquent premonitory voices in bioethics work with the assumption that their audience, whether civic or academic, possesses two capacities: (1) a common moral sense about the *borders* of *the human*; and, related to this, (2) a common moral sense that there is a more natural *prior* in *human history*—a time when this was not so.

There are many reasons for those wary of biotechno-logics to accept these two working assumptions about the definitive human and the human history. For one, the standard, almost universally default mode of medical ethical reasoning, as laid out in *The Principles of Bioethics*, assumes the moral neutrality of scientific advance and human identity.[12] The dominant assumption in the field of bioethical inquiry today is that the borders of *the human* are quite fluid. Is this embryo human? Maybe so. Maybe not. Is this fetus human? That depends. Is this newborn human? Well, that is a matter of some debate. Does using Ritalin to enhance a child's performance in school merely enhance his performance, or does it tinker with his natural personality? Is this next generation becoming more human due to anti-depressants, Viagra, and/or Lipitor, or are we relying on biotechnology to solve problems created by an increasingly unhealthy lifestyle? Or are the problems themselves cultural constructs, reflecting our discomfort with discomfort, flaccidity, and death? Is the psychotropic, silicone-implanted clone truly human? Well, perhaps she is even better—perhaps she is post-human. Wouldn't you want to be? The only absolute, not-to-be-crossed boundary in bioethics involves protecting the autonomy of the mature, rational, Western-educated adult.[13] The ever-expanding array of pharmaceutical goods and procedures are assumed to be neutral. It seems, given these working assumptions, quite salutary to ask deeper, more probing questions about how the culture of biotechnological consumption is changing our perspective about human existence itself. It seems important to find and to protect the definition of the "somebody" to whom we are responsible as neighbor.

However, I have three concerns about current debates on *Being Human*. The first concern, which has to do with the definition of *human* being, I will call the Katha Pollitt rejoinder. Pollitt is a columnist for *The Nation*, and she asks something along the lines of (and here I paraphrase) "Look around; does the United States seem like a country of people who recognize the dignity of each and every human life?" "Yeah, right" respond many critics from the left. My second concern has to do with human history—with the absence of a more pure prior. Dig more deeply into human history and one will find an infinite number of techniques for cordoning off, using, and exterminating creatures who certainly appear now, in retrospect, to be human. The third concern has to do with both the definition of human existence and the verity (or not) of human history. This third concern involves my suspicion that there is neither a more primal truth nor a definite *human* apart from the birth, life, death, and resurrection of one human in particular. I suspect that the pressing questions of biotechnology today require not so much that we dig deeper into humanity in order to find somebody to love, but that we discover ourselves as found by one who defines love itself. I will thus sketch what I hope might be a Christian, Kierkegaardian contribution to bioethics.

Savage Incongruities

In her July 21, 2001, *Nation* article on embryonic research "It's a Bird, It's a Plane, It's Superclone?" Katha Pollitt characteristically mocks religious concerns about the dignity of individual human lives and concludes, "The enemy isn't the research, it's capitalism." Pollitt's dismissive tone may distract from the bite of her piece. Her challenge may be summarized thus: So, Fukuyama, Kass, and McKibben, the biotechnological revolution will lead us to become a people who do not recognize the dignity and worth of each human life as given? You and your colleagues are concerned that life is going to become cheap? Isn't life already pretty cheap around here? Pollitt's perspective hit home for me recently while rereading Jonathan Kozol's *Savage Inequalities*. By my estimation, cloning human life is morally repugnant, but in a way that is formally identical to my repugnance at the disparity between rich and poor children in the American public school system. Life on the margins is already cheap—or expensive, depending on its use value. Will life in the United States become qualitatively less human if we proceed with procreative or therapeutic cloning? It is hard to argue along these lines, given patterns of current neglect. Consider this passage from Kozol:

> East St. Louis—which the local press refers to as "an inner city without an outer city"—has some of the sickest children in America. Of 66 cities in Illinois, East St. Louis ranks first in fetal death, first in premature birth, and third in infant death. Among the negative factors listed by the city's health director are the sewage running in the streets, air that has been fouled by the local plants, the high lead levels noted in the soil, poverty, lack of education, crime, dilapidated housing, insufficient health care, unemployment. Hospital care is deficient too. There is no place to have a baby in East St. Louis.[14]

This set of statistics merely touches on the plight of children living in forgotten neighborhoods across the country—neighborhoods that Kozol brings to the otherwise sheltered reader. This must provide reason to pause. Given the gap running through American public education and basic health, it seems almost obscene to argue that research on human embryos, genetic enhancement, or any biotechnological procedure will blow out the bridge spanning humanity. Many indigent women in the United States would counter that the bridge was never built. I expect that many of these women would read McKibben's *Enough* and wonder why bioethicists concerned with protecting human dignity did not holler *Enough!* quite a bit sooner.[15] Arguments against biotechnological enhancement or embryo research too often assume that we are a people who presently value human lives. The arguments draw on a consensus about human dignity that, seen from the underside, quite frankly does not exist.

Great Mountain Peaks of History

The second concern is related. Bioethics as a discipline has functioned more or less without attention to history. The past or the future function often at a rather fuzzy distance. While this is something of a caricature, it reveals something of the instincts at play in bioethics. *Critics* of genetic enhancement, to take one easy example, suggest that we are at a new moment—a time when humanity is at the cusp of a decision that will take us into an amoral, post-human realm. *Proponents* of genetic enhancement propose that we are at a new moment—a time when humanity is at the crossroads of a new era, a new, enhanced time of unparalleled promise.

During my own research into the development and marketing of bio-technological parenting, I came to suspect that both sets of arguments were off-kilter. To *proponents* of genetic enhancement, I submit that arguments about a qualitatively "new era" have been made before. One such argument was made not too long ago, during the "Atomic Age." Not long after Hiroshima and Nagasaki, Atomic Energy Commission chairman David E. Lilienthal was making a formally identical argument in *Collier's Magazine* about the relationship of the (then) present to the (then) future. Against the backdrop of a mural with a giant hand descending from the sky to deliver atomic power, Lilienthal explained:

> To me, atomic energy is more than something that in an indeterminate period will light electric bulbs or provide radioactive materials for our doctors. . . . I don't underestimate these coming advances. . . . But we will completely miss the point, and the whole effort will slacken and lose its drive if we think of it only in terms of immediate, practical gadgets and benefits. For as I see it, in the atomic adventure we sight one of those great mountain peaks of history, a towering symbol of one of the faiths that makes man civilized, the faith in knowledge. . . . Only a great people, a people alive to the meaning of what is happening in our own time, can make this a great adventure. And I believe we are a great people.[16]

This point was brought home again, eight years later, by Harold E. Stassen, Special Assistant on Disarmament to President Eisenhower, in a *Ladies' Home Journal* piece called "Atoms for Peace." The report ran with a highlighted promise across the top:

> Imagine a world in which there is no disease . . . where hunger is unknown . . . where food never rots and crops never spoil . . . where "dirt" is an old-fashioned word, and routine household tasks are just a matter of pressing a few buttons . . . a world where no one ever stokes a furnace or curses the

> smog, where the air everywhere is as fresh as on a mountaintop and the breeze from a factory as sweet as from a rose. . . . Imagine the world of the future . . . the world that nuclear energy can create for all of us.[17]

The particular promises are, in and of themselves, worth noting, but I wish to adumbrate the form of the argument itself. Both Stassen and Lilienthal promoted America's atomic project by appealing to a particular vision of history. Today is set as a turning point in human existence—the present and a qualitatively different future are linked inasmuch as the people at present are willing to move forward in faith, the "faith in knowledge," to quote Lilienthal.

Some arguments against biotechnology may be interpreted as a kind of mirror image of this vision. We are on the cusp of deciding whether we will be an enhanced, cloned, more-than-human people, or a people content to be linked together by the primal truths of limited, mortal, natural, human existence. The decision humans are making today regarding biotechnology is momentous, one of those turning points in human history. If we proceed, we will attenuate or even sever the links between humans, we will break with natural norms evident even in prehistory, and we will proceed up the slope toward a post-human existence. Again, I find these arguments compelling and perhaps even necessarily provocative, given the present climate of unfettered optimism regarding biotechnology. Yet I have found in my research that it is difficult to draw on a better human past prior to biotechnology; the human record is grim. There is arguably no prior point from which we may recollect a better present. By one (I believe sober) reading of human history, humans with the means to do so have severed ties between themselves and others at least as often as they have established them. The biotechnological revolution grants merely another means for doing so.

Manifestly Unfit

Moving backward less than a century into dominant American culture lands one in the middle of a decision regarding the humanity of a varied segment of the population. During the eugenic era, social workers, Protestant clergy, progressive politicians, and scientists joined forces to encourage a fitter, more wholesome future by cutting off the lineages of certain types of people. Immigrants who could not read English text, impoverished thieves, those judged by newly written tests to be "idiots" or "morons" (terms coined by a Quaker during the period), and women who had given birth to "illegitimate" children were all targeted by sterilization and/or immigration laws as parasites on the body politic. The basic assumptions of the era ran through Oliver Wendell Holmes's decision in Buck vs. Bell, decided by the Supreme Court in 1927:

> It is better for all the world, if instead of waiting to execute degenerate offspring for crime, or to let them starve for their imbecility, society can

prevent those who are manifestly unfit from continuing their kind. The principle that sustains compulsory vaccination is broad enough to cover cutting the Fallopian tubes. Three generations of imbeciles are enough.[18]

With characteristic clarity, Justice Holmes thus linked several key eugenic concepts. In order to prevent individual suffering, the state may compel the prevention of certain "kinds" of individuals. As an effective inoculation against degeneration, crime, and imbecility, the social body may "vaccinate" itself against the deleterious or parasitic "unfit." This death-dealing logic led to the sterilization of tens of thousands of people in the United States. The propaganda also lent an air of scientific legitimacy to long-established patterns of paranoia regarding Eastern European and Asian immigrants, those with mental or physical disabilities, and the unruly poor.

Whence to find the better old days? At what point did humans turn toward scientific knowledge in order to delineate the fit and unfit—the human and not-quite-human? With *in vitro* fertilization? With Charles Darwin? With Francis Bacon? With Aristotle? I fear that Martin Heidegger's fatal romantic error in harking back to a purer, more authentically human *prior* may be a temptation for others of us working in the field of bioethics. Pre-technological peoples may seem, under the influence of romantic recollection, patronizingly Edenic.

Interlude

Allow me to return to the question with which I opened this essay—the problem of the orphan in the woods. What if each human life is, humanly speaking, open to infinite interpretation? What if that assiduously avoided concept "sin" is sufficiently thoroughgoing to orphan not only the Down Syndrome fetus or the embryo in the vat or people of the Bikini Atoll, but each and every one of us? What if you and I are in the woods, without recourse to a more primal truth, definitive wisdom, moral repugnance, or, to employ a phrase used by Jürgen Habermas, an "ethical self-understanding of the species"?[19] What if each human life is, to paraphrase the character "A" from Kierkegaard's *Either/Or*, akin to the word *Schnur* in the dictionary—as easily a whisk broom as an entity due loving attention?[20] Again, to use the words of *Either/Or*'s "A," "What if everything in the world were a misunderstanding?"[21] What if we are but clay when in the hands of a masterfully human other? What if our lives and our loves are totally dependent on a divine gift that cannot be mapped, verified, or even comprehended? What if each life is sacred only inasmuch as held in God's pierced palm?[22]

I have begun to suspect that the answer to repro-biotechnological mastery may be the same answer as the one that might have been the answer to the abomination of Nazi Germany, had more Christians paid heed to the Barmen Declaration. I have begun to suspect that the answer today may be the one that might have been the answer to the atrocious presumption of Victorian England and, further back, the answer to the civilized racism of the Roman Empire. To put this in a slightly different, more explicitly Kierkegaardian way, if the proponents of biotechnology are involved in a kind of willed *hope* in the biotechnological future, and the opponents of biotechnology are involved in a kind of *recollection* of a pre-biotechnological past, perhaps what I propose is more akin to the possibility of received *repetition*. This does not mean that Kierkegaard, or one who reads Kierkegaard, has all the answers. I do not propose that repetition is a more effective tool with which to *eliminate* the moral conundrums sprouting from the soil of biotech. But repetition may help us better to *dig up* these conundrums. By the light of the hope of received, gratuitous existence, the problematic mastery of the present may appear more obvious. I hope to question the emergence of parental biotechnology by drawing on the possibility of sheer grace, rather than from the normativity of nature.

The Sober/Drunken Truth

> For my part, if I were a woman, I would rather be one in the Orient, where I would be a slave, for to be a slave—neither more nor less—is still always something compared with being "hurrah" and nothing. . . . If I were a woman, I would prefer being sold by my father to the highest bidder, as in the Orient, for a business transaction nevertheless does have meaning. . . . I would rather be a man and a little inferior, and actually be that, than be a woman and be an undefinable quantity and made blissful in fantasy.[23]

Kierkegaard's *"In Vino Veritas,"* which opens *Stages on Life's Way,* invites the reader into the belly of the beast. It may be read as Kierkegaard's demand that the aspiring assistant professor of ethics must first face the infinite malleability and vulnerability of the one beheld. In this, his take on Plato's *Symposium,* Kierkegaard narrates the perpetually drunken truth that insulates against the rude interruption of a recalcitrant—here female—other. By my reading of *"In Vino Veritas,"* Kierkegaard assembled characters that pre-exist in his pseudonymous corpus in order to indicate the prior and ongoing import of this amoral universe of perception. The arrangement of the banquet and each individual soliloquy narrate the well-constructed, self-perpetuating context underlying the exploits of Kierkegaard's other characters, including Constantin Constantius (of *Repetition*) and Johannes the Seducer (of *Either/Or*). Kierkegaard depicts with uncanny skill the construction of what the narrator, William Afham, calls "a new creation." The human other, in this case a creature called woman, is explicitly excluded in order that she might remain "an undefinable quantity," a cipher sufficiently vacant to allow each man to "wish" unencumbered (*SLW* 59). By envisioning the other in this manner, as nothing of real consequence, and by reconstructing meticulously every potential interaction as "only forgery," an individual may be, as Victor Eremita puts it, "better safeguarded than if he entered the monastery" (*SLW* 65).

The story and monologues of five men gathered for a meticulously orchestrated feast thus tell of the whimsy of beauty and the violability of the vulnerable, underscoring the malleability of any other when beheld by the masterful imagination. Inviolability (or not) and beauty (or not) are in the eye (or not) of the beholder. One may read the text as a sobering response to any formulation of the Kantian moral imperative. My response to the call of duty may be to redefine the other so that she is no longer due my reciprocal treatment, but rather disposal or consumption. Depending on my power to name the other, I may just as easily designate her as naught as designate her a daughter. Homing in on the material under the glass, I may just as easily deem her to be a pre-embryo, a blastocyst, a cipher for my dreams of perfect motherhood, a fertilized egg, or material for flushing.

There are other readings of the text, including readings that would allow for a Kierkegaardian Kantianism, a Kierkegaardian Thomism, or even a Kierkegaardian Calvinism. When Johannes the Seducer asserts in "*In Vino Veritas*" that there is "nothing more nauseating" than to have one's fantasies interrupted by "immediate" and "impertinent" actuality (*SLW* 23), one may read this (along with other cues) to indicate that there *is* such a thing as immediate, impertinent actuality that will interrupt a constructed, amoral universe. One may read clues in the text that there is indeed somebody to love, someone whose reality will become sufficiently clear as to thwart perpetual exploitation or total annihilation. There is another, less reassuring reading, for which I have argued elsewhere.[24] I suspect that Kierkegaard's variously baffled and menacing characters *are* indeed capable of existing without interacting—that they witness to the resilience of predation after the Fall. Constantin, Johannes the Seducer, the Fashion Designer—each testify to one's capacity to construct one's interaction with others to preclude the interruption of impertinent actuality. This story can be comic or tragic, depending. Indeed, several of Kierkegaard's most poignant characters (including the Young Man and the Diarist in *Stages on Life's Way*) exist alone in the barren world created as contingent reality fails to meet the expectations of their illusions about life and love.

For Kierkegaard, even the comedy of perpetuated self-deception teeters right on the edge of tragedy. I find this to be particularly the case when Kierkegaard narrates the cultured self-deception of polished domesticity. In my research into the normative biotechnologically timed and enhanced family, I am thus drawing also on a somewhat controversial reading of Judge William (as he appears both in *Either/Or* and *Stages on Life's Way*). My reading of William's position in the text is that "*In Vino Veritas*" is the outrageous outward manifestation of a philosophical system that is even more masterfully performed in the patriarchal cycle of the proper Danish home. By my reading of the holy housekeeping described in *Either/Or II* and *Stages on Life's Way*, Kierkegaard means William's home to be the epitome of a complete self-serving circle of utterly malleable reality. By this reading, William's narration of moral duty, aesthetic desire, and religious piety is even more menacing than the misdeeds of Johannes the Seducer. At least Johannes has no illusions about the verity of his love. He is quite aware that he has spun the web to catch the fly. William's domesticity seems, by all accounts including his own, to be thoroughly loving, dutiful, holy, and respectable.

In digging through the recent cultural history of holy housekeeping, reproduction, and biotechnological parenting in the United States, I have come to suspect that the human imagination, or at least the dominant *American* imagination, has quite the capacity for calculating the valence of a human life by its "fit" with prevailing norms of beauty and/or efficiency. This or that individual human life may or may not have been worthy of recognition, depending on the context and the will of those constructing the markers for definitive humanness. I have also discovered that some of the most blatant examples of willed inhumanity were tangled up in the organizing efforts of eminently respectable leaders to craft an orderly, manageable social body. This reading of American culture is perhaps as controversial as my reading of Kierkegaard's Judge William, for it involves the suspicion that holy domesticity, as defined by the mainline Protestant purveyors of good housekeeping in the United States, feeds off of a fear of being identified as disorderly, unproductive, accidental, backward, Pentecostal, dirty, poor, Roman Catholic, Black, or otherwise "other." Current patterns of biotechnological parenting reflect norms that are presently taken as holy givens by the judges of responsible or irresponsible parenthood and good or bad citizenship.

Bioethics and the Work of Love

In his chapter "The Work of Love in Recollecting One Who Is Dead" in *Works of Love*, Kierkegaard narrates in a different way the sense that each human life is vulnerably exposed to the reading of another.[25] There are many ways to read this section. One may find here irrefutable evidence of Kierkegaard's own fear of loving the living, or his fear of loving any living person in particular. But another fruitful way to read the text is as Kierkegaard's prompt that the dead beloved, who is *definitively* "no one," reveals much about the lover. When the other is as negligible as the shadow of one who once was, what becomes apparent is the tenacity of love within the lover. When the other is literally invisible, what becomes apparent is the beholder. How does one behold another when she is not definitively, solidly, measurably *there*? One way to read this section is as Kierkegaard's astute reading of the task of loving one who is indeed living, but whose very life is vulnerable to the masterful narration of others. Those so exposed, whether unplanned fetuses or unwanted immigrants, are almost as definitively no one as are the dead. Kierkegaard suggests here (as, I believe, elsewhere in *Works of Love*) that *there is no definitive other* in any meaningful sense until the other becomes, by my reckoning, a *neighbor*. If I go, intent to find someone who demands, by their very existence, my love, care, respect, or attention, I will not find her, unless I bring with me a third party. It is with a prayer to this third party that Kierkegaard opens *Works of Love*.

What might Kierkegaard's bleak and demanding narration of love's challenge and task have to say about bioethics? From my best reading, Kierkegaard calls for a different kind of bioethics, a kind of bioethics that calls into question (at least indirectly) the project of medical *ethics*. To use the words of Kierkegaard's pseudonym Johannes Climacus, most often "ethics" is performed "en masse with the help of a generation," in a way that allows one to "haggle" with "the requirement."[26] If today's generation is haggling with the requirement to find somebody to love, by way of newly perfected gauges and procedures, perhaps the answer is not more *ethics*, but rather the reception of the Gift that makes real the presence of the requisite third party. There are multiple possible riffs on Johannes Climacus's *Philosophical Fragments*, but one involves Kierkegaard's holy mischief of scrambling all attempts to map ourselves onto history by way of ethics.[27] In the little section called "Interlude," Kierkegaard gives a dense philosophical explication of the non-necessity of all that is, through the non-necessity of Christ. The question of the "Interlude," "Is the Past more Necessary than the Future? Or Has the Possible, by Having Become Actual, Become More Necessary than It Was?" differently situates the usual questions of determining the parameters of human life. Human life becomes, through the prism of non-necessity, a matter that is not up for human justification.

What if, as Climacus suggests in the "Interlude," "All Coming into Existence occurs in freedom, not by way of necessity"?[28] What might this mean about procreation and the turn to biotechnological reproduction? This particular question may bring us back again to the possibility of repetition. Through the potentially romantic recollection of a pretechnological past and through the hopeful optimism in an increasingly biotechnological future, Americans continue to try to locate ourselves, our children, and our nation on a map of either progress or moral degeneration. We continue to search for the big red arrow in time indicating *You are here*. But by Kierkegaard's mischievous reckoning in *Philosophical Fragments*, the Moment that ultimately matters enters time when *You are not*. By this reading, the various means today of justifying one's decision to "bring a child into the world" by way of carefully orchestrated quantity and quality control miss the sheer gratuity of each and every life. This may indeed have implications for how one perceives of "birth control," but it also has implications for how one perceives of various other efforts to justify oneself by way of one's better home and garden. Kierkegaard may be read as effectively upsetting history writ large *à la* Hegel and Fukuyama. He may as effectively be read as upsetting history writ small *à la* the Danish household and today's maternal obsession with familial "Scrapbooking."[29] Thus jumbled, my very existence may become again gratuitous, and time becomes, in a fundamental way, not my own to navigate morally and aesthetically. Much of my own writing in bioethics has to do with the hope that this knot of Kierkegaardian insights has much to say about everything from private schools to Ritalin to Baby Einstein videos to prenatal testing to Norplant.

No doubt the most incendiary implication, indeed, has to do with the status of the unborn human. By one reading of Kierkegaard's insight, no human life is totally open to being *located* by another, not even by the one in whose body she is formed. The biotechnological gauges by which women are increasingly pressured to evaluate their pregnancies may, in this light, come to seem inadequate to the task of proper expectation. Whether the designation is "illegitimate" or "accidental," it may not fully describe any given life, if Kierkegaard's christological insight about the sheer givenness of life is apropos. One line that Kierkegaard deleted from *Philosophical Fragments* may refute not only Hegel but the default account of existence evident in many conversations about the boundaries of human life:

> Too bad that Hegel lacked time; but if one is to dispose of all of world history, how does one get time for the little test as to whether the absolute method, which explains everything, is also able to explain the life of a single human being. In ancient times, one would have smiled at a method that can explain all of world history absolutely but cannot explain a single person even mediocrely.[30]

I do not mean to say that Kierkegaard would, if he were present today, picket for a change in abortion laws. I do not even know how to begin to ask what Kierkegaard would make of Roe vs. Wade. To begin to ask that question seems, perhaps, to miss Kierkegaard's boat altogether. But Kierkegaard did upturn his era's default mode of Christian Hegelianism in a way that may upturn the default domestic Darwinism at play in repro-biotechnology. To plot any individual embryo *in vitro* or fetus *in utero* according to its temporal legitimacy seems potentially to make a basic theological category error. Inasmuch as we are, each one of us, inexplicably unnecessary, the tools with which women are presently expected to plan, time, and evaluate seem, at the very least, *mediocre*, and perhaps even macabre. While it makes for uncomfortable conversation, Kierkegaard presses his readers to consider the concrete, radical implications of faith—not just to muse around the possibilities of existence, otherness, or givenness.

The radical implications of Kierkegaard's focused Christology extend beyond *in vitro* and *in utero*, and beyond the comfort zone of many Americans who would applaud the previous paragraph. The default mode of mainline Protestant evangelical reasoning most often assumes the goal of orderly domesticity. Will the tools of biotechnology be used by wholesome people to ensure good children to be brought up in seemly neighborhoods? (I believe that charismatic and Pentecostal Protestants witness more effectively to the potential chaos of a gospel of life.) Among the many Protestant shibboleths that Kierkegaard set out to debunk is the sanctity of the middle-class home, and I believe it fruitful to read in his authorship an extended quarrel with the sanctity of Protestant domesticity. Bringing the bleeding Christ into the better homes and gardens of Denmark, Kierkegaard called into question a soporific version of Protestant presumption. My extended project on American domesticity and the marketing of scientific technology is an attempt to pose pressing questions about a mainstream evangelical culture that loathes risk, disorder, and association with sinners. My driving suspicion is that behind many of the tools of procreative technology is another Protestant presumption—the presumption that a well-planned family is the outward manifestation of one's salvation. (Hence the Weberian subtitle of my current project *Conceiving Parenthood: The Protestant Spirit of Biotechnological Reproduction.*) This presumption has been and continues to be deadly for those judged as unplanned, irresponsible, or otherwise aberrant.

The project of finding somebody to love may require a rather risky turn to explicitly *Christian* bioethics. The task of finding each and every other to be someone to love may necessarily involve a turn away from publicly accessible descriptions of human history and human nature to a narration of the one who brings into our vision the neighbor who would otherwise be, in a sense, dead to us. The risk extends into life, as those who heed Kierkegaard may find themselves eschewing the very tools that designate one as a *better* parent today. The risk to which Kierkegaard calls the faithful may require the upwardly mobile to switch sides and actively seek association with children, mothers, and neighborhoods designated "at risk."

This may or may not be effective by either the gauges of Katha Pollitt and those who read *The Nation* or by the gauges of James Dobson and those who read *Focus on the Family*. Kierkegaard does not offer a resolution that makes previously wavering forms of human life reliably solid and safe from evaluation, violation, predation, or neglect. By my reading, *Works of Love* does not recommend a Christ who has discernibly set the calendar aright by any particular human alignment of history. The incarnation did not recalibrate temporality in a way that makes mere faith into muscular knowledge, as if Christ's work is akin to Julius Caesar's new, reliable, Roman calendar. (After all, even Julius's best-laid plan was soon undone by the hubris of Caesar Augustus in 8 BC, who was determined that his month be as long as July.) Kierkegaard does not deny in *Works of Love* the naked vulnerability of the malleable, intersubjective other, but offers an intersubjective context that makes love between self and each and every other a sheer gift from a third party—made possible by the gift of Christ. A Kierkegaardian answer to biotechnological mastery may run right through the heart of postmodern and postclassical relativity into the utter incalculability of any and every life created *ex nihilo* and redeemed by a profligate gift. His texts thus elicit love of each and every neighbor, not with certainty, but with hope.

NOTES

1. Patrick Goodenough, "Better for Old People to Kill Themselves than Be a Nuisance, Lawmaker Says," CNSNews.com, 14 December 2004; available from http://www.cnsnews.com/culture/archive/200412/CUL20041214a.html.

2. Aaron Patrick, "Abortion Justified for 'Better Babies,'" *The Age*, 6 July 2003.

3. Watson has gone on record in support of genetic engineering to eliminate physical suffering. He has also grown increasingly blunt in his support of genetic engineering of inheritable traits in order to avoid people who "really are stupid" and to make "all girls pretty." The relevant sentences, as reported by the London *Times*: "People say it would be terrible if we made all girls pretty. I think it would be great"; and "If you really are stupid, I would call that a disease." See Mark Henderson, "Let's Cure Stupidity, Says DNA Pioneer," *Times* (London), 28 February 2003, News 13.

4. For a longer discussion of selective termination rates, see Rayna Rapp, *Testing Women, Testing the Fetus* (New York: Routledge, 2000), in particular, 129, 223.

5. Robert Edwards, quoted by Lois Rogers, "Having Disabled Babies Will Be 'Sin,' Says Scientist," *Sunday Times* (London), 4 July 1999, News 28.

6. Polly Ross Hughes, "Groups Criticize Remark About 'Bad Gene Pools,'" *Houston Chronicle*, 26 October 2004, B4.

7. Maryann Mott, "Animal-Human Hybrids Spark Controversy," *National Geographic News*, 25 January 2005; available from http://www.news.nationalgeographic.com/news/2005/01/0125_050125_chimeras.html.

8. Bill McKibben, *Enough: Staying Human in an Engineered Age* (New York: Henry Holt, 2003), 114.

9. Martin Heidegger, "The Question Concerning Technology," in *Basic Writings*, ed. David Farrell Krell (San Francisco: Harper, 1993), 333. Quoted in Frances Fukuyama, *Our Posthuman Future: Consequences of the Biotechnology Revolution* (New York: Farrar, Straus and Giroux, 2002), 3.

10. Fukuyama is most explicit about the need to recover this layer in chapters 8 and 9, on "Human Nature" and "Human Dignity."

11. Fukuyama, *Our Posthuman Future*, 16–17.

12. Tom L. Beauchamp and James F. Childress, *Principles of Biomedical Ethics*, 4th ed. (New York: Oxford University Press, 1994).

13. Anne Fadiman's *The Spirit Catches You and You Fall Down* (New York: Farrar, Straus and Giroux, 1998) details precisely the collision of non-Western identity with the dominant Western system of dealing with bioethical conflict.

14. Jonathan Kozol, *Savage Inequalities: Children in America's Schools* (New York: Crown, 1991; HarperCollins, 1992), 20.

15. The week of the last edit of this essay, Bill McKibben published an essay in *Harper's Magazine* in which he firmly advocates for the national prioritization of poverty. I believe it to be a crucial addition to the conversation. See "The Christian Paradox: How a Faithful Nation Gets Jesus Wrong," *Harper's* (August 2005).

16. David Lilienthal, "Man and the Atom, An Introduction to a Golden Age," *Collier's*, 3 May 1947, 11.

17. Harold Stassen, "Atoms for Peace," *Ladies' Home Journal*, August 1955, 48–49.

18. Buck v. Bell, 274 U.S. 200, 207 (1927).

19. Jürgen Habermas, *The Future of Human Nature*, trans. Hella Beister (Cambridge: Polity Press, 2003). The phrase comes from the title of the second essay in the collection: "The Debate on the Ethical Self-Understanding of the Species."

20. Søren Kierkegaard, *Either/Or* 1, *Kierkegaard's Writings*, vol. 3, ed. and trans. Howard V. Hong and Edna H. Hong (Princeton, N.J.: Princeton University Press, 1988), 36.

21. Kierkegaard, *Either/Or* 1, 21.

22. This phrase, "God's pierced palm," is borrowed from poet Denise Levertov, from section 1 of her poem "The Showings: Lady Julian of Norwich, 1342–1416," in *The Stream and the Sapphire* (New York: New Direction Books, 1997), 50–51.

23. Søren Kierkegaard, *Stages on Life's Way*, vol. 11 of *Kierkegaard's Writings*, ed. and trans. Howard V. Hong and Edna H. Hong (Princeton, N.J.: Princeton University Press, 1988), 56, 58, 59; hereafter cited as *SLW*.

24. See Amy Laura Hall, *Kierkegaard and the Treachery of Love* (Cambridge: Cambridge University Press, 2002), esp. chaps. 5 and 6.

25. Søren Kierkegaard, *Works of Love*, vol. 16 of *Kierkegaard's Writings*, ed. and trans. Howard V. Hong and Edna H. Hong (Princeton, N.J.: Princeton University Press, 1998), 345–58.

26. Søren Kierkegaard, *Concluding Unscientific Postscript to Philosophical Fragments 1*, vol. 12 of *Kierkegaard's Writings*, ed. and trans. Howard V. Hong and Edna H. Hong (Princeton, N.J.: Princeton University Press, 1992), 346.

27. Søren Kierkegaard, *Philosophical Fragments*, vol. 7 of *Kierkegaard's Writings*, ed. and trans. Howard V. Hong and Edna H. Hong (Princeton, N.J.: Princeton University Press, 1985).

28. Kierkegaard, *Philosophical Fragments*, 75.

29. If you don't know the reference, ask your sister or wife; she will clue you in. You may also peruse any number of Web sites found by searching "scrapbooking" and "Christian," including: Inez Haythorn, "Preserving Memories Through Scrapbook Journaling," People of Faith.Com, available at *http://www.seedsofknowledge.com/scrapbook2.html.*

30. Kierkegaard, *Philosophical Fragments* (Supplement, Revision of Pap. V B 14), 206.

Contributors

Pamela Sue Anderson is Reader in Philosophy of Religion at Regent's Park College, Oxford University in England.

Bruce Ellis Benson is Professor of Philosophy at Wheaton College in Wheaton, Illinois.

John D. Caputo is the Thomas J. Watson Professor of Religion and Humanities at Syracuse University in Syracuse, New York. He is also David R. Cook Professor Emeritus of Philosophy at Villanova University in Villanova, Pennsylvania.

Ruthanne S. Pierson Crápo is completing her doctoral program at the Institute for Christian Studies in Toronto, Ontario.

Mark Gedney is Associate Professor of Philosophy at Gordon College in Wenham, Massachusetts.

Christina M. Gschwandtner is Assistant Professor of Philosophy at University of Scranton in Scranton, Pennsylvania.

Amy Laura Hall is Associate Professor of Theological Ethics and Director of the Doctor of Theology program at Duke Divinity School in Durham, North Carolina.

Bertha Alvarez Manninen is Assistant Professor of Philosophy at Arizona State University—West.

Edward F. Mooney is Adjunct Professor of Religion at Syracuse University in Syracuse, New York.

James H. Olthuis is Emeritus Professor at the Institute for Christian Studies in Toronto, Ontario.

B. Keith Putt is Professor of Philosophy at Samford University in Birmingham, Alabama.

Tyler Roberts is Associate Professor of Religious Studies at Grinnell College in Grinnell, Iowa.

Brian Treanor is Assistant Professor of Philosophy at Loyola Marymount University in Los Angeles, California.

Christopher Watkin is Junior Research Fellow, Magdalene College at Cambridge University in England.

Norman Wirzba is Professor of Philosophy at Georgetown College in Georgetown, Kentucky.

INDEX

Abraham, 53–55

agape, 8, 67–69, 73, 76, 79, 84, 85, 89, 93, 95,
112, 122–124, 127–129, 131, 172, 173,
193, 194, 204, 213, 215–217. *See also*
charity; Kierkegaard, Søren; love; Marion, Jean-Luc; Ricoeur, Paul

agnosticism, 123, 128, 129, 131–134

alterity. *See* Levinas, Emmanuel; other, absolute otherness of; other, relationship between otherness (alterity) and similitude
(sameness)

Aquinas, Thomas, 213

Augustine, 30, 107, 147

Badiou, Alain, 171–173, 175

being, 68, 187. *See also* God, as Being

beloved, 187, 188, 189. *See also eros*/erotic;
love; lover; Marion, Jean-Luc

bioethics, 9, 10, 240–247, 251. *See also* human, post-human

biotechnology, 9, 240–248, 250–253

Bonhoeffer, Dietrich, 32

Breton, Stanislas, 31

Bugbee, Henry, 18, 46

calculation. *See* economy; reciprocity

call, 123, 132, 133. *See also* other, response/
recognition of

Caputo, John D., 6, 7, 23, 130, 131, 135, 144–
145, 149, 153nn26,28, 163

Cavell, Stanley, 42, 43, 49

charity, 3, 4, 20, 185. *See agape*; love

child, 186, 192. *See also eros*/erotic; Marion,
Jean-Luc

Chrétien, Jean-Louis, 21

Christianity. *See* love, Christian conceptions
of

cogito, 124. *See also* Marion, Jean-Luc

Colossians, biblical book of, 165

command/commandment, 5, 6; to/of love,
63, 64, 67, 77, 78, 88, 89, 91–94, 103,

110–112, 113, 122, 144. *See also* Kierkegaard, Søren; Levinas, Emmanuel; love,
Christian conceptions of; love, relation of
to justice

communication. *See* other, identification/
naming of; other, relationship between
otherness (alterity) and similitude (sameness)

Corinthians, biblical book of, 3, 28–31, 32,
34, 35, 38, 108, 122, 123, 188. *See also*
Paul, the apostle

creation, 5, 7, 106, 108, 190, 194, 229; *ex
amore/ex nihilo*, 156, 167; as given reality, 16, 64, 65, 77

culture, 18

death, 5, 6, 92, 105, 106, 112–113, 182, 203,
213. *See also* Jesus/Christ, death of;
mother/maternal, death of

deconstruction, 6, 73, 80, 103, 110, 112, 113,
114, 115, 142–150, 173, 182. *See also*
Derrida, Jacques; ethics

deontology, 79

Derrida, Jacques, 4, 5, 7, 33, 41n38, 59n28,
63, 69, 73, 74, 78, 80, 109, 117n13, 121,
122, 126, 133, 142–146, 148, 160, 166,
173, 182. *See also* deconstruction; differ-
ence/différance; gift(s); justice

desire, 8, 144, 193, 208, 233; sexual, 212–213
(*see also* feminine/female, sexual desire
of). *See also eros*/erotic; Irigaray, Luce;
Levinas, Emmanuel; love

difference/différance, 6, 65, 66, 114, 115, 133,
180–181; sexual, 227, 229, 232–233. *See
also* Derrida, Jacques; Irigaray, Luce

distance. *See* love, distance of; other, as inde-
pendent/distant

divine. *See* God; love, divine

Dostoevsky, Fyodor, 147

duty, 6, 86, 89–90, 92, 95–97, 103, 110, 111,
112. *See also* command/commandment,

duty (*continued*)
  to/of love; Kant, Immanuel; Kierkegaard,
  Søren

Eckhart, Meister, 23, 104, 133, 164
economy, 76, 77, 186; of calculation/
  exchange, 3, 5, 69, 114; of the gift (exchange), 37, 78, 79, 110; of knowledge, 3,
  28–31, 38, 39; of law, 6, 103–106,
  107, 110, 115; of love, 3, 8, 31, 37, 38,
  39; market, 78–80. *See also* Derrida,
  Jacques; Levinas, Emmanuel; Marion,
  Jean-Luc
ego, 4, 21–23, 126, 127, 130, 131
eidos, 29. *See also* Plato
Electra, 9, 229. *See also* feminine/female;
  mother/maternal
Enlightenment, 206, 215
Ephesians, biblical book of, 132
equality. *See* economy; reciprocity; recognition
eros/erotic, 2, 8, 64, 65, 67, 69, 88–89, 92,
  112, 159, 173, 174, 185, 189–191, 193,
  204, 211–213, 216–217, 219; reduction,
  185, 189, 193. *See also* Kierkegaard,
  Søren; Levinas, Emmanuel; love, erotic;
  Marion, Jean-Luc
ethics, 73, 74, 76, 77, 111, 171, 182. *See also*
  Levinas, Emmanuel; other; responsibility
Exodus, biblical book of, 132, 134

faith, 38, 123–125, 128–131, 135
feminine/female, 227, 229, 233; economy,
  229–230; genealogy, 229, 231; identity
  of, 229–231; language of, 227–228;
  origin of, 230–231, 234; sexual desire of,
  208, 209, 230 (*see also* desire, sexual);
  subject, 229, 231, 232. *See also* Irigaray,
  Luce; masculine/male; mother/maternal
feminism, 207–208
flesh, 191
forgiveness, 63, 67–69, 80, 113, 215. *See also*
  gift(s); justice; love, relation of to justice
freedom, 36, 163, 164. *See also* other
friendship (*philia*), 69, 85, 89, 92, 94, 112,
  160, 204, 216

Gadamer, Hans-Georg, 24
Galatians, biblical book of, 37, 112, 113
Garff, Joakim, 44, 45, 50, 51, 53, 56
Genesis, biblical book of, 9, 16, 32, 98, 106,
  156, 159–163, 210, 214, 229–231, 233.
  See also creation

gift(s), 5, 10, 37, 38, 123, 131; of love, 67, 68,
  69, 80, 103–105, 110, 114–115, 127,
  132–134, 187, 188, 251, 253. *See also*
  Derrida, Jacques; economy, of the gift
  (exchange); Kierkegaard, Søren; love, relation of to justice; Ricoeur, Paul
Gilligan, Carol, 201, 210, 211, 218
gnôsis, 7, 29
God, 2, 6–7, 134, 185, 189–195; as Being,
  165–168; as condition of knowledge, 31;
  distorted image of, 33, 34; image of (*imago dei*), 3, 84, 97, 99, 230; known by, 31,
  37; love as/of, 16, 23, 64, 68, 91, 92, 98,
  108, 111, 115, 122, 130, 135, 156–168,
  193–195; naming/reducing of, 6, 7, 32,
  76, 132; relationship with, 6, 64, 66, 85,
  91, 93, 160, 163, 165–168; wisdom of,
  32. *See also* command/commandment,
  to/of love; creation; love, Christian conceptions of
Golden rule, 5, 77–78. *See also* gift(s);
  Ricoeur, Paul
Good Life, 10, 79
grace, 10, 247, 248. *See also* gift(s); Kierkegaard, Søren; love

Hadot, Pierre, 22
Hall, Amy Laura, 9, 85, 90, 98
hate, 89, 91. *See also* Kierkegaard, Søren; love
Hegel, Georg Wilhelm Friedrich, 65, 66, 203,
  208, 212, 232, 251
Heidegger, Martin, 4, 15, 22–23, 38, 68, 242
Henson, Richard, 85, 95
Herman, Barbara, 85, 94–96
hermeneutics, 47, 134–135; of love/trust/
  charity, 43–44, 55, 56, 78, 80, 127; of sus-
  picion/mistrust, 43, 44, 50, 52, 53, 55, 56.
  See also love, as a hermeneutical model;
  trust
horizon (of consciousness), 20, 124, 127, 129,
  131, 132, 134, 146, 189. *See also* Husserl,
  Edmund; intentionality; Levinas, Emmanuel; Marion, Jean-Luc
human/humanness, 240–243, 246, 250, 251;
  post-human, 242, 243, 245, 246. *See also*
  bioethics; biotechnology
humility, 3, 17
Husserl, Edmund, 129

idol/idolatry, 3, 28, 33, 37–39; of knowledge,
  32; taste for, 33–34
Imago Dei (image of God). *See* God, image of
impossible (*toute autre*), 142–150. *See also* de-

construction; love, as impossible; other, relative otherness of
"information age," 15
intentionality, 20, 124–127, 130, 132, 134. *See also* Husserl, Edmund; Levinas, Emmanuel; Marion, Jean-Luc
interpellation, 176–178, 180. *See also jouissance*; subjectivity; Zizek, Slavoj
intersubjectivity, 146, 228, 232, 233. *See also* Irigaray, Luce; Levinas, Emmanuel; Marion, Jean-Luc
Irigaray, Luce, 4, 9, 114, 227–234. *See also* difference/différance, sexual; feminine/female; masculine/male; mother/maternal; phallocentrism

James, William, 148
Janicaud, Dominique, 129–130
Jesus/Christ, 5, 6, 30, 36, 37, 38, 89, 94, 98, 106, 113, 123, 124, 127–128, 143, 177, 192, 194, 253; cross of Christ, 31; death of, 6, 107–108, 109, 111, 162, 176, 178, 181, 253; suffering of, 10, 165
John, biblical book of, 7, 17, 134, 167
jouissance, 111, 174, 175, 177, 179, 214, 215, 219. *See also* love, liberation/bondage of; subjectivity; Zizek, Slavoj
Judaism, 175, 176, 212
justice, 5, 63, 75, 76–78, 80, 146, 215. *See also* deconstruction; Derrida, Jacques; Levinas, Emmanuel; love, relation of to justice; other; Ricoeur, Paul

Kant, Immanuel, 5, 6, 86, 88–90, 94, 95–98, 99n1, 111. *See also* duty
Keller, Catherine, 160–162, 164
kenosis, 31, 128, 135, 145, 188, 194. *See also* Marion, Jean-Luc
Kierkegaard, Søren, 4, 5, 6, 10, 42–56, 78, 84–99, 107, 112, 145, 241, 247–253; on repetition, 248; *Concluding Unscientific Postscript*, 53, *specific passages cited*, 145, 251; *Either/Or*, 247, 249, *specific passage cited*, 247; *Fear and Trembling*, 53, 54, 55, 128; *Philosophical Fragments*, 88, 251, 252, *specific passages cited*, 88, 251, 252; *Stages on Life's Way*, 248, *specific passages cited*, 248, 249; *Works of Love*, 84, 85, 88, 250, 253, *specific passages cited*, 42, 85–87, 89, 91, 92, 93, 94, 95, 96, 97, 98, 99, 136n14, 239
Kingdom of God, 158, 228
knowledge, 2–4, 7, 22, 80, 209; scientific, 18–

20. *See also* economy, of knowledge; wisdom, in contrast to knowledge
Kristeva, Julia, 203, 204, 210–214, 216, 218

Lacan, Jacques, 172–174, 181. *See also* Irigaray, Luce; Zizek, Slavoj
language, 9, 16, 33, 64, 74–75, 77, 133. *See also* feminine/female, language of; masculine/male, language of
law. *See* command/commandment; economy, of law
Le Doeuff, Michèle, 204–211, 214–216, 218
Leviticus, biblical book of, 111, 112
Levinas, Emmanuel, 4, 5, 16, 20, 21, 26n14, 36, 37, 38, 73–78, 80, 111, 125, 142–144, 146, 159, 160, 164, 182; on heteronomy, 36; Saying, said, 74–76; *Otherwise than Being*, 73, 74, 80, *specific passages cited*, 21, 36, 37, 73, 74, 75, 76; *Totality and Infinity*, 111, 142–143, *specific passages cited*, 36, 75, 146. *See also* ethics; justice; love, relation of to justice; love, "wisdom of"; Marion, Jean-Luc; other; Ricoeur, Paul
logos, 31, 32, 167, 232
love: as blind/invisible, 121–130, 135; Christian conceptions of, 8, 17, 28, 77–78, 84–94, 96–98, 110–115, 122, 123, 128, 132, 134, 135, 143–147, 172, 173, 175–182, 213, 219 (*see also* command/commandment, to/of love); Christian love as a critique of bioethics, 9, 10, 244, 252, 253; declaration of love/war, 185–191; definition/logic of, 16, 38, 104, 105, 128, 143, 160; distance of, 5, 20, 66, 132; divine, 10, 16, 39, 68, 127–129, 162, 185, 193–195; erotic, 8, 88, 94 (*see also eros/erotic*); as a general philosophical method, 1–3, 10, 17, 18, 21–22, 25; as a hermeneutical model, 4, 42, 56 (*see also* hermeneutics, of love/trust/charity); human/divine relationship of, 6, 16, 25 (*see also* God, relationship with); as an identifying/individuating act, 7, 145, 147–149, 186–189, 192, 212; as impossible, 6, 114, 115, 130, 135, 142–150 (*see also* deconstruction; Derrida, Jacques); language of erotic, 186, 190–192; liberation/bondage of, 9, 201, 202, 204, 208–210, 214, 216, 218–220 (*see also* Irigaray, Luce; Kristeva, Julia); as militant, 7, 173, 180–182 (*see also* Zizek, Slavoj); non-reductive, 7, 16, 125; practice of, 3, 6, 7,

love (*continued*)
16, 84; primacy of for wisdom, 3, 15, 16,
17, 21; relation of to justice, 5, 6, 63, 73,
76–78, 79, 80 (*see also* justice); relation
of to knowledge, 28, 31, 37–39; self-love,
86, 87, 88, 89, 93, 94, 111, 186, 213,
215–218; as source and sustaining element of Creation, 16, 25 (*see* also creation, *ex amore/ex nihilo*); uncondi-
tional/preferential, 5, 84–99, 112; "wisdom of," 37, 80, 201, 202, 208–211, 214–
220, 229, 231 (*see also* wisdom). *See also*
command/commandment, to/of love;
economy, of love; gift(s), of love; God,
love as/of; Kierkegaard, Søren; Marion,
Jean-Luc; other, love of/for/to; phenomenology, of love; Ricoeur, Paul; sublimation, of love
lover, 186–191, 194, 216–219
Luke, biblical book of, 77, 78, 98
Luther, Martin, 107, 108. *See also* economy,
of law

Marion, Jean-Luc, 4, 7, 8, 20, 25n4, 32, 33,
37, 38, 123–135, 185–195; on givenness,
126, 127, 129, 130, 131; icon, 126, 127,
133; saturated phenomenon, 126–131,
132–135, 189; *Being Given*, 41n48, *specific passages cited*, 38, 125, 126, 132,
133, 134; *Erotic Phenomenon* (*Le phénomène érotique*), 8, 185, 191, *specific
passages cited*, 185–194; *God Without
Being, specific passages cited*, 32, 33, 38,
125, 127, 128; *In Excess, specific passages
cited*, 125, 127; *Prolegomena to Charity*,
189, *specific passages cited*, 20, 38, 124,
125, 126, 127, 128, 129, 135, 190, 194.
See also idol/idolatry; Levinas, Emmanuel; love; other
Mark, biblical book of, 128, 143
masculine/male, 9, 227, 228, 229, 231; economy, 231, 233; language of, 227; subject,
229–231. *See also* feminine/female
Matthew, biblical book of, 84, 111, 143, 144
metanoetic/*metanoia*, 22, 27n20
Midgley, Mary, 202, 203, 205, 206, 208, 218
mother/maternal, 206, 208, 209, 214, 215;
death of, 212, 213, 229, 230. *See also*
Electra; feminine/female; Irigaray, Luce;
Kristeva, Julia; love, liberation/bondage
of; patriarchy; Psyche, mythical figure of
Murdoch, Iris, 218–219
mystic(s)/mysticism, 17, 23

myth/mythological, 9, 202–205, 208–220.
See feminine/female; Kristeva, Julia;
mother/maternal; patriarchy

neighbor. *See* other, as neighbor
Nietzsche, Friedrich, 107
Noesis/noema, 124–126, 129

ontology, 73, 74, 76–80, 129, 166
other (others), 31, 75, 113, 177, 179, 185, 188,
212, 233, 234, 248; absolute otherness of,
7, 142–150; face/iconic gaze of, 20, 125,
126–129, 134; identification/naming of,
7, 127, 249; as independent/distant, 16–
17, 21, 66; love from, 67; love of/for/to,
16, 130, 142, 190–192, 233, 234, 253; as
neighbor, 7, 36, 250; reduction of, 7, 233;
relation of to "the third," 75–76; relationship between otherness (alterity) and similitude (sameness), 145, 150–151, 227,
228; relative otherness of, 145–150; re-
sponse/recognition of 21, 24, 132, 192,
233. *See also* Kierkegaard, Søren;
Levinas, Emmanuel; love, as blind/invis-
ible; love, as an identifying/individuating
act; love, unconditional/preferential;
Marion, Jean-Luc
overdetermination, 86, 95. *See also* Kant, Immanuel; Kierkegaard, Søren

patriarchy, 9, 204, 207–211, 213–215, 219,
229. *See also* feminine/female; mas-
culine/male
Paul, the apostle, 3, 6, 8, 28, 29–32, 34, 35,
37, 103, 104, 106–113, 122, 123, 129,
132, 135, 143, 171, 175, 180–182. *See
also* Corinthians, biblical book of
phallocentrism, 227, 228, 232; logic of, 229,
231. *See also* feminine/female; mas-
culine/male
phenomenology (phenomenological), 4, 8,
20, 73, 114, 123, 124, 129, 130, 132, 171,
185, 192, 193; of love, 103, 125, 127–
129, 131. *See also* love; Marion, Jean-Luc
Philippians, biblical book of, 104, 107, 145
philosophy. *See* love, as a general philosophical method; love, primacy of for
wisdom
Plato, 2, 18, 29, 67, 211, 248
politics, 76, 173, 177–182
Pope, Stephen J., 85, 88, 89
Post, Stephen, 85, 86, 93, 94
prayer, 191

Psyche, mythical figure of, 201, 202, 210–211, 214, 215
psychoanalysis, 204, 208. *See also* Irigaray, Luce; Kristeva, Julia; Zizek, Slavoj

question/questioning, 22. *See also* Socrates

reading, 4, 42
reason, 4, 22, 33, 203; instrumental, 2, 18
reciprocity, 187. *See also* economy
recognition, 66, 69, 207. *See also* other, response/recognition of
relationality, 164–168. *See also* creation, *ex amore/ex nihilo*; God, relationship with
repentance, 22
response. *See* other, response/recognition of
responsibility, 20, 36, 37, 75, 76, 80
revelation, 77; phenomenon of, 123, 134, 135. *See also* call; gift(s); Marion, Jean-Luc
Ricoeur, Paul, 4, 5, 63–69, 73–80, 204, 205, 215, 218; *Autrement*, 74–76, *specific passages cited*, 75, 76; *Penser la Bible*, *specific passages cited*, 65, 70n5; *Parcours de la reconnaissance*, 67, 74, 78–80, *specific passages cited*, 67, 68, 69, 74, 78, 79, 80; *Oneself as Another*, 77, 79, *specific passage cited*, 73. *See also* Kierkegaard, Søren; Levinas, Emmanuel; love; other
rights, 3, 35, 37
Romans, book of, 106–108, 113, 122, 165. *See also* Paul, the apostle
Rosenzweig, Franz, 63, 69, 72n22, 77. *See also* Levinas, Emmanuel; love

sacrifice, 8. *See also* love; suffering
Sanders, E. P., 107, 116n1
Shakespeare, William, 7, 121, 122
Simmons, William Paul, 76, 81n10
similitude. *See* other, relationship between otherness (alterity) and similitude (sameness)
sin, 17, 22, 37, 64, 68, 103, 175, 210, 214, 233, 249; original, 65–66
space, 227–228, 231–232. *See also* feminine/female; Irigaray, Luce; masculine/male; time
Spinoza, Baruch, 214, 216, 217
Socrates, 2, 22, 46
Socratic dialogue, 22

Song of Songs, biblical book of, 16, 63–67, 69, 77, 212
sophists/sophistry, 2, 10
sovereignty, 66
subjectivity, 172, 174–180. *See also* intersubjectivity; other
sublimation, 172–182; of desire, 175–177, 181; of love, 175–178, 180, 181. *See also* Zizek, Slavoj
suffering, 4, 10. *See also* Jesus/Christ, death of; Jesus/Christ, suffering of

teleology (*telos*), 79
temporality, 64, 181, 253. *See also* Ricoeur, Paul
theology (theological), 103, 105, 109, 110, 132, 142, 143, 166; mystical, 8, 191, 192
third, the. *See* other, relation of to "the third"
time, 227, 228, 231, 232, 251. *See also* feminine/female; Irigaray, Luce; masculine/male; space
Torah, 77
transcendence, 33, 35. *See also* ethics; other
trust, 43, 49, 50
truth, 148

understanding. *See* wisdom
universalism, 171, 179, 180

vocation. *See* call; Marion, Jean-Luc

War, metaphor of, 8. *See also* eros/erotic; love, declaration of love/war; love, erotic; love, as militant
Weil, Simone, 216, 218, 219
Westphal, Merold, 87, 89–90, 95
wisdom, 1, 2, 3, 9, 202–205, 207–209, 216, 218; in contrast to knowledge, 18, 19; intimate, 46; practical, 79, 80; pursuit of, 16. *See also* God, wisdom of; love, "wisdom of"
Woolf, Virginia, 207, 208

Zizek, Slavoj, 4, 8, 109, 123, 125, 127, 171–182; on the "fragile absolute," 178, 179; "Real," the, 173–177; *Puppet and Dwarf*, *specific passages cited*, 127, 174, 175, 176, 177, 180–182. *See also* interpellation; *jouissance*; subjectivity